INFORMATION SYSTEMS SERIES

INFORMATION SYSTEMS DEVELOPMENT:
A Database Approach

Second Edition

D.E. AVISON
BA, MSc, PhD, FBCS
Professor of Information Systems
Department of Accounting and Management Science
Southampton University, Southampton, UK

ALFRED WALLER LIMITED
HENLEY-ON-THAMES

Published by
Alfred Waller Ltd. Publishers
Orchards, Fawley, Henley-on-Thames
Oxfordshire RG9 6JF

First edition published 1985
Second edition published 1992
Reprinted 1993

© D. E. Avison 1985, 1992

British Library Cataloguing-in-Publication
Data
A catalogue record for this book is
available from the British Library

ISBN 0-632-03028-3

Printed and bound in Great Britain
by Hartnolls Ltd, Bodmin, Cornwall

To my Mother
Stella Avison

and the memory of my Father
Leslie Stuart Avison

Contents

Foreword   *xii*

Preface   *xiv*

PART ONE - INTRODUCTION

1   Introduction   3

    1.1   The Development of Computing   3

    1.2   Conventional Systems Analysis   8

    1.3   Problems with the Conventional Approach   11

    1.4   Answers to these Problems   15

    1.5   Why Databases?   23

    1.6   Early Database Experience   26

    1.7   The Difficulty of Modelling Reality   29

    1.8   The ANSI/X3/SPARC Architecture   30

    1.9   The Approach in Outline   32

    1.10   Further Reading   39

PART TWO - A DATABASE APPROACH TO INFORMATION SYSTEMS DEVELOPMENT

2   Business Analysis   43

    2.1   Introduction   43

    2.2   Goals of the Organisation   46

    2.3   Culture of the Organisation   50

    2.4   Structure of Management in the Organisation   51

    2.5   Roles of Key Personnel and Systems Planning Team   56

    2.6   Techniques for Investigation and Analysis   60

    2.7   Strategy for Information Systems Development   67

    2.8   Management and User Involvement   71

    2.9   Further Reading   74

3   The Conceptual Schema: Data Analysis and the Relational Model   75

    3.1   Introduction   75

3.2	Entity-Relationship Approach	77
3.3	Some Definitions	80
3.4	Phases in Entity Analysis	87
3.5	Alternative Approaches to Data Analysis	95
3.6	Relational Modelling	99
3.7	Normalisation	103
3.8	Further Normalisation	110
3.9	Further Reading	113
4	The Logical Schema: Relational, Hierarchical, Network and Object-Oriented Views	115
4.1	Introduction	115
4.2	The Relational Approach	116
4.3	Relational Algebra	118
4.4	Relational Calculus	125
4.5	The Hierarchical Approach	129
4.6	The Network Approach	133
4.7	Languages for Using Networks	138
4.8	Database Mapping	139
4.9	Object-Oriented Approach	141
4.10	Comparing Approaches to Logical Design	144
4.11	Further Reading	146
5	The Physical Schema: File Access and Organisation	148
5.1	Introduction	148
5.2	Traditional Methods of Organising Data on Backing Storage Media	148
5.3	B-Trees	154
5.4	Lists	156
5.5	Inverted Files	160
5.6	Conclusion	162
5.7	Further Reading	162
6	Implementing Applications	164
6.1	External View of Database	164
6.2	The Life-Cycle Revisited	166
6.3	Structured Systems Analysis and Design	168
6.4	Participation	175
6.5	Prototyping	181

	6.6	Multiview	184
	6.7	Further Reading	195

PART THREE - THE DATABASE ENVIRONMENT

7		Database Management Systems	199
	7.1	Introduction	199
	7.2	IMS - A Hierarchical DBMS	204
	7.3	IDMS - A Codasyl (Network) DBMS	209
	7.4	DB2 - A Relational DBMS	214
	7.5	Adabas - An Inverted File DBMS	217
	7.6	Ontos - An Object-Oriented DBMS	219
	7.7	Further Reading	221
8		SQL	222
	8.1	Introduction	222
	8.2	Data Definition	223
	8.3	Data Retrieval	226
	8.4	Data Update	229
	8.5	Views in SQL	230
	8.6	Embedded SQL	231
	8.7	Conclusion	232
	8.8	Further Reading	232
9		Microcomputer Databases and Database Machines	233
	9.1	The Development of Databases on Microcomputers	233
	9.2	dBaseIV	236
	9.3	OmnisV	239
	9.4	Database Machines	241
	9.5	Further Reading	243
10		Distributed Databases	244
	10.1	Introduction	244
	10.2	Principles and Requirements of Distributed Database Systems	246
	10.3	Distributed Database Design	249
	10.4	Implementation Issues	255
	10.5	Further Reading	258

11	Tool Support: Fourth Generation, Workbench, Case and Multi-Media Systems	259
11.1	Fourth Generation Systems	259
11.2	Components of a Fourth Generation System	263
11.3	Focus	267
11.4	Fourth Generation Systems - A Conclusion	270
11.5	Workbenches	272
11.6	Information Engineering Workbench (IEW)	273
11.7	Case (Computer-Aided Software Engineering)	275
11.8	Oracle	277
11.9	Multi-Media Systems	278
11.10	Use of Tools in the Database Approach	279
11.11	Evaluating Tools	281
11.12	Further Reading	282
12	Data Dictionary Systems	284
12.1	Introduction	284
12.2	Facilities of a Data Dictionary System	287
12.3	Advantages and Costs of Using a Data Dictionary System	290
12.4	ICL Data Dictionary System	292
12.5	DB2 Data Dictionary	293
12.6	Further Reading	294
13	Database Administration and Database Management	295
13.1	Introduction	295
13.2	Functions of a Database Administrator	297
13.3	Benefits of Database Administration	302
13.4	The Position of the Database Administrator in the Organisation	303
13.5	Further Reading	305

PART FOUR: THE APPROACH IN ACTION

14	An Application of the Database Approach	309
14.1	Introduction	309
14.2	Entity-Relationship Modelling	310
14.3	Logical Schema	318
14.4	Physical Schema	319
14.5	Implementing Applications	326

15   An Application of Multiview   328

Bibliography   354
Index   364

Foreword

The Blackwell Scientific Publications Series on Information Systems is a series of student texts covering a wide variety of topics relating to information systems. It is designed to fulfil the needs of a growing number of courses on, and interest in, computing and information systems which do not focus on the purely technical aspects, but seek to relate these to the organisational context.

Information systems has been defined as the effective design, delivery, use and impact of information technology in organisations and society. Utilising this fairly wide definition, it is clear that the subject is somewhat interdisciplinary. Thus the series seeks to integrate technological disciplines with management and other disciplines, for example, psychology and sociology. It is felt that these areas do not have a natural home, they are rarely represented by single departments in polytechnics and universities, and to put such books in a purely computer science or management series restricts potential readership and the benefits that such texts can provide. This series on information systems now provides such a home.

The books will be mainly student texts, although certain topics may be dealt with at a deeper, more research-oriented level.

The series is expected to include the following areas, although this is not an exhaustive list: information systems development methodologies, office information systems, management information systems, decision support systems, information modelling and databases, systems theory, human aspects and the human-computer interface, application systems, technology strategy, planning and control, and expert systems, knowledge acquisition and its representation.

A mention of the books so far published in the series gives a 'flavour' of the richness of the information systems world. *Information Systems Development: Methodologies, Techniques and Tools* (D.E. Avison and G. Fitzgerald), looks at many of the areas discussed above in overview form; *Information and Data Modelling* (David Benyon), concerns itself with one very important aspect, the world of data, in some depth; *Structured Systems Analysis and Design Method* (G. Cutts) looks at one particular information systems development methodology in detail; *Multiview: An Exploration in Information Systems Development* (D.E. Avison and A.T. Wood-Harper) looks at an approach to information systems development which combines human and technical considerations; *Software Engineering for Information Systems* (D. McDermid) discusses software engineering in the context of information systems; Information Systems Research: Issues, Techniques and Practical Guidelines (R.

Galliers (ed)) provides a collection of papers on key information systems issues; and *Relational Database Design* (P. Beynon-Davies) looks at relational database design in detail.

David Avison's new text adds to the strength of the series on the data and database aspect. Whereas David Benyon's book concentrates on data modelling and Paul Beynon-Davies' on relational databases, this new text describes and advocates a particular approach or methodology for database implementation, irrespective of the database model employed. The multi-disciplinary approach described is predicated on the database concept but is unusual in that it is not simply a technical view of implementation.

It begins with the business objectives and addresses such diverse aspects as organisational culture and management structures, topics not usually found in texts about databases. Data modelling, logical modelling and file access and organisation form other parts of the approach. There is also a chapter on the development of applications which might use the database. It integrates in one volume databases and an approach to their development with a large number of topics and issues that are normally only to be found in separate sources. The section entitled 'The Database Environment' is devoted to those important topics that give the reader an insight into the practice, and incorporates topics such as database management systems, database languages, Case tools, distributed databases, database machines, database administration, databases on microcomputers and data dictionary systems. This is reinforced by the two case studies that make up the final section. The book should find a home as the basic text for many database and information systems courses.

Guy Fitzgerald
Joint Consulting Editor
Information Systems Series

Preface to Second Edition

This text is designed foremost for students of computer science and business studies who are undertaking a second course in computing or data processing: one which covers database management and database applications. Readers are assumed to have completed a basic course in data processing or information technology or have had practical experience in the area. The book will also be of value to managers who may be contemplating a database path for their applications, and to programmers and systems analysts who wish to know more about the database environment. However, the book does not stress the technical aspects to the exclusion of human and organisational aspects. Indeed, I am pleased that this second edition of the book is in Blackwell Scientific Publication's Information Systems series which was announced sometime after the date of the original publication. There are a number of excellent texts available which cover the technical and formal aspects of database technology and database management systems in much greater detail than is possible here. This text looks at the database approach as a whole, and in particular describes a data-oriented methodology for implementing information systems using a computer database. This methodology begins at the stage of business analysis and ends at the stage of implementing the database on the computer system and the parallel development of applications using this database. The technical aspects only form a part of this process.

The book has changed greatly in structure and content since the first edition. This is firstly the result of developments in the field (seven years is a very long time in the database field); secondly the result of comments from academics and students in colleges, polytechnics and universities (and also database practitioners) who have used the book either as a text book for their courses on databases or to help in implementing database applications; and thirdly as a result of my own experience in teaching and researching the subject, and in using databases in computer applications in a number of consultancy projects over the time. The structure of the book is now split into four parts:

Part 1 Introduction
Part 2 Database approach to information systems development
Part 3 The database environment
Part 4 The approach in action

Following **Part 1**, the introduction, **Part 2** describes the approach to analyse, design, develop and implement the computer database along with the applications that use it. It has five phases: business analysis, conceptual modelling, logical modelling, physical modelling and applications development. Each of these phases forms a chapter in this part of the book. **Part 3** concerns itself with the technological and people support: the necessary infrastructure for database and the data resource of the organisation. Database management systems, the SQL language, microcomputer databases and database machines, distributed databases, tools (including fourth generation systems and Case tools), the data dictionary system and finally the role of the database administrator and the problems of managing the database system and applications development, all form chapters in this third part of the book. **Part 4** looks at the approach in action, describing both the development of a database system for a computer service company in Chapter 14 and the development of an information system using a database for a university department in Chapter 15.

We will now look at the chapters in more detail and note where this second edition differs from the first edition. In the **introduction**, the deficiencies of conventional systems analysis are discussed, along with problems and potential of the database approach, and readers are exposed to many of the ideas, techniques, tools and human and social activities described in this book. Users of the first edition will notice that along with the introduction of more recent developments, the ANSI/X3/SPARC architecture is described and this is put into the context of the approach used in the book.

Chapter 2, on **business analysis**, discusses the organisation - its goals, culture, the structure of management, and information requirements. It also looks at the roles of the people working, sometimes reluctantly, on the information systems project and the best strategy to adopt to ensure its effectiveness. Techniques for investigation and analysis, including information modelling, rich pictures and root definitions are described. There is a discussion of various strategies for information systems development. It is important to consider the needs of the organisation before attempting to solve a particular business problem, because an overall appraisal is more likely to lead to information systems which address the needs of the organisation as a whole rather than attempt to solve a particular short-term problem or a symptom of a different or much bigger problem. Yet this very important phase is often neglected by organisations attempting to implement a database system (and most texts on the subject). Users of the first edition will notice that this chapter has been greatly enhanced. For example, the work of Porter, Earl and others in the field has been incorporated and there is an additional section on the culture of the organisation which was neglected in the first edition. Sections on the roles of people have been considerably enhanced along with more recent developments in the range of techniques for investigation and analysis during this phase.

By using techniques of entity modelling and relational modelling, which are discussed in Chapter 3, a model of the organisation - or at least that part of the organisation in which we are interested - which is known as the **conceptual model**, can be designed. Later on, following this approach, the model created can be mapped onto a target database and database management system. Various approaches to data modelling are described and the entity-relationship model is emphasised. This is a diagrammatic approach, stemming from the work of Chen, which has proved very helpful in the modelling process. This chapter also looks at relational theory and normalisation, which originated in the database context through the contributions of Codd and Date. This material can be very theoretical, but this text describes these in a practical way. As in every chapter of the book, further references are provided at the end of the chapter for those readers who want to delve further. Users of the first edition will notice that much of the terminology has been standardised with common practice (though unfortunately there is still no agreed terminology for much of the field) and the examples provided have been developed further with the introduction of new concepts. Improved documentation is also suggested. The final section, on further normalisation, is new. This looks at refinements in normalisation beyond third normal form. It is the result of pressure from colleagues demanding a more complete description of the process for their courses (not complete, because extensions to normalisation seem to be never-ending). I wish to point out that my own experience would suggest that third normal form is usually adequate in practice.

The conceptual model so derived is mapped onto a target model used as the basic structure for the database management system. This is referred to as the **logical model** and can take a number of forms. Chapter 4 highlights the relational, hierarchical, network and object-oriented views (corresponding to relational, hierarchical, network and object-oriented databases) and shows how the conceptual model can be mapped (or transformed) into relational, hierarchical or network models. It is true that the relational model is the most common in modern computer database management systems and this is emphasised in this chapter. However, hierarchical and network database management systems are still used (and will be used for some time in the future) and the discussion of these models is also useful to highlight the strengths and weaknesses of the relational model. Object-oriented database management systems are comparatively new at the time of writing, but would seem to have the potential to make a considerable impact in the database world. Users of the first edition will notice that the descriptions of the relational and network approaches have been strengthened along with the new section on object-oriented databases. Other new sections include those describing the mapping processes and the final section compares approaches to logical design.

These database management systems can use a number of methods to organise and access the data on backing storage - the **physical model**. Traditional techniques, such as serial, sequential, indexed, indexed sequential, and random access files are introduced in the first section of Chapter 5. There are sections each for the major database techniques of B-trees, lists and inverted files. The section on B-trees is new to this edition.

Having developed the database, we look at **applications development** in Chapter 6 and this considers the ways in which the various information systems using the database are implemented. The first section looks at the various user views (or external views) which will be used by application programs. These will be subsets of the conceptual model. The ANSI/X3/SPARC model is re-introduced to show how the required data structures might be derived from the database. This section also discusses database access, that is, the methods and approaches by which applications might access and update data on the database. Section 6.2 looks again at the systems life cycle, but in the context of the database approach. Techniques of applications development, in particular, structured systems analysis and design, participation and prototyping are then described. The final section looks at Multiview, one approach to develop information systems applications which integrates many of the ideas described in this book. The sections on the user views of data and database access, the life cycle revisited and Multiview are new to the second edition. The section on tools has been scrapped, as there is now a new chapter on tools (Chapter 11).

Each part of the methodology could be looked upon as a piece of a jigsaw, and a failure to get each one right may cause disappointment to managers and staff of an organisation and eventual failure of the information systems and database project. Success will also depend on the technological and people support, and the next few chapters look at these and examine some of the issues involved.

Part 3 starts with a chapter on **database management systems**. These are the software systems supporting database use. Chapter 7 includes a description of one database management system of each type described in Chapter 4: IMS (a hierarchical system); IDMS (a network or Codasyl system); DB2 (a relational system) and Ontos (an object-oriented system), along with Adabas, which is an inverted file database management system. Some texts include inverted files in their classification of logical models. An inverted file, as shown in Chapter 5, is a way of physically organising data, but Adabas is included in Chapter 7 as an interesting database approach somewhat different from the others discussed. The methods used by each database management system to interact with application programs using conventional programming languages and query languages are highlighted. This chapter has also greatly changed from the first edition. The section on Ingres is dropped (though this database management system is described in Chapter 14 in the context of a case study) and the section relating to fourth generation databases is also dropped (but these are covered in Chapter 11). The sections on DB2 and Ontos are new, and the descriptions of the other database management systems have been strengthened and updated. The old Chapter 8 has been dropped but its contents, where relevant, will be found elsewhere in the new edition (in particular Chapters 9 and 10).

Chapter 8, on the query language **SQL**, is new. This language for querying and updating relations has become a standard or an option on most popular microcomputer, minicomputer and mainframe database management systems (including DB2, Oracle, Ingres, dBaseIV, Unify and many others), indeed it has been the subject of an ISO standards committee. Computer programmers and other database users are likely to need to know the basis of this interface to database systems. It is therefore reasonable in a database text to look at this language in particular. This chapter includes an examination of its strengths and weaknesses. There are separate sections on data definition, retrieval and update, followed by a look at user views in SQL, and embedded SQL, where access can be gained through the use of a host language, such as Cobol or Pascal, which have SQL commands embedded in the code.

Chapter 9, on **microcomputer database management systems** and **database machines**, is also a new chapter. The development of microcomputers is described because their early limitations necessitated very limited database management systems (in truth, file management systems). But the microcomputer environment is no longer so limiting, and many present-day microcomputer database management systems have most of the features and capabilities of their mainframe counterparts. Indeed, many mainframe systems have their personal computer versions, so that it is possible to prototype an application using a micro, and, once tested, install the operational version of the system on the organisation's mainframe. Overviews are given in this chapter of popular microcomputer database systems such as dBaseIV and Omnis. This chapter also includes a section on database machines. These are computers which are dedicated to database use and to which general-purpose computers have access when an application being processed needs to use the database. Such an arrangement can prove to be effective, providing speedier processing of database queries and efficient use of the computer resource as a whole.

Chapter 10, on **distributed database management systems**, is also new, although, like Chapter 9, has its roots in Chapter 8 of the first edition. Distributed database management systems have developed greatly in the last few years so that they are now a viable, if not too common, alternative to centralised database computer systems. The first section suggests circumstances where distributed database management systems may be a preferred alternative and suggests criteria on which to compare the two database architectures. A section on principles and requirements of distributed database management systems is followed by a section on their design. The final section examines some key implementation issues.

Chapter 11 is also new, and looks at the increasingly important area of **tool** support, for database analysis, design and implementation and for the development of applications that use the database. Following an introduction, the components of a fourth generation system, which might include a database management system, data dictionary, query language, report generator, screen painter and program generator, are described. An overview of Focus, a popular fourth generation system, is given. A section on workbenches, which includes a review of Information Engineering Workbench, is then followed by an extended section on Case (Computer-aided software engineering) tools. The Case tools of Oracle are then described. There is also a section on multi-media systems. The place of tools in the approach used in this book is followed by a section on tool evaluation.

Chapter 12, on **data dictionary systems**, is based on that of Chapter 9 in the first edition. The data dictionary system is another tool (indeed it is frequently part of a fourth generation or Case system) but it is of key importance because it provides information about the database, and the users and applications which reference it. Following the introduction, which suggests a wider data and process-oriented *system catalogue* (rather than a limited meta-data or 'data about data' view of the data dictionary), the possible facilities of a data dictionary system are outlined. The advantages and costs of using a data dictionary system are then examined, followed by a look at two systems in use: ICL's data dictionary system and the data dictionary part of the DB2 database management system.

Chapter 13, on the role of the **database administrator** and, in general, the problems of managing the data resource of the organisation, is based on that of Chapter 10 in the first edition, although readers of that edition will notice many changes. Following the introduction there is a section on the functions of the database administrator which includes a discussion on designing and loading the database, control of the database and maintenance of the database. The major problems of database security, back-up and recovery, integrity and the privacy of personal data are looked at in some detail. There are also sections outlining the benefits of database administration and the position of the database administrator in the organisation. The possible role of the data administrator, as against the database administrator, is also described.

Part 4 looks at the approach in action. It consists of two chapters, containing case studies based on two real-life projects. Chapter 14, similar to the Appendix of the first edition, describes an **application of the approach** described in Part 2 of this edition carried out at the Systems Development Division of Comshare Limited, a computer service company. Chapter 15, new to this text (but taken largely from Avison & Wood-Harper, 1990) describes the **development of an information systems application** (using a database at the Computer Science Department at Aston University) following the Multiview approach discussed in Chapter 6. Together, the two cases provide the reader with some interesting insights into the database approach discussed in this book as well as drawing together the pieces of the jigsaw described in this book into a unified whole.

Having described the objectives and provided an outline of the book, I wish to acknowledge its major limitation. Even though it is considerably expanded compared to the first edition, I have still not been able to look at many aspects in great depth. Each part of the methodology could be the basis of a separate book or advanced course. Inevitably I have omitted much of the detail or have simplified areas in order to stress the important elements of the methodology and to emphasise its unified nature. Following each chapter is a short and annotated list of references for further reading, which might be considered as a starting point to search for more information on the topics discussed in that chapter. At the end of the text, an extended bibliography is provided which can be used to help further fill in the detail once the overall approach is understood.

A number of people have helped me in writing this text. The first edition was greatly helped by Tom Crowe, now of Thames Information Systems, Guy Fitzgerald, now at Templeton College, Tom Gough of Leeds University, Gilbert Mansell of Huddersfield Polytechnic, Richard Veryard of James Martin Systems Limited and Bob Wood, now at Salford University. Students of Aston University have been influential in the design and content of both editions. They have repeatedly exposed my lack of knowledge and superficiality of thought, and I readily acknowledge my gratitude to members of the BSc and MSc courses over the last few years - they all deserve a mention, but this would not be practical. Many 1991 graduates carried out coursework in this area which was useful and these included M. Beak, C. Berger, B. Brownlee, D. Chahal, M. Chauhan, S. Clews, J. Cook, E. Coop, J. Earp, J. Forrester, T. Greenan, A. Meads, C. Mayne, J. Poulton, S. Prescott, R. Pringle, A. Sidhu, A. Stoner and S. Taurins. I am sure I have missed out some and I apologise for this. I would particularly like to thank ex-research students Paul Catchpole (now at Price-Waterhouse), Jayasri Chaudhuri (now at BIS Systems), Rob Hidderley (Birmingham Polytechnic), Mansoor Hassan (now of Bahrain University) and Hanifa Shah (now a lecturer at Aston), along with ex-colleagues Carol Byde, now at Bass Limited, Paul Gardner, now at Birmingham Technology and Paul Golder, along with Paul Beynon-Davies of Polytechnic of Wales, Cath Orange of Leeds Polytechnic and Hannah Searle at

Southampton University. They have all helped to shape this second edition. I am also grateful to many colleagues at polytechnics and universities who have commented on the first edition. Thanks also to Andrew Baker, a graduate of Aston, and Michael Coveney of Comshare for permission to publish the material given in Chapter 14, Trevor Wood-Harper for permission to publish the material presented in Chapter 15, and, again, many students and staff at Aston who contributed to the application described in that chapter. Most of all I wish to thank Marie-Anne and Thomas for their kindness and support.

David Avison,
Nérac and Southampton,
Summer and Autumn 1991.

PART ONE

_____

INTRODUCTION

Chapter 1
Introduction

_____

1.1 THE DEVELOPMENT OF COMPUTING

The early days of commercial computing were marked by great hopes but many disappointments. Business users in particular complained of broken promises. Sometimes the computer application was not ready when it was supposed to be operational. When it was operational, some of the features that were required were not implemented or did not work. This meant that there was a large problem in correcting and maintaining these systems. There were many reasons for these problems, but the main one was the lack of an acceptable methodology for implementing systems.

During the late 1960s, this need for a methodology was understood by the computing world. In the United Kingdom, the publication by the National Computing Centre (NCC) in 1968 and 1971 of their methodology for developing systems was a step in the right direction. It is typical of what is termed 'conventional systems analysis' in this text and based on the life-cycle of systems development (called the waterfall model in the United States). The NCC 'package' included systems training courses and documentation tools. These helped systems analysts to follow a step-by-step methodology which would lead to the implementation of applications which were more likely to conform to the requirements of the users. The results of this effort helped to improve the reputation of computer people and computer applications in business.

The applications that were implemented tended to concentrate on 'computerising' manual systems. Thus the standard data processing systems, previously clerical, such as payroll, sales order processing and invoicing, used the computer, wherever appropriate, so as to reduce the clerical burden. In these systems the computer procedures simulated the clerical procedures and the computer files contained the same facts as their clerical counterpart. Such systems frequently gained some of the advantages that computer systems could offer, in particular those of speed and reliability.

These systems were adequate for the 1970s and reflected the technology of the time. They may well be appropriate in many smaller organisations today and in situations in larger organisations where the processes are fairly stable, because one of their main drawbacks is inflexibility. If, for example, the function changes in some way or the needs of management change, it is difficult to adapt the system to meet the new requirements. From the point of view of the user, quite small changes seem to cause immense problems to computer people. 'How easy this change would have been on the old manual system' was a cry often heard. Data processing departments spend excessive effort on maintaining systems. This frequently amounts to over 75% of their time: time that could have been spent developing new applications. Sometimes the decision has to be made to develop and implement a new system which will replace the patched up old version. But this is an expensive solution and remains appropriate only until circumstances change again.

Over the last few years there have been a number of developments which have made it possible to offer an alternative methodology. With database systems, it is possible to hold the facts relating to parts of the organisation on a database. The 'organisation' in this context could be the whole business or, more likely, a part of it, such as a division or department. Perhaps the business database will be built up gradually, department at a time, so that eventually the whole organisation is reflected on the database. The various computer applications can use this as the data source. If the functions change, the data on the database will probably still be appropriate. If the facts change, then the database can be amended without redesigning the application systems. There is an element of **data independence** between the database and the applications that use it. The hardware and software can also be changed in order to reflect developments in the technology without requiring substantial changes in the application systems or the structure of the database.

Figure 1.1 illustrates three stages in the development of data processing. In Figure 1.1(a) the data is held on a document of some kind, the process carried out by the human being, and the result written down on paper. In Figure 1.1(b), the input source is the same but has been transferred to a medium which is suitable for computers to read. The process is performed by the computer which puts the result on computer output media such as line printer stationery. The system reflects the previous clerical system. Although there may well be more stages, data processing is likely to be quicker overall, due to the speed of the computer. Figure 1.1(c) represents something much more radical. The facts about the business are modelled on the computer database, and the various applications use the database as required. If the process needs to be changed in some way, the database will still be appropriate. The third option is likely to be the most rewarding, but there are risks attached to it because of the high cost and long term nature of its development.

A major problem is to construct the model of the organisation which will be held on the database. The real world is so complex that to model the organisation, or even part of it such as a department, is no easy task. This text proposes a methodology to help produce a model which proves a good basis for most applications. As Figure 1.2 shows, the methodology has a number of phases. The first stage is to get to know

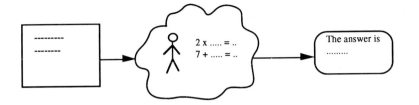

(a) Human being as data processor

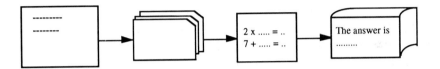

(b) The computer as data processor

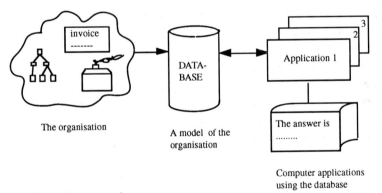

(c) The database approach

Fig. 1.1 Three ways of data processing

something about the organisation. This business analysis is necessary so that the analysts can gain a background knowledge of the organisation, such as the goals of the firm, the management hierarchy, and the various requirements that information systems may need to fulfil.

With a background knowledge of the organisation established, it is possible to develop a conceptual model. This is a formal model of the organisation which is achieved by using data analysis techniques, in particular entity-relationship modelling and normalisation. Interviews, observation and document appraisal can be used to

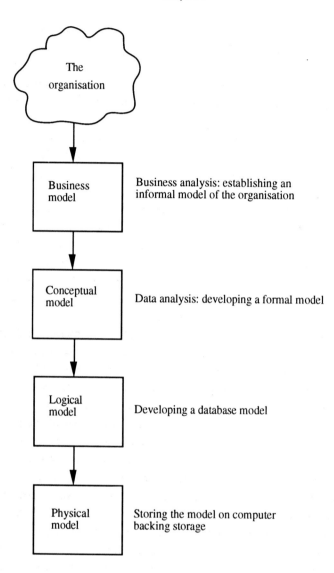

Fig. 1.2 The approach in outline (a)

establish the basic data and data relationships, and a model is constructed of the organisation either on paper or on computer files.

The next stage is to develop the logical model by mapping the conceptual model into a form required by the chosen database management system (DBMS). The form of this model will vary according to the DBMS used. The DBMS is the large piece of software controlling accesses to the database.

Finally the DBMS maps these data structures onto computer storage media. This is the physical model which is usually held on magnetic disks or another fast storage medium and will be accessed by the various applications that require data from the database. This access will be made using the facilities of the DBMS which might include a query language, for example, SQL, or a conventional programming language, for example, Cobol.

The complete methodology has other aspects which are necessary for successful information systems development, and these aspects are introduced in Section 1.9.

Using this methodology, the final version of the model, held on computer files, ought to be a fair representation of the organisation and should avoid some of the pitfalls which were a characteristic of early database use. The database can be the basis on which to build flexible information systems providing accurate information, at the appropriate time, and at the correct level of detail for management to use for improved decision-making. It will also be used for conventional data processing tasks such as payroll, sales ledger and invoicing. The database therefore should not be seen as a 'dump for all the data in the organisation'. The data is organised so that it might be accessed by a number of different users conveniently.

Before looking in more detail at the approach adopted in this book, this chapter looks at conventional systems analysis. Section 1.2 discusses the phases of the conventional approach and the following section looks at some of the problems that may be associated with applications developed in this way. Section 1.4 looks at some of the developments in hardware and software and in other tools and techniques which pave the way for improved systems analysis. Some of the reasons for choosing a database solution are given in Section 1.5. Unfortunately early experiences with databases and management information systems did not always prove successful, and reasons for this lack of success are discussed in Section 1.6. A particular problem, highlighted in Section 1.7, is the difficulty of modelling reality, that is, of representing the real world on computer files. Section 1.8 looks at the ANSI/X3/SPARC architecture, which has been very influential in database design, and shows how this fits into the approach described in this book. The final section of this chapter looks in more detail, but still in outline form, at the methodology adopted by this text. Although this methodology does not answer all the problems, it is hoped that the ideas, tools and techniques discussed and the use of a methodological way of proceeding are steps in the right direction.

Although this chapter discusses the opportunities open to the user of modern computing technology, it paints a rather negative picture of computing up to the 1970s and 1980s. This is perhaps unfortunate because the applications were appropriate to the technology of the time. However, it is useful to appreciate the weaknesses of the conventional approach in order to understand the necessity for the methodology discussed in this text. Without such a methodology, there are likely to be failures, or at least missed opportunities, associated with computing in the 1990s and beyond.

1.2 CONVENTIONAL SYSTEMS ANALYSIS

There have always been systems. If firms have employees, there needs to be some sort of system to pay them. If firms manufacture products, then there will be a system to order the raw materials from the suppliers, another to plan the production of the goods from the raw materials, and another to ensure that stock levels are reasonable. By 'reasonable' is meant that stocks are not so high that too much of the firm's capital is tied up in stock and not so low that the firm's products may go out of stock so that business is lost. There needs to be a system to deal with the orders for the firm's products from customers, and yet another to ensure that the products are transported, and another to send invoices to the customers and process their payments.

In the time before computers, these commercial systems were largely processed by clerical effort. The word 'largely' is appropriate, because the clerical workers would use adding machines, typewriters, and other mechanical or electrical aids to help the system run as efficiently as possible. The use of computers represents only an extension of this process. When used appropriately, computers possess advantages over clerical processing because of their speed and accuracy. If a clerical system proves inadequate in some way, a solution which involves the use of computers may well be contemplated. Data processing personnel are frequently called in to investigate applications where:
- Increasing workloads have caused strain on the clerical system
- Suitable staff are expensive and difficult to recruit
- There is a change in the type of work
- There are frequent errors detected.

The data processing personnel may well follow a methodology similar to that recommended by the National Computing Centre (NCC) in 1968 which was revised in 1971. This approach has the following phases:
- Feasibility study
- System investigation
- Systems analysis
- Systems design
- Systems development
- Implementation

- Review and maintenance.

These phases are frequently referred to in the literature as the systems development life cycle or the waterfall model. The use of the word 'cycle' is appropriate because at the review stage the decision could be made to start all over again because the system is already inadequate. The phases are seen in Figure 1.3.

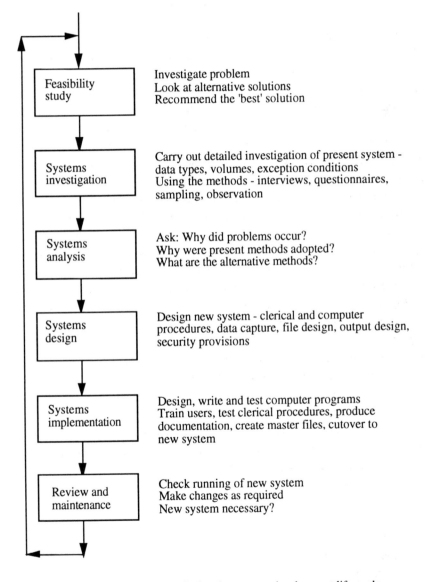

Feasibility study	Investigate problem Look at alternative solutions Recommend the 'best' solution
Systems investigation	Carry out detailed investigation of present system - data types, volumes, exception conditions Using the methods - interviews, questionnaires, sampling, observation
Systems analysis	Ask: Why did problems occur? Why were present methods adopted? What are the alternative methods?
Systems design	Design new system - clerical and computer procedures, data capture, file design, output design, security provisions
Systems implementation	Design, write and test computer programs Train users, test clerical procedures, produce documentation, create master files, cutover to new system
Review and maintenance	Check running of new system Make changes as required New system necessary?

Fig. 1.3 Conventional systems analysis - the systems development life cycle

The **feasibility study** looks at the system which is presently operating, considers its problems, and briefly looks at a range of alternative ways of doing the job. The list could include improved clerical systems as well as computer solutions. For each of these possibilities, a list of the costs and benefits is compiled and a 'recommended solution' presented to management. They will decide whether to follow this recommendation or to adopt another solution. Management will normally base this decision on the feasibility report along with a verbal presentation given by the systems analyst.

The next stage is a detailed fact finding or **systems investigation** phase. This aims to find out the objectives of the present system and whether these are being achieved, the range of data types and the volumes of data that have to be processed, exception conditions, and the problems associated with the present working methods. These facts are obtained by interviewing personnel (both management and clerical staff), sending out questionnaires, observing the area of interest, sampling, and looking at the records that are kept in the department or documents relating to any previous investigation work that has been compiled. The NCC approach uses a number of documentation aids which help to ensure that the investigation is thorough.

Armed with the facts, the systems analyst asks why any problems occurred, why certain methods of work were adopted, considers whether there are alternative methods, and decides on the likely growth rates of data. This **analysis** phase leads to the design of the new system. Although usually similar to the design accepted at the feasibility study stage, the new facts may lead to the analyst adopting a rather different design to that proposed at that time.

The **design** stage involves both the computer and clerical parts of the system. The design document will contain details of the input data and how the data is to be captured (entered into the system), the outputs of the system, the processes involved in converting the input to the output and the structure of the computer and clerical files which may need to be referenced in the system. Again, the NCC methodology provides documentation tools with which to detail the input, file and output formats, and to chart the procedures. Other features of the design will be the specification of the security and back-up provisions to be made, and the systems testing and implementation plans.

The next stage is to **implement** the new system. If the design includes computer programs, these have to be designed, coded and tested. Staff in the user department need to use the system and any difficulties experienced need to be ironed out. If the system is not fully tested at this stage there might soon be a loss of confidence in it as users find errors in the system when it becomes operational. This is likely to reduce its effectiveness. Manuals for the operations staff and the user staff will be produced and the live data, that is operational rather than test data, will be collected and validated so that the master files can be set up. Once all this has been carried out, the new system can be run as the operational system and the old one dispensed with. Frequently there is a period of 'parallel running' until there is complete confidence in the new system.

The final stage in the systems development cycle occurs once the system is operational. There are bound to be some changes necessary and some data processing staff will be set aside for **maintenance**. Their job will be to ensure the efficient running of the system and to make the changes required by the users. At some stage there will be a **review** of the system which will check that the system conforms to the requirements specified at the feasibility study stage, and the costs have not exceeded those predicted. A report should be produced. Sometimes the system has veered from the requirements definition significantly or new requirements have come to light and it may be sensible to consider whether it should not be replaced by yet another new system. The cycle will then come full circle as a new feasibility study gets under way.

This traditional systems development cycle has a number of features to commend it. In particular the use of documentation standards ensures that the proposals are complete, and that they are communicated to systems development staff, the users in the department, and the computer operations staff. Further, the user of the methodology ought to ensure that all the staff involved are trained to use the system in good time. The documentation helps this process as well. The methodology also prevents, to some extent at least, missed cutover dates and unexpectedly high costs and lower benefits. Early computing had a track record of these problems.

This conventional approach to systems analysis has a good track record, and it is still appropriate for many applications. But computer applications that have been implemented using this approach also have their limitations. Some of these limitations may stem from the way that the methodology is used or from the abilities of the analysts involved, but others stem from the methodology itself. Before discussing the alternative methodology suggested in this book, we will look at the problems of the conventional approach to systems analysis as represented by the early NCC methodology.

1.3 PROBLEMS WITH THE CONVENTIONAL APPROACH

The criticisms of some of the computer applications that are developed using the conventional approach include:
- Failure to meet the needs of business
- Inflexibility
- User dissatisfaction

- Problems with the documentation
- Incomplete systems
- Application backlog
- Maintenance workload.

This section looks at each of these problems which can occur in data processing applications.

As Figure 1.4 shows, although systems that are developed by this approach can successfully deal with operational processing such as sales order processing and the various accounting routines, there is a **failure to meet all the needs of business**. In particular, middle management and top management are being largely ignored by computer data processing. Management information requirements, such as the information to help make decisions about where to locate a new factory or which product range to stop producing or what sales or production targets to aim for, are being neglected. The computer is being used only for routine, repetitive tasks. Managers and computers are not mixing - apart from the 'lip-service' required to sanction the expenditure necessary to buy and develop mainframe computer systems. However, there is now a growing awareness amongst management that computers ought to be helping them more directly.

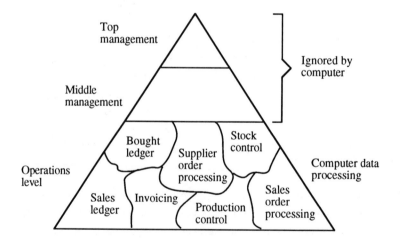

Fig. 1.4 Failure to meet all the needs of business

Another major problem is the **inflexibility** of the systems that are being implemented - conventional systems have a low responsiveness to change. Computer systems are very often replacing clerical systems which are proving inadequate. However, apart from using the new technology, their designs are similar to those of the existing system. They are not intended to be adaptive: they are expected to parallel existing systems. In order to reflect the present way of doing things, but using computers, the fundamental question 'is this the best way?' is not being asked, and there may be missed opportunities for improvement.

Inflexibility also occurs for another reason. The output of the new system is decided early in the systems development process. As Figure 1.5 shows, the design of the new system is 'output driven'. Once the output is agreed with user management, the other aspects of system design begin to fall into place. The development process may take some months to complete, and it is common and not unreasonable for users to require a change in the outputs even before the new system is operational. But because the system has been designed from the output backwards, such changes may necessitate a very large change in the whole system design. This can cause either a serious delay in the implementation schedule or an operational system that is unsatisfactory from the start.

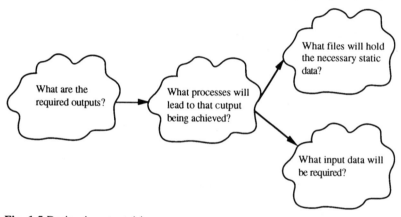

Fig. 1.5 Design is output driven

A third reason for the inflexibility of these systems - and here we re-introduce a key motivation for databases, is that there is no data independence. For example, the design of any file held on computer storage is replicated in the design of the file within all the application programs that use it. There cannot be multiple views of the data and if the design of the file needs to be changed, then all the programs which access that file also need to be changed.

User dissatisfaction, therefore, is a feature almost inherent in some computer applications. Frequently they are rejected as soon as they become operational. Users may have agreed the design of outputs with the systems analysts, but it is only when the system is operational that they see the repercussions of their decisions. Many data processing departments expect the users to 'sign off' their requirements at an early stage in the development of the system. At this time the users do not have the information to agree the exact requirements of the application. They may sign the completed documentation, even though these are not designed with the user in mind. On the contrary, they are designed for the systems analysts, operations staff, and programming staff who are involved in developing the system. Users cannot be expected to be familiar with the technology and its full potential. How can they usefully contribute to the debate? As a consequence, they are frequently disappointed with their computer systems, disillusioned with computers in general and fail to cooperate with the systems development staff. Conversely, because of this, computer people often regard users as 'bloody minded' and unable to make a decision.

In Section 1.2, one of the benefits of the NCC approach discussed was the documentation standards that were an integral part of that methodology. But there are **problems with the documentation**. The orientation of the documentation, as we have already seen, is towards the technologist and not the future users of the system. The main purpose of documentation should be to aid communication. A technically-oriented design is not ideal for this purpose. A further problem that occurs is that the forms tend to be completed rather reluctantly by the programmer or analyst. Completion is usually required by the data processing department, but it is infrequently done well. Furthermore, it is rarely updated when modifications to the system are made. This makes the documentation useless because it cannot be relied upon as an accurate reflection of the true system.

Computers are particularly good at processing a large amount of data quickly and accurately. They excel where the processing is the same for all items. Here the processing is structured, stable and routine. The unusual conditions, commonly known as exception conditions, are frequently ignored in the computer system and this leads to **incomplete systems**. The exception conditions are expensive to cater for. If they are diagnosed in the system investigation stage, then clerical staff may be assigned to deal with these exceptions. Frequently they are detected too late as the systems analyst finds out exactly what 'Joe Bloggs does in the corner'. He deals with the customer who is different from the rest and has to be dealt with separately. The new system, not catering for these special circumstances, crashes when the records of Joe Bloggs' customers are accessed, usually soon after the system is operational.

A further problem is the **application backlog** found in data processing departments. There may well be a number of applications waiting to be developed. Some users may have to wait two or three years before the development process can get under way and a further year before their system is operational. The temptation then will be to offer a 'quick and dirty' solution, particularly if the deadline set for cutover proves to be somewhat optimistic. It may be politically expedient to patch over a bad design rather than spend time on good design. However, poorly designed systems will be difficult to maintain and in many businesses the **maintenance workload** is over 75% of total data processing workload. The question is soon asked: 'should we start again with a new and more appropriate system?'.

1.4 ANSWERS TO THESE PROBLEMS

Over the last few years, a number of developments have been made. Advances have occurred in hardware, software, tools and techniques, and in the demands of managers and other users. These advances, which have enabled improvements to be incorporated in the conventional approach to data processing, have also enabled alternative methodologies to be developed which may be more appropriate in some circumstances. The improvements that are most relevant to the methodology described in this text are shown in Figure 1.6.

Although this text is about an approach to implement better systems for the user, such developments would not be possible but for the massive advances in hardware and software which seem to be never-ending. It is very difficult to keep up with the pace of change. Access times, memory size and reliability have all changed continuously and to the benefit of the user. Costs, for any particular computing power, have also shown a general movement downwards. The flexibility and power of the software now available also provides a necessary backcloth to the developments that are discussed in this text. Developments in data communications, microcomputers and workstations, operating software, database management software, fourth generation and computer-aided software engineering (Case) tools, and data dictionaries gain emphasis here only because of their special relevance to the database approach. The tools and techniques discussed, together with these technological developments, form the basis of the methodology. Data analysis, relational theory, new techniques of systems analysis and design, and object-oriented techniques, are highlighted because the use of these will improve the likelihood of the database project being successful.

The 'people' developments are also crucial. The willingness of non-computer people to become involved and contribute to the process of change, and management's will to demand these changes, also contribute positively. They are factors which are important in any computing project, but are particularly important in the long term and high cost projects discussed in this text. This section will look briefly at all these developments, but some will be re-introduced in the context of the overall methodology later in the text.

HARDWARE DEVELOPMENTS
- Data communications
- Microcomputers and workstations
- Distributed databases
- Database machines

SOFTWARE DEVELOPMENTS
- Real-time operating systems
- Database management systems
- Data dictionaries
- Fourth generation, Case and other tools
- Multi-media systems

TECHNIQUES
- Data analysis
- Relational theory
- Improved systems analysis and design techniques
- Object-oriented techniques
- Prototyping

PEOPLE DEVELOPMENTS
- Participation
- Management requirement

Fig. 1.6 Developments in computing

Data communications: The ability for computers to 'talk' to each other is now commonplace, even where these computers and their associated equipment are very different and made by different manufacturers. It has opened up many possibilities for users. It has facilitated the passing of information between users. It has also allowed data of all descriptions to be held in one place (the database) and accessed by a number of users in remote sites. Although access will sometimes be made to the central computer and database by users in the same building, very often the users are situated in other buildings, other towns, and other countries. With the development of microcomputers, local area networks (LANs) are being set up within businesses which ease the sharing of local data. The disk system of the file server, which is a hard disk microcomputer system usually dedicated to managing the network, might contain both the shared programs and data. With open systems architecture (OSA) or interconnection (OSI) any type of device and different models of each device can be hooked on to the network.

Microcomputers and workstations: Microprocessors and associated technology have led to computers costing a few hundred pounds which are more powerful than many mainframe computers of the 1970s which cost tens of thousands of pounds. They are also, by comparison, very small and some are portable. Typically, they can be placed on an office desk. Some come with packages which can perform word processing, graphics applications, spreadsheet and file management (often powerful enough to be called database management systems). One of their most important effects is to make every office worker and manager aware of computing. This awareness is a prerequisite for successful systems implementation. The technology on the office desk is no longer a 'dumb' terminal but a powerful workstation that can be used for the day-to-day work of the office. Further, microcomputers can be connected to other microcomputers and mainframes, so that their facilities can be brought in when needed. One of these facilities is likely to be the corporate database.

Distributed databases: With powerful microcomputers which can be linked together by networks, it is possible to distribute the database amongst the users over a number of different sites. Data can be held where it is used most. Each group of users can control 'their' particular part of the database, but other users can have access to it when required (assuming that they have the access privileges). Such a strategy may be suitable to organisations which are themselves dispersed, particularly where there is a tradition of local management independence. There may be other advantages, particularly those related to security, as the overall database is less vulnerable to a failure at one site (indeed, where it is so organised, less vulnerable to failure at a number of sites).

Database machines: Most database systems are implemented on general-purpose computers. These computers are used for many applications, some of which use the database and others which do not, and run systems software, including the database management system itself. The idea of a database machine is to locate the DBMS on a separate computer from the applications: this computer is dedicated to database work. Such an environment can increase overall efficiency, as whilst the database machine is searching the database, the applications computer can be executing programs. If the general-purpose machine is running a program waiting for data from the database machine, it can run another application program until the data has been received. Overall speed is also increased because the database machine can hold indexes to the data in main memory, indeed such computers are designed for efficient database processing and can be free of non-database processing responsibilities and facilities. Likewise, the applications computer is free of database processing responsibilities. Some installations have a dedicated database machine connected to a number of general-purpose computers. With a dedicated database machine, security of the database may be easier, and there may be cost advantages as well.

Real-time operating systems: Without multi-user and real-time operating systems, the applications discussed in this text would not have been possible. Such operating systems are now well established: indeed it is rare for operating systems to be single user, except in a microcomputer environment. Some mainframe computer systems are capable of processing many programs at the same time and handling a few hundred users connected to the computer. Some applications will be real-time systems, that is, changes to the 'real world' are reflected in the computer files almost immediately. The response time for the operating system to react to input needs to be very fast. Conventional systems were designed for batch processing, that is, the data for a system was put into batches, input to the system and processed together through the various programs. The application system could take an hour or more to process all the data. Frequently jobs were left overnight for processing on the computer. This processing time is not good enough for many applications.

Database management systems: A database is an organised and integrated collection of data. A large collection of books owned by the local council is not a public library. It only becomes one when, amongst other things, the books have been catalogued and cross-referenced so that they can be found easily and used for many purposes and by many readers. A database is also expected to be used by a number of users in a number of ways. In some companies the whole organisation is modelled on a database, so that, in theory at least, users can find out any information about any aspect of the organisation by making enquiries of the database. There needs to be a large piece of software which will handle the many accesses to the database. This software is the database management system (DBMS). The DBMS will store the data and the data relationships on the backing storage devices. It must also provide an effective means of retrieval of that data when the applications require it, so that this important resource of the business, the **data resource**, is used effectively. Efficient data retrieval may be accomplished by computer programs written in conventional programming languages such as Cobol, C and Fortran accessing the database. It can also be accomplished through the use of a query language which can be used by people who are not computer experts. These arrangements are shown in Figure 1.7.

Data dictionaries: Following the library analogy used in the previous paragraph, a data dictionary represents the catalogue. In other words, it is the directory showing what data is in the database. It will have information on each item of data held on the database, such as its name, who uses it, who updates it, and how it is validated. It will help to enforce standards - essential because of the shared nature of database use. The dictionary is therefore crucial to the success of the database project. Data dictionary

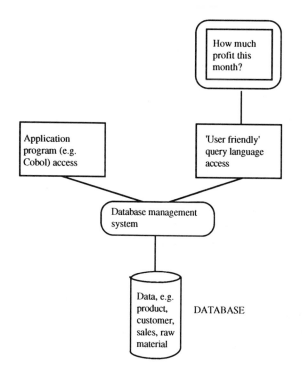

Fig. 1.7 The role of the DBMS intercepting data requests of users and application programs

systems have now become very sophisticated encyclopaedias, not only holding information about database use but also that relating to users, programs and application systems.

Fourth generation, Case and other tools: One of the problems mentioned in Section 1.3 was the application backlog. Writing programs in conventional programming languages such as Fortran and Cobol can be slow. A number of program generators and other tools have now been developed which can speed up the process of developing systems. These tools could be used to automate aspects of developing an application or designing the database. Some generate the Cobol code from the user's list of requirements using a library of subroutines, accessing the data dictionary and database where appropriate. The user's requirements might be expressed on forms, for example, on a 'soft copy' form (on the screen). Other tools aim to help design work, such as drawing diagrams, validating them and checking their consistency with other parts of the design. A fourth generation system is likely to include a database management system and data dictionary amongst its set of tools. The distinction between a Case and a fourth generation tool is somewhat confused in the market place, but the latter is often designed for use by users, whereas Case tools are normally designed for use by programmers and computer analysts.

Multi-media systems: These allow the storage, access and presentation of different forms and types of information, such as text (words and numbers, etc), images (graphical, photographic, video and animated) and audio (music and speech). Multi-media systems rely on the online storage of large amounts of data. CD-ROM and other improvements in storage systems have made this possible. The term 'database' in such environments will relate to audio and visual information as well as text. For example, data on personnel might include digitalised photographs; data on products might include video pictures showing the uses of the products; and data relating to sales orders might be input to the database by salesmen using voice.

Data analysis: The development of data analysis techniques has helped to bring out the structure and meaning of data in organisations. These techniques can be used as the first step of extrapolating the complexities of the real world into a model that can be held on a computer and be accessed by many users. The data can be gathered by conventional methods, such as interviews and studying documents. The results are usually represented in the form of an entity-relationship diagram. Entities are things of interest, such as customers, products and suppliers, and relationships might include that between customers and products (a customer orders products). There are a number of documentation and pictorial aids used in the process of data analysis and tools are available to help in the process. Some of these documents can be used as source documents for the data dictionary. The end result of data analysis can be mapped onto a database management system. This may sound a trivial task. However, modelling the organisation on a computer database is not easy. The whole organisation is usually too large as there will be too many things to be modelled. It takes too long and is unlikely to achieve anything concrete like an information system in a reasonable timescale. Managers want tangible results fairly quickly. A further consideration is that it is impossible to be totally objective and our task is rather to model a particular view of the organisation, one which proves reasonable and accurate for most applications and users in the problem domain, be it application, department or organisation.

Relational theory: As Figure 1.8 shows, relations are tables of data. The data of an organisation can be represented using a number of these relations. The relational model can be an end result of data analysis. It can also be used as input to most DBMS packages to describe the data structures. As far as the user is concerned, a relational DBMS is one which 'sees' the database as a collection of tables and provides a language to manipulate these tables. Relations are readily understood by computer experts and non-experts alike. This could not be said of the equivalent file structures used in conventional systems analysis which are difficult to understand by all but the trained computer user. However, so as to make the relations useful as a basis for modelling, certain rules are applied to them. These are collectively known as the rules of normalisation. Relations can be manipulated conveniently by computer programs. Certain aspects of two or more relations could be combined to highlight related sets of data or separated to highlight information contained in certain columns or rows which are of particular interest to the user. These requests to manipulate relations may be made within conventional programming languages or by users who have access to a relational DBMS using a database query language.

RELATION NAME: ORDER

NAME	PART-NUMBER	QUANTITY
Lee	36	12
Deene	38	18
Smith	30	96
Lee	57	20

RELATION NAME: COURSE

COURSE-NO.	COURSE-NAME	LEVEL	YEARS	STRUCTURE
B74	Computer science	BSc	3	Full-time
B75	Computer science	BSc	5	Part-time
C30	Computer science	MSc	1	Full-time
D70	Business studies	BA	3	Full-time
D75	Business studies	MBA	1	Full-time

Fig. 1.8 Relations: the tabular representation of data

Improved systems analysis and design techniques: Just as data analysis is a series of techniques to develop a data model, there is a parallel need to understand the functions that will be applied to the database when it is implemented. There has also been a series of improvements here. These techniques include the use of diagrammatic aids such as data flow diagrams and decision trees, and other techniques such as 'structured English'. The essential feature of these structured techniques is functional decomposition, that is the breaking down of large complex systems into smaller, more manageable and understandable subsystems. Many of these techniques have been incorporated into conventional systems analysis and have greatly improved its effectiveness. Other techniques aim to analyse and record less structured, but equally important, information and these techniques include rich pictures. All these techniques help in understanding the real-world processes and in communicating the knowledge acquired. Users can follow the analyst's documentation and confirm the analyst's understanding of the processes. Once there is agreement, the results can be converted into computer procedures as information systems applications using the database.

Object-oriented techniques: In object-oriented systems real-world objects are represented as objects. However, in order to support the richness of the real-world data represented, they are organised into classes such as complex objects. The object-oriented data model closely matches real-world entities, and languages to manipulate objects (such as Smalltalk) can be used as database languages so that object-oriented techniques are likely to impact on both data modelling and database management. Object-oriented databases are also likely to be of importance in those applications where relational databases have proved inefficient, for example, in the fields of computer-aided design and manufacture and office automation.

Prototyping: We have seen that many systems are implemented and then rejected by the users. One way to minimise this risk is to develop a prototype first. The users can see, using this 'quick and dirty' solution, what the outputs will be like. Ideas from users to improve the proposed system can be incorporated into the prototype until they finally give their approval. The operational system can then be developed with the analysts more confident that it is likely to be accepted by the users and therefore be successful. As we have seen, a number of computer aids are now available, such as program generators, report generators and screen painters, which facilitate the quick production of a prototype. These tools could be available in a fourth generation system or Case product. Prototyping can be incorporated into conventional systems analysis as an improved systems investigation technique. An alternative way of using a prototype is to use it as the operational system, once the user is satisfied with it. However there are maintenance and other problems with this approach, because it is difficult to build into the prototype the features necessary for a reliable operational system.

Participation: This is a practical philosophy aimed at providing solutions to user problems. In conventional systems analysis, the importance of user involvement is frequently stressed. However it is the technologist who is making the real decisions. The user, the person who will hopefully gain from the new system, frequently feels resentment about this lack of true involvement. When the system is implemented, the analyst may well feel pleased with the system, the users may not. If the users participated more in the design and development of the system, perhaps playing the leading role in the design, they are far more likely to be committed to the system once it is implemented. The role of computer analysts may then become more of a 'facilitator' than of decision-maker. The users may also try application packages rather than expect the data processing department to develop the applications. Through the use of a fourth generation system, users may develop applications themselves with little or no intervention from the 'specialist'.

Management requirement: In the past, top management have often avoided contact with computers. They have probably sanctioned the purchase of computer systems but have not involved themselves with their use, rather keeping themselves at a 'safe' distance. This cannot help achieve the goal of implementing successful computer applications. Managers need to participate in the change and this will also motivate their subordinates. However, there is now a growing awareness about computers and most managers will have used microcomputers in some way and can see that more sophisticated computer systems can be used to help them in their decision-making. Earlier computing concerned itself with the operations level of management within the firm. Modern computer applications concern themselves with decision-support as well. Top management and middle management, previously ignored by the computer (see Figure 1.4), are being helped by applications called decision-support systems and executive information systems. These applications are backed up by the corporate database. Managers realise that, without these computer applications, their businesses might lose out to competitors. Having said that, competitive advantage is not guaranteed with such systems! One possibility of organising computing for management is to connect the manager's microcomputer to the mainframe information system with its database; another is to provide a dedicated system, with database, which is used purely to provide information for executives. Some fourth generation systems, which usually incorporate a database, are designed for use by managers and others untrained in conventional computing. Most have sophisticated but easy-to-use tools for decision-support. Managers are now far more likely to demand sophisticated computer applications and play a leading role in their development. This will provide the clear sense of direction necessary for all large-scale projects.

These advances enable the growing and more mature use of information technology by organisations (Nolan, 1979). The scope of the application portfolio throughout the organisation moves from the narrow accounting systems to management information systems; the scope of data processing planning and control activities moves from an inward to external focus; and the level of user awareness moves from a passive to an active stance. An important indicator of growing maturity is the use of a database rather than single application files.

1.5 WHY DATABASES?

The database provides the data resource for the organisation. It is a major intangible asset of most organisations. The database management system is the software which manages this resource. Databases did not gain widespread use in the United Kingdom until the middle 1970s. Although database management systems were available before 1970, the systems available then were, by today's standards, somewhat rudimentary.

In the 1970s, a number of large firms with mainframe computers adopted the database approach. There were a number of reasons, for example to:

- Increase data shareability
- Increase data integrity
- Increase the speed in implementing applications
- Ease data access by programmers and users
- Increase data independence
- Reduce program maintenance
- Provide a management view of the organisation
- Improve the standards of the systems developers.

Increase data shareability: Large organisations, such as insurance companies, banks, local councils and manufacturing companies, had for some time been putting large amounts of data onto their computer systems. Frequently the same data was being collected, validated, stored and accessed separately for a number of purposes. For example, there could be a file of customer details for sales order processing and another for sales ledger. This 'data redundancy' is costly and can be avoided by the use of a database management system. In fact some data duplication is reasonable in a database environment, but it should be known, controlled and be there for a purpose, such as efficient response to some database queries. However, the underlying data should be collected only once, and verified only once, so that there is little chance of inconsistency. With conventional files, the data is often collected at different times and validated by different validation routines, and therefore the output produced by different systems could well be inconsistent. In such situations the data resource is not easily managed and this leads to a number of problems. With reduced redundancy, data can be managed and shared, but it is essential that good integrity and security features operate in such systems. In other words, there needs to be control of the data resource. Furthermore, each application should run 'unaware' of the existence of others using the database. Good shareability implies ready availability of the data to all users. The computer system must therefore be powerful enough so that performance is good even when there are a large number of users concurrently accessing the database.

Increase data integrity: In a shared environment, it is crucial for the success of the database system to control the creation, deletion and update of data and to ensure its correctness and its 'up-to-dateness' - in general, ensure the quality of the data. Furthermore, with so many users accessing the database, there must be some control to prevent failed transactions leaving the database in an inconsistent state. However, this should be easier to effect in a database environment, because of the possibilities of central management of the data resource, than one where each application sets up its own files. Standards need only be agreed and set up once for all users.

Increase speed of implementing applications: Applications ought to be implemented in less time, since systems development staff can largely concentrate on the processes involved in the application itself rather than on the collection, validation, sorting and storage of data. Much of the data required for a new application may already be held on the database, put there for another purpose. Accessing the data will also be easier because this will be handled by the data manipulation features of the database management system.

Ease data access by programmers and users: Early database management systems used well-known programming languages such as Cobol and Fortran to access the database. Cobol, for example, was extended to include new instructions which were used when it was necessary to access data on the database. These 'host language' extensions were not difficult for experienced computer programmers to learn and to use. Later came query languages and other software tools which eased the process of applications development in a database environment. Once the database had been set up applications development time should be greatly reduced.

Increase data independence: There are many aspects to data independence. It is the ability to change the format of the data, the medium on which the data is held or the data structures, without having to change the programs which use the data. Conversely, it also means that it is possible to change the logic of the programs without having to change the file definitions, so that programmer productivity is increased. It also means that there can be different user views of the data even though it is stored only once. This separation of the issues concerning processes from the issues concerning data is a key reason for opting for the database solution. It provides far greater flexibility.

Reduce program maintenance: Stored data will need to be changed frequently as the real-world that it represents changes. New data types need to be added, formats changed or new access methods introduced. Whereas in a conventional file environment all application programs which use the data will need to be modified, the data independence of a database environment, discussed above, circumvents the necessity of changing each program. It is necessary only to change the database and the data dictionary.

Provide a management view: With conventional systems, management do not get the benefits from the expensive computing resource that they have sanctioned. However, managers have become aware of the need for a corporate view of their organisation. Such a view requires data from a number of sections, departments, divisions and sometimes companies in a larger organisation. This corporate view cannot be gained if files are established on an application-by-application basis and not integrated as in a database. With decision-support systems using the database, it becomes possible for problems previously considered solvable only by intuition and judgement to be solved with an added ingredient, that of information, which is timely, accurate and presented at the required level of detail. Some of this information could be provided on a regular basis whilst some will be of a 'one-off' nature. Database systems should respond to both types of request.

Improve standards: In traditional systems development, applications are implemented by different project teams of systems analysts and programmers and it is difficult to apply standards and conventions for all applications. Computer people are reputed to dislike following the norms of the firm, and it is difficult to impose standards where applications are developed piecemeal. With a central database, it is possible to impose standards for file creation, access and update, and to impose good controls, enabling unauthorised access to be restricted and providing adequate back-up and security features.

1.6 EARLY DATABASE EXPERIENCE

Unfortunately not all the ambitions discussed in the previous section were realised in the early years of database systems. Data was frequently collected, input and validated more than once; sometimes data retrieval times were slower than those of conventional file access; the integrity and security of the databases were called into question; some database systems only supported batch processing and limited file handling facilities; and it was frequently difficult to incorporate new data structures without causing problems, which sometimes required the time-consuming process of reorganising the database. Database projects were very large and complex and the technology was not well understood. In short, the claims of the approach were not being substantiated.

Worse, this proved to be an expensive venture. The database software, the extra hardware required to support it, and the conversion of existing applications were all expensive. Organisations adopting the database approach were frequently surprised by the extra main memory required to hold the database software and the extra handling routines to support it. Frequently it was necessary to spend large sums of money on backing storage, much of which were needed for overheads consumed by the database management system, not for the company's data. Further, the database environment is a complex one. It requires sophisticated programming, back-up and recovery procedures and the computing installation becomes increasingly vulnerable in the event of failure.

There were a number of reasons for early problems with database systems. They included:

- Limitations of the software
- Limitations of the hardware
- Complexity
- Inexperience with the technology
- The lack of a data dictionary
- The lack of a database administrator
- Poor user languages
- The lack of management commitment
- The difficulty of modelling reality.

Limitations of the software: Some database systems were unable to express the complex logical structures of the data found in the applications. Many database management systems of the time saw data relationships only in terms of hierarchies and they had limits on the number of files that they could handle. Some of these limitations are not found in later versions of these systems or have been superseded by alternative models, and modern database management systems are, in general, much more sophisticated, but their early limitations proved a significant obstacle to successful implementation of database systems at the time.

Limitations of the hardware: On implementing the database software it was soon realised that it would be necessary to upgrade the hardware. In other words to gain the advantage of the approach, it was necessary to purchase extra disk capacity and sometimes to upgrade the computer itself with extra internal memory or a more expensive computer in the series with a faster processor. These monies may well not have been set aside by management who may be unwilling to invest further on the database project until it 'proves' itself. Without this extra hardware, this may be particularly difficult to achieve, leading to a sort of vicious circle.

Complexity: The support of database functions makes both the database system and its use very complex and difficult to manage. Sometimes poor physical design decisions, allied with this complexity, made the database project totally ineffective. Such failure had considerable impact, because the database project involved more departments in the organisation than a conventional application.

Inexperience with the technology: Systems development staff, that is programmers and systems analysts, were inexperienced with database technology and therefore had problems converting old applications to the new technology and in developing new ones. Computer people have a reputation for experimenting at the expense of the user. Attempts were made to implement applications using the new technology before the analysts were fully conversant with that technology and the problems that ensued eventually led to a lack of confidence in database applications. Many organisations were unwilling to invest in the human resources necessary for effective database development and use and there were not only technical problems but also political problems as there was no person appointed to help resolve the organisational conflict that comes from shared data. Yet, there was pressure to adopt a database path where, for example, competitors were using database technology and thought to be gaining competitive advantage.

The lack of a data dictionary: The need for a data dictionary was infrequently recognised and they were not normally provided with the database system in the early days. This meant that it was difficult for users to know what was already in the database and consequently difficult to avoid unnecessary data duplication and, in general, difficult to control database use.

The lack of a database administrator: The need for a database administrator was also not recognised. Standards for database use were rarely imposed, conflicting requirements of users unsatisfactorily resolved and the performance of the database system rarely monitored, so that few steps were made to improve performance. If such a role had been created, there were few facilities, such as data dictionaries, that would help the task being fulfilled successfully.

Poor user languages: Access to the database was gained through a host language rather than a query language. Host languages are suitable for computing professionals. It was therefore not possible for the users of the organisation to access the database themselves. Some of the expected gains of the database approach would only accrue if there was access to the database available to less experienced users. Non-procedural, natural language-like query languages only became generally available later.

Lack of management commitment: It was not usual for managers to become involved in computing. 'Computers were for experts', and, as we saw in the previous paragraph, there were no 'user-friendly' query languages available for database access on most systems. The database applications therefore continued to concentrate on operations level processing rather than on decision-support systems. Thus the real potential of the database approach was not being realised.

The difficulty of modelling reality: It is difficult to accurately reflect the organisation on computer files. How does the systems analyst hold on computer files the facts and rules that represent the organisation? Unless this is achieved, it is likely that the applications on the database will be incomplete and inaccurate. This was a difficult problem in the early days of databases and the problem is still with us. We will therefore consider this problem in some greater detail.

1.7 THE DIFFICULTY OF MODELLING REALITY

Most of the problems discussed in the previous section have been overcome. The technology has improved out of all recognition, and this applies to both hardware and software. Costs have continued to go down, whilst both capacities and speed of access improve. The technologist has learnt how to use the computer database environment to the good advantage of the organisation. 'User friendly' languages have been developed so that those users who are not computer experts may profitably access the database themselves. Managers are more involved with computing, partly as a result of their use of microcomputers, but also through their use of decision-support systems and executive information systems. Data dictionary systems have been developed which interface with the database packages and most organisations that use database systems have employed a database administrator. The final problem remains with us: how to model the real world onto a database. There are a number of aspects to this problem.

It is impractical to represent the whole organisation on a database. The analyst aims to hold only that relatively small part which will be a good basis for most applications. More fundamentally, however, is that a database can only be 'A' and not 'THE' model of the organisation. It cannot reflect reality completely and accurately for all purposes. It may present a distorted picture for some purposes and even if the modelling process has 'gone according to plan', the resultant database cannot be perfect. We can never fully know reality; our view of the real world is distorted by our perceptive process.

In a database project, we are aiming to produce the best model of the organisation that we can, and transform this on to a computer database that can be used for the information systems applications. This is difficult. The data on the database will be used by many applications and therefore it is important that it is well validated. However, no data can be guaranteed 100% accurate. It may be 'accurate enough' for some applications, but it will not necessarily be good enough for new applications which are added to the database later. The cost of ensuring 100% accuracy for all applications is prohibitive.

Another problem of which the reader ought to be aware is that in aiming to model the organisation, we are making a number of dubious assumptions. The data collected may not necessarily be useful at a later date. This is an expensive overhead on an already expensive enterprise. If it might be useful in the future, the data may then be out-of-date. Like many an attic, the database may contain a lot of rubbish. Utopian databases therefore do not exist.

In database projects we are attempting to achieve that which proves useful for most demands. In order to achieve this we need a positive methodology. This text aims to provide such a methodology, one that will harness some of the most sophisticated aspects of the new technology. It looks at the techniques, the role of the innovator, and the role of the manager, for, without considering all aspects of the processes and the people involved, the database project will fail ... and it will be a most expensive failure.

There are a number of stages in the methodology. These are stages in developing a data model which is almost natural to the user (**conceptual model**) through a series of mappings to other models before finally transferring it to a model which is natural to the machine (**physical model**). By 'natural' we mean readily understandable. These different views are necessary because it is not reasonable to expect a particular view to be natural to both man and machine.

We have used the term **model** without fully explaining what a model is. A model is a representation of the 'real world', often simplified, so that it represents only those aspects in which we are interested. We can use it to demonstrate features of the real world that are of interest to users or to see the effects of certain actions. Choosing and constructing appropriate models is difficult and the methodology described in this text uses a series of models and modelling techniques to derive the database model (physical model). This series of models begins with a very abstract model of the situation which is developed in the business analysis phase and is required to put all the relevant parts into perspective (Benyon, 1990, calls this type of model coarse-grained) whereas the physical model is more concrete, detailed and formal (fine-grained). We need intermediate models, the conceptual model and the logical model, to provide a smooth transition between the two. We also need models to provide different perspectives: for example, a process-oriented model, a data-oriented model or a people-oriented model and various combinations of these. We can also distinguish between different types of model of the same type, so that data models, for example, may contain information from the users' perspective (which Langefors & Sundgren, 1975, call the **infological** realm) or in a form suitable for implementing on the computer (**datalogical**). The former are likely to be graphical models (for example, annotated diagrams) whereas the latter needs to be formal (for example, relations). In the next section, we look at another model, the database architecture proposed by ANSI/X3/SPARC as it helps us to understand the situation of the database in relation to user programs and the computer system. This is put into the perspective of the methodology and its various modelling stages in Section 1.9.

1.8 THE ANSI/X3/SPARC ARCHITECTURE

The ANSI/X3/SPARC committee, established in 1972 with reports in 1975 and 1978 (ANSI/X3/SPARC, 1975, and Tsichritzis & Klug, 1978) suggested an architecture for database systems which has proved very influential in the database field. It will be frequently referred to in this book. As seen in Figure 1.9, the basic architecture of ANSI/X3/SPARC has three views. These are the external, conceptual and internal views of the database.

The external view is the view of the data as 'seen' by application programs and users. It will be a subset of the conceptual model which is a global or organisational view of the data. There may be a number of different user views and different users and programs may share views (Figure 1.9 shows that external view 1 is used by two applications). This arrangement enables aspects of the data in which a user may not be interested or does not have rights of access to be hidden from that user. There is a series of mappings or transformations between the external views and the conceptual view.

The internal view of the data describes how and where the data is stored. It will describe the access paths to the data storage and provide details of the data storage. There is again a mapping between the conceptual and internal views.

The conceptual view describes the whole database for the organisation (or community of users) in terms of entities, attributes and relationships. As we have seen, there is a series of mappings, from the conceptual view to the various external views and internal view and these mappings will be carried out by the database management system.

The separation of different views of the data enables the data independence, which we have considered so crucial to the database approach. It is possible to change the conceptual view without changing the external views (and the application programs that use them). This is known as **logical data independence**. It is also possible to change the internal view without changing the conceptual and external views. This is known as **physical data independence**.

The contribution of ANSI/X3/SPARC is important, in particular, because it enables us to understand the main functions of the database and demonstrates how data independence might be achieved using database systems. But it is not complete. We still need to consider how the conceptual view is formed. Some consideration of the organisation (business analysis) is necessary. We need also to consider how the conceptual view might be mapped to the various database systems. This is the logical view of relational, hierarchical, network and object-oriented databases. The database management system will map this on to the physical view of file organisation and access methods. We also need to know how the various applications using the database will be designed and which external views of the data might be appropriate for each application (applications development). These applications may access the database using conventional high level language programs or database query language programs.

The methodology described in this text puts the ANSI/X3/SPARC architecture into the overall perspective of a methodology for developing and implementing the database and the applications using it. This is outlined in the next section.

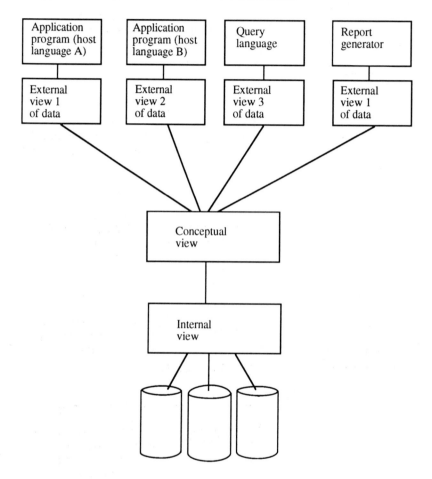

Fig. 1.9 The ANSI/X3/SPARC database architecture

1.9 THE APPROACH IN OUTLINE

The process of deriving a model of the business which is described in this text consists of a number of phases, most of which are shown in Figure 1.10. Further elements of the methodology and the various technological and human support necessary are

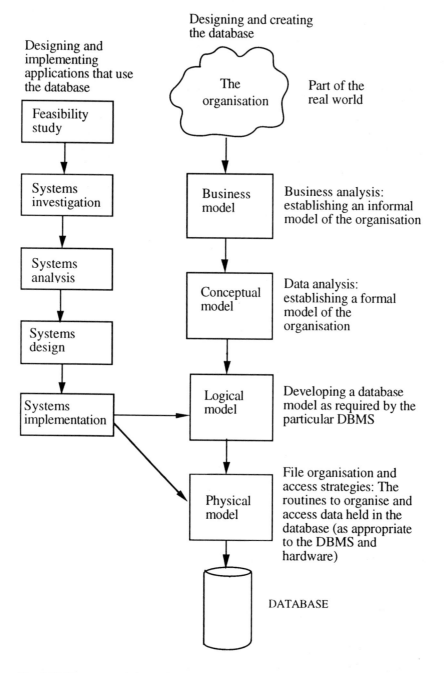

Fig. 1.10 The approach in outline (b)

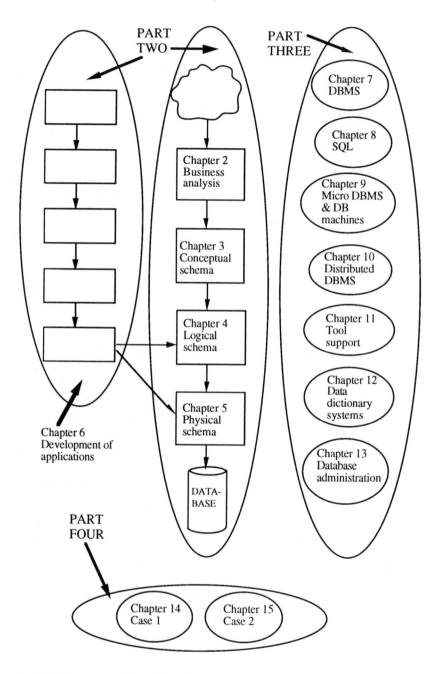

Fig. 1.11 The approach in outline (c)

illustrated in Figure 1.11, which also shows the chapter numbers in this text for the corresponding parts of the methodology.

Following this introductory chapter and first part, the book has three parts:

Part 2: Database approach to information systems development (Chapters 2-6)

Part 3: The database environment (Chapters 7-13)

Part 4: The approach in action (Chapters 14 and 15).

Part 2 describes the approach to analyse, design, develop and implement the computer database along with the applications that use it. A separate chapter is devoted to each of the five phases (business analysis, conceptual modelling, logical modelling, physical modelling and applications development). Part 3 concerns itself with the technological and people support for database and applications development. Database management systems, the SQL language, microcomputer databases and database machines, distributed databases, tools (including fourth generation systems and Case tools), the data dictionary system and finally the role of the database administrator and the problems of managing the database system and applications development, all form chapters. Part four looks at the approach in action, describing both the development of a database system for a computer service company in Chapter 14 and the development of an information system using a database for a university department in Chapter 15.

The first phase of the methodology consists of an overview of the organisation. It is important to consider the needs of the organisation as a whole, because an overall appraisal is more likely to lead eventually to information systems which address real needs than any attempt to solve a particular short-term problem. This may be a symptom of a different or much bigger problem. In the **business analysis** phase, the analysts find out about the organisational structure, including an outline description of the roles of management personnel. This will guide the analysts in determining who to interview, when to interview them, and what questions to ask. It is necessary to find out what are the goals of the firm. This will be helpful because it will then be possible to discover the types of information required for management to make better decisions. There are a number of diagrammatic aids which can be used at this time, including information modelling, rich pictures and root definitions, and these are all described in Chapter 2.

Another important feature of this business analysis phase is a political one. It is necessary to ascertain which strategies for informations systems implementation will be acceptable to the organisation and how best to approach the human problems associated with change. Some of the people associated with the database project may be doing so reluctantly and these problems are likely to be more difficult to solve than technical problems. Business analysis, therefore, lays the foundation for the work that follows.

Once business analysis is complete, it is possible to derive a formal model of the organisation, referred to as the **conceptual model**. At this stage the analyst identifies the various facts about the organisation and then analyses this data. The facts can be represented as objects of interest, called entities, and data about these objects of interest, called attributes. In a university department, courses, students, and lecturers, could be described as entities. The course entity will have attributes such as course name, description, level, and duration. The analyst will also be interested in relationships between entities. Thus students are likely to be taught by many lecturers. The model so formed is a more formal representation of the organisation, showing the data types and the data structures. The processes involved in deriving the conceptual model are collectively known as data analysis. The analysts will use interviewing, observation and other methods to obtain the information required. There are a number of documentation tools available, such as entity-relationship diagrams. These are useful aids to communication, help to ensure that the work is carried out in a thorough manner and ease the mapping processes that follow data analysis - the conceptual model will be mapped on to a target database management system. Entities can be represented as relations (see Figure 1.8) and Chapter 3 also looks at relational theory and the normalisation of relations.

Having derived the conceptual model, it is possible to map this model onto a computer database management system (previous stages have been carried out independently of any hardware or software considerations). This **logical model** can take a number of forms, depending on the database management system. In some database management systems, as we see in Chapter 4, the data model transferred to the system is defined in terms of relations. Other database management systems view the data relationships in terms of tree structures, known as hierarchies, or rather more complex structures called networks. The rules by which the conceptual model can be mapped (or transformed) into relational, hierarchical or network models are shown. Object-oriented database management systems are comparatively new at the time of writing, but would seem to have the potential to make a considerable impact in the database world, and the object-oriented model is also described in Chapter 4.

The next phase concerns the mapping of the data structures presented to the database management system onto computer storage media, usually magnetic disks. The ways by which the data is organised on disk files and the ways by which it is accessed are known as file organisation and file access respectively. Many database management systems offer alternative ways to organise and access the data, and the choice will depend on efficiency considerations. This **physical model** is discussed in Chapter 5. In this chapter, traditional techniques, such as serial, sequential, indexed, indexed sequential, and random access files are introduced, as well as the major database techniques of B-trees, lists and inverted files. There is a further mapping related to the very technical aspects of computer storage, involving the design of backing storage media, but this is considered outside the scope of this text being related to specific hardware devices and manufacturers and, in any case, not the concern of the applications analyst.

Once the database is created, the subsystems can be designed and implemented using the database. In Chapter 1 we have discussed the limitations of conventional systems analysis. In Chapter 6, we look at methods of **applications development** in a database environment. We look at the various user views (or external views) which will be used by applications. These will be subsets of the conceptual model and the ANSI/X3/SPARC architecture is re-introduced to show how the required data structures might be derived from the database. Database access, that is, the methods and approaches by which applications might access and update data from the database, is also described. We look again at the systems life cycle and discuss how the database approach might be integrated into application systems development. Approaches such as structured systems analysis and design, participation and prototyping are described. The final section looks at Multiview, one approach to develop information systems applications which integrates many of the ideas described in the book.

Although the database methodology described in Chapters 2 to 6 appears to suggest that data analysis and database creation will be completed for the organisation before any applications are implemented, this presents an unrealistic scenario. Management will want an earlier pay-off and it is much more likely that data analysis and database creation will be carried out in one local area (such as a department) at a time and applications implemented which are relevant for that department or division. In this way, the organisational database will gradually build up.

Each part of the methodology could be looked upon as a piece of a jigsaw, and a failure to get each one right may cause disappointment to managers and staff of an organisation and eventual failure of the information systems and database project. Success will also depend on the technological and people support, and the chapters in Part 3 look at these and examine some of the issues involved.

Part 3 starts with a chapter on **database management systems**. These are the software systems supporting database use. Chapter 7 includes a description of one database management system of each type described in Chapter 4: IMS (a hierarchical system); IDMS (a network or Codasyl system); DB2 (a relational system) and Ontos (an object-oriented system), along with Adabas, which is an inverted file database management system. The methods used by each database management system to interact with application programs using conventional programming languages and query languages are highlighted. Many database management systems offer host language access. Most database management systems will also offer some form of query language which will allow non-computer people to access the database. A query language may be suitable for the 'casual user', that is, someone who has little or no knowledge of computing, limited experience of using a computer, and has little time to practise skills in computing.

The most well-used query language is **SQL** and Chapter 8 is devoted to SQL. This language, for querying and updating relations, has become a standard or an option on most popular microcomputer, minicomputer and mainframe database management systems, indeed it has been the subject of an international standards committee (ISO). Computer programmers and other database users are likely to need to know the basis of this interface to database systems. It is therefore reasonable in a database text to look at this language in particular, including an examination of its strengths and weaknesses. There are separate sections on data definition, retrieval and update, followed by a look at user views in SQL, and embedded SQL, that is, access through the use of a host language which has SQL commands embedded in the code.

Chapter 9 looks at **microcomputer database management systems** and **database machines**. The development of microcomputers is described because their early limitations necessitated rudimentary database management systems (in truth, file management systems). But the microcomputer environment is no longer so limiting, and many present-day microcomputer database management systems have most of the features and capabilities of their mainframe counterparts. Indeed, many mainframe systems have their personal computer versions, so that it is possible to prototype an application on a microcomputer, and, once tested, install the operational version of the system on the organisation's mainframe. Overviews are given in this chapter of popular microcomputer database systems, including microcomputer versions of mainframe systems. This chapter also includes a section on database machines. As we saw in Section 1.6, these are computers which are dedicated to database use to which general-purpose computers access when an application needs to use the database. Such an arrangement can prove to be effective, providing speedier processing of database queries and efficient use of the overall computing resource.

Chapter 10 looks at **distributed database management systems**. These have developed greatly in the last few years so that they are now a viable, if not too common, alternative to centralised database computer systems. The first section suggests circumstances where distributed database management systems may be a preferred alternative and suggests bases on which to compare the two database architectures. A section on principles and requirements of distributed database management systems is followed by an examination of their design and a consideration of some key implementation issues.

Chapter 11 looks at the increasingly important area of **tool** support, for database analysis, design and implementation and for the development of applications that use the database. Fourth generation systems, workbenches, Case and multi-media systems are all described. The features of three commercial products, Focus, Information Engineering Workbench and Oracle are discussed. One section examines the place of tools in the overall approach used in this book and there is also a section on tool evaluation.

Chapter 12 looks at **data dictionary systems**. These are software tools for recording and processing information about the data that an organisation processes and uses. Originally these systems were designed merely as documentation tools but they have evolved as an essential feature of the systems environment (indeed, they are probably better named as system catalogues or encyclopedias) and are of particular importance to the database administrator who can use it to keep track of the data on the database and, in general, control its use.

It is essential that the organisation sets firm standards so that data which is shared by many users is not corrupted, privacy requirements are adhered to, and some users of the database are not using it to the detriment of others. The role of the **database administrator** (DBA) is discussed in Chapter 13. The major areas of database security, back-up and recovery, integrity and the privacy of personal data are looked at in some detail. There are also sections outlining the benefits of database administration and the position of the database administrator in the organisation.

Part 4 looks at the approach in action. It consists of two chapters, containing case studies based on two real-life projects. Chapter 14 describes an **application of the approach** described in Part 2 carried out at the Systems Development Division of Comshare Limited, a computer service company. Chapter 15 describes the **development of an information systems application** using a database at the Computer Science Department at Aston University. Together, the two cases provide the reader with some interesting insights into the database approach discussed in this book as well as drawing together the pieces of the jigsaw described in this book into a unified whole.

It must be emphasised that not all aspects of the methodology described in this text will be appropriate for all organisations and all applications. Furthermore, for different projects, different aspects take on different emphases. The approach is as flexible as possible within the overall framework.

1.10 FURTHER READING

Daniels, A & Yeates, D. A (1971) *Basic Training in Systems Analysis*, 2nd ed,

Pitman, London.
This text covers the conventional approach to systems analysis as proposed by the National Computing Centre in 1971. It describes the approach and its associated documentation standards.

Avison, D. E & Fitzgerald, G (1988) *Information Systems Development: Methodologies, Techniques and Tools*, Blackwell Scientific Publications, Oxford.
This text looks at the wide range of methodologies, techniques and tools associated with information systems development. Some can be looked at as alternatives to those described in this book, others can be used along with the database approach.

Nolan, R (1979) Managing the crises in data processing, *Harvard Business Review*, **57**, 2.
Galliers, R. D & Sutherland, A. R (1991) Information systems management and strategy formulation: the 'stages of growth' model revisited, *Journal of Information Systems*, **1**, 2.
Nolan's work postulated a standard growth pattern for organisations' use of information technology. Galliers and Sutherland's paper revises this model.

ANSI/X3/SPARC (1975) *Study Group on Data Base Management Systems, Interim Report*, ACM SIGMOD Bulletin, **7**, 2.
Tsichritzis, D. C & Klug, A (Eds) (1978) The ANSI/X3/SPARC Framework: Report of the Study Group on Data Base Management Systems, *Information Systems*, **3**.
These two documents are the interim and final reports of the ANSI/X3/SPARC group.

_____

PART TWO

A DATABASE APPROACH TO
INFORMATION SYSTEMS DEVELOPMENT

Chapter 2
Business Analysis

2.1 INTRODUCTION

Before we can carry out a detailed examination of the organisation in order to produce a data model which will then be implemented on a database, the analysts need to gain a general appreciation of the business (this term is interpreted broadly to include all types of organisation in the public and private sectors). This background information will include an examination of the goals of the organisation, the company structure and the roles of key personnel. Among other things, this will help the analysts to construct an interview plan. Following preliminary interviews, the analysts will be able to construct models and attempt to find out in outline the information needs of the organisation. This information will also be useful in deciding on the approach to adopt for information systems development. However, business analysis may often suggest altering business practices rather than always reveal a need for computer information systems.

Some practitioners argue that a very detailed analysis of the organisation should be carried out at this time. The danger here, however, is that analysing the working of the company to such a very detailed level early in the life of the project, might cause the analysts to be 'biased' towards the present methods of processing and, in general, to be superficial in the investigation and analysis stages. The analysts may, as a consequence, address the wrong problem by, for example:

* Mistaking a symptom of a problem for the problem itself
* Accepting people's statements of the problem at face value
* Posing questions that presuppose the nature of the problem
* Moving too quickly into 'solution mode'.

One of the main requirements of the analysts is that they view the organisation in a fresh and open way. Even so, an overall impression of the organisation is still necessary.

An important 'philosophical' base of this text comes from systems thinking. One of its ideas is that of **holism** - the whole is greater than the sum of the parts. The inter-relationships between the parts are of crucial significance. The systems approach focuses on the organisation as a whole and is concerned with the performance of the organisation and not on the specific requirements of any one department or application. However, it is usually difficult to persuade employees to see this organisation-wide perspective. One of the advantages of the database approach is that it permits the sharing of data. The database is viewed as a resource of the organisation as a whole. In conventional data processing, on the other hand, files are seen as a department or single application resource. Conventional files are not usually shared between applications.

The terms information and data represent different things. **Data** elements represent facts concerning people, objects, events, and so on. A person's date of birth or driving licence number are examples of data. '25786', '78700199' and '19873' are examples of data. They represent a man's date of birth, a driving licence number and an identity number. A date of birth (25/7/86) associated with a driving licence number (78700199) and an identity number (19873) could be used to give the **information** that a person whose identity number is 19873 possesses a driving licence, even though that person is under the minimum legal age for driving motor vehicles. The information comes from selecting data and presenting it in such a way that it is meaningful and useful to the user. Sometimes, as in this case, its value comes from its rareness or unexpectedness. The database will contain the facts of interest to the organisation. Each item of data on its own may not be useful to the police officer studying the data. Much has to do with the context in which the data is interpreted. The information system should transform the data and present these facts:

- Accurately (and consistently accurately)
- Relevant to the appropriate recipient
- In the correct level of detail
- Completely
- When required.

We have argued in Chapter 1 that computer databases offer advantages in storing and presenting the data over manual or computer file-based systems. But the analyst needs to know how best to design the database and the information systems that use it. Well designed information systems can give the information which will assist managers make better decisions, give their businesses competitive advantage or help them improve their cost structure or product base. A major prerequisite to successful information systems is therefore finding out what the organisation is about, what direction it is going and what information is required to support these goals. This issue is addressed in this chapter.

Although data does not appear at first sight to be a resource of the organisation, it certainly is a resource, as data is essential for the organisation to operate effectively. If a company 'lost' its accounts data, it would represent a serious loss and one which would be difficult to recover from. Some firms sell data, such as the names and addresses of their customers, which can be used by other companies for mailing lists. Data is costly to collect, store and keep up-to-date and it is also costly to transform data into information. The information systems will access data from the database and aim to transform it into information which the organisation can use. The value of information can be readily appreciated. For example, accurate information about future weather conditions will help the manager of a shop to determine whether to buy stocks of ice cream or stocks of soup. Here, information has the key role of reducing uncertainty. Poor information is likely to prove very costly for the shop owner through unsold stocks or missed sales opportunities. Such decisions, for example, as where and when to build a new warehouse, whether to buy out competitors or whether to change product structure, may have very long-term consequences and involve huge investments of money.

As can be seen from Figure 2.1, information systems are designed to help managers make better decisions. The model assumes that managers can specify their information requirements and that these can be predicted by the information system. The system then has to transform these requirements for information into requirements for data. The data will be retrieved from the database, assuming that it has already been collected and stored. Otherwise a data collection exercise is necessary to capture the data and store it in the database. Having retrieved the raw data, it needs to be transformed into the required information, perhaps by some preceding analysis work. The information can then be presented to the manager who now has the opportunity to make good or at least better decisions because the information on which the decisions are based will be of a better quality and more timely.

The information system aims to support decision-making and the decisions ought to be directed towards achieving the goals of the organisation. These are discussed in Section 2.2, along with a look at the universe in which the business is operating. In Section 2.3 we look at the system of values, beliefs and understandings that are shared by members of the organisation, that is, its 'culture'. We then look at the structure of management in the organisation in Section 2.4. A description of the roles of management (and of the users in general) and the information requirements supporting those roles is given in Section 2.5. The role of the systems planning team is emphasised. This will consist of the people involved in the technological change and they will play a major role in deciding what strategy to adopt and in following that strategy through. Just as 'the users' need to be defined, so do 'the analysts'. The systems approach to looking at organisations suggests mixed teams and we describe the roles of the various personnel likely to be involved: users and management as well as the business and technical analysts. There are a number of techniques that can be used to help in the business analysis phase, including interviewing strategies, information modelling, rich pictures and root definitions, and some of these are discussed in Section 2.6. The various strategies for developing information systems are outlined in

Section 2.7. The final section of this chapter stresses the importance of participation by managers and all users. The more radical strategies will not be feasible unless the political climate of the organisation is conducive to major change.

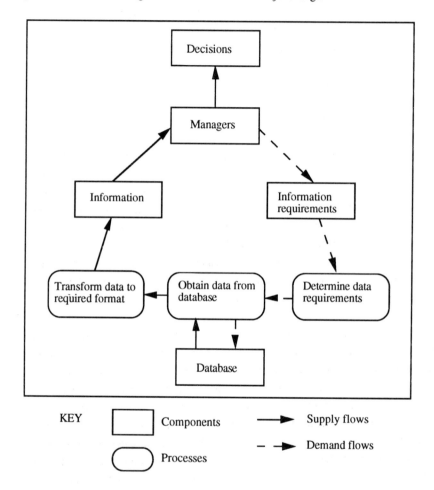

Fig. 2.1 The basic information system

2.2   GOALS OF THE ORGANISATION

The analysts cannot comprehend current or future information requirements unless the direction in which the organisation is going is identified. Management needs to ensure that the expensive and long-term project has a good strategic pay-off. The identification of the goals of the organisation is therefore essential.

Texts used to talk of organisations having just one goal, frequently profit maximisation. According to this view, the organisation was 'tuned' to maximise this one goal. The truth is that businesses have a number of goals. These could include:

- Increasing the size of their market
- Increasing the return on capital
- Increasing turnover
- Ensuring long term survival
- Improving the welfare of their employees
- Improving their public image
- Increasing profits.

Obviously most firms would readily sacrifice some profit if it meant that they were likely to be in business for some time. It could be that there are major goals which businesses fulfil, such as maximising the return on capital, whilst having shorter term aims, such as increasing turnover. During recent times, the main goal of many firms may have been long term survival. Much will depend on the general business climate and the particular business in which the organisation operates.

Some goals may conflict. In a retail organisation one of the goals, to increase sales targets, may conflict with others, such as reduce staff levels or increase profit margins. If sales levels do increase, it may be as a result of increasing sales staff or decreasing profit margins.

Many organisations do have a corporate mission statement which is a declaration of the company's 'reason for being'. It reveals the long-term vision of the organisation in terms of what it wants to be. The mission statement of a health authority may be to promote the health and hygiene of the people in its catchment area. Those of a church, hospital, business or charity are likely to be very different. This type of information may well be gleaned from interviewing members of the directorate - the chief executive, vice presidents, general managers and, perhaps, divisional managers. Other sources of information include the written company review and accounts, which is usually published annually as part of the statement to the shareholders or governors, and recruitment brochures. They will tend to stress long term objectives such as growth in assets, profitability, the degree and nature of diversification, earnings per share and social responsibility, and may specify the mission statement.

Medium (say, a period of six months to two years) and short term (less than six months) objective setting is usually the concern of the individual managers. They will be used as a basis for:

- Allocating resources
- Evaluating managers' performance

- Monitoring progress towards achieving long term goals
- Establishing divisional and departmental priorities.

All this company background can help the analysts get a 'feel' for the organisation, particularly if they are from outside the company. Information systems work is frequently carried out by external consultants or people recently recruited from outside, because they have had experience of such work elsewhere. We will look into the techniques of information gathering and analysis in Section 2.6.

According to Porter (1980 and 1985), the most important element is the industry in which the business competes. There are five competitive forces:

- The threat of new entrants coming into the same market
- The bargaining power of suppliers
- The bargaining power of buyers
- The availability of substitute products or services
- Rivalry among competitors.

Such a study enables a better understanding of the business and promotes new ideas for information systems. Figure 2.2 identifies where action needs to be taken either defensively or offensively to influence the forces in their favour in order to pursue the goals of that firm.

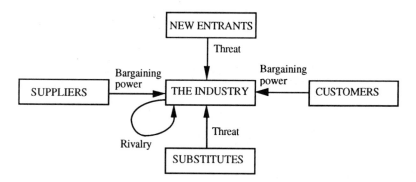

Fig. 2.2 Five forces of industry competition (adapted from Porter, 1980)

This is a useful and interesting view, even if it is rather narrow. It is also useful to look at the broader environment of the organisation, because the actions of trade unions, financial institutions, stockholders and the government, for example, as well as customers, suppliers and competitors, can have far-reaching effects on the business. Any information system needs to be sensitive to the present and future environment. Management should observe and react to changes in economic, social, cultural, demographic, geographical, political, legal, governmental, technological and competitive factors. These factors can affect consumer demand, types of product developed, the services offered and choice of business to acquire or sell. Although it is not always possible to record all this information in the modelling process, it is necessary to be at least aware of these factors. Figure 2.3 paints a sketch of the business universe having a number of major subsystems and environmental systems which relate to the business.

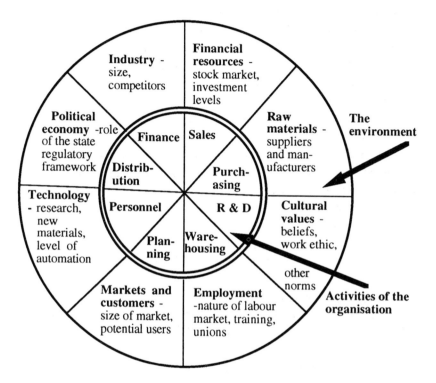

Fig. 2.3 The business universe

The analysis of the environment of an organisation, including the economic environment, needs to be supplemented by analysis of the political and cultural realities of the organisation, which may be at least as influential in the formation of the company goals and will be very important to the success of information systems. For example, the individual culture of organisations might explain why many firms opt for an expansionist policy in times of recession. It is important that the analyst detects the views and expectations of individuals and groups from within and around the organisation that exert power in it. These may be related to the history and age of the organisation, leadership and management style and its structure and systems. We will look at these human and social issues in the next section.

2.3 CULTURE OF THE ORGANISATION

The success of the database venture will depend to a large extent on the culture of the organisation, that is, its people and their values, beliefs and understandings. These will be shared by members of the organisation and set a pattern for its activities and actions. This is likely to have had a great influence on the goals and, in particular, the mission statement of the organisation which were discussed in Section 2.2. Essentially, the culture is a credible set of norms which employees, either consciously or unconsciously, use as guidance in meeting their specific job tasks.

Deal & Kennedy (1982) suggest that there are five elements of corporate culture:
- *Business environment:* the environment in which the organisation operates will determine what it must do to be a success.
- *Values:* these define what is seen as success by the organisation and establish standards of achievement within the organisation.
- *Heroes:* these suggest role models for employees to follow.
- *Rites and rituals:* the systematic routines in the company which define expected behaviour.
- *Cultural network:* the informal means of communication. The use of this network will be required in order to get things done.

A failure in an information systems project may be more due to a lack of recognition of or respect for the culture of the organisation than because of the technology itself. On the other hand, failure may be caused by the culture. Productivity gains expected may be seriously constrained because of ingrained attitudes which cause human behaviour to change slower than the potential rendered by technology or even go in a direction directly opposed to the requirements of the system. Culture can cause an inward-looking view which may lead to missed opportunities in changing external conditions.

The analysts will have to adhere to the cultural norms of the organisation in order to be successful with their database project. They have to deal with the attitudes to change found within the organisation, attempting to amplify positive attitudes and reduce negative ones. Deal & Kennedy suggest the following in situations where the culture may go against successful implementation:
- Position a hero in charge of the process
- Recognise a real threat from outside
- Make transition rituals the pivotal elements of change (for example, let people mourn old ways yet re-negotiate new values)

• Insist on the importance of job security in the transitional stage.

As has already been highlighted, there is a great deal more to successful database and information systems projects than the 'state-of-the-art' technology, and the analysts explore further these factors in the business analysis stage. Before the team of analysts engrosses itself into data analysis, which is partly carried out through interview and observation, it is necessary to consider the structure of the organisation and the roles played by members of the management team. Without this knowledge, it is not possible to decide on the people to interview, in which order they should be interviewed, and the level and subject matter of the questions to ask. We will look at these aspects in Sections 2.4 and 2.5. Section 2.6 looks at some techniques that the analysts might use to analyse the information gathered.

2.4 STRUCTURE OF MANAGEMENT IN THE ORGANISATION

In attempting to understand the organisation it is essential to realise that there is a trade-off between being simplistic and being practical. The management of organisations is very complex. We will first view organisations as having three layers of management because this traditional view proves useful as a basis for analysis. However, we should be aware of the greater complexity that really exists, and other structures, such as cell or matrix structures, have been proposed as being a more realistic reflection of management structure.

At the top of our three layer model, are the board of directors. They are responsible for the long range planning activities of the firm and they will set the overall goals. Middle management, typically heads of departments, will ensure that these policies are carried out and will act upon those conditions that veer from this norm (exceptional conditions). The operations level will be responsible for the day-to-day operations of the organisation. These people might include the chief clerks and foremen who control the daily ordering, production and distribution processes.

It is important to identify these individuals in the early stages of the project. Let us consider a retail company which has a number of department stores and warehouses. Strategic management for this business might include the directors of finance, trading, personnel and buying. Middle management might include the heads of the branches, branch accountants and warehouse managers. Operations management might include department managers, warehouse foremen and the head clerks. This structure is shown in Figure 2.4.

Top management is clearly very important to the organisation, and managers are realising that management information systems can help them make better decisions.

Although the euphoria associated with automatic decision-making has largely gone, the more realistic concepts of **decision-support systems** and **executive support systems** have certainly not disappeared. Management need these systems in order to help them establish sustainable goals and to provide information relating to the long-term decisions of the organisation. Competitive advantage can be gained from exploiting information at the strategic level so as to increase business efficiency or to highlight areas in the organisation which are particularly strong or weak, and thus lead to new business strategies.

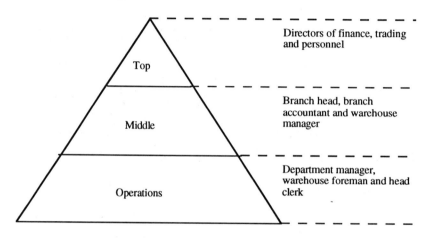

Fig. 2.4 The pyramid structure - layers of management for a retail company

Examples of the types of decisions that managers will make could include:
- Where to site new factories
- Whether to merge with other companies
- Whether to drop a product range.

Information to help top management make these decisions could be provided by the decision-support system. When the model of the organisation is implemented on a database, it will be possible for managers to make enquiries to the database. The types of information required will tend to be unpredictable and unstructured so that database access will need to be flexible. Such enquiries may be answered by getting data from a number of different areas in the database (for example sales, product and employee data to compare last year's with this year's performance).

Information systems should be integrated with the business plan at all three layers of the management hierarchy. Figure 2.5 shows the types of decision, Figure 2.6 examples of the decisions, Figure 2.7 the types of information required to support this decision-making, and Figure 2.8 examples of such information. A retail company with a number of 'High Street' departmental stores will be used as an example. As well as determining the information needed now and in the near future, some regard must be given to the difficult task of trying to foresee information needs in the longer term (Land, 1982). Priorities need to be assigned to information needs, and these priorities have to be assigned by management.

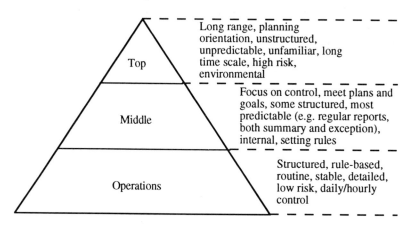

Fig. 2.5 Types of decision made by management

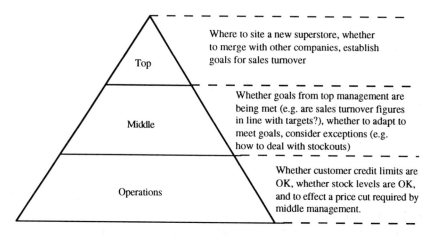

Fig. 2.6 Examples of decision for a retail company

Middle management will ensure that the goals set by top management are being met. Reports about performance will be produced regularly so that the results can be compared to the targets set, and the facilities of the database are also likely to be made available to managers with the help of a query language. The unusual, for example, products which are unavailable from stock, may also be reported on, so that managers may act on these exceptional conditions. This will allow **management by exception**. Much of the information required here will be predictable and internal. For example, each week the manager might want a list of those customers who have not cleared their debts. Decisions at the operations management level can frequently be made automatically. These decisions tend to be structured, rule-based and routine. For example, a computer system can check stock levels and produce a supplier's order request automatically in good time, and this will ensure that there are always supplies of products in stock.

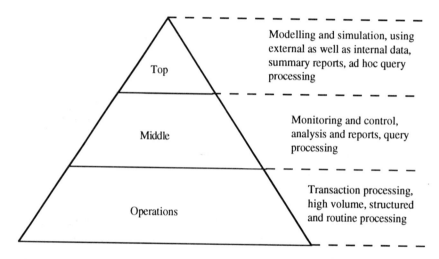

Fig. 2.7 Types of information required by retail company

Early in this section it was pointed out that not all organisations fit in easily to the three level structure. Some smaller firms may have a centralised functional structure where tasks and activities are arranged by business function such as:

- Production
- Finance
- Marketing
- Research and development (R & D)
- Personnel.

Some medium-sized firms will be decentralised and structured by divisions. Within that type of structure there are four ways of organisation:

- By product or service
- By geographic area

- By customer
- By process.

Functional activities will be performed centrally and in each division. The headquarters will be responsible for planning and corporate performance, and divisional managers for profits.

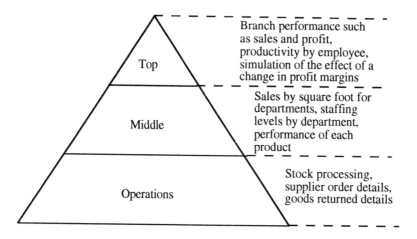

Top — Branch performance such as sales and profit, productivity by employee, simulation of the effect of a change in profit margins

Middle — Sales by square foot for departments, staffing levels by department, performance of each product

Operations — Stock processing, supplier order details, goods returned details

Fig. 2.8 Examples of information required by retail company

Many large firms have a matrix structure which is the most complex, since it is dependent on vertical and horizontal flows of authority and communication, as opposed to the divisional and functional structures which depend on vertical flows of authority and communication. Matrix structures exhibit dual lines of budget authority, dual sources of reward and punishment and dual reporting channels. Much of the discussion related to the three layered model above applies to these situations, but the analyst needs to be aware of other frameworks and recognise them when they occur.

It is important that the information given by the system is *relevant* to the particular recipient and therefore in the correct level of detail. This could be in summary form - **management by summary**. It must also be *accurate*, or at least accurate enough for the recipient, and *timely*, as information provided too late for the particular purpose is useless (and hence not 'information' at all). The system should also be *adaptable* so that it can respond to the changing needs of the user. This means that the data analysis stage is as crucial as the implementation stage of the computer applications. The most sophisticated technology is useless if the data is not appropriate; and the most accurate data collection exercise is useless if the technology does not support timely and adaptable systems.

2.5   ROLES OF KEY PERSONNEL AND SYSTEMS PLANNING TEAM

We have already discussed some of the roles of personnel, in particular the various levels of management. The information needs of the individuals in an organisation should be identified. The information requirements of some personnel may be inferred from their job description. It may be easy to find out formal descriptions of the roles of personnel. Many firms publish full job descriptions along with details of the reporting structure. Equally important is the informal structure. Important parts of the job could be carried out at break times or through telephone calls. Official communication channels may be side-stepped. The analysts therefore need a 'feel' for the informal as well as the formal system.

This exercise will also reveal the likely users of the information system. One fact will be immediately obvious: the users of the information system will not all be trained computer experts. Untrained computer users may make particular requests of the system or they might 'browse' through files. This type of casual usage is likely to grow. Therefore, although some access to the information system and therefore the database will be made by **professional users** through computer programs written in Cobol and other programming languages, some, perhaps most, access will be made by untrained users. Some of these will be **regular users**, that is they may make daily or weekly access to particular parts of the system and they may be willing to train in the use of particular facilities. Clerical staff who may be required to input data into the system will be expected to train in order to use the system. Others will be **casual users**, and these users, frequently middle or top managers, might have had little knowledge and experience of computing. Their use of the system will be varied. Each day's enquiries could be different and based on different parts of the database. It is therefore difficult to train such staff, even if they had the time and inclination to practise the skills necessary. For this reason, there must be query languages available which make it easy for untrained users to use the system.

Olle (1991) suggests nine key roles to the successful development of an information system:

- Executive responsible
- Development coordinator
- Business analyst
- Designer
- User's acceptor
- User
- Constructor's acceptor

- Constructor
- Resource manager.

The executive responsible is a member of the Board assigned to ensure the successful progress and completion of the project. We have already stressed the importance of senior managers demonstrating their commitment to the new system and this is therefore a key role. The development coordinator is responsible for the day-to-day control of the project and will report back to the executive responsible. The business analyst is responsible for the analysis of the business needs and the designer prepares the design of the information system. The user's acceptor represents the users and approves the specifications from the users' point of view before construction starts, and the user will use the operational system. As we saw in the previous paragraph, there are many kinds of user. The constructor's acceptor checks that the information systems design and 'product' conforms to the appropriate standards and the constructor writes the programs and other parts of the 'package' that is the information system. Finally, the resource manager ensures that the necessary resources are available for the project to develop smoothly. Of course the actual roles and how many people in each role will depend on the particular organisation; indeed, we will discuss other roles, such as that of the database administrator, but this suggested structure is a useful starting point.

We now discuss the role of the **systems planning team** whose main function is to coordinate and control the information systems project and ensure information systems are closely aligned with the goals of the organisation. With the growing emphasis on information technology for competitive advantage, systems planning may to some extent govern business plans and certainly influence them. It is important that the systems planning team is not dominated by the technologists, although it will certainly include them. Corporate experience, rather than technical expertise, should dominate. The information systems project will affect the whole organisation and, as we have seen, it is necessary to include top management in the team. This would suggest that the chairman of the systems planning team would be the 'executive responsible', who would carry the required status. Other management representatives of the systems planning team could include the production manager, marketing manager and other department heads. Such a high-powered team should ensure that the project has the prestige necessary to carry its proposals through the organisation. It should also help to get the management commitment behind the project and this will significantly increase the likelihood of its success. Top management will be seen to lead by example.

The information systems project will cause changes to the roles of employees and in working relationships. The systems planning team ought to anticipate problems that may occur. It is therefore necessary to include the personnel manager and a trade union representative in the systems planning team. As we shall see in Section 2.8, it is important to keep employees fully informed of the project. Many systems may be excellent from a technological point of view, but fail because of a lack of consideration given to 'people' issues. The new system may be seen as a threat to status and job. Frequently staff will resist the change in ways which may be less dramatic than sabotage, but be equally effective. Once the trust of the workforce has been lost, it is difficult to regain it, even if future change is perceived to be in the interest of employees.

Two of the most important representatives from the innovating group will be the database administrator and the chief analyst who is likely to be the project leader. The chief analyst should have both organisational and technical skills and be seen as linking the users and the technical group, and needs to possess good personal skills. This role is likely to be that of the 'business analyst' rather than 'designer', who will be concerned more about the technical aspects. In some circumstances the database administrator will be the project leader. The need for a database administrator is clearly recognised in the methodology, although the role is often filled late in the life of the project, perhaps when it is too late. The database administrator can help the systems planning team decide on standards for communication, documentation, project development and evaluation, and help to implement these standards.

Frequently the systems planning team also includes an outside consultant. This person will not have a background in the organisation, and a perceived lack of departmental bias will be useful when arbitrating on differences of opinion. Another reason for 'outsider' expertise could be the lack of internal expertise in projects of this kind. Figure 2.9 shows the possible membership of the systems planning team.

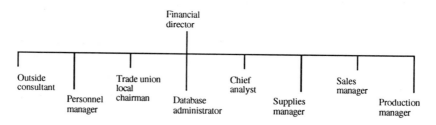

Fig. 2.9 The systems planning team

One of the most important tasks of the systems planning team is to determine the boundaries of the information system. The decision may be implicit by the membership of the team; even so, the boundaries must be defined explicitly. For a corporation like Unilever, which has a number of companies in its overall control, the boundary may be defined to include one or a number of these companies. With some organisations, the various subsystems may be so large that the boundary might be defined around accounts or personnel. This may be particularly appropriate where subsystems do not naturally relate, that is, there is little data travelling between them or where one or two areas, such as production/supply and invoicing, in the case of the electricity supply industry, dominate the business.

Once the overall information system's boundary has been fixed, it will be itself divided into lower-level systems (sometimes known as subsystems) for separate development. These arrangements will largely depend on the strategy adopted for the development of information systems. The determination of this strategy, a positive plan for the development of information systems, is a particularly important role of the systems planning team and is discussed separately in the next section. The data analyst has to know the boundary of the data analysis exercise and how much time to devote to it. The systems planning team will ensure that the subsystems are developed according to the plan which allows for some form of integration later. Each subsystem should be seen as a natural subsystem of the larger system. The priority for developing these subsystems will depend on *potential benefit, urgency of need, probability of success* or *natural precedence*, which could be described as the next 'piece of the jigsaw'.

Lederer & Mendelow (1989) suggest a number of guide-lines which should be considered when planning:

- *Develop a formal plan:* set objectives and policies in relation to the achievement of organisational goals and thereby enable the effective and efficient deployment of resources.
- *Link the information systems plan to the corporate plan:* provide an 'optimal project mix' which will be consistent with and link to the corporate plan, ideally over the same time period.
- *Plan for disaster:* ensure that dependencies are identified and damage likelihood identified.
- *Audit new systems:* evaluate present systems to identify mistakes and hence avoid their repetition and to identify areas where a small resource input might have led to a larger benefit.
- *Perform a cost-benefit analysis:* identify intangible and tangible benefits and costs before putting in the required resources.
- *Develop staff:* make use of and develop the skills of staff.
- *Be prepared to change:* as relationships, structures and processes change.
- *Ensure information systems development satisfies user needs:* understand the tasks and processes involved to establish the true user requirements.
- *Establish credibility through success:* build up user confidence through previous

success, thereby promoting cooperation and lowering barriers.

The systems planning team will overview the development of the project, although they will appoint a systems development team to control its day-to-day running. The constituents of the **systems development team** will depend on the degree of participation adopted, although it is usual, if not always desirable, that it is biased towards the technologists. The systems development team will include the chief analyst and the database administrator who are both likely to be members of the systems planning team. The project leader, who will be one of these two representatives, is likely to act as chairman of the development team. Other likely members of the systems development team will be data analysts who will be involved in developing the data model, and systems analysts, systems designers and programmers who will specify the needs of the users, and design and develop the various subsystems and programs (or choose and modify the application packages). The final constituents of the systems development team will be the representatives from the user departments. These are likely to include the department managers and possibly people who will use the system when it is implemented. We will say more about user involvement in Section 2.8 and further in Section 6.4.

2.6 TECHNIQUES FOR INVESTIGATION AND ANALYSIS

In this section we look at some techniques for finding out information about the business and for analysing this information. Some techniques could be described as formal and reasoned, and others as creative and informal. As stated earlier in this chapter, at this stage we are not looking for solutions but an understanding of the organisation. Some of these techniques stimulate the identification and representation of as many views and perspectives on the problem situation as possible. The analyst will be asking such questions as:

- What should be happening here?
- Who or what are involved and how are they affected?
- Who or what seems to be preventing the desired result?
- Why might this be happening?
- Are there associated problems that might be connected?
- Could this be a symptom of a more fundamental and deeper problem?

Rickards (1974) discusses a variety of techniques which will enable the problem-solver to view the situation from many perspectives and to widen the horizon of the study:

Goal orientation: the idea here is to think of goals and obstacles. Each situation should be approached by enquiring, for example, what are the goals involved, that is, 'what do I want?', what are the boundaries to the situation, that is, 'what constraints do I not want to challenge?', and what are the barriers to the goal, that is, 'what is blocking the path to where I want to be?'. In this way, situations can be redefined in ways which may be more useful for analysis.

Successive abstractions: these define the situation in terms of higher and lower levels of abstraction. If we consider the exercise-bicycle market shown in Figure 2.10, for example, we could move to a higher level of abstraction to new fitness machines and to lower levels of abstraction which can reveal a whole range of possibilities.

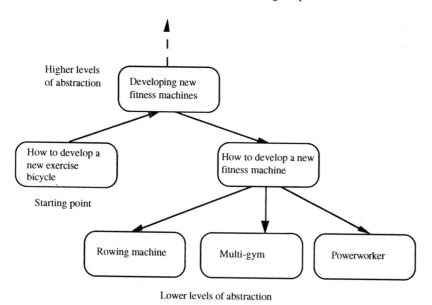

Fig. 2.10 Successive abstractions

Analogies and metaphors: these redefine the problem in an imaginative, non-literal fashion. The original problem definition of 'How to improve the sales team?' could be re-expressed as 'How to make the sales team perform like Newcastle United Football Club?' (an analogy which may suggest better team training or a new look at tactics) or 'How to address corporate turbulence?' a metaphor which may prompt ideas of inter-departmental conflict.

Wishful thinking: the statement 'If I could do anything I would implant the standards in his brain' may spark off more realistic ideas such as running a course to explain the standards (perhaps in a country hotel so as to make it a pleasant experience).

Non-logical stimuli: the first step here is to list as many aspects as can be thought of connected with the problem situation and to consider a completely irrelevant, unconnected object and to see how many ways that the object could affect the situation. For example, a production manager may be stuck about ideas on how to improve factory efficiency but looking at a potted plant on the desk might suggest an improved working environment or employees being given more wages (which may be seen as the equivalent of plant food).

Boundary examination: Here, the analyst writes a statement outlining the interpretation of boundaries and constraints which should then be critically examined for hidden assumptions and preconceptions.

Having an overall view of the nature of the business, the people in it, and its information needs, it is possible to construct an **information model**. This is largely a pictorial representation of the organisation in outline and it can be used as a basis for discussions with management. It combines a process-oriented view of the organisation (supplier ordering, warehouse management and stock control management) with a data-oriented view (goods to follow, stocks in warehouse and supplier orders). As a result of the discussions described in this section, the information model may well change in content.

It will show the major application systems of the organisation and the flows of resources between them. It is particularly useful in providing some **boundaries** and **interfaces** to the organisation. Some logical files have also been included in the model. These give the analyst ideas on what sort of data will be needed to support information systems. But all this information is in outline. It is not intended to suggest the detail of processes nor detailed data storage facilities.

Figure 2.11 shows one iteration in the creation of an information model for a retail business. The final version will be developed after several interviews with management personnel. I have included in the model some of the names of the smaller subsystems, sometimes referred to as modules, in each of the larger systems areas. These include stock control, supplier accounting, customer accounting and personnel. Within stock control, for example, are supplier ordering, warehouse management and quality control. The four major subsystems are carried out at different locations, by different personnel, and therefore formed 'natural' boundaries.

By the time the model has been constructed, the analyst has gained an appreciation of the business in outline. With this knowledge it will be possible to agree an appropriate 'strategy' for the systems project. This will be a decision of the systems planning team whose function will also be to oversee the development of the information systems project.

Many of the factors discussed in this chapter are seen in the information model, and

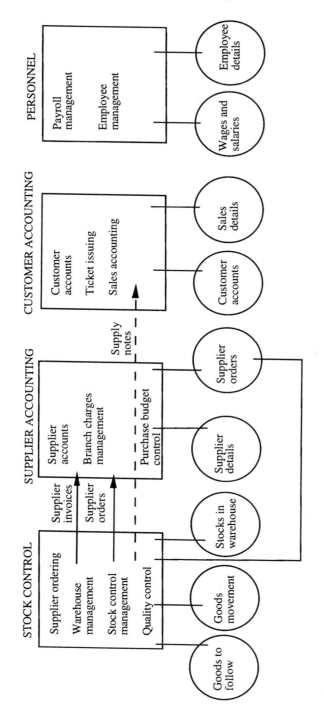

Fig. 2.11 Developing the information model for a retail company

these include interfaces, boundaries, subsystems and the control of resources. However, some factors are excluded, for example, organisational structure, roles of personnel, organisational goals, employee needs, issues, problems and concerns. Another technique is to construct a **rich picture**. This is a pictorial caricature of anorganisation and is an invaluable tool for helping to explain what the organisation is 'about'. It should be self-explanatory and easy to understand.

One may start to construct a rich picture by looking for elements of structure in the problem area. This includes things like departmental boundaries, activity types, physical or geographical layout and product types. Having looked for elements of structure, the next stage is to look for elements of process, that is, 'what is going on'. These include the fast-changing aspects of the situation: the information flow, flow of goods and so on. The relationship between structure and process represents the climate of the situation. Very often an organisational problem can be tracked down to a mismatch between an established structure and new processes formed in response to new events and pressures. The rich picture should include all the important hard 'facts' of the organisational situation, and the examples given have been of this nature. However, these are not the only important facts. There are many soft or subjective 'facts' which should also be represented, and the process of creating the rich picture serves to tease out the concerns of the people in the situation. These soft facts include the sorts of things that the people in the problem area are worried about, the social roles which the people within the situation think are important, and the sort of behaviour which is expected of people in these roles.

Typically, a rich picture is constructed first by putting the name of the organisation that is the concern of the analyst into a large 'bubble', perhaps at the centre of the page. Other symbols are sketched to represent the people and things that inter-relate within and outside that organisation. Arrows are included to show these relationships. Other important aspects of the human activity system can be incorporated. Crossed-swords indicate conflict and the 'think' bubbles indicate the worries of the major characters. Figure 2.12 shows a rich picture for part of a district health authority. Rich pictures are described fully in Avison & Wood-Harper (1990) as are associated techniques such as root definitions.

Root definitions can be used to define two things that are otherwise both vague and difficult. These are problems and systems. It is essential for the systems analysts to know precisely what **human activity system** they are to deal with and what problem they are to tackle. This is a concept which is an aid to thinking about and understanding, in the most general way possible, the organisation in which the information system is to operate. The root definition is a concise verbal description of the system, which captures its essential nature. Each description will derive from a particular view of reality. To ensure that each root definition is **well-formed**, it is checked for the presence of six characteristics. Put into plain English, these are *who* is doing *what* for *whom*, and to whom are they *answerable*, what *assumptions* are being made, and in what *environment* is this happening? If these questions are answered carefully, they should tell us all we need to know.

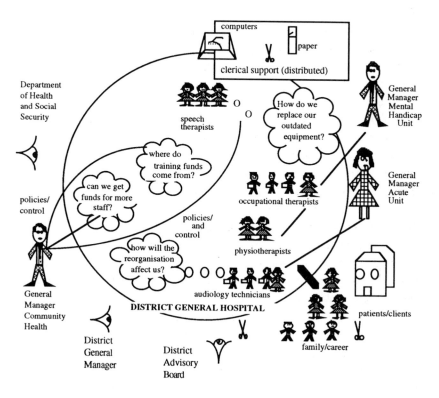

Fig. 2.12 Rich picture for part of a district health authority (from Avison & Wood-Harper, 1990)

There are technical terms for each of the six parts, the first letter of each forming the mnemonic **CATWOE**. We will change the order in which they appeared in our explanation to fit this mnemonic:

- **Customer** is the 'whom'
- **Actor** is the 'who'
- **Transformation** is the 'what'
- **Weltanschauung** or world view is the 'assumptions'
- **Owner** is the 'answerable'

- **Environment** (or environmental constraints) is kept as the 'environment'.

The first stage of creating the definition is to write down headings for each of the six CATWOE categories and try to fill them in. This is not always easy because we often get caught up in activities without thinking about who is really supposed to benefit or who is actually 'calling the tune'. We may question our assumptions and look around the environment even more rarely.

Even so, the difficulty for the individual creating a root definition is less than the difficulty in getting all the individuals involved to agree on the definition to be used. Only experience of such an exercise can reveal how different are the views of individuals about the situation in which they are working together.

Root definitions are particularly useful in exposing different views. We will look at an information system for a hospital to illustrate this. The different people involved in a hospital will look at the system from contrasting positions. Furthermore, these viewpoints in this problem situation are very emotive as they have moral and political overtones. In some situations this can lead to deliberate fudging of issues so as to avoid controversy. This is likely to cause problems in the future. Even if the differences cannot be resolved, it is useful to expose them.

Here are three different root definitions of a hospital system. They all represent extreme positions. In practice, anyone trying to start such a definition would make some attempt to encompass one or more of the other viewpoints, but any one of these could be used as the starting point for the analysis of the requirements of an information system in a hospital.

THE PATIENT

CUSTOMER	Me
ACTOR	The doctor
TRANSFORMATION	Treatment
WELTANSCHAUUNG	I've paid my taxes so I'm entitled to it
OWNER	'The system' or maybe 'the taxpayer'
ENVIRONMENT	The hospital

This could be expressed as 'A hospital is a place that I go to in order to get treated by a doctor. I'm entitled to this because I am a taxpayer, and the system is there to make sure that taxpayers get the treatment they need'.

THE DOCTOR

CUSTOMER	Patients

ACTOR	Me
TRANSFORMATION	Treatment (probably by specialised equipment, services or nursing care)
WELTANSCHAUUNG	I'll treat as many people as possible within a working week.
OWNER	Hospital administrators
ENVIRONMENT	National Health Service (NHS) versus private practice. My work versus my private life.

'A hospital is a system designed to enable me to treat as many patients as possible with the aid of specialised equipment, nursing care, etc. Organisational decisions are made by the hospital administrators (who ought to try treating patients without the proper facilities) against a background of NHS politics and my vision is of a lucrative private practice and regular weekends off with my family'.

THE HOSPITAL ADMINISTRATOR

CUSTOMER	Doctors
ACTOR	Me
TRANSFORMATION	To enable doctors to optimise waiting lists
WELTANSCHAUUNG	Create a bigger hospital within cash limits
OWNER	Department of Health and Social Security (DHSS)
ENVIRONMENT	Politics

'A hospital is an institution in which doctors (and other less expensive staff) are enabled by administrators to provide a service which balances the need to avoid long waiting lists with that to avoid excessive government spending. Ultimate responsibility rests with the DHSS and the environment is very political'.

All the techniques discussed in this section can be used to find out more about the organisation and to help determine the area for further work, the area for data analysis, database development and information systems development. The decisions relating to this strategy will be discussed in the next section.

2.7 STRATEGY FOR INFORMATION SYSTEMS DEVELOPMENT

There are a number of alternative strategies that the systems planning team may decide to adopt. It is essential that full consideration is given to the evaluation of which strategy or combination of strategies is appropriate for the organisation, so that information systems will align with business needs. Inadequate planning will lead to failure - however good the tools and techniques used in the database project. The particular strategy appropriate to the organisation will depend to a large extent on the political and financial circumstances of the organisation. Attempts in the past to implement change may have left scars, and the spirit of trust, confidence and cooperation necessary to implement radical change will be difficult to achieve. The organisation may not be used to changes: both with regard to the roles of personnel and the technology used.

Blumenthal (1969) suggests that six strategies are possible and these are discussed first, although the meaning of each has been changed somewhat to take account of the technological and other developments that have taken place since that text was published. These strategies should not be considered as mutually exclusive: usually the systems planning team decides that the best strategy for their organisation is one which is a combination of those discussed, and I have attempted to incorporate some of these possibilities.

One strategy for implementing information systems would proceed by breaking up the information systems project according to the departmental structure of the organisation. This **organisation chart approach** would be carried out by implementing each department's system in turn. In the retail organisation looked at earlier in this chapter, this could start at the sales office, then to accounting, warehousing, production, buying and personnel. This has the particular advantage of avoiding possible political problems that may have occurred if a more radical strategy had been adopted, because the workplace and working relationships will probably remain intact, although the roles of the employees in it may change. The management team is also likely to remain the same.

For the overall systems project to be successful, however, the design needs to allow for **integration later**. An opportunity will be lost if systems in the various departments cannot 'talk' to each other and share the same database. Thought has to be given to future integration at the initial design stage, otherwise subsequent integration will be very difficult and expensive. There will be no 'common language' between the systems. The systems planning team has a particularly important role to ensure a 'design for integration' and also to prevent any delay in this integration. The longer the delay, the more difficult integration becomes.

Nevertheless, applications in many organisations have been built up piecemeal in an unorganised, often chaotic way. They are often on different computers, with different capabilities, manufacturers, software and so on. It is not only a difficult job to attempt to integrate these but also one that might have opposition from users who would prefer to keep to a successful, if limited, system. Much will also depend on the structure of organisations: the benefit from integrating the databases of separate departments may not be as great as the costs involved.

With many organisations, following the departmental boundaries of the firm will not be a good strategy. Many processes, such as sales order processing, will cross departmental boundaries. The sales order may first enter the sales office, then be processed by the warehouse, then the production department, then distribution, and finally the accounts department. This reflects the following processes. The order is received by the sales office; checks are made in the warehouse to see if the sub-assemblies are in stock; a schedule is made in the production department and the products manufactured; the goods are despatched by the distribution department; and the invoice typed up in accounts and sent to the customer. It is not surprising therefore that the strategy for information systems development which follows the existing departmental structure of the firm may be the easiest politically but not the one that gains the most from the database and informations systems project. Even conventional processing is inter-departmental.

An alternative approach would break up the organisation according to some other criteria but implement each section in turn and allow for integration later. Again, without this design for integration it will be very difficult to achieve the expected gains of databases and information systems. This alternative design may be based on management needs, a sort of **top-down approach**. This approach can be a good strategy where the information required by top management is fairly stable in terms of content, level of detail and frequency. Designing the information systems project around management needs may, however, ignore the operational requirements. To fulfil operational requirements as well may lead to data being collected, validated and stored more than once. However, there are circumstances where management information cannot be derived from operational data.

Executive information systems, which are designed for strategic management, are usually of this type. They combine information from both external and internal sources. There are databases which can be bought in from outside (provided by government, consultancy and other organisations) and are as important a source for information as that gained from internal databases. Sophisticated analysis and model building tools enable the data to be converted into the information required to support decision-making by, for example, testing individual and organisational assumptions and values (discussed earlier in Section 2.3 on organisational culture).

In following the above approaches, there may be a tendency to design in terms of applications which mirror the present requirements of the business. There is a danger that these needs will change. The importance of developing the database without regard to applications has already been stressed. Applications requirements frequently change: data types and relationships are more stable. The **data collection approach** stresses the importance of data collection and analysis without regard to functions. The data is collected for an area of the organisation. It is then classified and the relationships between the data elements are recorded for use when required. One of the criticisms of this approach is that data may be collected which is never used subsequently. However, there is a two stage process: data modelling and mapping to the database. Data which is unlikely to be used need not be transferred to the database.

The **database approach** need not necessarily be associated with data collection and classification. Data analysis can be useful without databases. The process of modelling the organisation should result in a better understanding of the business. The data and data structures that have been identified can be mapped on to conventional computer files or clerical files and not necessarily databases. Similarly, the database can be built up piecemeal without an organised data analysis exercise. However, the resulting database system may well not prove as flexible nor as long-lasting as one formed by a preceding data analysis exercise.

This text therefore proposes that data analysis is followed by database implementation. The drawback associated with this approach is that data may be held indefinitely with no use being made of it. It is an important role of the database administrator to control attempts to keep data on the database indefinitely and to ensure that data entering the database is likely to be of use in the near future. The functions of the organisation should therefore be kept in mind in data analysis, even though in principle data analysis should attempt to look at the organisation independent of any processes.

Implicit in the discussion of this data analysis and database approach is that a **total system** is implemented. By this is meant that design, development and implementation will be for the organisation as a whole. The organisation is regarded as a 'green field', able and willing both to accept and adapt to a completely changed information systems environment. However, rarely can the political, social and other forces existing in the organisation countenance such change. Such an approach also assumes that management would be willing to pay for a large project, accept the risks involved and get little reward in terms of information systems for a number of years. Obviously this is not a realistic assumption. Further, the greater the inter-dependence, then the greater the complexity. Some of this complexity might be seen as unexpected side-effects. The systems planning team will have to ensure that rewards come during and not only after the full information systems project is implemented. The project must therefore be divided into chunks, and data analysis, database and information systems implemented in each of these divisions in turn, ensuring the success of each of these parts before the next subsystem is developed. Whilst doing so, the systems planning team must not lose sight of the overall plan, so that the benefits of the database approach, especially data sharing, can be achieved, and thus there can be better use of the information resource, greater flexibility in its use and an improved ability to meet new situations and applications.

The approach described in this book needs to be adapted flexibly as no single approach will work alone and compromises must be made. Earl (1989) researches into the reasons that UK companies undertake information systems strategy formulation:

- Sector exploitation of IT is posing strategic threats and opportunities
- The need to align IT investment with business needs is recognised
- The desire to gain some competitive advantage from IT is apparent
- The desire to change the appearance of systems development from data processing to IT activities is apparent.

These reasons may conflict and their emphasis change over time. No single approach will work alone and compromises must be made. Strategic development plans are best managed as portfolios, that is, during the development period early successes must be seen to be delivered, thus ensuring a continuous flow of systems products to maintain interest and commitment to the system from all users. We will look at this aspect in the next section.

2.8 MANAGEMENT AND USER INVOLVEMENT

The previous section has brought to light some of the difficulties of carrying out a radical approach to the development of information systems in many organisations. The reasons for failure in these projects tend not to lie in the technical side, though the technology is complex, nor in the economic side, though the cost of these systems is very high. The reasons for failure are more likely to be due to *people problems*, which may show themselves by the lack of cooperation when the information system is being developed and a resistance to the changes that occur when the application is implemented. These aspects have been touched upon throughout this chapter, but are now highlighted to emphasise their importance.

People may regard the change negatively. They may think that their jobs will be less secure, that they might lose the independence that they previously enjoyed, that their relationships with others will change for the worse and they might lose status, they may think the change unnecessary and they may simply fear change in itself. In reality, the changes may be positive for the staff, but they may be perceived as negative (there is also the possibility that change will be negative and resistance to change is therefore a positive thing).

During times of economic recession, especially, employees fear job losses and it is important to stress genuine reasons for the development of the database project which are not associated with cost savings. Employees fear the unknown and therefore early training, progress reports and user involvement in the change process will help. Managers and supervisors, who might fear a loss of status and authority, need also to be informed early and be involved in the training of their staff. They may feel particularly threatened, especially if they think that their power and responsibility may be given to the specialists involved directly with the technology. One possible move to counteract this is to ensure that the system proposer is a business analyst and not a technical analyst.

Unless steps have been taken to ensure that the people of the organisation are fully informed of the changes that are proposed, that they support the changes, and see themselves as gaining from them, then there is no reason to assume that they will cooperate with the changes: indeed, there is good reason to assume that they will try to ensure that the changes do not work. Their experience of the ways in which change has been effected in the past will also contribute to their present reactions. If the trust and confidence has been ruptured previously, it will be difficult to regain. The management climate within the organisation and the way in which grievances are heard and fears discussed are important. **Organisational learning**, where the 'organisation' stores experiences in forms, procedures and rules, and uses them to teach new staff and retrain others, can encourage adaptiveness to change. Such practices need to be established so that change becomes the norm, is expected, and is viewed positively.

The best strategy to counteract resistance is to ensure rational, self interest, where attempts are made to convince individuals that change is to their personal advantage. Such inducements as salary, status and job interest, could be used to ensure that staff might enjoy their new roles. The work force should be informed of the likely changes in good time. Rumours about impending changes will occur anyway, and staff not fully informed are likely to fear the worst. Those that can get jobs will leave, and these are likely to be the staff that the organisation wants to keep most. Further, resistance can be caused by fears which are not based on fact. Education, about what computers can and cannot do, will be more important than training in the early stages of the project.

We may be requiring a change in the **culture** of the organisation. As we have seen, it is a powerful influence on the actions and activities of the people in the organisation and will be one of the main influences on the attitude to change held by staff. A culture that promotes and encourages change will greatly influence the attitude to change held by staff. But changing the corporate culture is a very long term solution (up to ten years) and can be a very difficult period for all involved.

It is important to communicate to the user not only the potential advantages of the information systems approach, of relevant, timely, accurate, understandable, and up-to-date, information which is provided to the correct level of detail, highlighting critical factors which control the firm's success (critical success factors are discussed in Rockart, 1979), but also of potential pitfalls that should be avoided. More information is not necessarily better: it may be too detailed for 'digestion' or irrelevant to the particular decision-maker. Decision-making will not necessarily improve just because the information is available: it may be ignored as many managers will prefer to keep to the combination of intuition, experience and judgement to make decisions. There should be wide discussion within the organisation of these aspects so that management is aware of the pitfalls (Ackoff, 1967).

The database project is very expensive and difficult to justify in tangible terms. The major product is information, not tangible objects like stocks of goods which are easier to evaluate. What is the value of information? There are obvious advantages of the information which could include better costing, better cash flow, improved customer relations, and it should lead to better decisions being made by management, but it is difficult to put a monetary value on all this. Yet it is important to convince management of these gains, otherwise it will be extremely unlikely that the information systems projects will be given the go-ahead, and even if this is achieved, they are unlikely to be successful.

It is also important that top management are 'seen' to support the system, are committed to it and that they participate in the change. They should benefit most from the system, as they are the information 'requirers'. This commitment will encourage others to fall in with the change. A general air of good communications and user participation will also help. These users will include the clerical workers who will be concerned with the input of data to the system and the verification of its output. It is very important that user groups do contribute to the change and that their suggestions are not merely dealt with by paying lip service. Again, user involvement should help to lessen the likelihood of a general level of mistrust and a lack of confidence.

Earl (1989) argues that it is necessary to identify three issues in the business plan to help ensure the success of IT:

- Clarification of business needs and strategy in terms of IT requirements (which requires a methodological approach and teamwork)
- Evaluation of current systems, their provision and use (which requires involvement of users)
- Innovation of new strategic opportunities afforded by IT (which requires creative thinking and the identification of people who have this ability and others who will champion IT and have access to funds).

Business analysis should be looked upon as a two-way exercise - an opportunity to inform, help and convince, as much as an opportunity to find out about the organisation. It is therefore an important part of the methodology. It has helped in identifying the concerns of the business, its goals and its information requirements. It has identified the people concerned with information systems development. It has also helped in looking at the functions of the business in outline. This is enough to help the systems planning team draw limits to the data modelling exercise. It has set a strategy for the next stages in the development of the information systems and database project and, through the encouragement of user involvement and management participation, a 'style' likely to lead to its successful completion.

2.9   FURTHER READING

Blumenthal, S. C (1969) *Management Information Systems: A Framework for Planning and Control*, Prentice-Hall, Englewood Cliffs.
Although written over twenty years ago, the principles discussed in this text are still very relevant.

Benyon, D (1990) *Information and Data Modelling*, Blackwell Scientific Publications, Oxford.
Liebenau, J & Backhouse, J (1990) *Understanding information: an introduction*, Macmillan, Basingstoke.
The nature of data and information are explored in these texts.

Ackoff, R. L (1967) Management Misinformation Systems, *Management Science*, 14.
A critical look at management information systems.

Avison, D. E & Wood-Harper, A. T (1990) *Multiview: an exploration in information systems development*, Blackwell Scientific Publications, Oxford.
The techniques of rich pictures and root definitions are explored in this text.

Earl, M. J (1989) *Management Strategies for Information Technology*, Prentice Hall, Hemel Hempstead.
Explores the use and abuse of information technology in organisations.

Chapter 3
The Conceptual Schema: Data Analysis and the Relational Model

---

3.1   INTRODUCTION

Conventional systems analysis procedures were applied to single applications that were the first to be computerised in the organisation. When applications being developed are an integrated part of a total system, these techniques prove inadequate. The most obvious situation which requires a different approach is the development of a database. In a database environment, many applications share the same data. The database is looked upon as a common asset.

Data analysis techniques were largely developed to cater for the implementation of database systems, although that does not mean that they cannot be applied to non-database situations. Data modelling may be carried out as a step in conventional file applications. Data analysis can also be of interest to management as a way of understanding their organisation.

The methodology represents a significant change in the development of computing systems away from the technology, in particular, hardware and software (including programming techniques and algorithms), and towards data and the way it is structured. The emphasis on programming in earlier systems was natural: firstly because computers demanded considerable programming skill, and secondly because the professional was interested in the possibility of solving complex programming problems using the basic instruction set of the computer.

The emphasis has moved towards data because, if it can be made available in the correct form for applications, programming presents much less of a problem. Data is a very important resource of the business. The algorithms required for most data processing are relatively simple. As computer systems become more powerful, less stress needs to be paid to problems of implementation (availability of storage, for example) and more to problems independent of implementation.

One of the most important techniques of data analysis described in the text is entity modelling. Just as an accountant might use a financial model, the analyst can develop an entity model. The entity model is just another view of the organisation, but it is a particular perception of reality and it can be used to address a number of problems. The model produced provides an excellent and novel way of viewing the business. Systems analysis in general - and data analysis is a branch of systems analysis - is an art, not an exact science. There can be a number of ways to derive a reasonable model and there are a number of reasonable models (there are of course an infinite number of inadequate models).

A model represents something, usually in simplified form which highlights aspects which are of particular interest to the user, and is built so that it can be used for a specific purpose, for example, communication and testing. As we saw in Chapter 2, many types of model are used in information systems work. A model is a representation of real-world objects and events, and good entity models will be a fair representation of certain aspects of the 'real world'. The entity model is an abstract representation of the data within the organisation. It can be looked on as a discussion document and its coincidence with the real world is verified in discussions with the various users. However, the analyst should be aware that variances between the model and a particular user's view could be due to the narrow perception of that user. The model should be a global view. The size of that 'globe' - a department, a number of departments, a company or an organisation - having been agreed in the business analysis phase (Section 2.7).

An **entity-relationship model** views the organisation as a set of data elements, known as entities, which are the things of interest to the organisation, and relationships between these entities. This model enables the computer specialist to design appropriate computer systems for the organisation, but it also provides management with a unique tool for perceiving the business process. The essence of rational scientific problem solving is to be able to perceive the complex, 'messy', real world in such a manner that the solution to any problem may be easier. This model is 'simple' in that it is fairly easy to understand and to use.

Each entity can be represented diagrammatically by **soft boxes** (rectangles with rounded corners). Relationships between the entities are shown by lines between the soft boxes. A first approach to an entity model for an academic department of computer science is given in Figure 3.1. The entity types are STUDENT, ACADEMIC STAFF, COURSE and NON-ACADEMIC STAFF. The entity type STUDENT participates in a relationship with ACADEMIC STAFF and COURSE. The relationships are not named but it might be that STUDENT *takes* COURSE and that STUDENT *has as tutor* ACADEMIC STAFF. The reader will soon detect a number of important things of interest that have been omitted (room, examination, research and so on). As the analysts find out more about the organisation, entity types and relationships will be added to the model.

A mistake frequently made at this stage is to define the entities to reflect the processes of the business, such as stock control, credit control or sales order processing. This could be a valid model of the business but it is not an entity model and cannot be used to produce the flexible database for the organisation that we require. A database so created would be satisfactory for some specific applications, but would not be adequate for many applications. Where data analysis differs from conventional systems analysis is that it separates the data structures from the applications which use them. The objective of data analysis is to produce a flexible model which can be easily adapted as the requirements of the users change. Although the applications will need to be changed, this will not necessarily be true of the data.

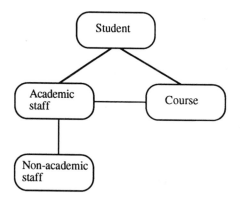

Fig. 3.1 Entity modelling - a first approach

The entity-relationship model is a data model, referred to in this book as the **conceptual schema** or **conceptual model**. The model reflects data in the business, not processes. It is concerned with the data that exists, not how it is used. The entities are quantifiable and can be represented as special tables, known as relations. These were introduced in Section 1.4 and typical relations were seen in Figure 1.8.

The data items (attributes) associated with each entity (or relation) can then be normalised. Normalisation is a set of rules applied to the relations which simplifies the model. These relations can then be mapped onto a database. The relational model and normalisation are explained in detail in Sections 3.6, 3.7 and 3.8.

3.2   ENTITY-RELATIONSHIP APPROACH

Probably the most widespread technique of data analysis is that proposed by Chen (1976). The major advances described in Chen's paper were helped by the preceding work of the Codasyl Committee (see Section 4.6) and Codd (1970). The information algebra proposed in the Codasyl report contained two important concepts: that of an entity as a thing that has reality, and that of joining records on equal values of keys. For modelling reality, it is essential to distinguish between different objects in the real world and understand how they are related to each other. The problem with the original Codasyl proposals was that there is no clear distinction made between the conceptual or user view and the physical or computer view. This distinction is most important because of the inherent flexibility that results from the separation of the logical and physical views. Codd's relational model is not dependent on any specific physical implementation, it is data independent.

In Chen's entity-relationship (E-R) model, the real world information is represented by entities and by relationships between entities. In a typical business, the entities could include jobs, customers, departments, and suppliers. The analyst identifies the entities and relationships before being immersed in the detail, in particular the work of identifying the attributes which define the properties of entities.

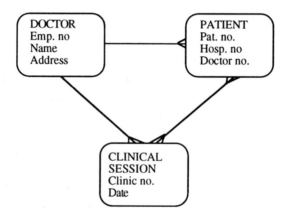

Fig. 3.2 An entity set relating to part of a hospital

Figure 3.2 relates to part of a hospital. The entities described are DOCTOR, PATIENT and CLINICAL SESSION. The relationships between the entities are also described. That between DOCTOR and PATIENT and between DOCTOR and CLINICAL SESSION are one-to-many relationships. In other words, one DOCTOR can have many PATIENTS, but a PATIENT is only assigned one DOCTOR. Further, a DOCTOR can be responsible for many CLINICAL SESSIONS, but a CLINICAL SESSION is the responsibility of only one DOCTOR. The other relationship is many-to-many. In other words, a PATIENT can attend a number of CLINICAL SESSIONS and one CLINICAL SESSION can be attended by a number of PATIENTS. The diagram also shows a few attributes of the entities. The particular attribute or group of attributes that uniquely identifies an entity occurrence is known as the key attribute or attributes. The 'employee number' (Emp. No.) is the key attribute of the entity called DOCTOR.

The technique attempts to separate the data structure from the functions for which the data may be used. This separation is a useful distinction, although it is often difficult to make in practice. In any case, it is sometimes useful to bear in mind the functions of the data analysed. A DOCTOR and a PATIENT are both people, but it is their role, that is what they do, that distinguishes the entities. The distinction, formed because of a knowledge of functions, is a useful one to make. However, too much regard to functions will produce a model biased towards particular applications or users.

Another practical problem is that 'global' (organisation-wide) data analysis may be so costly and time-consuming that it is often preferable to carry out entity analysis at a 'local' level, such as the marketing area. If a local entity analysis is carried out, the model can be mapped on to a database and applications applied to it before another local data analysis is started. This is far more likely to gain management approval because managers can see the expensive exercise paying dividends in a reasonable time scale. An important preliminary step is therefore to define the area for analysis and break this up into distinct sub-areas which can be implemented on a database and merged later. Again, the arrangement most suitable to the organisation should have been determined in the business analysis stage. Local data analysis should also be carried out in phases. The first phase is an overview which leads to the identification of the major things of interest in that area. At the end of the overview phase, it is possible to draw up a second interview plan and the next, longer, phase aims to fill in the detail.

Although it is relatively easy to illustrate the process of modelling in a book or at a lecture, in real life there are problems in deciding how far one should go and what level of detail is appropriate. The level of detail must serve two purposes:

1) It must be capable of explaining that part of the organisation defined for these purposes by business analysis, and

2) It must be capable of being translated into the physical model.

It is important to realise that there is no logical or natural point at which the level of detail stops. This is a pragmatic decision. Certainly design teams can put too much effort into the development of the model. Some of the levels of detail that are capable of expression using the method outlined are perhaps best left to implementation. An example of this could be entity occurrences of persons who are female, where they relate to:

1) Patients in a hospital

2) Students at university, and

3) Readers in a library.

In the patient example, the fact that the person occurrence is female is important, so important that the patient entity may be split into two separate entities - male patients and female patients. In the student example, the fact that the person is female may not be of great significance and therefore there could be an attribute 'sex' of the person entity. In the reader example, the fact that the person is female may be of such insignificance that it is not even included as an attribute. There is a danger here, however, as the analyst must ensure that it will not be significant in any application in the library. Otherwise the data model will not be as useful as possible. This type of debate can only be resolved when looking at the functions in some detail.

3.3   SOME DEFINITIONS

An **entity** is a thing of interest in the organisation, in other words it is anything about which we want to hold data. It could include all the resources of the business, including the people of interest such as EMPLOYEE, and it can be extended to cover such things as a SALES-ORDER, INVOICE and PROFIT-CENTRE. It covers concepts as well as objects. A SCHEDULE or a PLAN are concepts which can be defined as entities. An entity is not data itself, but something about which data should be kept. It is something that can have an independent existence, that is, can be distinctly identified. In creating an entity model, the aim should be to define entities that enable one to describe the organisation. Such entities as STOCK, SALES-ORDER and CUSTOMER are appropriate because they are quantifiable, whereas 'stock control', 'order processing' and 'credit control' are not appropriate because they are functions: what the organisation does, and not things of interest which participate in functions. *Entities will normally be displayed in small capitals.* Entities can also be quantified - it is reasonable to ask "how many customers?" or "how many orders per day?", but not "how many credit controls?". An **entity occurrence** is a particular example of an entity which can be uniquely identified. It will have a value, for example, 'John Smith & Son' and this will be a particular occurrence of the entity CUSTOMER. There will be other occurrences, such as, 'Plowmans PLC' and 'Tebbetts & Co'.

An **attribute** is a descriptive value associated with an entity. It is a property of an entity. At a certain stage in the analysis it becomes necessary not only to define each entity but also to record the relevant attributes of each entity. A CUSTOMER entity may be defined and it will have a number of attributes associated with it, such as 'number', 'name', 'address', 'credit-limit', 'balance' and so on. *Attributes will normally be displayed within single inverted commas.* The values of a set of attributes will distinguish one entity occurrence from another. Attributes are frequently identified during data analysis when entities are being identified, but most come later, particularly in detailed interviews with staff and in the analysis of documents. Many are discovered when checking the entity model with users. An entity may be uniquely identified by one or more of its attributes, the **key attribute(s)**. A <u>customer number</u> may identify an occurrence of the entity CUSTOMER. A <u>customer number</u> and a <u>product number</u> may *together* form the key of entity SALES-ORDER. The key attribute functionally determines other attributes, because once we know the customer number we know the name, address and other attributes of that customer. *Key attributes will normally be underlined.*

There often arises the problem of distinguishing between an entity and an attribute. In many cases, things that can be defined as entities could also be defined as attributes, and vice versa. We have discussed one example relating to the sex of people. The entity should have importance in itself, otherwise it is an attribute. In practice the problem is not as important as it may seem. Most of these ambiguities are settled in the process of normalisation (Sections 3.7 and 3.8). In any case, the analyst can change his model at a later stage, even when mapping the model onto a database. Entities participate in functions of the organisation and the attributes are those data elements that are required to support the functions. The best rule of thumb is to ask whether the data element has information about it, in other words does it have attributes? Entities and attributes are further distinguished by their role in events (discussed below).

A **relationship** in an entity model normally represents an association between two entities. A SUPPLIER entity has a relationship with the PRODUCT entity through the relationship supplies, that is, a SUPPLIER *supplies* PRODUCT. There may be more than one relationship between two entities, for example, in this case because a PRODUCT *is supplied by* SUPPLIER. *Relationships will normally be displayed in italics.*

The next stage in the development of an entity model, therefore, having defined the entities and 'fleshed' out the entities with attributes, is to associate related entities by relationships and thus put edges into the model. A relationship normally arises because of:

1) Association, for example 'CUSTOMER *places* ORDER'
2) Structure, for example 'ORDER *consists of* ORDER-LINE'.

The association between entities has to be meaningful, the relationship normally has an information content - CUSTOMER *places* ORDER. The action *places* describes the relationship between CUSTOMER and ORDER. The name given to the relationship also helps to make the model readable. As will be seen, the relationship itself can have attributes.

The **cardinality** of the relationship could be one-to-one, one-to-many, or many-to-many. A MEMBER-OF-PARLIAMENT can only represent one constituency, and one

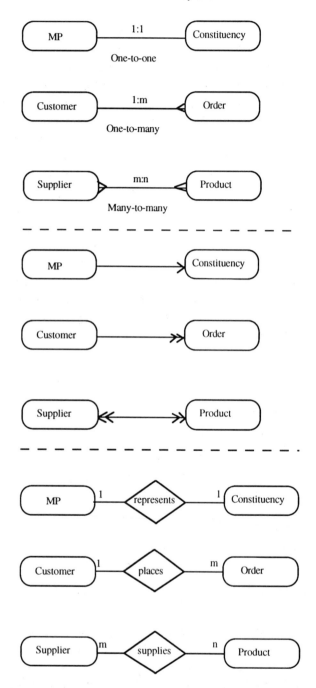

Fig. 3.3 Cardinality of a relationship: three ways of representing relationships

CONSTITUENCY can have only one MEMBER-OF-PARLIAMENT. A MEMBER-OF-PARLIAMENT *represents a* CONSTITUENCY. This is an example of a one-to-one (1:1) relationship. Figure 3.3 shows various ways of representing relationships. Very often, a one-to-one relationship can be better expressed as a single entity, with one of the entities forming attributes of the more significant entity. For example, the entity above could be MEMBER-OF-PARLIAMENT, with CONSTITUENCY as one of the attributes.

The relationship between an entity CUSTOMER and another entity ORDER is usually of a degree one-to-many (1:m). Each CUSTOMER can have a number of outstanding ORDERS, but an ORDER can refer to only one CUSTOMER: CUSTOMER *places* ORDER.

With a many-to-many (m:n) relationship, each entity can be related to one or more occurrences of the partner entity. A SUPPLIER can supply many PRODUCTS; and one PRODUCT could be supplied by a number of SUPPLIERS (SUPPLIER *supplies* PRODUCT; PRODUCT *is supplied by* SUPPLIER).

In this last example (of a many-to-many relationship), entity occurrences of the SUPPLIER entity could be 'Smith', 'Jones' and 'Wilson', and they could supply a number of products each. For example, Smith might supply wigits, ligits and sprigits; Jones might supply wigits and sprigits; and Wilson ligits and sprigits. This can be shown in the spaghetti-like manner of Figure 3.4.

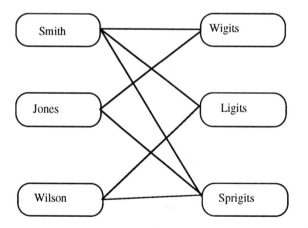

Fig. 3.4 Many-to-many relationship between SUPPLIER and PRODUCT

Frequently there is useful information associated with many-to-many relationships and it is better to split these into two one-to-many relationships, with a third entity created to link these together. Again, this should only be done if the new entity has some meaning in itself. The relationship between COURSE and LECTURER is many-to-many, that is, one LECTURER *lectures on* many COURSES and a COURSE *is given by* many LECTURERS. But a new entity, MODULE can be described which may only be given by one LECTURER and is part of only one COURSE. Thus a LECTURER *gives* a number of MODULES and a COURSE consists of a number of MODULES. But one MODULE *is given by* only one LECTURER and one MODULE *is offered to* only one COURSE (if these are the restrictions). This is shown in Figure 3.5.

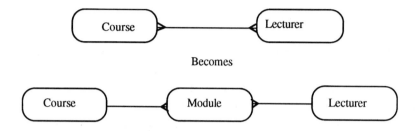

Becomes

Fig. 3.5 A many-to-many relationship represented as two one-to-many relationships

There are other distinctions and sophistications which are often included in the model. Sometimes a 1:m or an m:n relationship is a **fixed relationship**. The many-to-many relationship between the entity PARENT and the entity CHILD is 2:n (that is, each child has two parents); but a PARENT *can beget* more than one CHILD.

Whilst some relationships are **mandatory**, others are **optional**. An entity MALE and an entity FEMALE may be joined together by the optional relationship *married to*. Mandatory and optional relationships may be represented as shown in Figure 3.6.

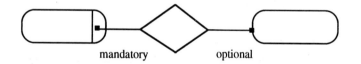

mandatory   optional

Fig 3.6 Representation of mandatory and optional relationships

Other structures include **exclusivity**, where participation in one relationship excludes participation in another or **inclusivity**, where participation in one relationship automatically includes participation in another.

A data structure may also be **involuted** where entity occurrences relate to other occurrences of the same entity. For an EMPLOYEE entity, for example, an EMPLOYEE entity occurrence who happens to be a manager *manages* other occurrences of the entity EMPLOYEE. This can be shown diagrammatically by an involuted loop, as in Figure 3.7.

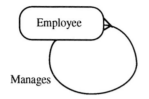

Fig. 3.7 An involuted relationship

Any relationship is necessarily linked to at least one entity. If it is linked to only one entity it is involuted, and such a relationship is also said to be **reflexive**. Where a relationship is linked to two entities (as in the case of the examples in Figure 3.3), it is said to be **binary**. If a relationship is linked to three entities, as in Figure 3.8, it is said to be **ternary**. Otherwise it is **n-ary**, with the value of 'n' equalling the number of entities.

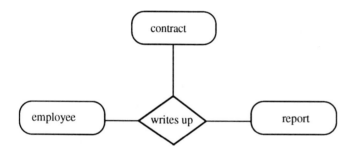

Fig 3.8 Example of a ternary relationship

Howe (1989) and Robinson (1989) discuss these variants and others, and their diagrammatic representation. Readers should note that the terminology is not always consistent in the literature. Howe, for example, in his excellent and thorough description of data analysis, uses the term 'degree' for what is referred to as 'cardinality' in this text.

Up to now, we have considered the data-oriented aspects of data analysis, but functional considerations are made in order to check the model. These are events and operations. Entities have to support the **events** that occur in the enterprise. Entities will take part in events and in the operations that follow events. Attributes are those elements which supply data to support events. 'Tom' is an occurrence of the entity EMPLOYEE. Tom's pay rise or his leaving the company are events, and attributes of the entity EMPLOYEE will be referred to following these events. Attributes such as 'pay-to-date', 'tax-to-date', 'employment status', and 'salary' will be referred to. **Operations** on attributes will be necessary following the event: an event triggers an operation or a series of operations. An operation will change the state of the data. The event 'Tom gets salary increase of 10%' will require access to the entity occurrence 'Tom' and augmenting the attribute 'salary' by 10%. Figure 3.9 shows the entity EMPLOYEE expressed as a relation with attributes. We have to check that the relation supports all the operations that follow the event mentioned.

Emp. no.	Name	Status	Pay-to-date	Tax-to-date	Salary
756	Tom	Full	754.30	156.00	14000

Does the entity support the operations necessary following events?
e.g.   employee leaves the company
          employee gets a pay rise

Fig. 3.9 Event-driven (functional) analysis

Some methodologies, for example, Merise (Quang & Chartier-Kastler, 1991) also define the **synchronisation** of an operation (Figure 3.10). This is a condition affecting the events which trigger the operation and will enable the triggering of that operation. This condition can relate to the value of the properties carried by the events and to the number of occurrences of the events. For example, the operation 'production of pay slips' may be triggered by the event 'date' when it equals '28th of the month'.

Some readers may be confused by the discussion of events (sometimes called **transactions**), which are function-oriented concepts, when data analysis is supposed to be function-independent. The consideration of events and operations is of interest as a checking mechanism. They are used to ensure that the entity model will support the functions that may use the data model. This consideration of the events and operations may lead to a tuning of the model, an adjustment of the entities and the attributes. It will also be useful information for later stages of the methodology. This event-driven analysis is frequently called **functional analysis**.

Another possible source of confusion is the similarity of the terms 'relations' and 'relationships'. Whereas relationships express the association between two entities, relations are a tabular representation of an entity, complete with attributes. Although the two names are similar, they represent two distinct concepts.

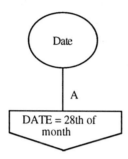

Fig. 3.10 Synchronisation of an operation

3.4   PHASES IN ENTITY ANALYSIS

We will now look at the stages of entity analysis which are:
- Define the area for analysis
- Define the entities and the relationships between them
- Establish the key attribute(s) for each entity
- Complete each entity with all the attributes
- Normalise all the entities to third normal form
- Ensure all events and operations are supported by the model.

We have looked briefly at all these elements apart from normalisation which is discussed in Section 3.7.

The first stage of entity analysis requires the definition of the area for analysis. This was discussed in Chapter 2 and is frequently referred to as the **universe of discourse**. Sometimes this will be the organisation, but this is usually too ambitious for detailed study, and as we have seen the organisation will normally be divided into local areas for separate analysis.

Then we have the stages of entity-relationship modelling. It is a top-down approach in that the entities are identified first, followed by the relationships between them, and then more detail is filled in as the attributes and key attribute(s) of each entity are identified.

For each local area, then, the entities are defined. The obvious and major entities will be identified first. The analyst will attempt to name the fundamental things of interest to the organisation. As the analyst is gathering these entities, the relationships between the entities can also be determined and named - sometimes they will be named in both directions. Their cardinality can be one-to-one, one-to-many or many-to-many. It may be possible to identify fixed relationships and those which are optional or mandatory. The analyst will be able to begin to assemble the entity-relationship diagram. The diagram will be rather sketchy, somewhat like a 'doodle', in the beginning, but it will soon be useful as a communication tool. There are now computer software tools which can help draw up these diagrams and make alterations easily. These are described in Chapter 11. The key of each entity will also be determined. The key attributes will uniquely identify any entity occurrence. There may be alternative keys, in which case the most natural or concise is normally chosen.

The analyst has now constructed the model in outline and is in a position to fill in the detail. This means establishing the attributes for each entity. Each attribute will say something about the entity. The analyst has to ensure that any synonyms and homonyms are detected. A product could be called a part, product or finished product depending on the department. These are all synonyms for 'product'. On the other hand, the term product may mean different things (homonyms), depending on the department. It could mean a final saleable item in the marketing department or a sub-assembly in the production department. These differences must be reconciled and recorded in the data dictionary (see Chapter 12). The process of identifying attributes may itself reveal entities that have not identified. Any data element in the organisation must be defined as an entity, an attribute or a relationship and recorded in the data dictionary. Entities and relationships will also be recorded in the entity-relationship diagram.

Each entity must be normalised to third normal form once the entity occurrences have been added to the model. This process is described in Section 3.7. Briefly, the rules of normalisation require that all entries in the entity must be completed (first normal form), all attributes of the entity must be dependent on all the key (second normal form), and all non-key attributes must be independent of one another (third normal form). The normalisation process may well lead to an increase in the number of entities in the model. This process puts the data model in a form more suitable for the next stage of the methodology.

The final stage of entity analysis will be to look at all the events within the area and the operations that need to be performed following an event, and ensure that the model supports these events and operations. Events are frequently referred to as transactions. For this part of the methodology, the analyst will identify the events associated with the organisation and examine the operations necessary on the trail of each of the events.

Events in many organisations could include 'customer makes an order' and 'raw materials are purchased from supplier' and 'employee joins firm'. If, say, a customer makes an order, this event will be followed by a number of operations. The operations will be carried out so that it is possible to find out how much the order will cost, whether the product is in stock, and whether the customer's credit limit is OK. The entities such as PRODUCT (to look at the value of the attribute 'stock') and CUSTOMER (to look at the value of the attribute 'credit limit') must be examined (see Figure 3.11). These attribute values will need to be adjusted following the event. You may notice that the 'product price' is not in either entity. To support the event, therefore, 'product price' should be included in the PRODUCT entity, or in another entity which is brought into the model.

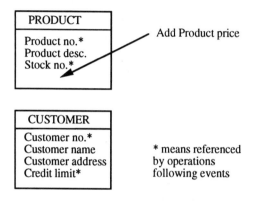

Fig. 3.11 Checking the entity model

Entity modelling has documentation aids like other methods of systems analysis. It is possible to obtain forms on which to specify all the elements of the data analysis process. The separate documents will enable the specification of entities, attributes, relationships, events and operations. These are shown as Figures 3.12, 3.13, 3.14, 3.15 and 3.16. Some completed forms, of a slightly different design, are shown in Chapter 14. These forms can be pre-drawn using software tools and their contents automatically added to the data dictionary.

As we have already stated, it may be possible to use completed documents directly as input to a data dictionary system so that the data is held in a readily-accessible computer format as well as on paper forms. A description of data dictionary systems is given in Chapter 12.

Entity modelling can be used as an aid to communication as well as a technique for finding out information. The forms discussed help as an aid to memory, that is, communication with oneself. The entity-relationship diagrams, which are particularly useful in the initial analysis and as an overview of the data model, prove a good basis

ENTITY TYPE SPECIFICATION FORM		
Entity name	*The standard name for the entity*	
Description	*A brief description of the entity type*	
Synonyms	*Other names by which the entity is known*	
Identifier(s)	*Name of the key attribute(s) which uniquely identify the entity occurrence*	
Date specified		
Minimum occurrences	*expected*	Maximum occurrences	
Average occurrences	*expected*	Growth rate %	*over time*
Create authority	*The names of the users who are allowed*	
Delete authority	*to access the entity in the manner*	
Access authority	*specified*	

Relationships involved cross reference

as shown in the entity-relationship diagram

Attributes involved cross reference
attributes which are found in other entities (to cross-reference different entities for access)

Functions involved cross reference
applications which require data contained in these and other entities

Comments

Fig. 3.12 Entity documentation

for communication with managers and users. They are much more understandable to non-computer people than the documents used in conventional data processing, although they are also a good communications aid between computer people. They provide a pictorial description of the business in outline, showing what the business is,

---

ATTRIBUTE TYPE SPECIFICATION FORM

Attribute name	Standard name for the attribute

Description *A brief description of the attribute*

Synonyms	Other names by which the attribute is known
Date specified	

Entity cross reference
Entities that include the attribute, including those where the attribute is a key or part of a key

Create authority   *The names of the users who are allowed*

Delete authority   *to access the attribute in the manner*

Access authority   *specified*

Functions involved cross reference

Uses of the attribute in the functions of the organisation

Format   *The type and length of the attribute*

Values   *The values that the attribute may have*

Comments

Fig. 3.13 Attribute documentation

not what it does. Managers and users can give 'user feedback' to the data analysts and this will also help to tune the model and ensure its accuracy. A user may point out that an attribute is missing from an entity, or that a relationship between entities is one-to-many and not one-to-one as implied by the entity-relationship diagram. The manager may not use this terminology, but the data analyst will be able to interpret the comments

RELATIONSHIP TYPE SPECIFICATION FORM	
Relationship name	Standard name for the relationship
Description	A brief description of the relationship
Synonyms	Other names by which the relationship is known
Date specified	
Entities involved (Owner) (Members)	The owner and member entity(ies)
Occurrences	The numbers of each entity type involved in an occurrence of a relationship and the occurrence of that relationship

Cardinality (1:1, 1:m, m:n)	Optional Mandatory	Conditions governing the existence of the relationship

If exclusive: **state paired relationship name**

If inclusive: **state paired relationship name
                      and first existence relationship name**

Create authority	The names of the users who are allowed
Delete authority	to access the relationship in the manner
Access authority	specified
Comments	

Fig. 3.14 Relationship documentation

made. Data analysis is an iterative process: the final model will not be obtained until after a number of tries and this should not be seen as slowness, but care for accuracy. If the entity model is inaccurate so will be the database and the applications that use it. On the other hand, the process should not be too long or 'diminishing returns' will set in.

EVENT TYPE SPECIFICATION FORM	
Event name	*Standard name for the event*
Description *A brief description of the event*	
Frequency	*of the event*
Date specified	
Operations following event *The procedures that are triggered by the event*	
Synchronisation *The condition of the event that effects the trigger*	
Pathway following event *A diagrammatic representation of the processes following the event through the entity types accessed*	
Create authority *The names of the users who are allowed*	
Delete authority *to access the event in the manner*	
Access authority *specified*	
Comments	

Fig. 3.15 Event documentation

The entity-relationship diagram given in Figure 3.17 shows the entities for part of a firm of wholesalers. Included in the figure are the attributes of the entities. The key attributes are underlined. Perhaps you would like to verify that you can understand something of the organisation using this form of documentation. It is a first sketch of the business, and you may also verify the relationships, add entities and relationships to

OPERATION TYPE SPECIFICATION FORM

Operation name	*Standard name for the operation*

Description
A brief description of the operation

Access key	
Date specified	

Entities involved	*Entity names and processing carried out on those entities*

Events preceding operation	*Events caused by operation*
Response time required	
Frequency	
Privacy level	

Create authority	*The names of the users who are allowed*
Delete authority	*to access the operation in the manner*
Access authority	*specified*

Comments

Fig. 3.16 Operation documentation

the model or attributes to the entities, so that the model is more appropriate for a typical firm of wholesalers. For example, I have not included payments in this interim model.

A more realistic example for an academic department is shown as Figure 3.18 (discussed fully in Chapter 15).

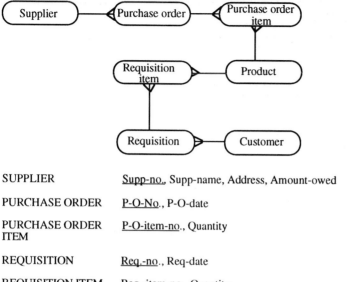

SUPPLIER	<u>Supp-no.</u>, Supp-name, Address, Amount-owed
PURCHASE ORDER	<u>P-O-No.</u>, P-O-date
PURCHASE ORDER ITEM	<u>P-O-item-no.</u>, Quantity
REQUISITION	<u>Req.-no.</u>, Req-date
REQUISITION ITEM	<u>Req.-item-no.</u>, Quantity
CUSTOMER	<u>Cust.-no</u> Cust.-name, Address, Amount-owing, Credit-limit
PRODUCT	<u>Product-no.</u>, Description

Fig. 3.17 Entity-relationship diagram - a first approach for a wholesaler

3.5   ALTERNATIVE APPROACHES TO DATA ANALYSIS

The entity-relationship approach to data analysis is **interview-driven**, that is most information is obtained through interviewing members of staff. It is also **top-down**, in that the entities are identified first and then more and more detail filled in, as where the attributes of the entities are identified. An alternative approach is **document-driven**, where most of the information comes from a study of documents. These documents could be the input forms used in the system and output reports, both hard copy and soft copy designs. In order to make the model flexible, the investigation will include reports likely to be required in the future.

Though this approach includes a formal technique to derive the model, other information gathered in the investigation phase can be incorporated in the final model so derived. The methodology has the following steps:

1) Identify the documents that most typify the area under investigation. Each of these is processed in turn, starting with the most significant. These are usually the ones

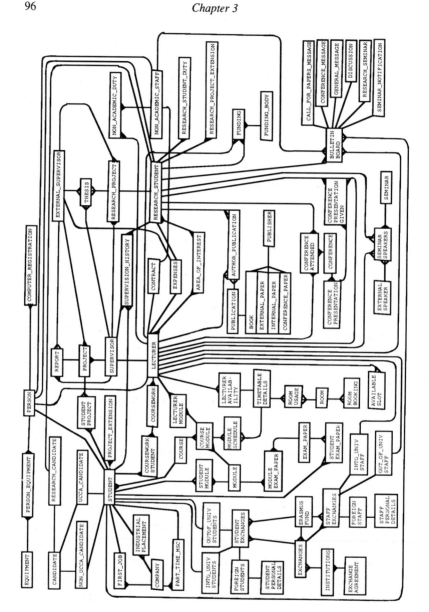

Fig. 3.18 An entity model for an academic department (from Avison & Wood-Harper, 1990)

that carry most data.

2) Identify the data elements on these documents and attach names to each of these. Ensure that synonyms and homonyms are recognised. This may well necessitate

interviewing people in the department concerned. Construct and develop the data dictionary.

3) Draw data usage diagrams for each of these documents. These diagrams highlight the relationships that the documents reflect, in particular any hierarchical structure that the document shows.

4) Separate each level of the diagram as a relation with attributes. Find the identifying (or key) attributes. Modify the relations so that they conform to the rules of normalisation.

5) Combine the relations obtained in the present document with the set obtained from previous documents. This may imply adding new relations to the set, adding data elements (attributes) to one or more of the relations, or breaking up one relation into two or more relations. As more and more documents are processed, the less likely will subsequent documents effect a change in the overall model.

The methodology is best illustrated by an example which is taken from Avison (1981). Figure 3.19 shows an online enquiry and its associated **data usage diagram** (DUD). The first level of the DUD relates to jobs and the second level to orders for parts, because for each occurrence of the job data, there can be many occurrences of order data. The key of the second level consists of the key of the first level (job-number) plus the identifier of the second (part number). Therefore the relations JOB and ORDER are as follows (with key attributes underlined):

JOB (Job-number, sales-area, representative-number)

ORDER (Job-number, part-number, part-description, quantity-ordered)

Figure 3.20 gives another report to be analysed and its DUD. This shows that for each sales area there may be a number of representatives. The JOB relation will have to be modified and a SALES relation formed.

JOB (Job-number, sales-area)

SALES (Sales-area, representative-number, sales-amount)

The process is continued, developing and tuning the set of relations, until all the documents have been processed.

In practice, it is rarely possible to thoroughly analyse all the documents of the organisation in this way. The process is too slow. The first few documents will be used to create the initial model. Later documents will be perused rather than analysed thoroughly in the hope that any new information is revealed in the process.

The major criticism of this approach is that it assumes that all information about the organisation is kept in documents. For this reason it is best to consider the approach document 'driven'. In other words, whilst analysing documents, other information, such as that gained from interviews, can be incorporated into the model. A knowledge of the firm could soon reveal, for example, that the 'part-description' in the

PARTS REQUIRED BY EACH JOB NUMBER					
Job no.	Sales area	Rep. no.	Part	Description	Quantity
1051	3	7	1	Screw 1	300
			2	Screw 2	100
			7	Bolt 1	50
1053	7	9	1	Screw 1	300
1054	14	16	8	Screw 6	20

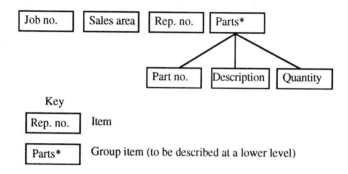

Key

Rep. no.	Item

Parts*	Group item (to be described at a lower level)

Fig. 3.19 Forming data usage diagram from output document

SALES OF REPRESENTATIVE		
Sales area	Rep. no.	Sales (£,000)
3	7	5300
	8	1007
14	15	750
17	9	3004
	11	20
34	116	220
	119	35

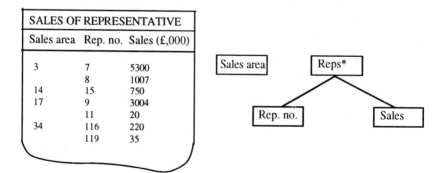

Fig. 3.20 Analysing a second document

ORDER relation is dependent on the 'part-number', not the whole key. This does not conform to the rules of normalisation (attributes must give facts about all the key). There should therefore be another relation formed relating to PART, and the ORDER relation modified.

PART (<u>Part-number</u>, part-description)

ORDER (<u>Job-number</u>, <u>part-number</u>, quantity-ordered)

Rather than use the document-driven approach as the main approach to data analysis, I use this method to verify the model obtained from the entity-relationship approach.

A further approach, also a data collection approach, works by collecting the facts of interest to the enterprise. The attributes are then combined into normalised relations. Like the Data Collection Approach, but unlike the entity-relationship approach, it is a **bottom-up** procedure. As we have seen, the entity-relationship approach looks at the major things of interest first. This is a **top-down** technique. Although bottom-up approaches work for simple cases, there usually proves to be too large a number of attributes to analyse in more realistic situations.

3.6 RELATIONAL MODELLING

In 1970 Ted Codd published his influential paper 'A Relational Model for Large Shared Data Banks'. This has had a profound effect on systems analysis and database design. Most of the early work in data processing had been done pragmatically with developments taking place in the data processing applications environment rather than in the research and academic environments. Little or no formal techniques were being used or developed: problems were solved by rule of thumb and guess-work.

However, by the 1970s the early pioneering days of computer data processing were over and more sophisticated integrated systems were being developed. Large integrated files were needed. Customer files, for example, were being developed which included data relevant to more than one system. These could include sales order, sales ledger and bad debt processing. Later came databases. Codd's research was directed at a very real problem, that is the deletion, insertion and update of data on these very large files.

Being a mathematician, his approach to the problem was mathematical. In describing the work in this text, however, it is intended to avoid a formal mathematical treatment.

The relational model is stressed in this text for a number of reasons:

* The model is understandable by users as well as technologists
* The model is transferable into other data models
* The model is not computer-oriented
* The model is not biased towards particular user requirements
* The model is derived by the processes of data analysis

• Different users can see different views of the model.

It is a model which is *understandable* by the technologists, and also, more importantly, by managers and users. They can far more readily appreciate the meaning of the data relationships illustrated in a tabular form than they could in the file and record specification forms of conventional systems analysis. These are computer-oriented. I have found more difficulty teaching the relational model to computer students (who want to think in terms of computer jargon and are looking for complications that do not exist) than to management students. It is not necessary to know anything of computers or computer file structures to understand the relational model and to use it. Everyone has used tables, and relations are tables.

Relations are *transformable* into other models, such as hierarchies or networks, which are other ways in which database management systems can view data structures. Increasingly, however, relational database management systems are being used so that they are now by far the most common database management systems. These systems expect data to be presented to them in terms of relations and normally present results to users in the form of relations.

The relational model is *not computer-oriented*. It is not biased by any particular physical storage structure that may be used. From a user point of view, the model stays the same whether the storage structures are held on magnetic tape, disk or main storage. It is not biased towards the way that the data may be accessed from storage media. If the target system is a computer system, it could be mainframe, minicomputer or microcomputer.

It *does not show bias towards particular users*, either particular user enquiries, enquiry types, or the enquiries from a particular (perhaps powerful) user. Many systems make some questions easier to ask and answer, particularly where the structure of these matches the design of the database. This is not true of the relational model itself. The database administrator may choose to optimise the performance of some query type which is posed frequently, but these considerations are not made when building the data model.

The relational model can be *derived from data analysis*. Most data analysis techniques derive their data model as a set of entities which can be represented as relations. It maintains the truths of the universe it represents. Thus it can represent that part of the real world that was modelled in the data analysis process. It can also be adapted to reflect changes in the organisation and 'readily adapted', if the relations have been normalised (because normalisation leads to a much more flexible model).

Although the model represents the organisation as a whole, it can be adapted so that a particular part of the model can appear in a *different form to different users*. There will be one overall model, the **conceptual schema**, but in the logical model, the various user views can be represented as **sub-schemas** (particular user or external views). Such flexibility allows users to see only that part of the data model that interests them and avoid an otherwise over-complicated view of the model, and supports other requirements such as privacy and security.

NAME	PART	QUANTITY
Lee	25	12
Deene	38	18
Smith	38	9
Williams	87	100

Fig. 3.21 The relation 'SALES-ORDER'

As seen in Figure 3.21, a relation is a flat file. This relation is called SALES-ORDER and it could show that Lee ordered 12 of 'part number' 25, Deene and Smith ordered 18 and 9 respectively of 'part number' 38, and Williams ordered 100 of 'part number' 87.

The entities and relationships identified in the entity-relationship model can both be represented as relations in the relational model. The many-to-many relationship between COURSE and LECTURER in Figure 3.22 can be represented as three relations: COURSE, LECTURER and TIMETABLE. Here, COURSE and LECTURER come from the original entities and TIMETABLE stems from information about the coincidence of the two, that is, their relationship. The key of the TIMETABLE relation is taken from the key of the COURSE relation (course-number) and that of the LECTURER relation (lecturer-number). The processes involved in mapping these to relations are described more fully in Section 4.8.

We will now introduce some of the terminology associated with the relational model. Each row in a relation is called a **tuple**. The order of tuples is immaterial, although they will normally be shown in the text in a logical sequence so that it is easier to follow their contents. No two tuples can be identical in the model. A tuple will have a number of **attributes**, and in the SALES-ORDER relation of Figure 3.21, 'name', 'part' and 'quantity' are attributes. All items in a column come from the same **domain** - there are circumstances where the contents from two or more columns come from the same domain. The relation ELECTION-RESULT (Figure 3.23) illustrates this possibility. Two attributes come from the same domain of Political Parties. The number of attributes in a relation is called the **degree** of the relation. A relation with two attributes is known as a binary relation. The number of tuples in a relation define its **cardinality**.

Each tuple in a relation is distinguished from another because one or more attributes in a relation are designated **key attributes**. In the SALES-ORDER relation, the key is

Chapter 3

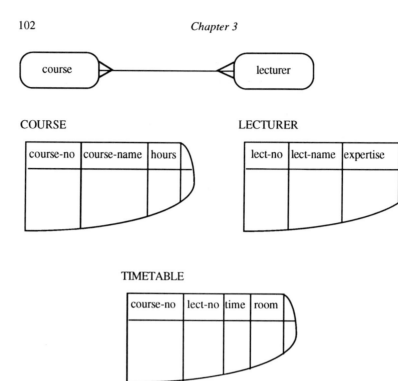

Fig. 3.22 Many-to-many relationship mapped as three relations

'name'. It might be better to allocate numbers to customers in case there are duplicate names. If the customer may make orders for a number of parts, then 'part' must also be a key attribute as there will be several tuples with the same 'Name'. In this case, the attributes 'name' and 'part' will make up the **composite key** of the ORDER relation.

What is the key for the ELECTION-RESULT relation? On first sight, 'election year' might seem appropriate, but in 1974 there were two elections in a year, and even if all three attributes were part of the key, there are still duplicate relations. It is necessary to add another attribute or replace 'year' by 'election date' to make each tuple unique (there will not be two elections of the same type on the same day). Alternatively the composite key 'election year' and a new attribute 'election number in year' will be adequate.

There may be more than one possible key. These are known as **candidate keys**. 'Customer name' and 'customer number' could be candidate keys in a CUSTOMER relation. In this circumstance one of these is chosen as the **primary key**. An attribute which is a primary key in one relation and not a primary key but included in another relation is called a **foreign key** in that second relation.

The structure of a relation is conventionally expressed as in the following examples:

SALES-ORDER (<u>name</u>, part, quantity) and

ELECTION-RESULT (<u>elect-year</u>, <u>elect-number</u>, first-party, second-party)

ELECTION RESULT

ELECTION YEAR	FIRST PARTY	SECOND PARTY
1966	Labour	Conservative
1970	Conservative	Labour
1974	Labour	Conservative
1974	Labour	Conservative
1979	Conservative	Labour
1983	Conservative	Labour
1987	Conservative	Labour

Fig. 3.23 Relation 'ELECTION RESULT'

3.7   NORMALISATION

The process of normalisation is the application of a number of rules to the relational model which will simplify the relations. This set of rules proves to be a useful guideline because we are dealing with large sets of data and the relations formed by the normalisation process will make the data easier to understand and manipulate. The model so formed is appropriate for the further stages in the methodology and the database will be shareable, a fundamental justification for the database approach. On the other hand, normalisation can lead to an increase in the number of relations and to data duplication so that relations can be joined on the primary key and foreign key.

Codd developed three nested levels of normalisation, and the third and final stage is known as **third normal form** (TNF). It is this level of normalisation that is usually used as the basis for the design of the data model, as an end result of data analysis, and for mapping onto a database (the logical schema). There are a few instances, however, when even TNF needs further simplification, and these are looked at in Section 3.8 which may be skipped on first reading. TNF is usually satisfactory in practice.

Normalisation is the process of transforming data into well formed or natural groupings such that one fact is in one place and the correct relationships between facts exist. The relations formed by the normalisation process will make the data easier to understand and manipulate. As well as simplifying the relations, normalisation also reduces anomalies which may otherwise occur when manipulating the relations in a relational database. Normalised data is stable and a good foundation for any future growth. It is a mechanical process, indeed the technique has been automated (see Chapter 11), but the difficult part of it lies in understanding the meaning, that is, the semantics of the data, and this is only discovered by extensive and careful data analysis. Automation of the normalisation process still requires this information to be supplied to the particular tool.

There are three stages of normalisation:

First normal form

Ensure that all the attributes are atomic (that is, in the smallest possible components). This means that there is only one possible value for each domain and not a set of values. This is often expressed as the fact that relations must not contain repeating groups.

Second normal form

Ensure that all non-key attributes are functionally dependent on (give facts about) all of the key. If this is not the case, split off into a separate relation those attributes that are dependent on only part of the key.

Third normal form

Ensure that all non-key attributes are functionally independent of each other. If this is not the case, create new relations which do not show any non-key dependence.

A rather flippant, but more memorable, definition of normalisation can be given as 'the attributes in a relation must depend on the key, the whole key, and nothing but the key'. This is an oversimplification, but it is essentially true and could be kept in mind as normalisation is developed.

A more detailed description of normalisation is now given. A key concept is **functional dependency**, which is often referred to as **determinacy**. This is defined by Cardenas (1985) as follows:

'Given a relation R, the attribute B is said to be functionally dependent on attribute A if at every instant of time each value of A has no more than one value of B associated with it in the relation R.'

Thus, if we know a 'customer-number', we know the associated 'customer-name' and 'customer-address' if they are functionally dependent on 'customer-number'. Functional dependency is frequently illustrated by an arrow. The arrow will point from A to B in the functional dependency illustrated in the definition. Thus, the value of A uniquely determines the value of B.

Before normalising the first relation given as Figure 3.24, it is necessary to analyse the meaning of the relation. Knowledge of the application area gained from data analysis will provide this information. It is possible to make assumptions about the inter-relationships between the data, but it is obviously better to base these assumptions on thorough analysis. In the relation COURSE-DETAIL, there are two occurrences of 'course', one numbered B74 called computer science at the BSc. level and the other B94 called computer applications at the MSc. level. Each of these course occurrences has a number of module occurrences associated with it. Each 'module' is given a 'name', 'status' and 'unit-points' (which are allocated according to the status of the 'module').

(a) COURSE DETAIL

COURSE	COURSE-NAME	LEVEL	MODULE	NAME	STATUS	UNIT-POINTS
B74	Computer science	BSc	B741	Programming 1	Basic	8
			B742	Hardware 1		
			B743	Data processing 1		
			B744	Programming 2	Intermed.	11
			B745	Hardware 2		
B94	Computer apps.	MSc	B951	Information	Advanced	15
			B952	Microproc.		
			B741	Programming 1	Basic	8

(b) COURSE DETAIL

COURSE	COURSE-NAME	LEVEL	MODULE	NAME	STATUS	UNIT-POINTS
B74	Computer science	BSc	B741	Programming 1	Basic	8
B74	Computer science	BSc	B742	Hardware 1	Basic	8
B74	Computer science	BSc	B743	Data processing 1	Basic	8
B74	Computer science	BSc	B744	Programming 2	Intermed.	11
B74	Computer science	BSc	B745	Hardware 2	Intermed.	11
B94	Computer apps.	MSc	B951	Information	Advanced	15
B94	Computer apps.	MSc	B952	Microproc.	Advanced	15
B94	Computer apps.	MSc	B741	Programming 1	Basic	8

Fig. 3.24 First normal form

First normal form: The first stage of normalisation includes the filling in of details. This is seen in the example in Figure 3.24(a) and is a trivial task. You may note that in Figure 3.24(a), the order of the tuples in the unnormalised relation is significant. Otherwise the content of the attributes not completed cannot be known. As we have already stated, one of the principles of the relational model is that the order of the tuples should not be significant. The relation seen in Figure 3.24(b) could be in any order. First normal form really converts unnormalised data or traditional file structures into relations or tables.

The key of the relation of Figure 3.24(b) is 'course-number' and 'module-number' together (a composite key) and the key attributes have been underlined. A composite key is necessary because no single attribute will uniquely identify a tuple of this relation. There were in fact a number of possible candidate keys, for example, 'module-name' and 'course-name', but we chose the primary key as above.

Further work would have been necessary if the following was presented as the unnormalised relation:

COURSE, COURSE-NAME, LEVEL, MODULE-DETAILS

'Module-details' has to be defined as a set of atomic attributes, not as a group item, thus it has to be broken down into its constituents of 'module-name', 'status' and 'unit-points':

COURSE, COURSE-NAME, LEVEL, MODULE-NAME, STATUS, UNIT-POINTS

will be the result in first normal form, with all the details filled out.

Second normal form: This is achieved if the relations are in first normal form and all non-key attributes are fully functionally dependent on all the key. The relation course-detail shown in Figure 3.24(b) is in first normal form. However, the attributes 'status', 'name' and 'unit-points' are functionally dependent on 'module'. In other words, they represent facts about 'module', which is only part of the key (known as partial dependency). We may say that if the value of module is known, we can determine the value of 'status', 'name', and 'unit-points'. For example, if module is B743, then 'status' is basic, 'name' is data proc 1, and 'unit points' is 8. They are not dependent on the other part of the key, 'course'. So as to comply with the requirements of second normal form, two relations will be formed from the relation and this is shown as Figure 3.25.

But the relation course-module is still not in second normal form because the attributes 'course-name' and 'level' are functionally dependent on 'course' only, and not on the whole of the key. A separate COURSE relation has been created in Figure 3.26. The course relation has only two tuples (there are only two courses), and all duplicates are removed. Notice that we maintain the relation COURSE-MODULE. This relation is all key, and there is nothing incorrect in this. Attributes may possibly be added later which relate specifically to the course-module relationship. The relation is required because information will be lost by not including it, that is, the modules which are included in a particular course and the courses which include specific modules. The relations are now in second normal form.

Third normal form (TNF): Second normal form may cause problems where non-key

(a) COURSE-MODULE

<u>COURSE</u>	<u>MODULE</u>	COURSE-NAME	LEVEL
B74	B741	Computer science	BSc
B74	B742	Computer science	BSc
B74	B743	Computer science	BSc
B74	B744	Computer science	BSc
B74	B745	Computer science	BSc
B94	B951	Computer apps.	MSc
B94	B952	Computer apps.	MSc
B94	B741	Computer apps.	MSc

(b) MODULE

<u>MODULE</u>	NAME	STATUS	UNIT-POINTS
B741	Programming 1	Basic	8
B742	Hardware 1	Basic	8
B743	Data processing 1	Basic	8
B744	Programming 2	Intermed.	11
B745	Hardware 2	Intermed.	11
B951	Information	Advanced	15
B952	Microproc.	Advanced	15
B741	Programming 1	Basic	8

Fig. 3.25 Towards second normal form: course-module needs further normalisation

attributes are functionally dependent on each other (a non-key attribute is dependent on another non-key attribute). This is resolved by converting the relations into TNF. In the relation module, the attribute 'unit-points' is functionally dependent on the 'status' (or level) of the course, that is, given 'status', we know the value of 'unit-points'. So 'unit-points' is determined by 'status' which is not a key. We therefore create a new relation STATUS and delete 'unit-points' from the relation MODULE. The third normal form is given in Figure 3.27.

Sometimes the term **transitive dependency** is used in this context. The dependency of the attribute 'unit-points' is transitive (via 'status') and not wholly dependent on the key attribute 'module'. This transitive dependency should not exist in third normal form.

The attribute 'status' is the primary key of the STATUS relation. It is included as an attribute in the MODULE relation, but it is not a key. This provides an example of a foreign key, that is, a non-key attribute of one relation which is a primary key of another. This will be useful when processing the relations as 'status' can be used to

join the STATUS and MODULE relations to form a larger composite relation if this is
required by the user. But we are now drifting to the next stages of the methodology.

(a) COURSE-MODULE

COURSE	MODULE
B74	B741
B74	B742
B74	B743
B74	B744
B74	B745
B94	B951
B94	B952
B94	B741

(b) COURSE

COURSE	COURSE-NAME	LEVEL
B74	Computer science	BSc
B94	Computer apps.	MSc

(c) MODULE

MODULE	NAME	STATUS	UNIT-POINTS
B741	Programming 1	Basic	8
B742	Hardware 1	Basic	8
B743	Data processing 1	Basic	8
B744	Programming 2	Intermed.	11
B745	Hardware 2	Intermed.	11
B951	Information	Advanced	15
B952	Microproc.	Advanced	15
B741	Programming 1	Basic	8

Fig. 3.26 Second normal form

Codd developed three nested levels of normalisation, and this third and final stage
is known as TNF. It is this level of normalisation that is usually used as the basis for
the design of the data model, as an end result of data analysis. As we shall see in
Section 3.8, there are a few instances when even TNF needs further simplification, and
Kent (1983) and Date (1990) describe these extensions. TNF is usually satisfactory,
however, and readers may avoid further extensions if they wish, that is, skip the next
section.

(a) COURSE-MODULE

COURSE	MODULE
B74	B741
B74	B742
B74	B743
B74	B744
B74	B745
B94	B951
B94	B952
B94	B741

(b) COURSE

COURSE	COURSE-NAME	LEVEL
B74	Computer science	BSc
B94	Computer apps.	MSc

(c) MODULE

MODULE	NAME	STATUS
B741	Programming 1	Basic
B742	Hardware 1	Basic
B743	Data processing 1	Basic
B744	Programming 2	Intermed.
B745	Hardware 2	Intermed.
B951	Information	Advanced
B952	Microproc.	Advanced
B741	Programming 1	Basic

(d) STATUS

STATUS	UNIT-POINTS
Basic	8
Intermed.	11
Advanced	15

Fig. 3.27 Third normal form

Relations are normalised because unnormalised relations prove difficult to use. This can be illustrated if we try to insert, delete, and update information from the relations not in TNF. Say we have a new 'module' numbered B985 called Artificial Intelligence and which has a 'status' in the intermediate category. Looking at Figure 3.24, we cannot add this information in COURSE-DETAIL because there has been no allocation of this 'module' occurrence to any 'course'. Looking at Figure 3.25(b), it could be added to the MODULE relation, if we knew that the 'status' intermediate carried 11 unit-points. This information is not necessary in the MODULE relation seen in Figure 3.27(c), the TNF version of this relation. The TNF model is therefore much more convenient for adding this new information.

If we decided to introduce a new category in the 'status' attribute, called coursework, having a 'unit-points' attached of 10, we cannot add it to the relation MODULE (Figure 3.25(b)) because we have not decided which 'module' or modules to attach it to. But we can include this information in the TNF model by adding a tuple to the STATUS relation (Figure 3.27(d)).

Another problem occurs when updating. Let us say that we decide to change the 'unit-points' allocated to the Basic category of 'status' in the modules from 8 to 6, it becomes a simple matter in the TNF module. The single occurrence of the tuple with the key Basic, needs to be changed from (Basic 8) to (Basic 6) in Figure 3.27(d). With the unnormalised, first normal or second normal form relations, there will be a number of tuples to change. It means searching through every tuple of the relation COURSE-DETAIL (Figure 3.24(b)) or module (Figure 3.25(b)) looking for 'status' = Basic and updating the associated 'unit-points'. All tuples have to be searched, because in the relational model the order of the tuples is of no significance. This increases the likelihood of inconsistencies and errors in the database. We have ordered them in the text to make the normalisation process easier to follow.

Deleting information will also cause problems. If it is decided to drop the B74 course, we may still wish to keep details of the modules which make up the course. Information about modules might be used at another time when designing another course. The information would be lost if we deleted the course B74 from COURSE-DETAIL (Figure 3.24(b)). The information about these modules will be retained in the module relation in TNF. The TNF relation COURSE will now consist only of one tuple relating to the 'course' B74 and the TNF relation COURSE-MODULE will consist of the THREE tuples relating to the COURSE B94.

3.8   FURTHER NORMALISATION

In Section 3.7 we regarded third normal form as the end of the normalisation process and this is usually satisfactory. Further, the process of normalisation to third normal form is neither difficult nor obscure. However, much of the database literature discusses further levels of normalisation.

Boyce-Codd normal form (BCNF): One criticism of third normal form is that by making reference to other normal forms, hidden dependencies may not be revealed. BCNF does not make reference to other normal forms.

In any relation there may be more than one combination of attributes which can be chosen as primary key, in other words, there are candidate keys. BCNF requires that all attribute values are fully dependent on each candidate key and not only the primary key. Put another way, it requires that each **determinant** (attribute or combination of attributes which determines the value of another attribute) must be a candidate key. As any primary key will be a candidate key, all relations in BCNF will satisfy the rules of third normal form, but relations in TNF may not be in BCNF.

It is best explained by an example. In fact, the third normal form relations in Figure 3.27 are also in BCNF, so we will extend the example used so far. Assume that we have an additional relation which is also in TNF giving details about the students taking modules and the lecturers teaching on those modules. Assume also that each module is taught by several lecturers; each lecturer teaches one module; each student takes several modules; and each student has only one lecturer for a given module. This complex set of rules could produce the relation shown as Figure 3.28.

STUDENT	MODULE	LECTURER
Bell	B741	Dr. Smith
Bell	B742	Dr. Jones
Martin	B741	Dr. Smith
Martin	B742	Prof. Harris

Fig. 3.28 Relation in TNF but not BCNF

Although this relation is in TNF because the 'lecturer' is dependent on all the key (both 'student' and 'module' determine the lecturer), it is not in BCNF because the attribute 'lecturer' is a determinant but is not a candidate key. There will be some update anomalies. For example, if we wish to delete the information that Martin is studying B742, it cannot be done without deleting the information that Prof. Harris teaches the module B742. As the attribute 'lecturer' is a determinant but not a candidate key, it is necessary to create a new table containing 'lecturer' and its directly dependent attribute 'module'. This results in two relations as shown in Figure 3.29. These are in BCNF.

LECTURER	MODULE
Dr. Smith	B741
Dr. Jones	B742
Dr. Smith	B741
Prof. Harris	B742

STUDENT	LECTURER
Bell	Dr. Smith
Bell	Dr. Jones
Martin	Dr. Smith
Martin	Prof. Harris

Fig. 3.29 BCNF

Fourth normal form: We will illustrate fourth normal form by looking at a relation which is in first normal form and which contains information about modules, lecturers and text books. The example is based on that found in Date (1990). Each tuple has a module name and a repeating group of text book names (there will be a number of texts recommended for each module). The module can be taught by a number of lecturers, but each will recommend the same set of texts.

MODULE	LECTURER	TEXT
B741	Dr. Smith	Database Fundamentals
B741	Dr. Smith	Further Databases
B741	Dr. Jones	Database Fundamentals
B741	Dr. Jones	Further Databases
B742	Dr. Smith	Database Fundamentals
B742	Dr. Smith	Systems Analysis
B742	Dr. Smith	Information Systems

Fig. 3.30 Redundancy where relation is in BCNF but not in fourth normal form

The relation seen as Figure 3.30 is in BCNF (and therefore TNF) and yet it contains considerable redundancy. If we wish to add the information that Prof. Harris can teach B742, three tuples need to be added to the relation. The problem comes about because all three attributes form the composite key: there are no functional determinants apart from this combination of all three attributes.

The problem would be eased by forming from this relation the two all key relations shown as Figure 3.31. There is no loss of information, and there is not the evident redundancy found in Figure 3.30.

MODULE	LECTURER
B741	Dr. Smith
B741	Dr. Jones
B742	Dr. Smith

MODULE	TEXT
B741	Database Fundamentals
B741	Further Databases
B742	Database Fundamentals
B742	Systems Analysis
B742	Information Systems

Fig. 3.31 Fourth normal form

The transition to fourth normal form has been made because of **multivalued dependencies** (Fagin, 1977). Although a module does not have one and only one lecturer, each module does have a pre-defined set of lecturers. Similarly, each module also has a pre-defined set of texts.

Although these examples are valid, in that they do show relations which contain redundancy and yet are in TNF and BCNF respectively, the examples are somewhat contrived. The reader will have seen that in both examples it was necessary to make a number of special assumptions. The implication is that such problems will not be found frequently by analysts when carrying out data analysis and therefore that TNF will normally be a reasonable stopping point for normalisation. Many academics take normalisation even further. In order to provide an example of fifth normal form, Date has to bring in what he calls a 'bizarre constraint'. He goes on to suggest that 'such relations are pathological cases and likely to be rare in practice'. We will stop at fourth normal form!

3.9   FURTHER READING

Benyon, D (1990) *Information and Data Modelling*, Blackwell Scientific Publications,

Oxford.

Bowers, D. S (1988) *From Data to Database*, Van Nostrand Reinhold, Wokingham.

Howe, D. R (1989) *Data Analysis for Data Base Design*, 2nd ed, Arnold, London.

Kent, W. A (1978) *Data and Reality*, North Holland, Amsterdam.

Robinson, H (1989) *Database Analysis and Design*, 2nd ed, Chartwell-Bratt, Bromley.

Veryard, R (1984) *Pragmatic Data Analysis*, Blackwell Scientific Publications, Oxford.
Alternative books on data modelling.

Date, C. J (1990) *An Introduction to Database Systems, Vol 1*, 5th ed, Addison-Wesley, London.

Cardenas, A. F (1985) *Database Management Systems*, 2nd ed, Allyn and Bacon, Boston.

Elmasri, R & Navathe, S. B (1989) *Fundamentals of Database Systems*, Benjamin/Cummings, Redwood City, Ca.

McFadden, F. R & Hoffer, J. A (1991) *Database Management*, 3rd ed, Benjamin/Cummings, Redwood City, Ca.
The classic text of Date on the technology of database management, followed by some excellent alternatives.

Chen, P. P. S (1976) The Entity-Relationship Model - Toward a Unified View of Data, *ACM Transactions on Database Systems*, **1**.

Codd, E. F (1970) A Relational Model of Data for Large Shared Data Banks, *Communications of the ACM*, **13**.

Kent, W (1983) A Simple Guide to Five Normal Forms in Relational Theory, *Communications of the ACM*, **26**, 2.
Three 'classic' papers, the first being an early statement of the entity-relationship approach, in the second Codd defined the basic tenets of normalisation theory and in the paper by Kent, the basic steps are extended.

Chapter 4
The Logical Schema: Relational, Hierarchical, Network and Object-Oriented Views

---

4.1 INTRODUCTION

Having formed an agreed conceptual schema, a model which represents the enterprise reasonably well and is independent of any type of physical system (computer or otherwise), it is possible to transfer or 'map' this model on to a database management system (DBMS). The use of a DBMS is not necessary to develop information systems, but it is part of the methodology for implementing information systems discussed in this text. Thus the entity model is mapped into a form required by the particular DBMS used. This is the **logical schema**. Most DBMS require the data structures to be presented in one of three ways: as relations, hierarchies, or networks, but more recently, object-oriented DBMS have begun to appear. Although most DBMS fall into one of these design types, some do not. This will be looked at in Chapter 7 where a number of commercial DBMS are investigated. Some writers distinguish another type of database, the inverted file. This distinction is more related to the physical schema (the next stage of developing the data model) and a discussion of inverted files is therefore given in Chapter 5.

It should be emphasised that the data model which we have called the conceptual schema was developed independently of both machine and software considerations. It represents the integrated user views of the data and the data relationships in the area chosen. This means that the best possible data model can be formulated with the knowledge that it can be mapped on to a DBMS. Its conversion to a logical schema can then be made and this will be in the form required by the target DBMS. Some DBMS accept more than one data model type, for example, both relations and hierarchies. Whatever the form of the logical model, the accuracy of the mapping from conceptual schema to logical schema is crucial to the success of the database project: there should be no loss of information.

In order to put this mapping of conceptual to logical schema into perspective (and therefore the place of this chapter in the overall methodology), the next step (discussed in Chapter 5) is a further mapping to the storage level representation of data, the ways in which the data is stored on disk. However, this mapping will be largely transparent to the user, in other words the DBMS will usually take care of physical mapping onto storage media and file organisation. This may be carried out following intervention by the database administrator, who will choose between the alternative file organisation methods offered by the DBMS (if any) as appropriate for the particular data and users. Such alternative methods may include linked lists, indexes, inverted files, random access, B-trees or other methods of file organisation. This is the concern of the physical schema. DBMS therefore have two views of the data: the logical schema, which is the view given to them by the user, programmer or database administrator, and the physical schema. The position of the DBMS, acting as a cushion between the logical views of the data structure and the physical schema, is shown in Figure 4.1.

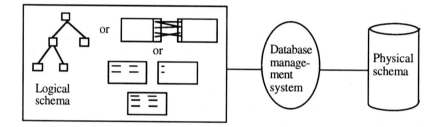

Fig. 4.1 The logical schema and the database management system

DB2, IMS and IDMS are DBMS which are examples of different database types (we will look at object-oriented DBMS separately, they have only recently been available). DB2 is a relational DBMS, that is data structures are presented to it in the form of tables; IMS views the data structures in terms of hierarchies; and IDMS in terms of networks. This chapter discusses these forms of the logical schema and also shows how the data structures might be described to the database. This description is usually called the **Data Definition Language** (DDL) of the particular DBMS. An introduction to a DDL for each type of system is discussed below along with a description of the ways in which the data could be accessed and updated using the **Data Manipulation Language** (DML). These features will be developed further in Chapter 7 when we look at particular commercial DBMS.

4.2   THE RELATIONAL APPROACH

The relational model was described in Chapter 3 and therefore it is not proposed to repeat this description here. The model is an excellent means of describing the data structures in an enterprise, independently of the requirements of a particular DBMS or any other computer-oriented factor. Many DBMS, such as Oracle, Rapport, Ingres,

DB2 and dBaseIV, are relational, and therefore can take advantage of the particular features of the relational structure. This does not mean that the logical model needs to be relational, but it is obviously convenient to use a relational DBMS when using the methodology described in the text.

We will look at database mapping in detail in Section 4.8, but in principle, when converting the conceptual schema to the relational model, entities become relations (entity occurrences being the tuples); the attributes are mapped directly, the key attributes of an entity will be the same as those of the relation; and the relationships also become relations, their keys being derived from the keys of the relations taking part in the relationship. The result is a set of normalised relations mapped on to the target DBMS.

Although the conceptual schema will be a set of normalised relations, it may be efficient to have a logical design specified to the DBMS which has some non-normalised relations. If a particular group item is always associated by users with a relation, it may be reasonable to specify a non-normalised relation. This will be a decision of the database administrator. Relations may also be stored which are derived from the primary set of relations. Thus, from a basic EMPLOYEE relation

EMPLOYEE (emp-num, emp-name, dept-num)

and a basic DEPARTMENT relation of

DEPARTMENT (dept-num, dept-name, no-of-staff, head)

an EMPLOYEE-DETAILS relation consisting of

EMPLOYEE-DETAILS (emp-num,emp-name,dept-num,dept-name,dept-head)

may be derived. There may be good grounds, such as a requirement to frequently access this data, to include this unnormalised and derived relation on the database.

In most DBMS, tables are easy to create. The DBMS may have a CREATE command, such as:

```
CREATE RELATION EMPLOYEE
(EMP-NUM,10,C
EMP-NAME,30,C
SALARY,5,N)
```

This will set up the structure of a relation called EMPLOYEE which has three attributes. The 'employee number' is 10 characters long, the 'employee name' is 30 characters long, and the 'salary' is a 5 digit number. No links need be set up in a relational database between relations. The links are set up temporarily by the DBMS at run time following a user request for this information. This will be effected using the relational Data Manipulation Language (DML) of the DBMS. The DML is the database language which is used to join relations together and pick out selected tuples or domains as requested by the user.

One of the most interesting aspects of relational databases are their data manipulation languages. Codd (1970) developed a series of operators to manipulate relations. These operators include those to merge relations and to separate out some columns or some rows. The set of operators are known together as the **Relational Algebra**. Other DMLs, such as the Relational Calculus and Query-by-Example (QBE), are usually translated into relational algebra by the DBMS before executing the request using the database. The relational algebra is a procedural language. The operators manipulate the relations using a series of steps to perform the user's requirements. As we shall see, the relational calculus is less procedural, and the database system is expected to translate this into the procedural steps of the relational algebra.

In a relational system, *the result of any operation on one or more relations is itself a relation.* This gives the relational model advantages over other models. The language reflects the design of the system. The relational algebra is also **relationally complete**, that is, it is possible to perform <u>any</u> data manipulation on the relations required by the user using one or more of the relational algebra operators. The language is also executed dynamically. In other words the access paths for joining or separating relations are not set up with the data. They are set up each time when the operation is required at run time. This has particular advantages where the user requests are not predictable, but is less efficient when compared to hierarchical and network systems in situations where the access paths are predictable. For this reason, many commercial relational DBMS enable links to be set up as an option and therefore they can be set up beforehand and executed each time they are required. The database administrator (DBA) is given the opportunity to set up indexes at data creation time and this will increase the speed by which data is retrieved. We now look at the relational algebra and the relational calculus in more detail. Many DML implementations are based on one of these specifications.

4.3   RELATIONAL ALGEBRA

The relational algebra is a collection of operators on relations. It includes the traditional set operators union, intersection, difference and product. The UNION of two relations is the set of all tuples (rows) belonging to either or both of the relations. The INTERSECTION of two relations is the set of all tuples belonging to both of the relations. The DIFFERENCE of two relations is the set of all tuples belonging to one relation but not the other. Thus A MINUS B is the set of tuples belonging to relation A and not B. The PRODUCT of two relations concatenates each pair of tuples on the original tables. Thus, if the first table has R rows and the second table r rows, then the product of the

LECTURER-MODULE

MODULE	LECTURER-NAME	N0-OF-WEEKS
1	Clarke	10
1a	Goodwin	10
1b	Goodwin	10
2	Knight	10
2a	Collins	10
2b	Baker	10
2c	Jagger	10
3	Fisher	10
3a	Oldham	10
4	Glenn	20

ATTENDANCE

STUDENT -NAME	MODULE	LECTURER -NAME
Ashworth	1	Clarke
Ashworth	1b	Goodwin
Ashworth	2	Knight
Ashworth	2a	Collins
Ashworth	3	Fisher
Ashworth	3a	Oldham
Ashworth	4	Glenn
Atkins	1	Clarke
Atkins	1a	Goodwin
Atkins	2	Knight
Atkins	2b	Baker
Atkins	3	Fisher
Atkins	3a	Oldham
Atkins	4	Glenn
Johnson	1	Clarke
Johnson	1a	Goodwin
Johnson	2	Knight
Johnson	2c	Jagger
Smith	1	Clarke
Smith	1b	Goodwin
Smith	2a	Collins
Smith	3	Fisher
Smith	3a	Oldham
Smith	4	Glenn
Perkins	3	Fisher
Perkins	3a	Oldham
Perkins	4	Glenn

Fig. 4.2 The relations associated with an MSc course

two relations will be R x r rows. This operator is infrequently used because it is indiscriminate in the way it joins tuples together. (Usually the JOIN operator is more appropriate, as we shall see later in this section.) These are all traditional set operators and they require that all relations included in one operation have the same **degree**, that is, they have the same number of columns (referred to as **union compatibility**).

(a)

A

STUDENT-NAME	MODULE	LECTURER-NAME
Ashworth	3	Fisher
Atkins	3	Fisher
Smith	3	Fisher
Perkins	3	Fisher

B

STUDENT-NAME	MODULE	LECTURER-NAME
Ashworth	2a	Collins
Smith	2a	Collins

(b) Result of union

STUDENT-NAME	MODULE	LECTURER-NAME
Ashworth	3	Fisher
Atkins	3	Fisher
Smith	3	Fisher
Perkins	3	Fisher
Ashworth	2a	Collins
Smith	2a	Collins

(c) Result of intersection

STUDENT-NAME	MODULE	LECTURER-NAME
Ashworth	3	Fisher
Smith	3	Fisher
Ashworth	2a	Collins
Smith	2a	Collins

(d) Result of subtraction

STUDENT-NAME	MODULE	LECTURER-NAME
Atkins	3	Fisher
Perkins	3	Fisher

Fig. 4.3 Results of operations on relations

So as to illustrate the use of the various operators, we will consider the two relations in Figure 4.2. They give information about an MSc. course which consists of four parts, three of which have a ten week compulsory unit and a choice of options. The relation LECTURER-MODULE gives the module number (each compulsory unit and option is termed a module) the name of the lecturer presenting the module and the number of weeks it lasts. One course has no options, it runs the full 20 weeks. Finally, ATTENDANCE gives the student name, the modules that the student has chosen and the lecturer of that module.

Consider the ATTENDANCE relation. If A is the set of students attending module 3, and B is the set of students attending module 2a (see Figure 4.3(a)), then

A UNION B

is the set of students tuples (Figure 4.3(b)) who attend either module 3 or 2a (or both); and

A INTERSECT B

will be the set of student tuples (Figure 4.3(c)) who attend both module 3 and 2a. The DIFFERENCE between the two relations

A MINUS B

will be the set of tuples (Figure 4.3(d)) who attend module 3 but not module 2a.

Such operations may be useful for timetabling, classroom allocation and for making examination arrangements. The results are in tabular form and are therefore understandable to the user.

The other basic operations in the relational algebra are not traditional set operators. They are PROJECT, SELECT, JOIN and DIVIDE. The SELECT operator in the relational algebra is different from the SELECT statement of SQL which is described in Chapter 8. It allows a choice to be made of the tuples in a relation and takes a horizontal subset of an existing table. For example:

SELECT ATTENDANCE WHERE MODULE = 3a

will derive the relation shown as Figure 4.4. The part of the statement 'WHERE MODULE = 3a', is called the **conditional** part of the statement.

STUDENT -NAME	MODULE	LECTURER -NAME
Ashworth	3a	Oldham
Atkins	3a	Oldham
Smith	3a	Oldham
Perkins	3a	Oldham

Fig. 4.4 Result of select

The statement:

SELECT LECTURER-MODULE WHERE NO-OF-WEEKS GREATER THAN 10

will give a one tuple relation shown as Figure 4.5:

LECTURER-MODULE

MODULE	LECTURER-NAME	N0-OF-WEEKS
4	Glenn	20

Fig. 4.5 Result of second select

The PROJECT operator will choose specified attributes of a relation and eliminate others. It therefore forms a vertical subset of an existing table by extracting columns. It also removes any duplicate tuples that may have been formed by the operation. Hence:

PROJECT LECTURER-MODULE OVER MODULE, NO-OF-WEEKS

will give the relation shown in Figure 4.6(a). The PROJECT operator may also be used to change the order of attributes written in the relation, for example:

PROJECT LECTURER-MODULE OVER NO-OF-WEEKS, MODULE

will give the relation shown in Figure 4.6(b).

MODULE	N0-OF-WEEKS
1	10
1a	10
1b	10
2	10
2a	10
2b	10
2c	10
3	10
3a	10
4	20

N0-OF-WEEKS	MODULE
10	1
10	1a
10	1b
10	2
10	2a
10	2b
10	2c
10	3
10	3a
20	4

(a)   (b)

Fig. 4.6 Result of projects

In using the relational algebra, SELECT and PROJECT statements are important because many queries will require information from only some of the tuples or attributes in a relation. But users may also have queries where the data comes from two or more relations. The JOIN operator will form a relation from others where there is the same value in a common domain. This common domain might be a key in one relation and a non-key attribute (called a **foreign key**) in another. In order that tables can be joined, the value of the foreign key must exist as a primary key in another relation or be null (this is a rule of relational modelling known as **referential integrity**). Null values are usually permitted because in some situations the value will not yet have been allocated. Dealing with null values is one of the problems that extensions to Codd's original relational model do take into account.

The result of a JOIN operation is a new wider table in which each row is formed by concatenating the two rows that have the same value in the common domain. For example:

JOIN LECTURER-MODULE AND ATTENDANCE OVER MODULE

will result in Figure 4.7 (the relationship between LECTURER-MODULE and ATTENDANCE is one-to-many).

MODULE	LECTURER-NAME	NO-OF-WEEKS	STUDENT-NAME
1	Clarke	10	Ashworth
1	Clarke	10	Atkins
1	Clarke	10	Johnson
1	Clarke	10	Smith
1a	Goodwin	10	Atkins
1a	Goodwin	10	Johnson
1b	Goodwin	10	Ashworth
1b	Goodwin	10	Ashworth
2	Knight	10	Ashworth

Fig. 4.7 Result of join

In some relational systems, the operation will be written as:

JOIN LECTURER-MODULE AND ATTENDANCE WHERE
MODULE=MODULE

and some less refined systems repeat information in the relation that is derived from the operation so that the result is a relation consisting of the following columns:

MODULE LECTURER-NAME NO-WEEKS STUDENT-NAME MODULE
LECTURER-NAME

In its simplest form, DIVISION is defined as an operation between a binary relation (the dividend) and a unary relation (the divisor) which produces a unary relation (the quotient) as its result. To form a binary relation consisting of student-name and module, we first carry out a projection:

PROJECT ATTENDANCE OVER STUDENT-NAME AND MODULE GIVING
DEND

which will produce Figure 4.8(a). Let the divisor DDR be Figure 4.8(b), then:

DIVIDE DEND BY DDR OVER MODULE:

DEND

STUDENT-NAME	MODULE
Ashworth	1
Ashworth	1b
Ashworth	2
Ashworth	2a
Ashworth	3
Ashworth	3a
Ashworth	4
Atkins	1
Atkins	1a
Atkins	2
Atkins	2b
Atkins	3
Atkins	3a
Atkins	4
Johnson	1
Johnson	1a
Johnson	2
Johnson	2c
Smith	1
Smith	1b
Smith	2a
Smith	3
Smith	3a
Smith	4
Perkins	3
Perkins	3a
Perkins	4

(a)

DDR

MODULE
2c

(b)

RESULT

STUDENT-NAME
Johnson

(c)

DDR

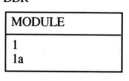

(d)

RESULT

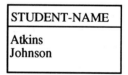

(e)

Fig. 4.8 Results of two divide operations

gives the single tuple of Figure 4.8(c). There is only one student-name who takes module 2c. If the divisor DDR was the two tuple relation of Figure 4.8(d), then:

DIVIDE DEND BY DDR OVER MODULE

will produce the relation shown as Figure 4.8(e). Atkins and Johnson both take modules 1 and 1a.

Retrieval requirements may necessitate a combination of operations in order to obtain the desired result. For example, a typical retrieval request may be to find the names of students who attend any module given by Goodwin. This can be achieved by the following:

SELECT ATTENDANCE WHERE LECTURER-NAME = 'GOODWIN' GIVING TEMP

followed by:

PROJECT TEMP OVER STUDENT-NAME GIVING RESULT..

TEMP   RESULT

STUDENT-NAME	MODULE NAME	LECTURER-NAME
Ashworth	1b	Goodwin
Atkins	1a	Goodwin
Johnson	1a	Goodwin
Smith	1b	Goodwin

STUDENT-NAME
Ashworth
Atkins
Johnson
Smith

(a) Following select   (b) Following project

Fig. 4.9 Two-stage retrieval

The temporary relation TEMP is shown as Figure 4.9(a) and RESULT as Figure 4.9(b).

To insert a new tuple into the relation, the operator UNION could be used. If, for example, 'Zed' was the name of a new student in the first year, then we might add those details to the STUDENT relation by:

STUDENT UNION ('ZED', '1') GIVING STUDENT

and to delete a student:

STUDENT MINUS ('ATKINS', '1') GIVING STUDENT

These procedures are rather awkward and most languages based on the relational algebra 'cheat' and have an ADD and DELETE operator as well as the standard operators discussed above, although strictly these are not necessary.

The relational algebra is fairly simple and powerful. One criticism, particularly when compared to the relational calculus, is that it is somewhat procedural and the user will need some programming experience to be able to formulate a particular request. Many requests may be very involved, with a number of individual statements. For this reason, it should not be looked on as an end user language.

4.4 RELATIONAL CALCULUS

When compared to the relational algebra, the relational calculus is more oriented towards expressing the user requests in a way that the user may construct. Users specify their needs rather than having to construct the procedures to retrieve the required data. 'Pure' relational calculus is difficult for non-mathematicians, but more user-oriented languages which are based on the relational calculus are easier to use. The QUEL data manipulation language of Ingres is a well used DML which is based on the relational calculus. Ingres and QUEL are described in Chapter 14 in the context of a case study. The original specification, Codd's Data Sub Language called DSL ALPHA, has the general retrieval format:

GET INTO workspace (target list) option list

where, workspace is the name of the area where the retrieved data is to be put; target list gives details of the relation; and option list gives the particular restrictions on the target list. In some implementations of the relational calculus, GET INTO is replaced by RETRIEVE. An example will make this easier to understand:

GET INTO W (ATTENDANCE,STUDENT-NAME)
WHERE (LECTURER-NAME='CLARKE')

Here we are putting into the workspace 'W' the names of students held in the relation called 'ATTENDANCE' who are taught by the lecturer called 'CLARKE' (see Figure 4.2). The result in W will be as Figure 4.10.

STUDENT -NAME
Ashworth Atkins Johnson Smith

Fig. 4.10 Result of GET statement

The option list can contain < or > (for less than or greater than) as well as = (for equal to).

If a particular relation is frequently referred to in a particular run, then the use of the 'RANGE' statement can reduce the work of the user. For example:

RANGE ATTENDANCE A and
RANGE LECTURER-MODULE L

will allow the user to specify the ATTENDANCE relation using 'A' and LECTURER-MODULE using 'L' as abbreviations. For example:

GET INTO W (L.MODULE) WHERE (L.NO-OF-WEEKS>10)

will give Figure 4.11:

W

MODULE
4

Fig. 4.11 Result of GET statement

(Module 4 is the only module which lasts longer than 10 weeks).

It is possible to search through many relations, indeed the whole database, and the RANGE command can be used to restrict such access by only allowing users to refer to relations defined in a RANGE statement.

DSL ALPHA was specified as a host language system. This means that the programs could be written in Cobol (the host language) and when data is to be retrieved from the database, the special DSL ALPHA commands will apply. QUEL is not a host language system, but a self-contained query language. It uses the RETRIEVE command rather than GET INTO, but this performs a similar function.

SQL, which stands for structured query language, is a calculus-based language used on a number of database systems, for example, DB2 and Oracle. It has become a particularly popular query language for relational DBMS. The American National Standards Institute have defined standards for the language. Indeed, it has become so well used in relational DBMS that it is described in a separate chapter of this text (Chapter 8). Queries are defined using the:

SELECT/FROM/WHERE

construct, so that a request:

LIST PARTS ISSUED IN 1985

would be formulated as:

SELECT	PART NAME, QUANTITY	(data items)
FROM	PARTSFILE	(a relation)
WHERE	YEAR=1985.	(qualifiers)

Note that this SELECT is very different from (and more powerful than) the SELECT statement of the relational algebra.

The qualifications on the data retrieved can include ANDs and ORs. As with QUEL, the user has to know the names of the relevant attributes and key them in explicitly. The user has also to construct a path through the relations thus setting up the linkages required at run time. SQL also provides a CREATE VIEW command which sets up alternative views of the data derived from other tables and selected rows and columns. This is useful when setting up different sub-schemas (which adhere to the security and privacy requirements defined by the database administrator).

Lacroix and Pirotte (1977) have proposed an alternative calculus which is named the domain calculus in which the fundamental base is that of a domain variable. Using this method, variables range over domains rather than over relations. Languages using this principle include Query-by-Example (QBE). This has gained popularity with the QMF (Query Management Facility) which is an option to DB2 (SQL is the standard interface).

QBE, proposed by Zloof in 1974 is designed for users with little or no programming experience. This cannot be said of the relational algebra and it is more 'user friendly' than a straight relational calculus language such as QUEL or SQL. The intention is that operations in the QBE language are analogous to the way people would naturally use tables. Many databases which use SQL provide a QBE interface so that inexperienced users can formulate queries quickly (the data definition will usually have been carried out by a more experienced user using SQL and complex queries will also use SQL). The QBE query is formulated by filling in **templates** of relations. The user enters the name of the table and the system supplies the attribute names. The system then details the attributes in which the user has indicated an interest. Many systems are menu-based and it is not necessary to recall the relation names. This means that minimal training is necessary. However there are severe limitations to retain flexibility unless the database is not very complex.

(a)

EMPL NO	NAME	STATUS	PAY/DATE	TAX/DATE	SALARY

(b)

EMPL NO	NAME	STATUS	PAY/DATE	TAX/DATE	SALARY
P:756	P	P			P

(c)

EMPL NO	NAME	STATUS	PAY/DATE	TAX/DATE	SALARY
756	SMITH	FULL			12000

Fig. 4.12 QBE example

A session could begin with the user requesting a template of the EMPLOYEE relation. The template could be as seen as Figure 4.12(a). The user may then request details of the tuple for employee whose employee number is 756. The user also marks with a P (for print) any other entries for that employee that are required (Figure 4.12(b)). The system then supplies the information required (Figure 4.12(c)). The user can also specify retrievals to be made on a range of values, for example, all tuples where the salary is greater than 10000 and also use ANDs, ORs and so on. Joins are effected by filling in fields from more than one relation. We will look at QBE in greater detail in Section 7.4 in the context of the relational DBMS DB2.

4.5 THE HIERARCHICAL APPROACH

In the hierarchical model the data structures are represented by *trees* with the top entity referred to as the *root* (of which there can be only one per hierarchy). Subordinate entities are connected to the root and further subordinates connected to them. These are often referred to as parent/child relationships.

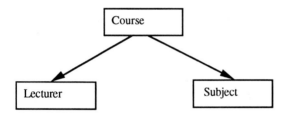

Fig. 4.13 Hierarchy with siblings

Figure 4.13 shows the basic structure. The link between the entity types COURSE and LECTURER and that between COURSE and SUBJECT represents a one-to-many relationship. For every occurrence of the parent (which must be ordered), there can be any number of occurrences (including zero) of the child (which must also be ordered). However, a child will have only one parent. In Figure 4.13 LECTURER and SUBJECT are known as 'siblings' because they are of the same level but of different types. If they were occurrences of the same type, they are usually referred to as 'twins'. As the details of a parent are only held once, though it can have many children, these details can be integrated with the details of any subordinates as required, and this introduces redundancy. The complexity of the model will depend on how the database administrator interprets the conceptual model, and increasing flexibility in use may lead to increases in complexity of the logical model and slower access times.

The connections or links are explicit in the hierarchical model. Pointers are used to explicitly relate elements of the model. Trees are normally described using linked lists. There are overheads when defining and manipulating hierarchies, and this is particularly apparent when comparisons are made with the relational approach. This becomes worse when hierarchies are made realistically complex to reflect real-world data relationships.

Many real-world data structures fit into the hierarchical pattern, however, and they are also readily understood. The speaker at many a company induction course will illustrate his organisation or departmental structure using a hierarchical diagram. Many DBMS, including IMS, are based on the hierarchical approach. Nevertheless, the approach has been included in this text with reservations. The network approach, which will be discussed in Section 4.6 can deal with hierarchies as well as networks (many-to-many relationships), and these structures do occur frequently. For example, a lecturer can teach on a number of courses and a course may use a number of lecturers. This network cannot be expressed by one hierarchy.

It is possible to express many-to-many relationships using the hierarchical model, but only by creating two hierarchies. Figure 4.14(a) shows that one course can be given by a number of lecturers and Figure 4.14(b) illustrates that one lecturer can lecture on a number of courses. These form the many-to-many relationship shown in Figure 4.14(c). This means that there is likely to be considerable data duplication when using a hierarchical database.

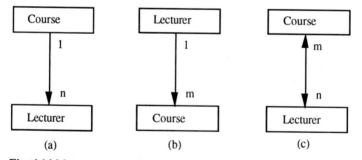

Fig. 4.14 Many-to-many relationships expressed as hierarchies

The order of the tree is significant. In Figure 4.15, the fact that LECTURER is placed to the left of SUBJECT, even though they are on the same level, means that the former will be processed first in any search. In the hierarchical model, each node represents a record type (it is an entity) and each entity occurrence is an occurrence of a record (for example, that for the lecturer J. Smith).

Of course there may be a number of levels in a hierarchy. Figure 4.15 shows such a possibility. Sometimes it is necessary to include intermediate nodes, which do not

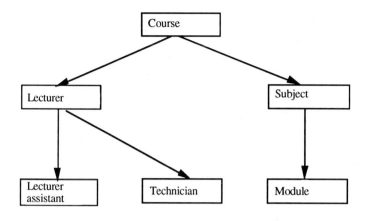

Fig. 4.15 Hierarchy with a number of levels

actually represent records, but are included to maintain the correct hierarchical structure, so that they will be processed in the required order.

The inclusion of SENIOR LECTURER requires such an intermediate node on the right hand side so as to keep SUBJECT at the level of LECTURER who, along with SENIOR LECTURER, will be responsible for the teaching of the SUBJECT. This is shown in Figure 4.16.

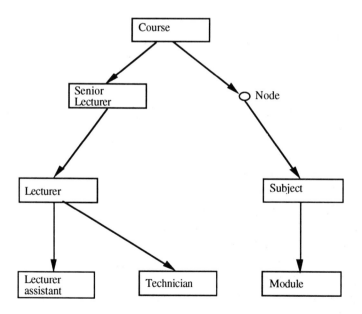

Fig. 4.16 Hierarchy with intermediate node

When manipulating data in hierarchies, it is necessary to specify to which level a request refers. For example if the next record is requested, is it the next at that level or at a parent level or at some other level?

There is a convention to hierarchical sequence, the ways of visiting trees. The routine is as follows:

VISIT

LEFT and call routine: VISIT

                        LEFT and call routine, and so on

                        RIGHT and call routine, and so on

RIGHT and call routine, and so on.

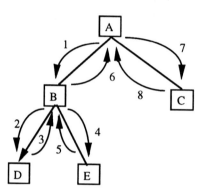

Fig. 4.17 Hierarchical sequence

The routine will terminate when there are no more branches. It is easiest to understand by following the example given in Figure 4.17. The sequence here will be A (the root) then left (1), visit B then left (2), visit D, no more left, so back to B (3) and right (4), to visit E, no more left so back to B (5), back to A (6) to right (7) and visit C, back to A (8), no more right and, as it is the root, stop. Thus A,B,D,E and C, is the natural hierarchical sequence in the above hierarchy.

Inserting and deleting records also presents a problem. Insertions must be connected to a parent record. Thus to insert a lecturer record, it is necessary to choose a senior lecturer to whom that lecturer reports. Deleting a record may also present problems. If the lecturer to be deleted is the only one that reports to a particular senior lecturer, then the information that the senior lecturer did supervise a lecturer is lost if the lecturer record is deleted. One way to avoid losing this information, but perhaps not an ideal solution, is to keep an empty 'lecturer' record for that particular senior lecturer.

The relations developed by data analysis can be readily converted into hierarchies. Each relation is an entity and if a domain is a key in one relation and an attribute or part of a key in another, this would represent a one-to-many hierarchical relationship. Where a many-to-many relationship is implied hierarchies would need to be created for both directions if the model is to represent the 'real world' accurately. In IMS terminology (see Section 7.2), the entities are converted to segments, the attributes to fields, and the relationships are represented by hierarchies. Each hierarchy is an IMS 'database'.

For example, the following two relations in Figure 4.18, COURSE and SUBJECT, both have course as the key, but the latter has it as only part of the composite key with subject. Thus COURSE to SUBJECT represents two record types having a one-to-many relationship.

COURSE   Course, Lecturer-in-Charge

SUBJECT   Course, Subject, Title, Lecturer, No-of-Hours

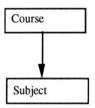

Fig. 4. 18 Relationship between COURSE and SUBJECT

In other words, a particular course might have a number of subjects associated with it. The addition of a LECTURER relation:

LECTURER Lecturer, Room-no

and also a LEC-SUBJ relation:

LEC-SUBJ Lecturer, Course, No-of-times-given

would be implying, because Course is also part of the key, that a lecturer can teach a number of courses. This also implies a many-to-many relationship between the hierarchical record types COURSE and LECTURER.

A DDL for setting up the user views or external schemas and a DML for the processing of hierarchies (applications using the data) is described in Section 7.2, in the context of IMS.

4.6 THE NETWORK APPROACH

As seen in Figure 4.19, the relationship between COURSE and LECTURER is a many-to-many relationship and not a hierarchical one. This can be represented as a network as

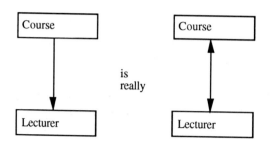

Fig. 4.19 COURSE-LECTURER relationship

shown in Figure 4.20. The days of the week in which the lecturer works and gives a course are given in **link records** which need to be set up in these diagrams. In fact, the relationship between two record types is again one-to-many, but the construct of link records enables convenient representation of many-to-many relationships. Implied in the diagram is that one LECTURER can give more than one COURSE (Fred, for example, gives business studies and computer science) and one COURSE is given by more than one LECTURER (maths by Tom and Dave, for example) - a many-to-many relationship. Each link record is on two chains which connect the COURSE and LECTURER to it. These link records, sometimes called **connector records**, are usually meaningful in themselves. The link records in the above example could be called TIMETABLE and contain details of the particular class, for example, day, time, room number and so on.

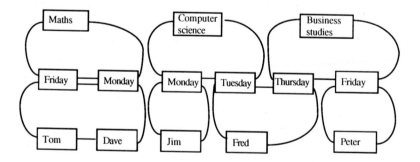

Fig. 4.20 Network with link records

The occurrences of the records linked together have been represented by pointers. In this approach, as with hierarchies but unlike the relational model, there are explicit links between related entity occurrences. This is a clear way of showing the relationships, but it can be misleading as the linked list with pointers is not the only tool that can be used to link record occurrences. Indeed the means by which record occurrences are related physically is irrelevant to the logical schema. An alternative, data structure diagram technique to relate records, is shown in the case study found in Chapter 14.

Although the network approach does answer some of the problems of the hierarchical approach, particularly in that it deals with many-to-many relationships, it is more complex. Nevertheless there are a number of DBMS, possibly the most well known being IDMS, which are of this type.

The approach became particularly important after the publication of the Database Task Group (DBTG) report of the Codasyl Committee in April 1971. Codasyl (COmmittee of DAta SYstems Languages) originally set up in 1959 is a group of commercial and government computer users in the United States, and representatives from the computer manufacturing world. Its essential purpose is to set up standards for computing which reflect the users' requirements rather than manufacturers' convenience. It was largely responsible for defining the business-oriented Cobol computer language. One of the main uses of computers in commercial data processing is for file and record processing and the DBTG grew out of this concern. A number of reports define a common set of standards for database systems and also feature an analysis of DBMS and distributed database technology (see Codasyl 1973, 1978a and 1981). The Cobol host language interface is defined in Codasyl (1975 and 1978b).

In the terminology of Codasyl, the data item is equivalent to an attribute value, and these can be aggregated (a non-normalised group item) and referred to as a repeating group data aggregate. A record is an ordered collection of data items and/or data aggregates, the equivalent of a tuple.

One of the main features of the 1971 report is the **set** concept. A set consists of a one-to-many relationship between two record types (relations in the relational model). If we assume that a LECTURER can only teach one COURSE, and many LECTURERS teach on one COURSE, then the 'closed loop' shown in Figure 4.21 represents such a set. Each set type is named. This set type is called CLEC. Figure 4.21(a) is not acceptable from a Codasyl standard: it does not include a set name. Figure 4.21(b) is Codasyl. Set occurrences are shown in Figure 4.21(c) The set type has COURSE as the owner record type and LECTURER as the member record type. There can be zero or more occurrences of a member for each occurrence of the owner. Thus a set type can be defined as a named relationship between record types. The latter is a form of entity, such as COURSE, LECTURER, SUBJECT, and ROOM.

The rules of sets are as follows: a set is a collection of named record types and any number of sets can be defined to the database. A set must have a single owner type. A record type can be a member of one or more sets and can be both owner and member

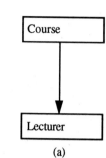
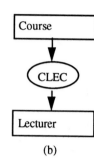

(a)   (b)

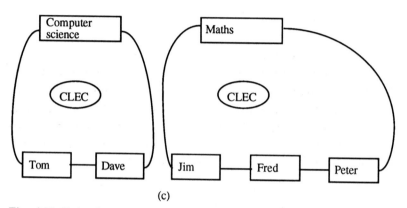

(c)

Fig. 4.21 Codasyl sets

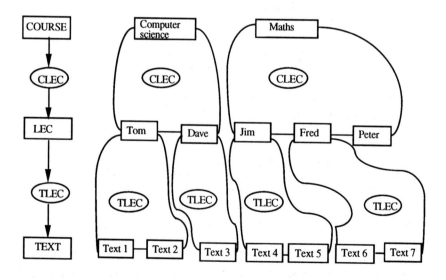

Fig. 4.22 Set occurrences at three levels

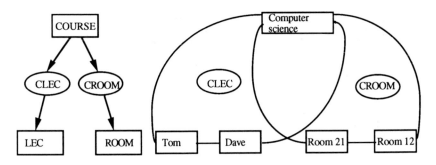

Fig. 4.23 Two set occurrences

but not of the same set. A set must also have a specified order.

The model can be developed showing more than one level, as in Figure 4.22 and further, by having more than one type of record at a particular level, as in Figure 4.23. In Figure 4.22, LEC is a member of set CLEC and an owner of set TLEC. In Figure 4.23, COURSE is a record type which is the owner of more than one set of the same type. However, a record type cannot be a member of more than one set of the same type, and no record type can be both owner and member of the same set type.

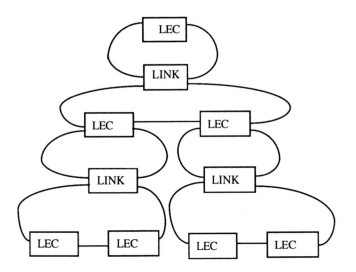

Fig. 4.24 Use of link records - one record type at a number of levels

One of the problems that the DBTG dealt with was the possibility of having one type of record at a number of levels. Thus a LECTURER could be at a 'head of department', 'course tutor' and 'tutor' level (we used the term involuted relationship in Chapter 3). To cater for this possibility, link records need to be set up. This is shown in Figure 4.24. As we saw earlier, this technique of setting up link records is used to represent networks.

The link record is usually not redundant, that is, it contains useful information in itself (in the relational model, it may well have been specified in any case, as a separate relation formed from a relationship in the data analysis phase).

Although the network model is more flexible than the hierarchy, the overall structure is fairly complex to implement and requires extra storage space to handle the pointers. As a first approach to converting the conceptual schema to the Codasyl model, the entities are mapped to records, attributes to data items, one-to-many relationships to sets, and many-to-many relationships to two sets connected by a link record type.

4.7   LANGUAGES FOR USING NETWORKS

The DBTG specification proposed a language for manipulating the files. This data manipulation language (DML) is embodied in a host language. The host language was originally Cobol but the DML extensions to other host languages have been specified. The DBTG also specified a language to set up the logical schema, called the data description language (DDL) and a DDL to set up particular user views (sub-schemas) of the data structures. The sub-schema DDL and the DML are extensions to the Cobol language, but even the schema DDL has a Cobol 'flavour', though it is supposed to be language-independent. The sub-schema DDL *has* to be compatible with Cobol (or the chosen language) as it will be embedded in it.

The DBTG report did not suggest a standard for the **Device and Media Control Language** (DMCL), that is the language controlling the physical access to storage devices, because this would be dependent on the particular hardware used. However the original Codasyl proposals were considered by many to have a "physical schema flavour" as well as presenting a standard for the logical schema. In the later report of 1978, a **Data Storage Description Language** (DSDL) was proposed and this included many of these physical (that is implementation) aspects. It corresponds to a DMCL in part.

The Schema DDL is the language to set up the global data description. The language is distinct and self-contained and it is not dependent on an established programming language. It enables the specification of the various record types (including the individual data items such as 'lecturer', 'name', and 'age' in the LECTURER record) and the specification of set types relating these records. It is envisaged in the report that a database administrator would be responsible for this overall schema data definition and at least oversee the setting up of the user views, that is, the external views in ANSI/X3/SPARC terminology, via the sub-schema DDL. This was certainly perceptive, and most practitioners would argue strongly for strengthening the role of the DBA.

The concept of *areas* which is proposed in the Codasyl report is also an interesting one. Although it is associated with the Schema DDL, it is an important consideration in the physical storage of the data. It is a named portion of accessible storage space in which records are to be stored. It may contain occurrences of records, or sets, or parts of sets. This concept is one of the features of the original report which is most open to criticism because it is specifying 'physical' considerations at the logical level (the Schema DDL) and therefore may sacrifice some of the data independence of the model. When assigning records to areas, the DBA has to reconcile a trade-off. On the one hand, increasing the number of areas allows files to be distributed on a number of areas of storage. This will optimise performance and increase integrity and security, so that concurrent access to areas can be prevented. Further, as back-up and restore procedures are carried out by areas, a program with exclusive access to a particular area will not exclude access to other areas. The price to be paid for this is the consequent complexity of the procedures. In view of these considerations, particularly its implementation aspect, it is not surprising that the area concept was removed in the later specification.

The sub-schema DDL allows the setting up of particular user views of part of the schema, such as the specification of privacy locks, and the renaming and redescription of data items and records. Some sub-schemas could overlap.

The data manipulation language represents extensions to the Cobol language specification. This allows data on the database to be manipulated. It thus includes GET and FIND for reading records on the database (equivalent to the Cobol READ) and STORE and INSERT which are equivalent to the WRITE statement. ERASE is similar to the Cobol DELETE statement. It removes records from the database. We will look at these languages in more detail in Section 7.3, which discusses IDMS, a Codasyl-oriented DBMS.

4.8 DATABASE MAPPING

The mapping or transformation rules to convert the conceptual model in the form of entities, attributes and relationships, to a logical model which could be relational, hierarchical or network has already been touched on in the relevant sections. In this section we bring the basic rules together. Although much of the mapping is relatively straightforward to automate because it is rule based, there are exceptions and therefore the mapping in a real database application is not quite so straightforward as implied here.

In the case of mapping to a relational DBMS, the identifier or key of the entity remains the key, the properties or attributes of the entity remain as attributes, the entity becomes a relation and the relationship also becomes a relation. The key of the relation in the latter case is made of the identifiers of the entities of the conceptual data model which the relationship links. If the relationship is itself a carrier of properties, these become attributes of the relation. There are slight variances in these generalities depending on whether the relationships are binary or n-ary and on the cardinality of the relationship (Quang & Chartier-Kastler, 1991, pp 103-107 and Elmasri & Navathe, 1989, pp 329-334 give details).

In the case of mapping to a Codasyl DBMS, each of the entity occurrences of the conceptual model becomes a record, the owner record in the set corresponds to the entity at the 'one' end of the relationship, with the other record as the member, the identifier or key of the entity remains the key of the records of the logical model, and the properties or attributes of the entity remain as data items or fields of the records. The mapping of relationships also depends on whether the relationships are binary or n-ary and on the cardinality of the relationship. In a one-to-many binary relationship, where the relationship linking the entities is the carrier of attributes, these migrate to the member record and the relationship disappears. In a many-to-many binary relationship, the relationship becomes a member record, its key is made up of the identifiers of the entities of the conceptual data model which the relationship was linking and if the entity is the carrier of attributes, these become fields of that record. In the case of n-ary relationships, the relationship becomes a member record, each of the entities linked by the relationship becomes an owner, their keys are made up of the identifiers of the entities of the conceptual data model which the relationship was linking and the attributes of the entity become fields of the records generated. Again, there are some exceptions (Quang & Chartier-Kastler, 1991, pp 111-116 and Elmasri & Navathe, 1989, pp 334-338).

In the case of the hierarchical data mapping, the one-to-many relationship types can be represented as parent-child relationships but many-to-many relationships are more difficult to represent and lead to duplication. In this case the relationship is treated as if it were a one-to-many relationship, but the records on the 'many side' are duplicated because each record can be related to several parents. There are a number of alternative ways of dealing with many-to-many relationships, all of which lead to either duplication or unnatural restrictions on the model (that is, the model does not represent the real-world accurately). The various options are discussed in Elmasri & Navathe,

1989, pp 338-344).

4.9 OBJECT-ORIENTED APPROACH

The development of databases is sometimes perceived as having three generations:
1) File management systems
2) Hierarchical database systems
3) Network and relational database systems
to which can now be added a fourth:
4) Object-oriented database systems.

This way of seeing the development of databases can be misleading because it should <u>not</u> be implied that either each new generation will replace the previous generation (all these systems will be used for some foreseeable time in the future) or that each new generation is necessarily better than the previous one (the appropriateness or otherwise of an approach will depend on the organisation and its applications). Nevertheless, object-oriented database systems are an interesting newer development which is having considerable impact on the database world. Further, the object-oriented approach is likely to impact on data modelling, so that some database applications may be developed through object modelling (rather than entity-relationship modelling and relational modelling) mapped to object-oriented databases (rather than relational databases). Nevertheless, it is perhaps premature to regard object-oriented design as a comprehensive methodology, though it has potential to become one.

An object-oriented DBMS (OODBMS) is one which supports an object model. In an object-oriented database all data is represented as an object, though to support the richness of the data such DBMS need to support object-oriented programming language concepts such as complex objects, object identity and inheritance. We will look at these concepts later in the section, but it should be noted that not all 'object-oriented DBMS' presently support all the concepts associated with object-orientation. As well as distinct OODBMS now being available, some relational DBMS have object-oriented extensions.

According to Loomis (1990a), the appeal of OODBMS comes from two major factors:
- The data model more closely matches some real-world entities. Objects can be stored and manipulated directly: there is no need to transform application objects into tables. Data types can be defined by the user, rather than being constrained to certain pre-defined types. Thus, whereas in the relational model information about the object customer would be scattered over a number of relations (which could be:

customer, holding customer name and address information; sales ledger, holding details about the debts of the customer; invoice, holding details of payments due), in the object-oriented model there would be one object, customer, reflecting all this information.

- The database language can be integrated with an object-oriented programming language (in particular Smalltalk, but also Traits and Eiffel, and extensions of programming languages such as Object Pascal, Object Lisp, and C++), which means that the programmer deals with a single uniform model of objects. It is not necessary to have different languages for database access (such as SQL) and a host language (such as Pascal) for the complex programming tasks using the data collected.

The first factor is important in that it brings some applications within the database world (for example, computer aided design, computer aided manufacture, architectural design, software design (Case) and office automation), previously ill-served by relational databases because of the performance of relational database systems and because the relational model itself is unsuitable for those domains. Now engineers, for example, can also share information because it can be held on the object-oriented database. The object model more naturally represents their real world (the relational model proves particularly suitable for data processing and accounting applications). The correspondence between real-world and database objects means that the objects do not lose their integrity and identity, and therefore can be identified conveniently and operated upon.

The second factor is important because it should lead to improved productivity of application developers, as it is no longer necessary for them to know diverse languages, environments and command sequences. As Khoshafian (1990) argues, by combining database functionality with object-oriented concepts, OODBMS become the ideal repository of information that is shared by multiple users, multiple products, and multiple applications on different platforms (hardware and software environments).

We have been aware for some years that the relational model and relational database systems have not been able to represent some real-world concepts and activities, and there have been many papers and conferences devoted to the study of extensions and refinements to the original model of Codd (1970). The entity-relationship model of Chen (1976), Codd's own extended relational model (Codd, 1979), known as RM/T, and the functional data model of Shipman (1981) are three of the most well-known. These extensions to the relational model are known as **semantic data models** (see, for example, Hull & King, 1987), and they represent the results of many efforts to enhance the richness of the relational model. They aim to generalise from the relational model by capturing as much semantic information from an application domain as possible. (The role model of Bachman & Daya, 1977, attempts to extend the network model in a parallel way). Although these models are able to represent more complex situations, to some extent this has been at the cost of reduced elegance and simplicity and only the entity-relationship model of Chen is widely used as a data modelling tool. In the approach used in this text, the E-R model is used in conceptual modelling because it is much more semantically rich than the relational model, but this is mapped to a relational model because most commercial databases are relational and it is more convenient for logical mapping. A more fundamental criticism of semantic data models has been that although there is increased support for data definition, there is no parallel increased support for data manipulation. By specifying the operations that can be performed on each data object, the object-oriented approach attempts to model the dynamic as well as static aspects of the world being modelled.

The object-oriented approach increases both the semantic and manipulation capability of database systems and therefore offers more than semantic data models. The uniform group of objects that the programmer has when using an object-oriented model, also reduces the sting of the 'elegance and simplicity' argument used against the proponents of semantic data modelling. Therefore, even if complex real-world situations can only be represented by complex models, the proponents of the object-oriented model argue that it is only as complex as it need be to represent these situations on computers and to manipulate those representations for the purpose of processing queries. Indeed, many argue that its concepts allow even complex situations to be expressed easily and naturally and that the associated techniques and tools enable the construction of complex software systems for those applications.

In the object-oriented model, **objects** represent some aspect of interest in the application area: they could be physical entities, concepts, ideas or events. Typically an object is a producer or consumer of information or an item of information. This has its parallel with entities in the entity-relationship model, which will be represented as relations in the relational model. However, there are major differences.

The concept of **object identity** provides one distinction. Conventionally, a record or tuple is identified by one or more attributes that uniquely identify that occurrence. This causes problems if, for example, there are two customers with the same name or the value of that identifier changes (a customer name change, for example). In the object model, the object's current value can change, but its identity is unique, system generated, never reused and identifies an object for its lifetime. Any attribute of an object can be changed without destroying its identity. Hence an object can be a dynamic structure, changing when being manipulated, indeed its form may not be known by the system in advance.

An object may contain any type of data: text, sound, photographs and video, and multi-media systems (Section 11.9) may be based on objects. Unlike alternative modelling approaches, the object model models data, data definitions and processes as objects, the same basic element of the model. All this provides a flexibility not found in other models.

Another area of distinction is that the object model can represent an abstraction and generalisation (Smith & Smith, 1977). An animal is an object and there are many kinds of animal (dog, cat, cow). We could say that an animal is a group of things which are related in some way. Using the terminology of object-orientation, animal is a **class** or **abstract data type**. This is a set of objects with the same representation. Within the class are sub-objects (birds, mammals). These are also objects in their own right. We can also bring similarities together by generalising. In the object-oriented model, the features of a cat are added to the features of a mammal (to which sub-class cat belongs) and the features of a mammal include the features of all animals (the class to which mammal belongs). This is the object-oriented concept of **inheritance**, that is, characteristics received from an ancestor in a class hierarchy. They also **specialise**, by adding extra features to the object. Thus objects include a much wider list of things than entities: indeed, a database schema or a data dictionary are themselves objects. This generic type object gives the object-oriented approach advantages for data manipulation, as a number of related objects can share operations (called **methods** in object-oriented terminology). Thus, objects can inherit operations, enabling code sharing and reusability among software modules, as well as characteristics.

A full description of the object-oriented model would be inappropriate here, but as Kim & Lochovsky (1989) and many others show, the approach provides a very rich language to model complex real-world objects.

There have been a number of approaches proposed to design and develop object-oriented systems. These include object-oriented development (Booch, 1991), hierarchical object-oriented design (developed by the European space agency) and object behaviour analysis (Gibson, 1990).

4.10 COMPARING APPROACHES TO LOGICAL DESIGN

Of the approaches to database design, relational databases are possibly the most flexible, as access paths can be defined as and when necessary using the JOIN operator. This means that the exact nature of queries need not be predicted during database design. Further, there is less need for an experienced programmer or database administrator to access the database as there are languages available which are easier to use, such as QBE. A full justification of the relational model was given in Section 3.6.

However, relational DBMS require the user to be aware of the relations that have been set up in order to obtain information from the database, including keys and foreign keys used to join relations. The user also needs to know the operations that can be applied to the relations so as to carry out the desired retrievals. Speed of access may also be worse, as the links between relations are set up at run time and not at data definition time. Slow retrieval speed has led to a partial withdrawal of relational database systems in a few organisations as well as the late appearance of commercial relational DBMS which came many years after their research counterparts. The incorporation of query optimisation techniques are an important feature of any relational DBMS. Some organisations have database machines, dedicated to efficient database use, running along with general-purpose computers which process all non-database processing. For this reason, pre-ordering of relations (strictly, tuples need not be in any pre-defined order in the relational model) and the use of indexes to increase speeds of particular accesses, are both options in many DBMS to improve their overall performance. Storage space may also be greater (for example, for foreign keys enabling joins of relations), unless the other approaches use a large number of pointers to support database use.

One of the advantages of the relational model is its simplicity, and this makes relatively simple query languages, such as SQL, Quel and QBE, feasible. On the other hand, this simplicity has its price in that the model proves unsuitable for some applications (hence, the drive towards semantic data models and object-oriented data models). For example, attributes should be atomic (they cannot be divided into sub-attributes). In a personnel system, for example, names will be divided into surname and first names, where searches such as 'give me all people with surname Jones' or '...first name David' are easy, but the request 'give me all people with name David Jones' requires a connection between first name and surname which make queries more complex. Further, repeating groups do occur in applications (values in a ledger, for instance), but the normalisation process does not permit representation as an array.

In the network and hierarchical DBMS the access paths are defined by the DBA before the database is set up and these are often referred to as **navigational** systems (Bachman, 1973). Although these access paths can be changed at a later date, this can usually be achieved only with considerable difficulty. It will probably necessitate reorganising part of the database and, therefore, navigational systems are rather inflexible once the design has been implemented. Relational databases do not have this problem.

The hierarchical database only allows downward access paths, and a member at one level cannot be an owner of a record at a higher level. The network system allows access paths to be defined at any level and thus allows much greater flexibility. The penalty paid for this is increased complexity when setting up the pointers and accessing and updating the database. A more fundamental criticism is the requirement that databases should facilitate unplanned access as well as planned retrieval to the database.

In assessing DBMS there are other factors to bear in mind and not all DBMS of each 'type' follow the ideal. Some have options which enable the user to correct many of the disadvantages of the type.

Object-oriented DBMS are much newer and appeal because of two major factors. The first is that the data model more closely matches some real-world entities. Objects can be stored and manipulated directly: there is no need to transform application objects into tables. Generalisation and abstraction, which reflect real-world relationships where objects can inherit properties from their parents, are supported. Secondly, the database language can be integrated with an object-oriented programming language (such as Smalltalk), which means that the programmer deals with a single uniform model of objects. When object-oriented database systems become more widely available, there may be a number of application domains where their advantages make them a good choice. However, at the time of writing, object-oriented DBMS are still in their infancy, with no system accepted as a standard (indeed present systems differ greatly in their exact data model, query language and mapping schema). Commercial systems include Ontos, GemStone and OrionII. They require navigation through the class hierarchy (rather like hierarchical and network DBMS) and though this may well be appropriate for some applications, it is not appropriate to all.

4.11 FURTHER READING

Benyon, D (1990) *Information and Data Modelling*, Blackwell Scientific Publications, Oxford.
Bowers, D. S (1988) *From Data to Database*, Van Nostrand Reinhold, Wokingham.
Howe, D. R (1989) *Data Analysis for Data Base Design,* 2nd ed, Arnold, London.
Quang, Pham Thu & Chartier-Kastler, C (1991) *Merise in Practice*, Macmillan, Basingstoke.
Robinson, H (1989) *Database Analysis and Design*, 2nd ed, Chartwell-Bratt, Bromley.
These texts cover the data modelling aspects in some detail and some also include sections on data mapping.

Date, C. J (1990) *An Introduction to Database Systems, Volume 1,* 5th ed, Addison-Wesley, London.
Elmasri, R & Navathe, S. B (1989) *Fundamentals of Database Systems,*

Benjamin/Cummings, Redwood City, Ca.

McFadden, F. R & Hoffer, J. A (1991) *Database Management*, 3rd ed, Benjamin/Cummings, Redwood City, Ca.

Oxborrow, E (1989) *Databases and Database Systems*, 2nd ed, Chartwell-Bratt, Bromley.

These texts provide an analysis of the types of logical model and their associated data definition and data manipulation languages.

Beynon-Davies, P (1992) *Relational Database Design*, Blackwell Scientific Publications, Oxford.

Provides a thorough description of relational database design.

Codasyl (1971) *Programming Languages Committee (DBTG) Report*, BCS and ACM.

Codasyl (1978) Data Description Language Committee, *DDL Journal of Development*.

These two publications of Codasyl (and others) define the basic standard.

Booch, G (1991) *Object-oriented design with applications*, Benjamin/Cummings, Redwood City, Ca.

Gibson, E (1990) Objects - born and bred, *Byte*, October.

Khoshafian, S (1990) Insight into object-oriented databases, *Information and Software Technology*, **32**, 4.

Loomis, M. E. S (1990a) OODBMS: the basics, *Journal of Objected Oriented Programming*, May/June.

Loomis, M. E. S (1990b) OODBMS vs relational, *Journal of Objected Oriented Programming*, July/August.

The above texts and articles cover the object-oriented model.

Chapter 5
The Physical Schema: File Access and Organisation

5.1 INTRODUCTION

The **physical schema** represents the various file organisation methods that are supported by computer systems. It is sometimes referred to as the **internal schema**, for example, by ANSI/X3/SPARC (1975). **File organisation** refers to the way that the records have been structured on disk, that is, record storage and how the records are linked together. **File access** refers to the way that the records can be retrieved for the purpose of reading the data, changing it, adding to it and deleting it. In common with most texts, this book uses the term file organisation to mean both the data storage structure and access methods.

As we can see from Figure 5.1, the physical schema represents a mapping from the logical view. This mapping may be carried out automatically by the DBMS; indeed there may not be any options open to the user. On the other hand, some DBMS enable alternative ways for the data to be stored and accessed, and the decisions will most likely be made by the database administrator, possibly with the help of optimising and efficiency information provided by the DBMS.

Figure 5.1 also illustrates that there is a further mapping to the machine view of the data (sometimes called the device and media model (see also Section 4.6)) in terms of blocks, pages, disks, tapes and so on. This is not discussed in this text as it is dependent on the particular hardware chosen.

5.2 TRADITIONAL METHODS OF ORGANISING DATA ON BACKING STORAGE MEDIA

We will first look at traditional methods of file organisation. This will enable us to understand the issues relating to file organisation, and in Sections 5.3, 5.4 and 5.5 we look at those structures most suitable for database work.

Serial files are the simplest form of file organisation. The records are not stored in any particular sequence apart from that of first in, first out. This is simple to create, but makes the retrieval of any particular record slow as the file has to be searched until the required record is found. Because database systems require fast retrieval, this method

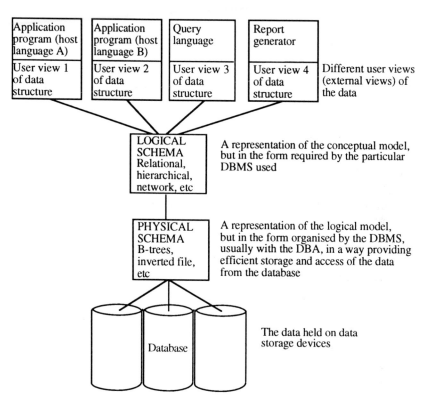

Fig. 5.1 The place of the physical schema

of organising data is unlikely to be appropriate, apart from, perhaps, the storage of historical or back-up files.

A second method of file organisation is to store records in a particular sequence. A file of lecturers may be stored in 'lecturer number' or 'lecturer name' sequence. The records need to be sorted in order of a particular (key) field before storing the data on to the file. Sequential files are easy to use, they will support records of variable length and they use the backing storage media space efficiently. **Sequential** organisation has the major advantage that the records are stored in a logical order, presumably that sequence to which the records are normally required for printing and for soft copy reports. However, sequential ordering still does not cater for the particular requirements of most database uses. It may be used for printing or processing information on a large number of records on the file (where there is a high **hit rate**), but is inappropriate where the required hit rate in a run is low (say, less than 6%). Particular records cannot be searched for directly. A search has still to be carried out of the file until the particular record required is found. Tape files can only be accessed in this way (Figure 5.2) and therefore tapes can only be used for serial or sequential files.

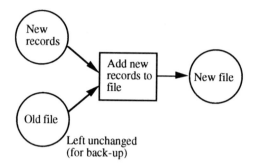

Fig. 5.2 Adding new records to a sequential file

If the file is stored on disk, however, there are possible answers to the problem. One solution would be to store an **index** (Figure 5.3). This will contain the key alongside a **pointer**, which is a field used to identify the location or **address** where the data is stored. The record address can be retrieved following an index **look-up** operation. With the address known, the record can be located. This address could be an actual physical address, that is, the disk cylinder, track and block number where the data is held, or some sort of relative address: relative, that is, to the beginning of the file.

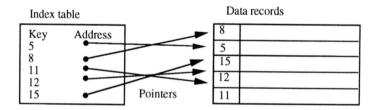

Fig. 5.3 Indexed files

The process of (a) searching the index to find the address of the required record, and then (b) going directly to that address, will be considerably faster than searching through all the records on a sequential file.

Sometimes the index is sorted, making access quicker, particularly when using the **binary chop** method of searching. Here, the key of the record to be accessed is compared to the key of the middle record on the index. If the desired key is higher than this, the key is compared to the third quartile record (if less, to the first quartile record).

The process continues until the matching key is found. Figure 5.4 shows the method. Four searches of the index table are required in order to find the address of record 30. Serial searching will take eleven accesses of the index. In a large file, normally the case in database systems, the savings in time will be marked.

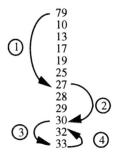

Fig. 5.4 Binary search (or binary chop)

The **indexed sequential** method of file organisation which is common in conventional files may be appropriate for some database uses. This method is based on a combination of the sequential and the index methods described earlier. The file is created in sequential order of a key field. It can therefore be processed sequentially, and this may be best for some of the applications which use the file. An index is created at the same time. Unlike the examples of indexing discussed previously, an index to every record need not be held. Instead there is a reference to only one record for each block of data. The key of this record will be the highest in that block, which usually corresponds to a track on a disk.

Figure 5.5 shows an indexed sequential file of three blocks of data. The index contains the keys of the records ending each block along with the address of the beginning of that block. If the key requested is 24, then the index table will be searched to see in which block it is to be found. The address of the beginning of the relevant (third) block can then be found, located, and searched through sequentially until the required record is located. Thus index sequential files, even when processed by key, do not eliminate sequential processing, but limit it to one block. With large files, there will frequently be a cylinder index added as a first level index. The particular track index can then be located. Even then, if a file is very large, it may spread over a number of disks. In that case there will be a further preliminary search through a disk index.

Access speeds may still be slow for many purposes in a database environment. Updating and deleting are straightforward. The record is accessed (as previously described), changed or deleted (or marked 'for deletion'). The addition of a record to

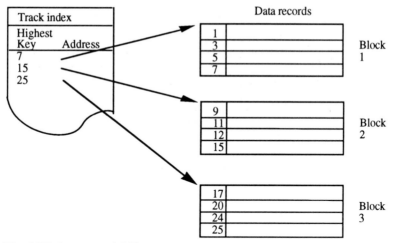

Fig. 5.5 Index sequential file

the indexed sequential file can present difficulties, however. Indeed, it will require complete reorganisation of the file unless precautions are taken, because the records should be retained in sequential order to permit sequential access. One usual method is to leave gaps at the end of each block so that records can be inserted into a block (with only slight reorganisation of the records in that block to maintain the correct order). Figure 5.6 illustrates how a record with key number 5 can be inserted. Problems will occur when a block becomes full.

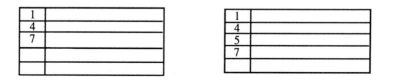

Fig. 5.6 Index sequential files - record insertion

Another possible way of allowing for addition is to set up a special block, called the **overflow block** (see Figure 5.7). When a data block overflows, a pointer will be maintained to point to the address of the overflow block. Eventually, however, reorganisation of the complete file is necessary to avoid poor performance.

A true **direct access** file is one where there is a direct relationship between the key field of a record and a unique address on disk. Processing is therefore minimal and the records will be stored in sequence. Keys have to be numeric and space has to be

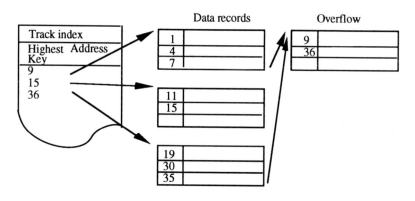

Fig. 5.7 Index sequential files - overflow block

reserved on disk to hold records of every key that can possibly exist in the defined range. If many keys do not have records associated with them, then there is wastage in storage space. Indeed, few files seem in practice to conform to this requirement. Random access is more usual, and these files are often called (mistakenly) direct access files.

Random access offers another way of organising data on disk for quick access. The DBMS allocates space on disk and a record is allocated to a particular slot via a **randomising** (or **hashing**) **algorithm** which is designed to use the allocated space efficiently. This translates the key of the record to a physical address on disk and the system places the record there. The advantage of random access files lies in the speed of accessing a particular record via the algorithm (which will not produce files in sequential order). There is a wide range of possible algorithms. The designer has to choose one which is appropriate for the file.

Random access files can present problems mainly because an appropriate randomising formula is often difficult to construct. A good formula will depend on the area on disk available and the particular spread of keys. By 'good' we mean two things:

1) The area on disk allocated for the file is well used - very critical for large files. This is referred to as a high **packing density**.

2) There are not many **synonyms**. A synonym occurs when the application of the randomising formula to two or more keys gives the same address. In this case, most systems look for the next available space when storing the data or the record is moved to an overflow area. If synonyms occur frequently, it can slow down access speeds considerably, and therefore the advantage of random access is lost.

The file organisation methods so far discussed do not respond to all the desired features of database systems. In particular, a database user may want to search a file in a number of ways, according to a particular application. A file of lecturers, for example, may be searched for according to 'lecturer number', 'lecturer name', 'status', or 'qualification'. A possible solution, but one which contains considerable data duplication and certainly does not conform to the aims of the database approach, would be to store the files in a number of ways. In other words to have a file of lecturers in lecturer number order, another in name order, another in status order, and yet another one according to qualification. Sorting records for each application would also be too slow. This solution would be very inefficient in storage space and, if data changed, it would be necessary to update a number of files.

Assuming that the DBMS permits a number of alternative file organisation techniques (which is normally the case), the actual organisation chosen for any particular data structure will depend on which is the most efficient for that particular application, and this decision is likely to be made by the database administrator. The file organisation method chosen for some files could even be serial or sequential, particularly if the data is likely to be accessed in batch mode. Most DBMS can process data both in real-time and batch mode. If the use of the data changes, then its organisation should be capable of being changed without the users being aware of it (known as **physical data independence**), apart, that is, from the gains in speed. The systems of file organisation most suited to database management systems are B-trees, the various forms of list organisation and the inverted file. These are discussed in the following sections.

5.3   B-TREES

The B-tree represents a development from the index sequential file with its multi-level indexes (for example, track, cylinder and disk). As we saw, the necessity for overflow records presents problems with index sequential files. B-trees are also multi-level indexes but they have a tree-structured index and perform much better (particularly in the way they can absorb new records). There are many variants on the basic structure, the B+-tree being the most used variant of the standard B-tree. Most DBMS support some form of B-tree and they represent the most common database storage structure. Like index sequential files, but unlike random access files, B-trees support sequential access. We will follow Date (1990) and illustrate B-trees through the variation proposed by Knuth (1973a) which is a B+-tree. This is shown in Figure 5.8.

The basis of the B-tree is the multi-level index and the levels of index form the tree structure from which the file organisation method is part-named. The 'B' stands for

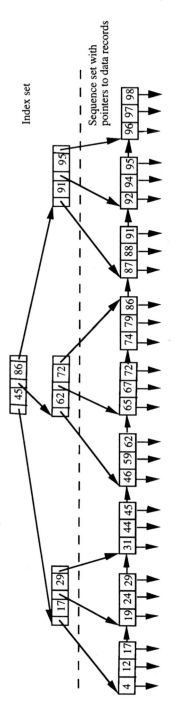

Fig. 5.8 Part of a B-tree (modified from Knuth, 1973a and Date, 1990)

balanced, meaning that all 'leaves' (the sequence set) are the same distance from the root. A non-leaf node that has x children will have $x-1$ keys (in the example, three children and two key values).

The index has two parts, the sequence set and index set. The former consists of an index to the data and, as can be seen from Figure 5.8, enables sequential processing through the data files. The index set enables fast access to a particular part of the sequence set (and hence a particular data record). It is the index set which represents the B-tree and with the sequence set forms the B+-tree.

In Figure 5.8, each value is a value of the indexed field and those of the top node have two values (45 and 86) and three pointers. Data records with index fields less than or equal to 45 can be found by following the left pointer; greater than 45 and less than or equal to 86 can be found by following the middle pointer; and records greater than 86 by following the third pointer. The same principle applies at each level. Having reached the sequence set, there is a pointer to every data record. The leaf node therefore has a different structure to index nodes. Leaf nodes contain data pointers and index nodes contain pointers down the tree. As Date points out, this is a simplified version of a B-tree, because the nodes of a B-tree need not contain the same number of data values and they normally contain free space.

Additions and deletions can be made which always leave the tree balanced. If we wish to add a new value, then we search for that node which is the lowest level of the index set in which it belongs. If there is free space it is inserted at the correct node. Otherwise, the node is split into two nodes containing the lowest and highest values respectively. There may now be a place, but if not, this process can be repeated up the tree until a place is found for the new value. In this way, the correct sequencing is maintained. Thus there is no repeat of the search through overflow areas and/or frequent reorganisation that might be necessary to support index sequential processing.

It therefore has major advantages for some application domains: it enables quick access to individual records; it enables sequential access; and modifications are made easily.

5.4   LISTS

One of the obvious ways of organising the data on physical storage media is by using lists. In fact the Codasyl DBTG started life as the List Processing Task Group but changed its name on investigating the wider issues of their task. A list structure joins a sequence of data elements by including along with each data element a pointer, which is itself a field, relating to the next data element in the list. This pointer could refer to the actual address, for example, the cylinder, track and head number on a disk. Usually it refers to a relative address, the location of the next record when compared to the address of the record being presently processed. Alternatively, it may be a symbolic address, which is converted to an actual address via some form of key transformation scheme. This logical identifier has to uniquely identify the record, and its actual address can also be obtained by looking up a table containing the addresses of all the identifiers.

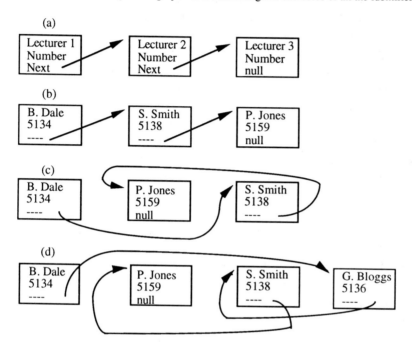

Fig. 5.9 Linked lists

Figure 5.9 (a) shows a list of lecturers with details completed in Figure 5.9 (b). 'Next' represents a pointer to the address of the next record in the list. The word 'null' marks the end of the list. Obviously much of the data relating to each lecturer (such as department, salary, address, telephone number, courses taught) has been omitted. These records need not be held in this 'logical' sequence (see Figure 5.9(c)), as long as the files are held on direct access storage devices. One of the advantages of list processing is that data can be processed sequentially without the records themselves being stored sequentially.

Records are added by changing the pointer references (see Figure 5.9(d)). If George Bloggs of number 5136 was added to the list then the pointer contained in B Dale's record should be changed to point to 5136 (and not to 5138) and the pointer in

Bloggs should contain 5138. This maintains the required sequence. Deletion requires the reverse of this exercise.

| B. Dale 5134 null Last (address of B) Next (address of D) null | D. Jones 5159 First (address of A) null null Prev. (address of C) | S. Smith 5138 First (address of A) Last (address of B) Next (address of B) Prev. (address of D) | G. Bloggs 5136 First (address of A) Last (address of B) Next (address of C) Prev. (address of A) |

Fig. 5.10 Records with a number of pointers

   To facilitate easier access it may also be necessary to add other pointers (Figure 5.10), such as a pointer to the beginning of the list or to the previous record as well as the next one. It may be convenient for the last record to have a pointer which points to the first record in that list, in which case the list is a circular list, ring or chain (see Figure 5.11).

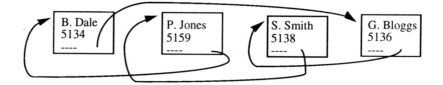

Fig. 5.11 Circular lists

   For most DBMS applications, the lists required will be more complex. For one thing, there are likely to be various levels. These will support the tree structures (Figure 5.12) that databases frequently are required to represent. DBMS are therefore expected to support multiple linked lists if they adopt the list processing method of file organisation.

   Tree structures can be balanced or unbalanced. Each node in the former will have the same number of 'children'. Binary trees are balanced, each node having two children and two pointers. This can result in fast access if the application files lend themselves to this type of structure.

   To implement a network, it is necessary to have a series of pointers at each record occurrence. A realistic example would therefore have a considerable overhead in space for pointers, and the time necessary to access a record through a list may be slow. Modifying the database will also be complex. The above example could support a network. Both the department head lists will hold the same pointers downward as the

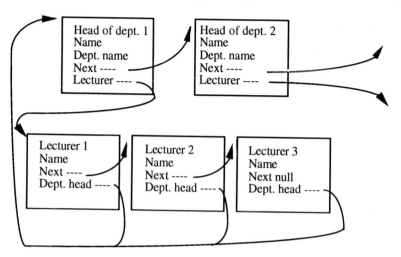

Fig. 5.12 List processing - tree structures

lecturers hold upwards, that is, all types of access between the two 'levels' are permitted.

The various records are likely to contain more data. The lecturer records might contain the age, qualifications, years of experience, salary, and so on. The list structure allows other fields within records to be linked (though this flexibility is paid for in terms of complexity and other overheads). There may, for instance, be a requirement to join together lecturers of a similar qualification or age group.

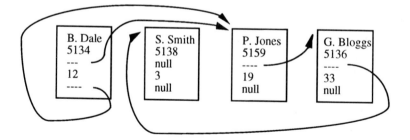

Fig. 5.13 Records with a number of lists

In Figure 5.13 there is one list of four records joining the lecturers together. There are also three lists joining lecturers within similar age groups. The first of these (less than 10 years) has only one record, S.Smith. The second list joins two records, that of B. Dale and P.Jones, who have less than 20 years experience. The final list (over 20 years experience) contains only the one record, that of G. Bloggs.

Frequently there will be other pointers. In a hierarchy, a pointer is likely to refer to the owner record - on each lecturer record there could be a pointer to its owner, the head of department. This would be useful to support quick processing of enquiries.

The negative aspect of providing this flexibility is the added complexity, in particular to support insertions, deletions and updates. Pointers have to be maintained for each of these operations, so time will be spent maintaining pointers as much as updating data. Furthermore, the software to support this requirement will also be fairly complex. It is essential that links are not lost when maintaining pointers. The database administrator has to think very carefully when setting up numerous lists as to whether their use will justify the overheads.

5.5 INVERTED FILES

In some applications the list structure has serious drawbacks. One type of enquiry which is slow in list processing but which inverted files deal with much more efficiently is illustrated by the example: 'Is there a lecturer with a name Perkins on the staff?'. In a list file, this request requires access to all records on the 'lecturer name' list until the Perkins occurrence is found (if at all). This simple enquiry, which a user may 'feel' ought to have an immediate response, might take some seconds to process.

With inverted files the records are held in a data area on disk, but there is also an index which contains values or a range of values for some of the data. These will be the nominated key fields. Along with these are associated pointers containing the addresses of the record(s) with those corresponding field values. Normally the pointers are relative, rather than actual, addresses. This allows for changes of physical location without changing the index, thus providing some level of data independence. Another possible gain in efficiency is to hold the indexes of the inverted file in sequential order so that the binary search (discussed in Section 5.2) can be applied.

Many queries can be answered by simply accessing the index. Fields which may be frequently accessed may be designated key fields by the database administrator and held on the index, to facilitate this easy access. There are overheads in storing these indexes and this factor needs to be weighed with ease of access. Record insertion, deletion and update may involve high costs. Large files will have a number of inverted indexes. Sometimes there is an overall key index, and pointers to the relative addresses of the particular key indexes are required to be searched. A further possibility is to combine the list and inverted file. The inverted file will have an index which points to lists of certain types of record.

Index		
Key name	Key value	Address
Qual.	BA	50
		80
	MSc	60
	PhD	40
Dept	Comp sci	40
		80
	Maths	60
	Business	50

Data records	
Address	Data
40	J. Smith
	PhD
	Comp. sci.
	1947
60	T. Davis
	MSc
	Maths
	1961
80	R. Jones
	BA
	Comp. sci.
	1954
50	T. Hanes
	BA
	Business
	1945

Fig. 5.14 Inverted file

There may be a number of data items in a record that are chosen to be indexed. In Figure 5.14, a lecturer's qualification and department are indexed but not name or date of birth. Of course there is a price to pay. The 'ideal' 100% inversion, where all data items are keys and therefore all items are contained in an index as well as a data record, will be very inefficient in many respects. When deleting a record, not only has the data record to be deleted but all mentions of it in the indexes have also to be deleted. For additions, the record is created and the index must include references to it where appropriate. When updating, care has to be exercised when the field updated is one which is indexed.

Yet there are considerable advantages of such an approach. Queries of the type 'Are there?' or 'How many?' become simple if the information is held in the index. For example: 'Do any lecturers have a PhD?' or 'How many lecturers are in the Computer Science Department?' can be answered by accessing the index only. If there are expected to be a number of queries of the type 'How many lecturers are over 40 years of age?', the database administrator may well consider using date-of-birth as a key for inclusion in the index. More complex queries requiring 'and' and/or 'or' can be described such as 'Is there a lecturer who has a PhD and is in the Business Department?'. The answer can also be obtained by access to the index without recourse to the data storage area.

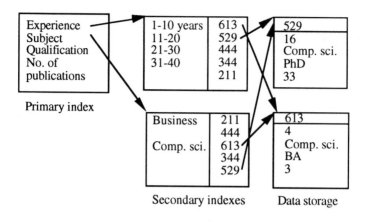

Fig. 5.15 Use of secondary indexes

When there are a large number of keys, it may be convenient to have a secondary index as shown in Figure 5.15.

5.6 CONCLUSION

If the database administrator has the choice of file organisation then that chosen will depend on the application. Some database management systems support a number of file organisation methods and many will help the database administrator by simulating the requirements of the application on various file organisation types. Some DBMS support a combination of the above approaches, such as, secondary indexes with chains. Some DBMS, however, only support one file organisation technique. Many will use compression techniques which will reduce the amount of data storage needed for any collection of stored data and thereby, and more importantly, reduce access times because the data requires less space and therefore fewer input-output operations.

5.7 FURTHER READING

Dodd, G. C (1969) Elements of Data Management Systems, *Computing Surveys*, June.
Provides a clear, concise account of some of the basic methods of file organisation and access.

Knuth, D.E (1973) *The Art of Computer Programming, Vol III, Sorting and Searching*, Addison-Wesley, Reading, Mass.

A technical book which discusses the various searching algorithms for data held on disk.

Date, C. J (1990) *An Introduction to Database Systems, Volume 1*, 5th ed, Addison-Wesley, London.

Elmasri, R & Navathe, S. B (1989) *Fundamentals of Database Systems*, Benjamin/Cummings, Redwood City, Ca.

McFadden, F. R & Hoffer, J. A (1991) *Database Management*, 3rd ed, Benjamin/Cummings, Redwood City, Ca.

These texts provide a more detailed discussion of the various file organisation methods used by DBMS.

Chapter 6
Implementing Applications

6.1   EXTERNAL VIEW OF DATABASE

As reference to Figure 6.1 (a modification of Figure 5.1) makes clear, the external view of the database is that which each user 'sees'. It is derived from and is a subset of the logical schema (Chapter 4), which is the overall view of the database in a form required by the DBMS used, and which is itself a mapping from the conceptual schema (Chapter 3). The external schema is the subset of the database which is relevant to the particular user, and though it may be a summarised and a very restricted subset, the user may think that it represents the whole view, because it is the whole view as far as the user is concerned. Its format may also be different from the logical schema. The presentation and sequence of the data will also suit the context in which it is presented. The format will depend on the particular host language, query language, report writer or other software used. Indeed, there may well be several external views, perhaps as much as one per application or user that accesses the database. Different user languages will be described in the context of particular DBMS in Chapter 7. But whatever the description given to the user, the underlying data described by the logical schema will be the same. In other words, there is **program data independence**, and the description of the data in the programs can change without the descriptions in the database changing, and vice versa.

Readers should note that the ANSI/X3/SPARC architecture described in Section 1.8 is slightly different to that shown in Figure 6.1 as in that architecture the external view is mapped onto a conceptual view. There is no intermediary logical view as we have in our methodology (this text describes a methodology for designing databases and developing database applications, whereas the ANSI/X3/SPARC proposals describe an architecture to view database applications). As we saw in Chapter 4, the logical schema proves to be a useful stage for database design and separates the conceptual model, which is independent of any hardware/software factors, from the physical model.

External views may be presented to the user through the use of host language programs or a query language but they may also be obtained through a dialogue, which approaches a natural language dialogue, or via a menu. In Figure 6.2, the users pass through a number of menus to indicate which system and which part of the system they require to use. The options are provided in the menu: the user has only to select the

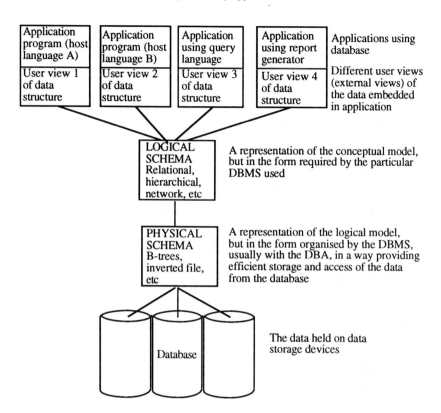

Fig. 6.1 The place of the external views

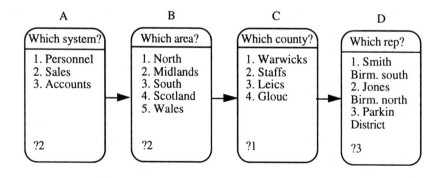

Fig. 6.2 Sequential menus

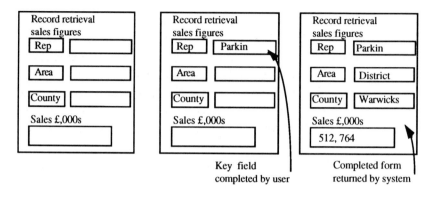

Fig. 6.3 Form processing

option required by pressing the appropriate key (following the question mark).

Alternative approaches which are also easy to use include a soft copy form presented to the users who 'fill in the forms' to state their requirements (see Figure 6.3) or icon/mouse systems, which use graphical symbols (icons) representing such requirements as filing (file cabinet), deleting (wastepaper basket) and so on. The user specifies the option required by pointing the mouse to the icon and pressing a button on the mouse to activate that process.

In this chapter we look at the ways to develop the applications which use the database, including an analysis of data requirements, and in Chapter 7 we look at setting up different external views in the context of different DBMS. Section 6.2 looks again at conventional applications development, but in the overall context of a database approach, and then we look at alternative ways of developing applications, again in a database environment. In Section 6.3 we look at structured systems analysis and design, in Section 6.4 at participation and in Section 6.5 at prototyping. Finally, in Section 6.6 we look at Multiview, a blended methodology for developing applications, using the methods, techniques and tools which are appropriate for a particular situation. Although not necessarily used with a database, it proves suitable in that environment and in Chapter 15 a case study is described of an application developed with a database.

6.2   THE LIFE-CYCLE REVISITED

In a database environment, many applications are large operational systems, such as sales order processing, sales ledger, production control, stock control, and invoicing. These systems have to be designed and implemented. In Section 1.2 some critical comments were made of conventional systems analysis. Some of these criticisms applied because of their file orientation. This type of criticism should not apply in a database environment. Here there should be a separation of data aspects from processing aspects. Sets of data which may be required in a number of applications need not be collected more than once. The data will be shared on the database. Further, modifications to applications are likely to be much easier to make, because files are external to the program. Changes to the data may only involve changing the relevant parts of the database, and the many programs that may use the data will not need to be changed.

There are a number of points in favour of the conventional approach. The six stages (feasibility study, systems investigation, systems analysis, systems design, implementation, and review and maintenance) associated with conventional systems analysis have been well tried and tested. At the end of each stage the analyst and management have an opportunity to review progress in the development of the application. There are a number of documentation aids to help the analysis, design and implementation processes, particularly in helping to ensure that the work is thorough and can be communicated to interested parties.

Another argument in its support is that many of the developments in systems analysis, such as structured systems analysis, participation and prototyping which are discussed later in this chapter, can be incorporated into the conventional approach. This can make the conventional approach perfectly adequate for some systems development work.

But as we saw in Section 1.3 there are limitations to the approach. There is a danger that the new system merely 'computerises' the clerical system used previously as the analysis phase is often neglected. Frequently it is designed quickly in order to solve a problem that has occurred with the old system. A 'quick and dirty' solution may be politically expedient but may well cause considerable problems, particularly with regard to the maintenance workload. The new design may be unambitious, not tested properly, and unlikely to take full account of the potential of the technology used. The conventional methodology tends to pay lip service to user involvement. There is no mechanism to enforce user involvement and it is therefore often ignored or at best lip-service paid to it. This frequently results in the system being rejected by the users.

This rejection of the system may be a result of poor analysis: the systems analyst has not found out the user requirements. The users may not have been involved to the extent of being able to see the repercussions of the system design they had 'agreed' with the analyst. The documentation provided is oriented towards computer people and it is difficult for users to translate many of these forms used in conventional systems documentation into their 'language'. If systems are developed without the involvement of the users, they may be unwilling to accept the new systems because they feel they have been imposed on them. Systems may therefore be rejected as soon as they are implemented.

The database approach is long term and costly, and therefore top management should not risk its failure by sticking to outdated methods of applications development. The failure of one application could jeopardise all applications. For this reason it is essential to pay regard to different methods of applications development. Participation and prototyping could be used independently in some applications and in others it may be appropriate to use the conventional approach modified by incorporating these tools and techniques. Similarly, the techniques and tools of structured systems analysis can be incorporated into the conventional approach or can be seen as forming part of an alternative methodology for applications development.

6.3 STRUCTURED SYSTEMS ANALYSIS AND DESIGN

The term 'structured' is very fashionable in computing. It has been adopted by many authors and consultants and it seems to mean many things, depending on the author and context. However, the essential feature of structured techniques is the breaking down of a complex problem into smaller manageable units in a systematic (disciplined) way. The techniques may use a number of pictorial methods for presenting results and these can be understood by users and analysts alike.

Structured techniques are relevant to systems analysis <u>and</u> design. Systems analysis could be described as 'what is' and 'what is required' whilst systems design is 'what could be'. Using the technique of **functional decomposition**, a very complex problem can be broken down into a number of fairly complex parts and then further to less complex parts until, at the bottom level, all the parts are fairly trivial and therefore easy to understand.

As can be seen in Figure 6.4, 'produce weekly payroll' at the top level can be broken into 'validate weekly return', 'calculate gross wage', 'calculate deductions' and 'print wages slip'. Each of these boxes is separate and, when at the program level, can be altered without affecting the other boxes. Each of these steps can be further broken down, a process also referred to as **stepwise refinement**. For example, 'calculate deductions' can be broken down into 'calculate tax', 'calculate national insurance contribution' and 'calculate loan repayments'. Eventually this 'top down' approach can lead to the level of a few simple English statements or a small amount of programming code.

This technique has had a great deal of impact in computer programming where it has led to more reliable programs which are easier to maintain, and it is also important

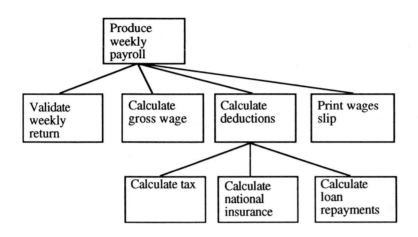

Fig. 6.4 Functional decomposition

in systems analysis and design. Books by Gane & Sarson (1979) and DeMarco (1979) have had considerable impact. To some extent these books propagate a series of techniques. These techniques are a great improvement on more established techniques, such as flowcharting, which typify conventional systems analysis. Most of these newer techniques of systems analysis and design have in fact been with us for some time, but were not brought together until the publication of the above texts. The techniques include data flow diagrams, data structure diagrams, decision trees, decision tables and structured English.

The improvements on conventional systems analysis resulting from the use of these techniques is gained both from the point of view of understanding the real-world processes that they represent and in communicating the knowledge acquired. Structured analysis documentation includes documents describing the logical (real-world) analysis of the processes and not just their physical (implementation) level designs. In other words, there is a clear distinction between application logic and the computer representation of that logic. There will be a separation of any data that the system is likely to want to input, output, process, or store, and the physical record, that will be part of the computer database. The analysis documentation will include the system inputs, outputs and data structures as well as the processing logic.

Data Flow Diagrams (DFD) are a particularly useful aid in communicating the analyst's understanding of the system. They do so by partitioning the system into independent units of a size that enable the system to be easily understood. The user, whether the operator of the system when it is operational or the manager of the department it is aimed to help, can readily check that the DFD is accurate because it is so graphical. DFDs can be converted to computer procedures.

There are four parts to the DFD. This is standard, though there are a number of different graphical conventions in showing them. The convention used here is suggested by Gane and Sarson. The arrow represents a data flow from one part of the system to another. In Figure 6.5 an example of a data flow is the delivery notes passing from one supplier to the process 'check note against order'. A second part of the diagram is represented by 'bubbles' or rounded boxes which are used to denote processes. A third element is the data store, such as the store of purchase orders in Figure 6.5.

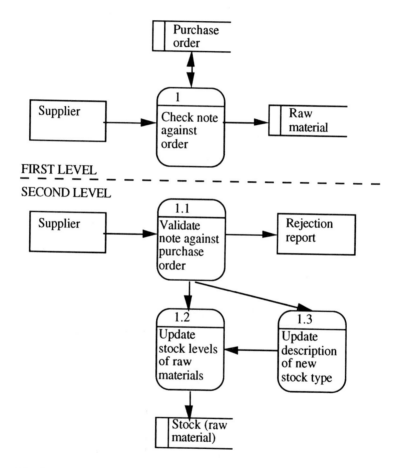

Fig. 6.5 Data flow diagram - top level and more detailed second level

A fourth part of data flow diagrams is 'sources' and 'sinks', usually external, such as a customer, a supplier or the Inland Revenue. We are not interested in them as such (they are outside the boundary of the investigation), but we are interested in what they give. For example, it is not the customers themselves which are important in the context of this particular data flow, but their orders. Similarly it is not the warehouse that is important, but the drain on stock. These are represented by boxes. One of the main features of data flow diagrams is the ability to construct them in levels (reflecting functional decomposition of the process). For example, the process contained in a soft box in one level could be a whole DFD in another. This is illustrated in Figure 6.5. Note that the process numbered 1 in the top part of the diagram is represented by 1.1, 1.2, and 1.3 in the more detailed version below. Further examples are found in Chapter 15.

Data flow diagrams prove to be a good communication tool and only the major features of systems are drawn to help clarity. In drawing a data flow diagram, the analyst will start by drawing a 'doodle' attempt of the whole system, and a number of lower level 'doodles'. These are then refined iteratively to the analyst's satisfaction. This version is then presented to the users for their comment. Further iterations of the diagram are therefore likely before the final versions are produced.

Another technique used in structured methodologies is the **structure chart** or **diagram** (DeMarco, 1979). The basic function diagram, for example, Figure 6.4, shows the links as a function is decomposed into its constituent modules. **Structure charts** or **diagrams** are more sophisticated.

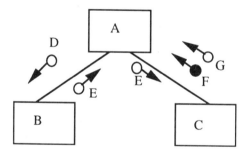

Fig.6.6. Structure diagram

The structure chart is a series of boxes (representing processes or modules) and connecting lines (representing links to subordinate processes) which are arranged in a hierarchy. The basic diagram is shown as Figure 6.6. This structure chart shows that:

- Module A can call module B and also module C. No sequencing for these calls nor whether they actually occur is implied by the diagraming notation. When the subordinate process terminates, control goes back to the calling process.
- When A calls B, it sends data of type D to B. When B terminates, it returns data of

type E to A. Similarly, A communicates with C using data of types E and G.

- When C terminates, it sends a flag of type F to A. A flag is used as a flow of control data.

A number of examples of their use is seen in Chapter 15.

Structured English, decision trees and decision tables are alternative methods of describing process logic. They are appropriate in different circumstances but each provides simple, clear, and unambiguous ways of describing the logic of what happens in a particular process. Natural language is ambiguous and long-winded and these techniques are much superior.

Structured English, for example, is very like a 'readable' computer program. It is not a programming language though it can be readily converted to a computer program, because it is a strict and logical form of English and the constructs reflect structured programming. Structured English is a precise way of specifying a function and is readily understandable by the systems designer as well as being readily converted to a program. An example is given in Figure 6.7. Structured English uses only a limited subset of English and this vocabulary is exact. This ensures less ambiguity in the use of natural language English by the analyst. Further, by the use of text indentation, the logic of the process can be shown more easily.

Structured English has an:

> IF condition 1 (is true)
> > THEN action 2 (is to be carried out)
> ELSE (not condition 1)
> > SO action 1 (to be carried out)

construct. Conditions can include equal, not equal, greater than, less than, and so on. There are alternative languages such as 'Pseudo Code', and 'Tight English'. These vary on their nearness to the machine or readability to users.

CREDIT RATING POLICY

IF the customer is a trade customer
    and IF the customer is customer for 5 or more years
        THEN credit is accepted up to £5000
    ELSE credit is accepted up to £1000
ELSE (the customer is private customer)
    SO: no credit is given

Fig. 6.7 An example of structured English

A **decision tree** illustrates the actions to be taken at each decision point. The actions follow each decision point via a branch of a tree whereas each condition will determine the particular branch to be followed. The techniques of showing decisions and actions are graphical and easy to understand unless it becomes so large that it is difficult to follow. An example of a decision tree is given in Figure 6.8. They are constructed by first identifying the conditions, actions, unless/however/but structures from narrative. Each sentence may form a mini decision tree and these will be joined together to form the version which will be verified by the users. Decision trees prove to be a good method of showing the basics of a decision, that is, what are the possible actions that might be taken at a particular decision point and what set of values leads to each of these actions. It is easy for the user to verify whether the analyst has understood the procedures.

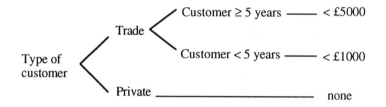

Fig. 6.8 Decision tree

Decision tables are less graphical but are concise and have an in-built verification mechanism so that it is possible to check that all the conditions have been catered for. An example of a decision table is shown as Figure 6.9. Decision tables can be used as computer input, programs being produced directly from them, and there are a number of packages available for this purpose.

Figure 6.9 shows the decisions that have to be made by drivers in the U.K. at traffic lights. The table has four sections. The condition stub has the possible conditions 'red', 'amber' and 'green'. Condition Entries are either Y for yes (this condition is satisfied) or N for no (this condition is not satisfied). Having three conditions, there will be 2 to the power of 3 (2 x 2 x 2 = 8) columns. The easiest way of proceeding is to have the first row as YYYYNNNN, the second row as YYNNYYNN and the final row as YNYNYNYN. If there were four conditions, we would start by eight Ys and eight Ns and so on.

All the possible actions are listed in the Action Stub. An X placed on a row/column coincidence in the Action Entry means that the action in the action stub should be taken. A blank will mean that the action should not be taken. Thus, if a driver is faced with Red (Y), Amber (Y) and Green (Y), the first column indicates that the driver should stop and call the police. All combinations, even invalid ones, should be considered. The next column Red (Y), Amber (Y) and Green (N) informs the driver to stop. Only the Red (N), Amber (N) and Green (Y) combination permits the driver to go with caution.

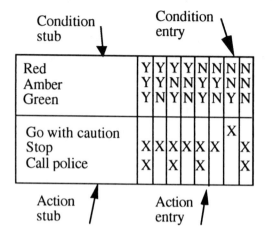

Condition stub   Condition entry

Red	Y	Y	Y	Y	N	N	N	N
Amber	Y	Y	N	N	Y	Y	N	N
Green	Y	N	Y	N	Y	N	Y	N

Go with caution						X		
Stop	X	X	X	X	X	X		X
Call police	X		X		X			X

Action stub   Action entry

Fig. 6.9 Decision table

In systems analysis, there are likely to be requirements to specify actions where there are a large number of conditions. A set of decision tables is appropriate here. The first will have actions such as 'GO TO Decision Table 2'. Each of these may themselves be reduced to a further level of decision tables. The technique therefore lends itself to functional decomposition.

Structured methodologies use techniques most of which can be followed by analysts and users alike. In the past, systems analysts were first and foremost computer people. Now, to some extent at least, they are talking a language that the rest of the organisation can understand. This is important in getting the willing participation of users. Most of the documentation aids are graphic representations of the subject matter. This is much easier to follow than text which is long-winded and frequently ambiguous or file designs or programming flowcharts which are understandable only to the computer professional.

Gane & Sarson and other writers on structured analysis also advocate the use of data dictionaries (discussed in Chapter 12 of this text) and other tools of data analysis, such as normalisation (discussed in Sections 3.7 and 3.8). Forms for detailing the data elements and data stores are also provided. In this text, we have attempted to separate these data-oriented aspects, particularly data analysis and databases, from the process-oriented aspects. In practice, the distinction is never clear-cut.

As well as improved communication tools, the methodology usually incorporates **structured walkthroughs**. These are team meetings where the analysis and design specifications and other documentation are exposed to review by the members of the team. It is usual that they represent meetings of peers and that 'management' are not involved. This is to avoid the type of criticism which may have repercussions on the team member's status or salary. A peer review is likely to reveal errors, omissions, ambiguities and weaknesses in style, and also help to motivate and train the staff involved.

Questions that the peer group are likely to ask of a design could include:

- Can bespoke programs use library routines?
- Is the user interface simple, understandable, consistent?
- Does the design fulfil the specification fully?
- Will it work?

Structured walkthroughs should avoid the late detection of errors and flaws in logic and hence greatly reduce the risk of failure when the system is running.

Structured systems analysis and design need not only be seen as an alternative to the conventional approach. The different authors of the approach do not view structured analysis in the same way. Some regard the techniques as a useful alternative to many techniques of the conventional approach, and which therefore should be incorporated in the conventional approach. Other writers, for example Gane and Sarson, emphasise a 'structured methodology' which should replace the conventional approach. DeMarco regards these techniques as in the realm of analysis only and considers design to be a separate process where the analyst uses his experience and imagination to 'invent' a new system. Gane and Sarson suggest that the techniques can be used to specify the system design and help in the implementation process. They discuss query types and their implication for physical design. They also ask users to construct a 'wish list' defining their requirements and providing a menu of alternatives. Writers in the structured school also emphasise different techniques, although some techniques are common to all. It is functional decomposition which really separates the structured systems approach from other approaches.

6.4 PARTICIPATION

This is a practical philosophy aimed at providing solutions to user problems. The belief here is that people have a basic right to control their own destinies and that, if they are allowed to participate in the analysis and design of the system that they will be using, then the implementation, acceptance and operation of the systems are more likely to be successful.

In the conventional systems analysis methodology, the importance of user involvement is frequently stressed although it is not 'built in' to the methodology as are, for example, the various documentation requirements. However, the computer specialist is the person who is making the real decisions. In practice participation may mean (a) 'doing a public relations job to placate the staff' and (b) 'once that is done train them to use the system'. This is not what we mean by participation. This section is about ways to encourage participation in the systems development process.

Systems analysts are trained in and knowledgeable of the technological and economic aspects of computer applications but far more rarely on the human aspects which are at least as important. The person who is going to use the system frequently feels resentment. Further, top management may do little more than pay lip-service to computing.

When the system is implemented, the systems analyst may be happy with the system. This is of little significance if it does not meet the expectations of the users, who are the customers. This may be due to poor analysis - the analyst may not have understood fully the present system or the users' requirements. On the other hand, many systems may 'work' in that they are technically viable, but fail because of 'people problems'. Users may feel that the new system will make their job less secure, will make their relationship with others change for the worse, or will lead to a loss of the independence that they previously enjoyed.

As a result of these feelings, users may do their best to ensure that the computer system will not succeed. This may show itself in attempts to 'beat the system'. Frequently it manifests itself when people blame the system for difficulties that may well be caused by other factors. Some people may just want to have 'nothing to do with the system'.

These reactions against a new computer system may stem from a number of reasons, largely historical, but they will have to be corrected or allowed for if future computer applications are going to succeed. Users may regard the computer department as having too great powers, and controlling (by technology) other departments which were previously controlled by people within the user department. Computer people seem to have great status in the eyes of top management and are not governed by the same codes as the rest of the company. Pay scales seem to be much higher for computer staff, particularly when seen in the light of the length of time that computer staff have worked with the firm. In any case, the track record of computer applications - missed cutover dates, greater costs, fewer benefits, and designs which seem to be very different from that promised - should have led to reduced salaries and status, not the opposite.

Some of these arguments are valid, others less 'objective', but the poor communications between computer staff and others in the organisation, caused by the use of jargon or a lack of training and education, have not helped. Somehow these barriers have to be broken down if computer applications are really going to succeed.

One way to help this process is to involve all staff affected by computer systems in the computing process. This includes the top management of the organisation as well as departmental staff. In the past, top management has avoided much contact with computer systems. Managers have probably sanctioned the purchase of computer hardware and software but have not involved themselves with their use. They preferred to keep themselves at a 'safe' distance from computers. This cannot lead to successful implementation of computer systems: managers need to participate in the change and this will motivate their subordinates.

Attitudes are changing, partly because managers can see that without their involvement computer systems are unlikely to succeed, and because they believe that computer systems should be able to help them in their decision-making. Earlier computing concerned itself with the operations of the firm; modern systems concern themselves with decision-support as well. Without decision-support systems, firms will lose out to their competitors. Managers are now therefore far more likely to demand sophisticated computer applications and to play a leading role in their development and implementation.

Communications between computer and non-computer people within the organisation must also improve. This should establish a more mutually trusting and cooperative atmosphere. Training and education of all staff in the organisation about computers are therefore important for the success of the computing venture. Of course data processing staff should also be aware of the various operating areas of the business. This should bring down barriers caused by a lack of knowledge and by technical jargon and encourage users to become involved in the technological change.

Involvement should mean much more than agreeing to be interviewed by the analyst and working extra overtime hours as the operational date for the new system nears. If the users participate more, perhaps being responsible for the design, then they are far more likely to be satisfied with and be committed to the system once it is implemented. It is 'their baby' as well as that of the computer people. This environment is one where the users and analysts work as a team rather than as expert and non-expert. There is less likely to be a misunderstanding by the analyst which causes a poorly designed system. The user will also know how the new system operates by the time it becomes operational, with the result that there are likely to be fewer 'teething troubles' with the new system.

Borovits *et al* (1990) look at some of the benefits of participation on the finished system. Two important aspects of group work are identified: communication patterns and working procedures. Traditional models consist of the transfer of information from one person to another, for example, from user to designer and from manager to designer. Working independently, there is little opportunity for discussion and feedback. In contrast, participation is characterised by communication amongst all members of the group working together towards a common goal, in a friendly, informative atmosphere with open discussion and the swapping of ideas. This may be an idealised picture, but group participation is likely to be more successful. It is argued that participation will result in:

- More efficient use of resources
- The elimination of poor ideas more quickly
- More accurate performance feedback as it comes from a number of sources
- A higher level of commitment.

The role of the computer analysts may be more of facilitator than designer, helping to realise the users' wishes. This can be aided by the use of application packages which the users can try out and choose what is best for them. Another possibility is for the user or the analyst (or both) to develop a 'prototype'. There are prototyping packages available which will set up screen layouts and bring in blocks of code for validating and presenting data. The users can compare all these possibilities and develop a prototype before making up their minds on a final design. This can then represent the specification for the new system. Prototyping is discussed fully in Section 6.5.

A very interesting case study relating to a successful application of participation at Rolls Royce is given in Mumford & Henshall (1979). The approach recognises that the clerks who will eventually use the system ought to have a major design role. This includes the form of work structure into which the computer aspects of the system are embedded. The final system design is evaluated on the basis of job satisfaction of those working on it as well as its efficiency. A likely result of taking job enrichment into account is the reduction of monotony usually associated with the clerical tasks of computer systems. It is particularly interesting, however, to discover that a small group of white collar workers at Rolls Royce did not want an intellectually taxing job and provisions were made for them in the final design.

Mumford distinguishes between three levels of participation. **Consultative participation** leaves the main design tasks to the systems analysts, but tries to ensure that all staff in the user department are consulted about the change. The systems analysts are encouraged to provide opportunity for increasing job satisfaction when redesigning the system. It may be possible to organise the users into groups to discuss aspects of the new system and make suggestions to the analysts. Most advocates of the conventional approach to systems development would accept that there is a need for at least this level of participation.

Representative participation requires a higher level of involvement of user department staff. Here, the 'design group' consists of user representatives and systems analysts. No longer is it expected that technologists dictate the design of the system to the users. They have equal say in the decision. Representative participation does assume that the 'representatives' can represent the interests of all the users affected by the design decisions.

Finally, **consensus participation** attempts to involve all user department staff throughout the design and development of the system. It may be more difficult to make quick decisions, but it has the additional merit of making the design decisions those of the staff as a whole. This is the approach particularly favoured by Mumford, although it is not always appropriate. Sometimes the sets of tasks in a system can be distinguished and those people involved in each task set make their own design decisions.

Frölich & Krieger (1990) report on a survey of participation in Europe following 4654 interviews. This extends Mumford's three levels of participation to five:

- *No worker participation:* management plans and implements new technology without any participation.
- *Information:* management informs employees in writing or at joint meetings.
- *Consultation:* joint committees are set up where users are given information and can state their opinions, and in the case of differing view, can expect management to explain its reasoning.
- *Negotiation:* contractually binding conclusions are worked out in joint negotiation committees.
- *Full participation:* decisions require the agreement of all parties.

In the survey, one of the two higher forms of participation was recorded by only 20% of those surveyed. About half thought that their organisation used the second form of participation, that employees were kept informed. Although not a high form of participation, employees were likely to be informed of the reasons for change, how and when it will be implemented, what the new system will mean to them and its benefits. Even where the level of participation was highest, its emphasis was stressed at the implementation, operation and evaluation phases of the development of a project, very rarely in any earlier planning phase. The report suggests that the time taken for decision-making and the quality of the decisions were largely unaffected by participation, but the utilisation of skills, the general feeling of empathy with the organisation, the working atmosphere and the employees' acceptance of technology all improved in general. However, many organisations require a change in their culture (Section 2.3) to enable effective participation.

Although the human and social aspects of change are emphasised in this section, the technical aspects are also important. As Hirschheim & Newman (1988) argue:

'Resistance is more likely to occur in systems which are cumbersome, 'unfriendly', unreliable, lack functionality, and slow. If users find the technical quality of the system to be low, they are unlikely to welcome it, with the result that they will be disinclined to use it.'

One approach which can support user participation is that of the **information centre**. By giving users ready access to appropriate tools and guidance from the data processing department, user departments could, it is proposed, develop systems themselves. A user request for a system <u>may</u> lead to standard data processing work - procedural language solutions, high volumes of data to be processed, critical response times .... and a long development time. But the user request may alternatively be followed by advice on how users can themselves make use of facilities available, such as microcomputers, terminal access, query languages, and other packages, such as report generators, graphics, spreadsheet and file management systems, so that users can design their own technical system.

One of the very positive aspects of the information centre is that it provides choice rather than immediate solutions (which may not match the requirements). A number of alternatives are provided and the user exercises choice between these alternatives which will have social as well as technical repercussions. User groups can discuss social issues such as retraining, new departmental structures and new job responsibilities as well as issues such as terminals and the particular package required. In view of this, it should be a prerequisite for users to decide on the social/human and technical objectives before approaching the information centre. Only then will the users be able to rank particular solutions.

The information centre needs to be a centre of education - what computers can and cannot do, the importance of good standards, security provision and so on - as well as a source of training, reference material and advice on particular problems or the appropriateness of particular hardware and software solutions. Data processing professionals are much more facilitators in this environment, and they may be brought in to assist on tasks such as detailed debugging.

In the first chapter we discussed the problems of the application backlog, where user departments may have to wait years for the implementation of systems. The information centre alternative can speed up the development of applications and maintenance (as the users should be able to maintain the systems as well as develop them). On the other hand, care has to be taken to prevent the scope of applications being limited, as users cannot be expected to know all the possibilities that computers offer. Furthermore, there is a danger that if testing, documentation, validation, back-up and recovery procedures are not thorough, the quality of the final systems will be poor. This will reduce the possibilities of sharing data, with consequent data duplication and the possibility of inconsistency. The role of the facilitators is therefore crucial. It should not be the intention of the data processing department to 'wash their hands of the applications' if the major role in decision-making related to their development rests with the users.

The participative approaches to information systems development discussed in this section are pragmatic but they require consensus on the part of the technologists and users. Sometimes the technologists may 'agree' to the approach but resent it: they feel that they have lost their power in the firm. Sometimes users resent the time taken from their usual work: they may ask why they should spend their time on 'computers' when they are employed to work on their application. But it is surely generally accepted that some level of participation is necessary whatever approach to systems design and development is adopted. Otherwise there is a very real risk that new systems will be rejected by the people who are expected to use it.

6.5 PROTOTYPING

We have seen that many systems are implemented but then rejected by the user department. When analysts talk to users about their needs it is difficult for them to envisage the hypothetical - much easier to talk about how the present system works - and it is therefore difficult to think of all their future needs in any new system and the full consequences of their requests. One way to reduce this possibility is to develop a prototype first so that the users can see what the output of the final system could be like. If comments are unfavourable, ideas from the user can be implemented on the prototype until the users are happy with it. Users are frequently unsure about what they want from the system, and the prototypes can guide them towards a knowledge and communication of their requirements. Again, prototyping can be incorporated into the conventional approach to developing applications, but it can also be seen as a systems development methodology in its own right.

There are many reasons for organisations using prototypes when developing applications:

- *Avoid incorrect requirements specification:* As discussed in Section 6.4, users often find it difficult to communicate their requirements, and design based on incorrect requirements specification will be costly to correct.
- *Provide a tangible means of assessment:* It provides a tangible means of evaluating a potential application system and for suggesting improvements.

- *Provide a common base line:* Prototyping represents a common reference point for both users and analysts by which to identify potential problems and suggest improvements.
- *Encourage user participation:* Prototyping proves to be a practical way to cultivate and achieve user participation and commitment to the project.
- *Improve user/analyst relationships:* Users and analysts gain an improved appreciation for each other's roles and thereby develop better communications.

Frequently it is only possible to develop a prototype having some of the features of the final system. However, this may be all that is needed, the analysts wishing to examine only those areas where they are unsure of the user requirements or about how to build the system. To some extent, therefore, prototyping can be seen as an improvement in the techniques of systems investigation.

A prototype is frequently built using special tools such as **screen painters** which facilitate the quick design of data entry screens and **report generators** which can be used to design reports from files. These reports, which can be soft copy (screen) as well as hard copy (paper) reports, are expected to conform to the basic layouts offered by the system. This leads to an acceptable design in quick time. If the screen layout is not entirely satisfactory, the prototype can be quickly redrawn using the tools available. As with word processing systems, the gains accrue when making changes. Only the areas to be changed need to be redrawn, not the whole screen. Tools supporting prototyping are discussed fully in Chapter 11.

Sometimes a microcomputer will be used to develop the prototype although the actual system will be run on a mainframe computer. Some packages are designed for microcomputer use. Omnis and dBaseIV are database management systems popular on microcomputers which can be used in this way to set up reports and enquiry runs from files.

Frequently a prototype system can be developed in a few hours, and it rarely takes more than 10% of the time to develop the operational system. This is surely a good investment of time if it means ensuring that the final version does provide the users with a system that they want. Some systems teams use the prototype as the user 'sign off'. Once the users are content with the prototype output, it will used as the basis on which the actual outputs will be designed. This is likely to be a much better basis for a user decision than the documentation of conventional system analysis.

A possible drawback of prototyping is that many users question the time taken to develop the operational system when they know that the prototype was developed so quickly. This discrepancy will be due to a number of reasons. The final system will have to deal with all possible types of data and processing and the prototype may only have included the main types of data. The final version must be documented thoroughly. It needs to be programmed efficiently, whereas efficient coding of a prototype is not a prime concern. The validation routines in the implemented system have to be thorough. The users may need convincing that these considerations, which delay the system in their eyes, are necessary.

Some users and technologists could also argue that the time, effort and money spent in developing a prototype is 'wasted'. This is also said of user participation. It is often difficult to persuade busy people that this effort does lead to better information systems and it possibly needs management encouragement to provide 'weight' behind this argument.

One of the problems is that prototyping is frequently oversold leading to unrealistic user expectations and thereby unmet user expectations and disappointment. A prototype will normally have limited capabilities, capturing only the essential features of the proposed system. Further, the nature of prototyping, developing through user feedback in ways sometimes unpredicted, makes it difficult to manage and control. Avison & Wilson (1991) suggest some possible ways of controlling prototyping. It is also difficult to prototype large information systems, because of the complexity, and in most cases constraints in time and project resources determine the boundaries and scope of prototyping.

Prototyping could be used as a basis for a methodology of systems development in the organisation. This may have an analysis phase which could use structured techniques to understand the present system and suggest the functional requirements of an alternative system. This can be used to construct a prototype for evaluation by users. In response to the resulting user comment, the prototype can be re-tuned and the process continue until the prototype represents the wishes of the user. Once this has been established, the target system can be designed and developed with the prototype being part of the systems specification. Prototyping, used as an integral part of the systems development process, is discussed in Dearnley & Mayhew (1983).

Many prototypes are discarded as they will be inefficient and poorly designed and documented. They will not integrate into the other operational systems. The prototype may incorporate techniques which are impractical for the operational system. They are used only as a development tool. But as we have seen, a prototype may not always be developed merely as a learning vehicle. It could be used as part of the final system, the final prototype being the basis for the operational system. The system has evolved by an iterative process. If this is the expected role of prototyping, the analysts must be aware of robustness, documentation and efficiency when developing the prototype. The prototype must be able to handle the quantities and variety of live data that are unlikely to be incorporated in the test runs which are used to give the user an idea of the systems output and capabilities. Otherwise there is danger that prototyping will not improve the quality of systems analysis.

Used carefully, however, prototyping can help systems development in a number of ways. It is possible to test ideas without incurring huge costs, allow the user to look at a number of alternatives and see the opportunities that information systems can provide. Further by reducing the application development time and costs, it may make the acceptance of the final system more likely.

6.6   MULTIVIEW

This section looks at one application development methodology called Multiview. It has been chosen because it incorporates many of the aspects of systems development discussed in this chapter, including the use of structured methods, participation and prototyping, and follows the tenets of this text.

Whilst the larger database project is developed (following Chapters 2-5), the applications might be developed using the Multiview approach. It is a contingency approach in that it is flexible in its use and will be adapted according to the particular situation in the organisation and the application. The section is modified from Avison & Wood-Harper (1990). Chapter 15, also adapted from that text, provides a case study of the application of Multiview in a database environment.

The stages of the Multiview methodology and the inter-relationships between them are shown in Figure 6.10. The boxes refer to the analysis stages and the circles to the design stages. The arrows between them describe the inter-relationships. Some of the outputs of one stage will be used in a following stage. The dotted arrows show other major outputs. The five stages are:

1) Analysis of human activity
2) Analysis of information (sometimes called information modelling)
3) Analysis and design of socio-technical aspects
4) Design of the human-computer interface
5) Design of technical aspects.

They incorporate five different views which are appropriate to the progressive development of an analysis and design project, covering all aspects required to answer the vital questions of users. These five views are necessary to form a system which is complete in both technical and human terms. The outputs of the methodology, shown as dotted arrows in Figure 6.10, are listed in Figure 6.11, together with the information that they provide and the questions that they answer.

Because it *is* a multi-view approach, it covers computer-related questions and also matters relating to people and business functions. It is part issue-related and part task-related. An issue-related question is: "What do we hope to achieve for the company as a

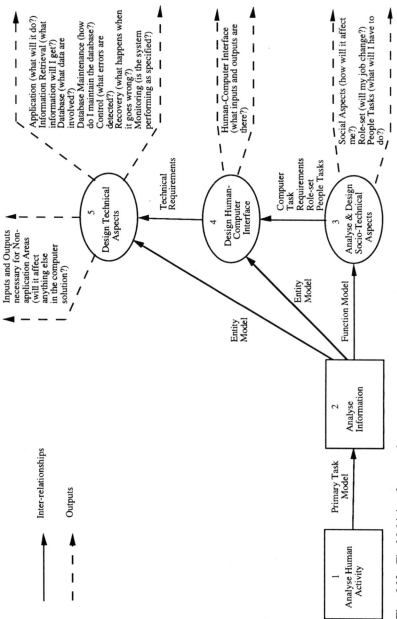

Fig. 6.10. The Multiview framework

Outputs	Information
Social Aspects	How will it affect me?
Role-set	Will my job change? In what way?
People Tasks	What will I have to do?
Human-Computer Interface	How will I work with the computer? What inputs and outputs are there?
Database	What data are involved?
Database Maintenance	How will I maintain the integrity of data?
Recovery	What happens when it goes wrong?
Monitoring	Is the system performing to specification?
Control	How is security and privacy dealt with? What errors are detected?
Information Retrieval	What information will I get?
Application	What will the system do?
Inputs and Outputs necessary for Non-application Areas	Will it affect anything else on the computer subsystem?

Fig. 6.11. Methodology outputs

result of installing a computer?". A task-related question is: "What jobs is the computer going to have to do?".

The distinction between issue and task is important because it is too easy to concentrate on tasks when computerising, and to overlook important issues which need to be resolved. As we saw in Section 1.3, too often issues are ignored in the rush to 'computerise'. But, you cannot solve a problem until you know what the problem is! Issue-related aspects, in particular those occurring at stage 1 of Multiview, are concerned with debate on the definition of system requirements in the broadest sense, that is 'what real world problems is the system to solve?'. It takes in many of the issues discussed in Chapter 2, on business analysis. On the other hand, task-related aspects, in particular stages 2-5, work towards forming the system that has been defined with appropriate emphasis on complete technical and human views. The system, once created, is not just a computer system, it is also composed of people performing jobs.

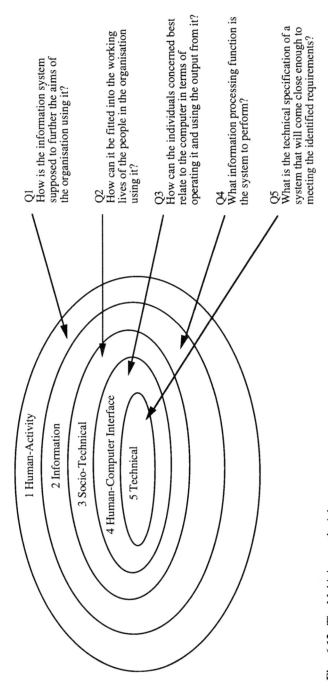

Q1
How is the information system supposed to further the aims of the organisation using it?

Q2
How can it be fitted into the working lives of the people in the organisation using it?

Q3
How can the individuals concerned best relate to the computer in terms of operating it and using the output from it?

Q4
What information processing function is the system to perform?

Q5
What is the technical specification of a system that will come close enough to meeting the identified requirements?

1 Human-Activity

2 Information

3 Socio-Technical

4 Human-Computer Interface

5 Technical

Fig. 6.12. The Multiview methodology

Another representation of the methodology, rather more simplistic but useful in providing an overview for discussion, is shown in Figure 6.12. Working from the middle outwards we see a widening of focus and an increase in understanding the problem situation and its related technical and human characteristics and needs. Working from the outside in, we see an increasing concentration of focus, an increase in structure and the progressive development of an information system.

Stage 1 - Analysis of human activity

This stage is based on Checkland (1981). The very general term human activity is used to cover any sort of organisation. This could be, for example, an individual, a company, a department within a larger organisation, a club or a voluntary body. They may all consider using a computer for some of their information systems.

The central focus of this stage of the analysis is to search for a particular view (or views). This Weltanschauung will form the basis for describing the systems requirements and will be carried forward to further stages in the methodology. This world view is extracted from the problem situation through debate on the main purpose of the organisation concerned, sometimes described using the terms 'raison d'etre', 'attitudes', 'personality' and so on. Examples of world view might be: "This is a business aimed at producing maximum long term profits" or "This is a hospital dedicated to maintaining the highest standards of patient care".

The phases within the methodology of this stage are shown in Figure 6.13. These sub-stages can be grouped into four main ones:

1) Perceiving the problem situation (sub-stages 1-3)
2) Constructing systems models (sub-stages 4-7)
3) Comparing the systems models to perceived reality (sub-stage 8)
4) Deciding on the comparison and then implementing the consequences of these decisions (sub-stages 9 and 10).

This is a simplification because there are several iterations not appearing in the diagram. Firstly, the problem solver, perhaps with extensive help from the problem owner, forms a rich picture of the problem situation. The problem solver is normally the analyst or the project team. The problem owner is the person or group on whose behalf the analysis has been commissioned. The 'picture', described in Section 2.6, represents a subjective and objective perception of the problem situation in diagrammatic and pictorial form, showing the structures of the processes and their relation to each other. Elements of the rich picture will include the clients of the system, the people taking part in it, the task being performed, the environment, and the owner of the system. This picture can be used to help the problem solver better understand the problem situation. It is also a very useful tool with which to stimulate debate, and it can be used as an aid to discussion between the problem solver and the problem owner. There are usually a number of iterations made during this process until the 'final' form of the rich picture is decided. The process here consists of gathering, sifting and interpreting data which is sometimes called 'appreciating the situation'. Drawing the rich picture is a subjective process. There is no such thing as a 'correct' rich picture. The main purpose of the diagram is to capture a holistic summary of the situation.

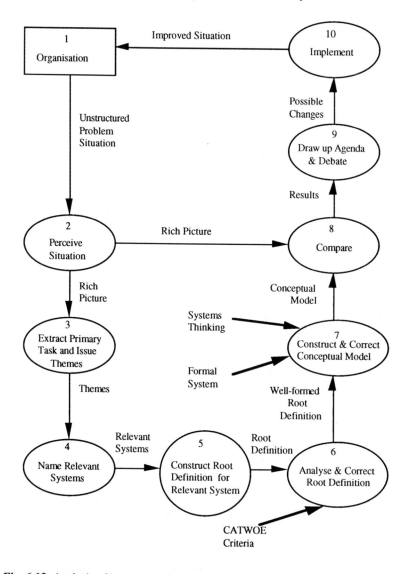

Fig. 6.13. Analysis of human activity systems to depict processes and products

From the rich picture the problem solver extracts problem themes, that is, things noticed in the picture that are, or may be, causing problems and/or it is felt worth looking at in more detail. The picture may show conflicts between two departments, absences of communication lines, shortages of supply, and so on.

Taking these problem themes, the problem solver imagines and names relevant systems that may help to relieve the problem theme. By relevant, we mean a way of looking at the problem which provides a useful insight, for example:

Problem theme   =   conflicts between two departments
Relevant systems   =   conflict resolution system or
                                     system for redefining departmental boundaries.

Several different relevant systems should be explored to see which is the most useful. It is at this stage that debate is most important. The problem solver and the problem owner must decide on which view to focus, that is how to describe their relevant system. For example, will the conflict resolution system be 'a system to impose rigid rules of behaviour and decision-making in order to integrate decisions and minimise conflict' or will it be 'a system to integrate decisions of actors through increased communication and understanding between departments' or even 'an arbitration system to minimise conflict between departments by focussing disagreements towards a central body'?

Once a particular view or root definition (also described in Section 2.6) has been decided upon, it can be developed and refined. Thus, by using the CATWOE check-list, the root definition can be analysed by checking that all necessary elements have been included. For example, have we identified the owner of the system? all the actors involved? the victims/beneficiaries of the system? and so on.

When the problem owner and the problem solver are satisfied that the root definition is well formed, a conceptual model (or activity model) of the system is constructed by listing the "minimum list of verbs covering the activities which are necessary in a system defined in the root definition.....". At this stage, therefore, we have a description in words of what the system will be (the root definition) and an inference diagram of the activities of what the system will do (the conceptual model).

Aids to forming the conceptual model include the check-list technique of comparing the system described against a formal systems model. This is a compilation of features which have to be present if a set of activities is to comprise a system capable of purposeful activity. This checking process ensures that no vital elements have been excluded. (Note that provided that the root definition has been well formed according to the CATWOE criteria, it is unlikely that discrepancies will occur at this stage.)

The completed conceptual model is then compared to the representation of the 'real world' in the rich picture. Differences between the actual world and the model are noted and discussed with the problem owner. Possible changes are debated, agendas are drawn up and changes are implemented to improve the problem situation.

In some cases the output of this stage is an improved human activity system and the problem owner and the problem solver may feel that the further stages in the Multiview methodology are unnecessary. In many cases, however, this is not enough. In order to go on to a more formal systems design exercise, the output of this stage should be a well formulated and refined root definition to map out the universe of discourse, that is the area of interest or concern. It could be a conceptual model which can be carried on to stage 2 - the analysis of entities, functions and events.

Stage 2 - Analysis of information
The purpose of this stage is to analyse the entities and functions of the application. Its input will be the root definition/conceptual model of the proposed system which was established in stage 1 of the process. Two phases are involved: the development of the functional model and the development of an entity model.

1) *Development of a functional model:* The first step in developing the functional model is to identify the *main* function. This is always clear in a well formed root definition. This main function is then broken down progressively into sub-functions (functional decomposition), until a sufficiently comprehensive level is achieved. This occurs when the analyst feels that the functions cannot be usefully broken down further. This is normally achieved after about four or five sub-function levels, depending on the complexity of the situation. A series of data flow diagrams, each showing the sequence of events, are developed from this hierarchical model. The hierarchical model and data flow diagrams are the major inputs into stage 3 of the methodology, which is the analysis and design of the socio-technical system.

2) *Development of an entity model:* In developing an entity model, the problem solver extracts and names entities from the area of concern. Relationships between entities are also established. The preceding stage in the methodology - analysis of the human activity systems - should have already given this necessary understanding and have laid a good foundation for this second stage. The entity model can then be constructed. The entity model, following further refinement, becomes a useful input into stages 4 and 5 of the Multiview methodology. Much of this stage will have already been carried out in the overall database project and this stage of Multiview will be minor compared to the development of the functional model under these circumstances. But it will still be carried out as a checking mechanism. Some data elements and relationships may have been missed in the earlier organisational data modelling exercise or the organisation itself may have changed in some way since that time and the data structures should reflect this change.

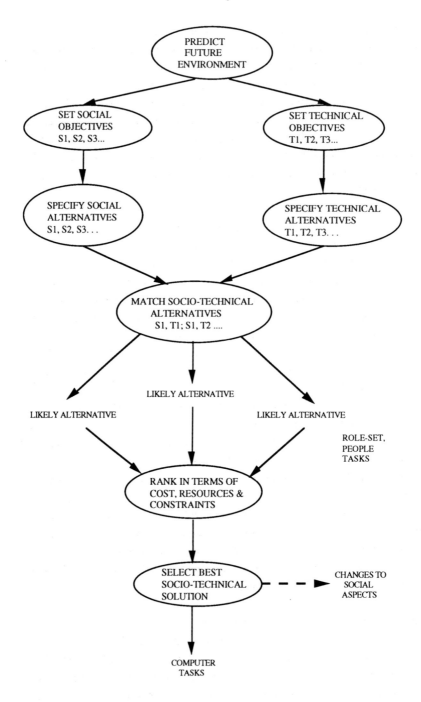

Fig. 6.14. Outline of socio-technical analysis and design

Stage 3 - Analysis and design of the socio-technical aspects

The philosophy behind this stage is that people have a basic right to control their own destinies and that, if they are allowed to participate in the analysis and design of the systems that they will be using, then the implementation, acceptance and operation of the system will be enhanced. It takes the view therefore that human considerations, such as job satisfaction, task definition, morale and so on, are just as important as technical considerations. The task for the problem solver is to produce a 'good fit' design, taking into account people and their needs and the working environment on the one hand, and the organisational structure, computer systems and the necessary work tasks on the other.

An outline of this stage is shown in Figure 6.14. The central concern at this stage is the identification of alternatives: alternative social arrangements to meet social objectives and alternative technical arrangements to meet technical objectives. All the social and technical alternatives are brought together to produce socio-technical alternatives. These are ranked, firstly in terms of their fulfilment of the above objectives, and secondly in terms of costs, resources and constraints - again both social and technical - associated with each objective. In this way, the 'best' socio-technical solution can be selected and the corresponding computer tasks, role-sets and people tasks can be defined.

The emphasis of this stage is therefore *not* on development, but on a statement of alternative systems and choice between the alternatives, according to important social and technical considerations.

It is also clear that, in order to be successful in defining alternatives, the groundwork in the earlier stages of the methodology is necessary and, in order to develop and implement the chosen system, we must continue to the subsequent stages.

An important technique applicable to this stage is **future analysis** (Land, 1982). This aids the analyst and user to predict the future environment so that they are better able to define and rank their socio-technical alternatives.

The outputs of this stage are the computer task requirements, the role-set, the people tasks, and the social aspects. The computer task requirements, the role-set and the people tasks become inputs to the next stage of the methodology, that is the design of the human-computer interface. The role-set, the people tasks, and the social aspects are also major outputs of the methodology.

Stage 4 - Design of the human-computer interface

Up to now, we have been concerned with what the system will do. Stage 4 relates to how, in general terms, we might achieve an implementation which matches these requirements. The inputs to this stage are the entity model derived in stage 2 of the methodology, and the computer tasks, role-set and people tasks derived in stage 3. This fourth stage is concerned with the technical design of the human-computer interface and makes specific decisions on the technical system alternatives. The ways in which users will interact with the computer will have an important influence on whether the user accepts the system.

A broad decision will relate to whether to adopt batch or on-line facilities. In on-line systems, the user communicates directly with the computer through a terminal or workstation. In a batch system, transactions are collected, input to the computer, and processed together when the output is produced. This is then passed to the appropriate user. Considerable time may elapse between original input and response.

Decisions must then be taken on the specific conversations and interactions that particular types of user will have with the computer system, and on the necessary inputs and outputs and related issues, such as error checking and minimising the number of key strokes. There are different ways to display the information and to generate user responses. The decisions are taken according to the information gained during stages 1 and 2 of Multiview.

Once human-computer interfaces have been defined, the technical requirements to fulfil these can also be designed. These technical requirements become the output of this stage and the input to stage 5, the design of technical subsystems. The human-computer interface definition becomes a major output of the methodology.

Stage 5 - Design of the technical aspects
The inputs to this stage are the entity model from stage 2 and the technical requirements from stage 4. The former describes the entities and relationships for the whole area of concern, whereas the latter describes the specific technical requirements of the system to be designed.

After working through the first stages of Multiview, the technical requirements have been formulated with both social and technical objectives in mind and also after consideration of an appropriate human-computer interface. Therefore, necessary human considerations are already both integrated and interfaced with the forthcoming technical subsystems.

At this stage, therefore, a largely technical view can be taken so that the analyst can concentrate on efficient design and the production of a full systems specification. Many technical criteria are analysed and technical decisions made which will take into account all the previous analysis and design stages. The final major outputs of the methodology are shown in Figure 6.15. These are the application, and information retrieval, database maintenance, control, recovery and monitoring aspects, and the database. The inputs and outputs necessary to support these are also defined.

It is likely that as a result of developing the database using the stages of this text described in Chapters 2 to 5, the database has already been created and the application uses the database without further amendment. On the other hand, the limited entity modelling phase of Multiview may have revealed data that is needed but which is not already held on the database. This will need to be collected, validated and stored on the database. The maintenance, control, recovery and monitoring of the database is described in this text in Chapters 12 and 13.

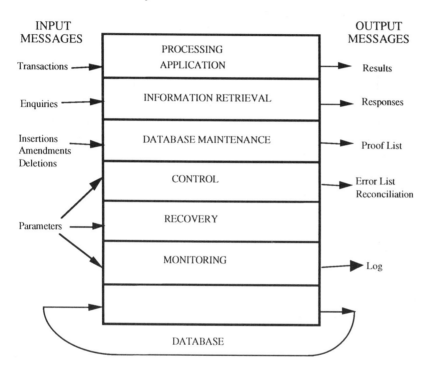

Fig. 6.15. Outline of the requirements for the technical specification

6.7 FURTHER READING

Avison, D. E & Fitzgerald, G (1988) *Information Systems Development: Methodologies, Techniques and Tools*, Blackwell Scientific Publications, Oxford. This text looks at a number of approaches to developing applications, including a more detailed description of the various techniques discussed in this chapter.

DeMarco, T (1979) *Structured Analysis and Systems Specification*, Prentice Hall,

Englewood Cliffs.

Gane, G & Sarson, T (1979) *Structured Systems Analysis*, Prentice Hall, Englewood Cliffs.

These two texts give a full description of the techniques used in structured analysis and design.

Mumford, E (1981) Participative Systems Design: Structure and Method, *Systems, Objectives and Solutions*, **1**.

Mumford, E (1985) Defining Systems Requirements to meet Business Needs: A Case Study Example, *Computer Journal*, **28**, 2.

Mumford, E, Land. F. F & Hawgood, J (1978) A Participative Approach to Computer Systems, *Impact of Science on Society*, **28**, 3.

Three papers which look at the participative approach to information systems development

Avison, D. E & Wilson, D (1991) Controls for Effective Prototyping, *Journal of Management Systems*, **3**, 1.

Dearnley, P. A & Mayhew, P. J (1983) In Favour of System Prototypes and their Integration into the Systems Development Cycle, *Computer Journal*, **26**, 1.

These two papers discuss different aspects of prototyping.

Avison, D. E & Wood-Harper, A. T (1990) *Multiview: an exploration in information systems development*, Blackwell Scientific Publications, Oxford.

This text describes Multiview in detail and presents six case studies where the approach was used.

PART THREE

THE DATABASE ENVIRONMENT

Chapter 7
Database Management Systems

7.1 INTRODUCTION

This chapter examines database management systems (DBMS). These are software packages which manage large and complex file structures. Fourth generation languages (4GL) and computer assisted software engineering (CASE) are looked at separately in Chapter 11. We will look at DBMS in general first, and then look at five DBMS products. These are IMS, IDMS, DB2, Adabas and Ontos. IMS is a hierarchical system (Section 7.2); IDMS a network system based on the Codasyl proposals (Section 7.3); DB2 is a relational system (Section 7.4); Adabas is a DBMS based on inverted files (Section 7.5); and finally we look at the object-oriented DBMS Ontos (Section 7.6). Oracle, which includes a relational DBMS as part of its facilities, is a fourth generation system/Case tool discussed in Chapter 11. The microcomputer DBMS products dBaseIV and Omnis are discussed in Chapter 9 which addresses database applications in a microcomputing environment.

DBMS make databases available to a large number of users and the sharing of data can reduce the average cost of data access as well as avoiding duplicate and therefore possibly inconsistent or irreconcilable data. Databases hold large amounts of data and the operations required on it can be complex. Correspondingly, DBMS are large, complex pieces of software. Users of databases do not directly access the database. Instead they access the DBMS which translates the data requirements into accesses to the database, makes the accesses required, and returns the results to the user in the form that the user requires.

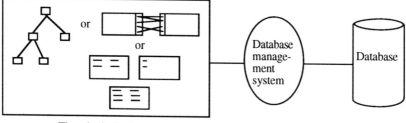

Three logical schema

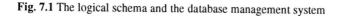

Fig. 7.1 The logical schema and the database management system

In Figure 7.1 the logical schema represents the view of the overall database seen by the database administrator. Codasyl called this overall view the schema. It could take a number of forms, for example, relational, hierarchical and network, depending on the particular database management system.

As we saw in Chapter 6, the user programs see only subsets of the logical schema, and these are called external views. The various users accessing the database via the DBMS may be user department managers and clerks as well as data processing professionals. These different users may require subsets of the logical schema, presented in different ways. They may access the database using 'user friendly' query languages on their systems. Access may also be made via user programs written in a conventional programming language such as Cobol or PL/1 which act as **host languages**. The subset of the host language which is used to access the database is usually called the data manipulation language. These host languages are procedural and the programmer has to know the set of logical procedures required to fulfil a particular request. This requires an in-depth knowledge of the language, but if the knowledge of the language has been acquired, the requests for database access need not be complicated nor difficult to write.

Query languages are usually somewhat less procedural and may be suitable for untrained computer users who may be making *ad hoc* enquiries of the database. A useful distinction between programming languages and query languages is to look at the former as concerned with the *how* of an operation, and the latter as being concerned with the *what*. One area of possible confusion is that 'query' languages are badly named in that they do usually offer ways of updating (changing) the data as well as accessing it in the form of a query. Many query languages are more difficult to use and more procedural than the 'ideal'. The most well known, SQL (Chapter 8), is somewhat disappointing in these respects though it has become a standard.

As we saw in Chapter 6, there are a number of formats for the interface between the query language and the user. Many require the user to use special commands; others a choice between options in a series of menus. These clearly make available the alternatives open to the untrained user, although they are less flexible than some alternative ways of specifying user requirements. Some DBMS require the users to state their requirements on a soft copy 'form', perhaps by using a light pen on the screen rather than the more conventional keyboard.

Perhaps the most 'user friendly' are those which use a near natural language interface. However there are lots of 'false friends', that is words in the query language having different meanings than their natural language meanings. Natural language is ambiguous, and computers require unambiguous input. Such systems usually require long and tedious clarification dialogues. Although query languages can be easy to use and are usually geared towards fast response, they can be less flexible, sometimes rather limited, and may also be less efficient than conventional programming languages.

Many DBMS provide alternative ways of access. This can be a useful facility as there are many types of user. Users can be untrained and intermittent in their use of the system. These casual users should be encouraged by its ease of use. Regular users may make frequent, perhaps daily, use of the database and are usually willing to learn a simple syntax. Other users will be professional users who are data processing people and will apply their long experience as computer and database users, and be concerned about efficiency of their work.

An important human intermediary will be the database administrator (DBA) who will be responsible for the design of the overall data structure (schema) and for ensuring that the required levels of privacy, security and integrity of the database are maintained. The DBA could be said to be the manager of the database and, because the design of the database involves trade-offs, will have to balance these conflicting requirements and make decisions on behalf of the whole organisation, rather than on behalf of any particular user or departmental objective. The role of the database administrator is discussed separately in Chapter 13.

The data model, which we have called the conceptual schema, was developed independently of both machine and software considerations. This means that a good data model can be formulated with the knowledge that it can be mapped on to a DBMS at a later stage. Its conversion to a logical schema can then be made and this will be in the form required by the particular DBMS used, usually a set of relations, hierarchies or networks. Some DBMS accept more than one data model type, for example, the user can input the data and data structures in the form of relations or hierarchies. The DBMS will also take care of the physical mapping onto storage media and its file organisation. This may be carried out using instructions from the DBA, who will choose between the alternative file organisation methods offered by the DBMS, as appropriate for the particular data sets.

These aspects are not the concern of the applications users. The DBA is involved in these decisions so as to ensure that the system is efficient. The separation of the physical storage structures from the user gives the user a high degree of data independence. Thus the users need not concern themselves with decisions relating to the storage structures and access strategies which were discussed in Chapter 5. It also means that if a data item type (say a field called customer name) is added to the database it will not be necessary to change programs that use the database, apart from those that are directly interested in the customer name. With conventional systems, all programs accessing a file containing a changed data structure (the customer file in this case) will have to be modified and recompiled.

This data independence means that even when the pointers, character representation, record blocking or access method are changed, this is not noticed by the users. Data independence is normally seen as one of the great advantages of DBMS. The degree of data independence will depend on the particular DBMS, but will at least imply that the user will be screened from changes in physical location of the data, changes in parts of the schema which are not of interest to the user and changes in the form of the data held. The appropriateness and sophistication of the data dictionary system used alongside the DBMS (Chapter 12) will also affect the degree of data independence of the system.

There are other advantages of the database approach which offset their cost and the complexity of setting them up. The degree of data duplication may well be reduced significantly. The DBA should be aware of any data duplication that does exist and be able to control it. There may be data duplication for good reason. If the same data is frequently required in two formats, it may well be efficient to store the data in both formats. Another example of efficient data duplication occurs where aggregates are stored. A particular total may be required frequently and therefore it is more efficient to store the aggregation than to calculate the total from its constituent elements each time it is required. The key factor is that the duplication is known to the DBA and is justifiable.

A DBMS may enable access to the data by a number of users who may be using different host languages and query languages. The sharing of data reduces the average cost, because the whole community pays for the data. New applications ought to be able to use the database conveniently. They may require separate external views to be defined, but the database may already cater for the data needs of the new applications. As we shall see in later chapters, the role of both the DBA and the data dictionary system are very important in helping to fulfil this function.

The database approach makes it possible to exercise a high degree of control in the use of the data resource. This control will help to maintain the quality and integrity of the data and allow security measures to be enforced. The DBMS is likely to provide help to the DBA in the form of validation checks, logs and copying facilities which will enable a successful restart should the system fail. Reports to the DBA will also be provided to help him maintain an efficient database.

In the following sections we look at a number of DBMS. A thorough discussion of the facilities of any DBMS would take a book in itself and therefore only a 'flavour' of the systems can be given here. Further, it is not intended to be a 'best buy' survey. Some features that are mentioned in regard to one DBMS are available in others but are not mentioned again to avoid repetition.

There are of course many criteria that ought to be used in evaluating DBMS. Three obvious criteria which we have already discussed are the user interface, the logical model type and the file organisation supported. Other important criteria are:

Cost: The cost of the software package itself and of maintaining it and keeping it operational. There is also the cost of any extra CPU (central processor) power, main memory and backing storage memory which will be necessary to ensure the efficient running of the database. There is also the personnel cost of training users and acquiring specialised staff.

Adaptation required: Although generalised DBMS are intended for most users, there will be some work required in adapting it to the particular installation and installing it. This will have cost and time implications. In this text we have ignored 'tailor made' DBMS, that is, a database system designed and developed for a particular organisation to be used only by that organisation. Situations are very rare where this would be more efficient than the purchase of a generalised DBMS package.

Help to database administrator: DBMS are usually large programs and can be slow and memory-hungry. Most systems provide usage statistics so that performance can be monitored. Some provide facilities to enable design alternatives to be simulated. This will enable the DBA to see which is the 'best' for the organisation. A further consideration is the help that the DBMS gives the DBA to enforce standards of database use. Its relationship with the data dictionary system is also important. Some DBMS have a data dictionary interface and the DBMS/DDS/DBA are expected to work together. Connected with this is the level of support that it offers to ensure that access cannot be gained by users who have not got access rights. Most DBMS will require password access to all levels of data. This will help to maintain the integrity (accuracy) of the data and the privacy of confidential information. The DBMS must also have good security features so that recovery can be made from a malfunction of the hardware or software.

Flexibility: Some DBMS are very flexible in that they can be used in batch or real-time mode, can be used by a number of types of user who require different language interfaces and styles of interface, and can run on a number of operating systems and hardware configurations. Database use will vary over time as the company expands or applications change. It is important that the investment in one DBMS is not lost because of such change.

Utilities: As well as the data dictionary system, a DBMS will provide utilities to perform some of the tasks necessary for database use such as back-up, file organisation, report generation, data compression and performance monitoring.

7.2   IMS - A HIERARCHICAL DBMS

IMS is somewhat out of date now (though still used) and has been replaced in many
IBM installations by DB2 (there are packages available which facilitate the migration of
IMS files to DB2 ones), but IMS is included here - even if briefly - as an example of a
hierarchical DBMS. IMS is a large package capable of processing many large files and
numbers of simultaneous users; it has database management, communications
management and other features. Like most texts, however, IMS will be equated with
the database system. IMS has been marketed by IBM since 1967 and the company has
improved the system over the years so that a data dictionary, database design aid,
performance analyser and monitor are now available.

The users' access to the database is made via IMS commands in DL/1 (the database
facility in IMS) which will be embedded in a host language such as Cobol, PL/1 or
IBM assembly language. IMS does not have an integrated query language: access to the
database is made using a user-written program. However IMS can be used with other
packages which will provide the required query language interface. An alternative
hierarchical DBMS called System2000 does have an integrated query language and the
user need only know the System2000 command language to access the database.

The DL/1 programs will include the users' particular view of their part of the
database (external view). This will be translated by IMS into the logical model, referred
to in IMS as the 'physical database'. There is a further mapping to the files on disk,
which means that there is a significant degree of data independence.

As for the physical storage of data, IMS provides for a number of file organisation
methods: sequential, indexed sequential, indexed direct access and direct access. IMS
also provides for inverted file structures (called secondary indexes in DL/1
terminology) for all these database organisation methods (with the exception of
sequential). The large number of options add to the complexity of the system, though
they are usually specified by the DBA and therefore this need not be looked on as a
fault. System2000, mentioned earlier, is a hierarchical system that uses only one
method, that of inverted files. These are also offered by Adabas, which is discussed in
Section 7.5.

In IMS terminology, each hierarchical structure defined to it is called a database.
Each record type in the structure is called a segment type and its attributes are called
fields. Thus for each IMS database, there will be a root segment type, ordered
according to a sequence field, followed by a number of child segments. In the original
'pure' hierarchical version of IMS, no child segment type could have more than one
parent segment type - m:n relationships could not be specified. The occurrences of the
root segment must be ordered, but the occurrences of child segments need not be

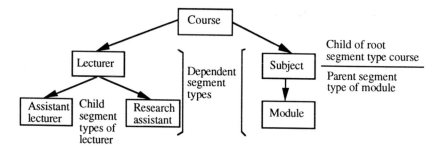

Fig. 7.2 A physical database type: course details

ordered. Figure 7.2 illustrates the IMS data model and its associated terminology.

In the figure, COURSE is the root segment type. LECTURER is both a child of the root segment type and parent of the ASSISTANT LECTURER and RESEARCH ASSISTANT segment types. These are child segment types of LECTURER. SUBJECT is a child of the root segment and parent of MODULE. Figure 7.3 shows one occurrence of the physical database which relates to the MSC1 course. Another occurrence is implied by the MSC2 root segment. Normally there will be pointers set up connecting the parent segment to the first occurrence of one of its child segments. Thus there will be a pointer from MSC1 to Clark and to Algol and also from Algol to Algol60, and so on. There will also be pointers within a segment, for example, between Clark and Jones.

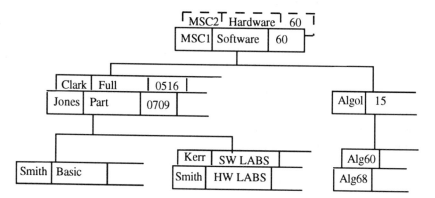

Fig. 7.3 Sample physical database occurrence

In later versions of IMS the strictly hierarchical approach has been contravened to allow users to link IMS databases. If, for example, there are two databases set up, one for courses and another for lecturers, the user might want to connect these as shown in

Figure 7.4. The link between the LECTURER segment type and the SUBJECT record type gives the latter two parents. In IMS terminology, COURSE, being on the same database, is said to be the 'physical parent', and LECTURER the 'logical parent' of SUBJECT. SUBJECT is the 'logical child' of LECTURER and the physical child of COURSE. The structure is still limited, as a segment type can have only one logical parent as well as only one physical parent. But this solution to the situation where two trees share a common segment type avoids some data redundancy.

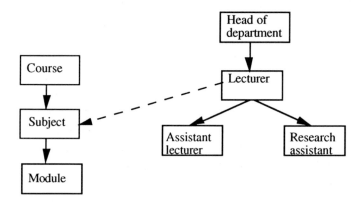

Fig. 7.4 IMS - logical parent

Each of these physical databases is defined by a Database Description (DBD). This is usually set up by the database administrator. In the DBD, the database and then each segment type is named. The size of the segment followed by details of all the fields (data elements) belonging to the segment are then provided. The sequence of these statements is important as the order of segments in the DBD reflects the hierarchical structure.

```
1  DBD      NAME=COURSEDB,ACCESS=HIDAM
2  SEGM     NAME=COURSE,PARENT=0,BYTES=31
3  FIELD    NAME=(COURSENO,SEQ,U),BYTES=4,START=1,TYPE=C
4  FIELD    NAME=CRSENAME,BYTES=20,START=5,TYPE=C
5  FIELD    NAME=CRSELGTH,BYTES=3,START=25,TYPE=C
6  SEGM     NAME=LECTURER,BYTES=31,PARENT=COURSE,BYTES=57
7  FIELD    NAME=(LECNAME,SEQ),BYTES=25,START=1,TYPE=C
8  FIELD    NAME=LECTIME,BYTES=4,START=26,TYPE=C
9  FIELD    NAME=LECTNO,BYTES=4,START=30,TYPE=C
10 SEGM     NAME=ASSTLECT,BYTES=25
```

etc.

20 LCHILD NAME=(SUBJECT,SUBJNO)

etc.

34 DBDGEN

35 FINISH

36 END

Statement 1 in the DBD names the database as COURSEDB and gives its access method (in this case HIDAM, or hierarchical indexed direct access method). Statement 2 names the root segment (COURSE) and gives its length in bytes. The root segment is the only segment that does not have a parent (parent=0). Statements 3 to 5 define the fields of a segment - their name, length, starting place in the database definition and type (characters in this case). COURSEDB has been defined as the field for ordering the data within the root segment. Thus record occurrences within the COURSEDB will be ordered (SEQ) in ascending value of COURSEDB, which will be unique for each segment occurrence (U means unique). The alternative (M) means multiple, which implies that there can be more than one occurrence of the given segment type under a common parent occurrence.

The number of bytes specified gives the size in characters of each segment and field. The reader may regard this method of specifying the field sizes as being somewhat machine-oriented. Child segments may be in a particular sequence if required (the LECTURER segment is ordered). The DBD and DBDGEN statements mark the beginning and end of the physical database description. FINISH and END are instructions to the IMS control programs to end the IMS job. IMS sub-schemas are defined in a similar (though not in exactly the same) way.

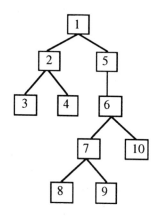

Fig. 7.5 IMS - hierarchical sequence

The hierarchy is specified by the sequence of the statements, from top to bottom and left to right. In Figure 7.5 the sequence follows the pattern of starting at the root segment and goes next to 2, being below it and to the left. As 2 is not at the bottom of that path, control passes below and to the left of it to 3. This is at the bottom of the path, so control passes to the parent of 3 and below right to 4. This segment is at the bottom of that path and its parent 2 is then called. This has no more paths to the bottom right and control passes to the root segment 1 and thereby to 5, 6, 7, to 8, back to 7 for 9 and back to 7 and then 6 for 10. At this point all the segment types have been processed.

Once the hierarchy has been set up, it is possible for users to access, update, add and delete the data using the DL/1 language within the host language program. The DL/1 statements in the data manipulation language (this term is not used by IBM) are extensions to the host language to call the database. The GET statement in the Cobol extension is used to access data on the database and can be in one of many forms, partly due to the complexities of hierarchies themselves. The GET UNIQUE (GU) retrieves the segment directly, at least it appears that it does to the user but it may be retrieved in fact via a search through pointers. GET NEXT (GN) retrieves the next record in the hierarchy according to the hierarchical sequencing scheme discussed above. GET NEXT WITHIN PARENT (GNWP) follows sequential segment retrieval under the current parent occurrence. This type of command allows a user to navigate around a database using the access paths that have been defined in the Data Definition Language. Unlike relational database systems, all access paths which might be needed have to be specified in advance when constructing the database.

The host language has to ensure that a user work area is provided where the instructions are embedded and for holding the data transferred to and from the database.

If it is required to REPLACE (REPL) or to DELETE (DLET) the segment, it must first be HELD to prevent others accessing it before the alteration is made. The GET statement becomes a GET HOLD statement such as GHU, GHN or GHWP. The add command INSERT (ISRT) is also used for database maintenance.

IMS offers a number of alternate ways to map the data structures to storage devices. These include sequential, indexed sequential, direct access and indexed direct access. A particular access method has to be chosen for each physical database (hierarchical data structure). Hierarchical Sequential Access Method (HSAM) provides sequential access to the entire database and is intended for magnetic tape files and is not therefore widely used. For the indexed sequential method (HISAM), the root segment type key is the prime key and it is also possible to allow the child segments of the root segment to be indexed or accessed sequentially.

For the direct access method (HDAM), the user has to supply a convenient randomising algorithm to be applied to the key of the root segment. In the case of a HIDAM file (indexed direct access), the root segments are stored in ascending order of key and accessed in a separate index. Other, lower level segments, are stored and accessed using pointer chains from their parent segment. Backward pointers are also catered for if required by the users.

Thus, although HDAM gives better direct root access and update time, root segments cannot be accessed sequentially by key as in the case of HIDAM. The range of choice does give the database administrator a considerable workload. Fortunately IMS provides tools which can help the designer by simulating the performance of IMS under different load conditions and design parameters. This design task is critical for the efficient working of the system.

7.3   IDMS - A CODASYL (NETWORK) DBMS

IDMS is probably the leading DBMS to be modelled on the Codasyl Database Task Group (DBTG) proposals and is available on a range of computers. It is capable of handling network data structures as well as hierarchies. IDMS terminology is similar to that used in the Codasyl reports. The record or record occurrence is the basic unit of addressable data which is itself sub-divided into data items. Similar record occurrences belong to a record type and related record types belong to a set type where one record is the owner and others are members. The records in a set are linked together using pointers. The owner points (NEXT) to the first member and so on. A chain is established because the last record points to the owner record. There may also be backward pointers (PRIOR) and pointers for all member records to the OWNER.

Hierarchies are established by a member (a record type) of one set being the owner of another set, indeed it can be the owner of a number of sets. Networks are established because multiple membership is allowed as well as multiple ownership. IMS' extension allows only one secondary membership. IDMS supports m:n relationships using the link records discussed in Section 4.6.

The schema, which is the Codasyl and IMS term for the logical model, is set up using the schema DDL commands, and this provides a complete description of the database. It names and describes all the areas, set occurrences, record occurrences, data items and data aggregates (groups of data items) that exist in the database. An example of part of a DDL run follows:

SCHEMA NAME IS WHOLESALER.
AREA NAME IS SUPPLIER-AREA.

PRIVACY LOCK FOR PROTECTED UPDATE.
AREA NAME IS CUSTOMER-AREA.
PRIVACY LOCK FOR EXCLUSIVE RETRIEVAL.

RECORD NAME IS SUPPLIER
   LOCATION MODE IS DIRECT SUPP-NO
      DUPLICATES ARE NOT ALLOWED
   WITHIN SUPPLIER-AREA.
   02 SUPP-NO   TYPE IS CHARACTER 8.
   02 SUPP-NAME   TYPE IS CHARACTER 25.
   02 SUPP-ADDRESS   TYPE IS CHARACTER 75.
   02 SUPP-AMNT-OWING TYPE IS INTEGER 10.

RECORD NAME IS CUSTOMER......etc.

The AREA concept, defined in earlier Codasyl reports, relates to physical storage aspects and hence reduces the data independence expected in a DBMS. It has been retained by IDMS although it was dropped by Codasyl in its 1978 Report. The record occurrences are stored on a page, which is a convenient, user-specified, unit of storage. These pages are grouped together into the area, a sub-division of the overall database. The privacy clause can be associated with each area so that they may be protected for retrieval or update or both. The clause is also available at the record level.

   A record's allocation to a particular page is located by one of the following 'location modes': CALC, VIA and DIRECT. If the CALC option is used, the record occurrence is stored on a page calculated by IDMS using a hashing (randomising) algorithm. The VIA location mode places the record via a particular set. This location mode is particularly suitable where the retrievals of the record type are carried out primarily as a member of the named set. If the DIRECT location mode is used, as in the above example, then the record is placed on or as close as possible to a user (that is, application program) specified page in an area. These location modes were specified in the original Codasyl proposals but dropped in the 1978 Report because, like the area concept, these are physical aspects of the database and do not relate to its logical design.

   Some records on the database may be required directly for some applications (CALC) and sequentially (VIA) for others. The DBA may exercise the power of assigning priorities to the conflicting procedures and may choose the option with the highest priority. Another possibility is to use the option VIA, and create an indexed set with the key of the record as the owner and the actual record as the member (Figure

7.6). This will improve retrieval times, but it does cause added complexity in the updating procedures. This trade-off between retrieval times and updating speed ought to be a prime consideration when defining set relationships.

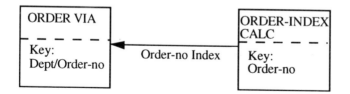

Fig. 7.6 The use of VIA with an index

Having set up the areas and records, it is necessary to describe the relationships between the records by set definitions.

SET NAME IS PURCHORD-SUPPLIER
   OWNER IS SUPPLIER
   ORDER IS SORTED BY DEFINED KEYS
      DUPLICATES ARE NOT ALLOWED
   MEMBER IS PURCHASE-ORDER
      INSERTION IS AUTOMATIC
      RETENTION IS FIXED
   KEY IS ASCENDING PONUM IN PURCHASE-ORDER

SET NAME IS PURCHORD-PRODUCT
   OWNER IS PURCHASE-ORDER
   MEMBER IS PRODUCT.......etc.

This definition is followed by END SCHEMA.

The first line names the set, and the owner and member records of the set are then named. Duplicate values for keys are not permitted in this particular set definition. The order statement specifies where member records are 'placed'. This is a logical not a physical placement. The INSERTION statement defines rules for record creation and the RETENTION statement defines rules for record retention. The key is used as a sort control for a member record of a sorted set.

Set membership can be explicitly established by a CONNECT statement. If set membership is automatic, the member record is made a member of the set whenever an occurrence of a member record is stored in the database using the STORE statement of the DML. Another aspect of set descriptions is the way in which records are placed in a set. They can be ordered and the order FIRST indicates that new members are placed at the beginning of the list. Member records can also contain pointers backwards (PRIOR) and to owner records. There is also a privacy mechanism for a set and there can be a lock for FIND, ORDER, INSERT or REMOVE.

Each record in IDMS is actually divided into two parts: a prefix area, which contains the pointers necessary to maintain the data relationships with other records, and the data area. Each record is connected by pointers to the other records in a set occurrence. The pointer consists of the page number and the line number of the stored record. In fact the Device and Media Control Language (DMCL) was not specified in the Codasyl proposals and is defined in IDMS in order to set up the mapping of the logical pages described above to physical blocks on disk and other physical considerations. Its exact format will depend on the particular hardware used.

As well as the SCHEMA DDL, IDMS (like Codasyl) provides a SUBSCHEMA DDL (to describe the external, user views of the data) in Cobol which consists of a:

1) TITLE DIVISION, which names the subschema and identifies the underlying schema
2) MAPPING DIVISION, which defines the aliases which the user wishes to give to sets, records, and data items
3) STRUCTURE DIVISION, which has three sections as follows:
   - REALM SECTION, the realm being the logical subset of the schema database
   - SET SECTION, which lists the set types
   - RECORD SECTION, which list all the schema records required by the user, with details of the items in the records, such as type and length.

The list is followed by the statement END SUBSCHEMA.

IDMS, then, is similar to the Codasyl proposals in most respects, having a schema and subschema data definition language which are processed by three 'compilers'. The term compiler here is not inappropriate as the language specified by Codasyl does not seem totally unfamiliar to applications programmers used to Cobol Data Division formats. However, much of the terminology, for example, sets, areas, and schema, will be new to Cobol programmers not working in a database environment, because the original Cobol language is file-oriented, not database oriented.

Although the Codasyl DBTG proposed a host language data manipulation language embedded originally in Cobol, IDMS has added to this basic system a report generating system called IDMS/CULPRIT which will write reports on the contents of the IDMS database and an ON-LINE QUERY FACILITY. Nevertheless, IDMS is essentially a host language system. Access to the database by applications will normally be made using Cobol, PL/1 and other languages having a 'CALL' statement. The programs are preprocessed by an IDMS preprocessor before compilation in the host language. This changes DML commands into IDMS subroutine calls.

The IDMS DML commands correspond very much to the Codasyl data manipulation language proposals with one or two minor changes such as the addition of a command OBTAIN (which is a combination of FIND and GET in Codasyl terminology). FIND and GET can still be used separately. The FIND function locates the required record occurrence and GET puts it into a user-defined working storage area.

Unlike IMS, which does not have OPEN and CLOSE statements because they are carried out automatically by the IMS system, IDMS has four control statements: INVOKE, OPEN, CLOSE and IF. The sub-schema is specified by the INVOKE statement and the OPEN statement makes available areas within the sub-schema to be accessed. The OPEN statement has a number of options depending on the type of access (update, retrieval), and the levels of protection which will depend on whether other users should be locked out whilst the present user has access. The CLOSE statement closes all areas previously opened and the IF statement tests whether a set occurrence is, or is not, empty.

A fundamental concept in IDMS and the Codasyl DML is that of **currency**. As we saw in Chapter 4, the user navigates using pointers around the database and the position at any point is the current record in a current set. This also places it in relation to the parent record in a set type.

The FIND statement (or, if preferred, the OBTAIN statement) has a number of options depending on the type of access. Many options relate to the current record. However, the direct access form is:

FIND record name RECORD USING keyname

Once within a particular set or area, the FIND statement can include NEXT, PRIOR, LAST, nth (an integer), or FIRST record of a particular set or area, or OWNER of a set. The options NEXT or PRIOR relate to the record presently being processed: the next record on the list or the previous record. The options FIRST, LAST or nth refer to that particular record in a set or area. The OWNER locates the owner record in a set. All these options relate in one way or another to the current record.

Pointers are required to be able to support these alternatives. These are addresses, usually relative addresses, of the record to which the pointer relates. Each pointer requires four bytes; therefore one record occurrence participating as a member of two set types requires pointers to owner, next and prior for the first set type and next and prior pointers for the second set type, a total of 20 bytes reserved for set linkage. GET FIRST and GET LAST can be processed by going through a number of GET PRIOR or GET NEXT statements.

There are also five modification statements in the IDMS data manipulation language

(DML). These are STORE and DELETe (for adding or deleting a record on the database), MODIFY (to replace a record in the database), INSERT or REMOVE (to make or cancel a record as a member of an occurrence of a set type). In some versions, there are CONNECT and DISCONNECT statements.

The facility of locating a particular record is, like IMS, complex because of the way a record is searched for in the set structure. However, IDMS has the particular advantage of being based on the Codasyl proposals which are a well-respected standard for DBMS. In addition, it provides a number of routines for the database administrator, on-line access and the report generator Culprit.

There is now a version of IDMS which has the features mentioned above, but with relational capabilities, called IDMS/R. However, we will look at relational systems using DB2 as an example product.

7.4   DB2 - A RELATIONAL DBMS

Having looked at hierarchical and network DBMS, we consider DB2 which is IBM's relational DBMS product. Many users of IMS (Section 7.2) opted for DB2 either as a replacement (because relational systems are more flexible and easier to use) or as well as IMS, keeping the latter for large applications. However, as the efficiency of relational systems improves, it is expected that in such situations IMS will eventually be phased out. An IBM utility exists, called Data Extract (DXT) which extracts data from IMS databases and converts it to a sequential file which in turn can be loaded into a DB2 database.

The main interface with DB2 is SQL, and in view of its importance we devote the whole of Chapter 8 to SQL. The discussion of DB2 will therefore be rather cursory. Readers should note that although SQL is a 'standard' there are many variants on this standard. The version of SQL discussed in Chapter 8 is based on that of DB2. Chapter 8 describes how relations (or tables in DB2 terminology) are created, changed and deleted through the data definition part of SQL. It also shows how data is retrieved through the SQL SELECT statement and updated, deleted and added to using the various SQL data manipulation commands. Further, the DB2 base and view tables are also described (base tables are physical relations which are stored physically, and views are logical relations which are derived from base tables for user convenience, but are not stored physically). We will therefore not consider the detailed SQL commands in this chapter.

There are many components of DB2, but four are evident to the users. These are the precompiler, the 'bind' component, the run time supervisor and the stored data manager.

- *Precompiler:* SQL in DB2 can be used interactively (as the term query language implies), but SQL statements can also be embedded in a host language such as Cobol, PL/1, Fortran or IBM Assembler. The SQL statements will be recognised by the precompiler and replaced by the appropriate CALL statements in the host language to the database.

- *Bind:* This combines the SQL statements (which could be from a host language or ad hoc query language) and optimises these statements into an efficient application plan.

- *Run time supervisor:* This oversees the application, that is, the running of the SQL statements, at run time, ensuring that the application plan produced at the bind stage is followed.

- *Stored data manager:* This manages the physical database. It stores and retrieves records according to the application plan.

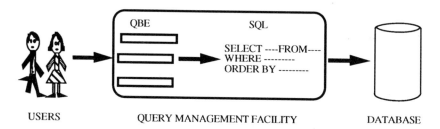

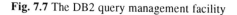

USERS   QUERY MANAGEMENT FACILITY   DATABASE

Fig. 7.7 The DB2 query management facility

DB2 is often run with a separate IBM product called the Query Management Facility (QMF). As seen in Figure 7.7, this is used as a front-end to DB2, in other words the user uses the QMF facilities and the QMF requests are translated into SQL statements which perform the database manipulations. QMF has a report generator (see Section 11.2) and also a Query-by-Example (QBE) facility. This is used as an interface for specifying queries, but rarely data definitions, which are normally specified using SQL. QBE was introduced in Section 4.4.

We saw in Section 4.4 how the QBE system can generate templates which are filled in by the user to produce a report. The user enters the name of the table and the system starts to fill in the template by supplying attribute names. The user requests information on particular attributes (marked with a P) and the system provides the information required. Figure 7.8 is a modification of Figure 4.12, in that a conditional statement has been added: that only tuples where the attribute 'pay/date' is more than 1500 are printed. This 'pay/date' figure is not included in the report. Further, the tuples are listed in ascending order of employee number ('AO'). Aggregation functions, such as sum, average, minimum and maximum values can also be requested using QBE.

(a)

EMPL NO	NAME	STATUS	PAY/DATE	TAX/DATE	SALARY

(b)

EMPL NO	NAME	STATUS	PAY/DATE	TAX/DATE	SALARY
P: AO	P	P	> 1500		P

(c)

EMPL NO	NAME	STATUS	SALARY
756	SMITH	FULL	12000
787	JONES	FULL	15000

Fig. 7.8 QBE example

A variety of conditional statements are possible using QBE. An additional constraint to that shown in Figure 7.8, ('= PART'), could be placed in the status box so that only part-time employees are included in the report. The user might also specify a range of values, such as 'pay/date' >1500 and <2500, and only records which conform to that range are printed. In this case, the user requests two 'pay/date' columns and one of the conditions in the range is placed in the first and the other in the second. Sometimes conditions may be quite complex, and QBE provides a separate condition box for specifying these conditions.

Updates can be performed on the tables. Thus to effect a salary increase of 20% 'across-the-board', the user keys in the statement '_*1.2' under the column headed 'salary'. In this case the user has to denote this by 'U' for update (as against 'P' for print). Queries that are frequently required can be stored by name and recalled as required.

QBE proves much easier to use than SQL. Commands are not necessary. It is 'natural' to use because the user interface is in the form of tables. The user specifies requests in a tabular form and receives responses in tables. Again, compared to SQL, there are far fewer key strokes necessary. But the requests need to be relatively simple for QBE to be effective.

Like most commercial DBMS, the DB2 product also includes facilities to ensure the security of data in the database, that the privacy of personal or key commercial data is respected and measures are available to prevent the possibility of two or more users updating the same data at the same time where data is shared between users (concurrency control). The System Catalog part of DB2 provides information, such as the definitions of base tables, views, indexes, users and applications and can itself be queried using SQL. In other words it has many of the features expected in a data dictionary (Chapter 12), but not all!, to support the work of the database administrator (Chapter 13).

7.5   ADABAS - AN INVERTED FILE DBMS

Adabas is a DBMS based on inverted file structures (Section 5.5). It can also support relational, hierarchical and Codasyl-type logical data structures. It does use tables although there is no 'official' relational data manipulation language. Tables are joined (or 'coupled' in Adabas terminology) on a common attribute. This also allows hierarchies and networks to be defined to the database.

Like many other DBMS, it has opted for a host language DML, again those languages having a CALL facility. However, there is a query language provided called 'Adascript'. The data is mainly stored physically as partially inverted files, although direct access may be used to retrieve records. It is an unusual system in that when records are added to the database they are allocated a permanent internal sequence number (ISN) which is used both to access records and to couple files. Adabas also compresses data so that the extra storage overhead for ISNs is not evident. Thus spaces in an alphabetic item or leading zeros in a numeric item will be compressed out of data held in storage but edited in again for users when accessed by them.

In Figure 7.9, the inverted list shows the internal sequence numbers of the keys. There is one occurrence of Jones (ISN is 3) and three occurrences of Brown (ISNs of 1, 4, and 6). Access to the inverted file may provide the answer to a query (for example, 'How many people called Brown are on the database?'). If other information in the record is required, the ISN is converted to an actual address via the address convertor (ISNs 1 and 2 are in block 1) and so the data record can be accessed.

To set up data relationships between records it is necessary to define one or more keys (called 'descriptors') which ensure its inclusion in the index. A descriptor can be a field, a number of fields or a part of a field. A record type may have one or more descriptors. Files can be coupled on the basis of this descriptor. Two files are shown in Figure 7.10. If Student Number is a descriptor of both, the coupled search 'What are the names of students who passed the exams?' could be made. Table (file) 2 can be

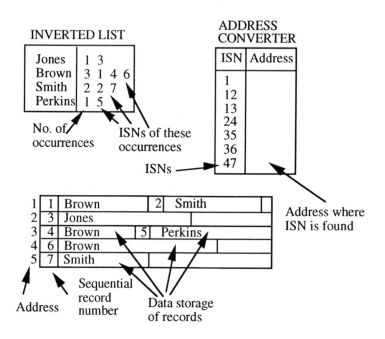

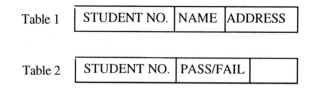

Fig. 7.9 Adabas record storage system

used to find the student numbers of those who passed, and with these descriptors, their names can be obtained from table 1.

If name on table 1 and pass/fail on table 2 were also made descriptors, that is, kept in the inverted files, the above request could be fulfilled without access to the data storage areas.

Table 1

STUDENT NO.	NAME	ADDRESS

Table 2

STUDENT NO.	PASS/FAIL	

Fig. 7.10 Two Adabas tables to be coupled

If files are coupled so that a particular value of a descriptor occurs once on one file and a number of times on another, a hierarchy is defined. If another value of the same descriptor occurs more than once on the first file and once on the second, a network is described. Adabas does not differentiate - and checks are not made - to ensure that particular key values are not repeated.

Data manipulation via a host language is achieved using a CALL statement with parameters which will specify: the command to be executed, file number, format of records or fields to be retrieved, space for the record retrieved, information on the search itself (the Boolean operators AND, OR, BUT NOT, TO (value) of top field value required), and the descriptor values. The command can specify any sorting that is to be carried out before returning the values. The number of ISNs satisfying the enquiry is returned and this enables the user then to choose whether only some or all of the 'hits' need be retrieved.

There are five basic commands for Adabas data manipulation: FIND, READ, UPDATE, ADD and DELETE.

The FIND command retrieves a list of ISNs that satisfy the search criteria (descriptor values) specified as part of the command. As described above, it may include Boolean operators and may sort the hits, as well as keeping a count of the ISNs found. These searches may be the result of coupling, as well as from one file.

The READ command retrieves from a file an entire record or selected fields from it. Using the ISN, the required record can be obtained randomly. Frequently, such a command follows a FIND, where records to be READ are identified. The READ statement can be used to retrieve all records in the file in the sequence in which they are stored. This will be efficient as the address convertor is not used at all. The READ statement can also be used to sort the items retrieved.

The UPDATE command modifies fields in a record having specified its ISN, the ADD command adds a new record to a file, and the DELETE command deletes the record with a given ISN.

The privacy and security features of Adabas are thorough. For example, files and fields can be protected against unwarranted access by passwords and these may be 'scrambled', that is, ciphered so that a copy of the contents of the storage area would not help in searching for a password. Users are given an authorisation level for a file and a field. There is a separate allocation for access (read) and update (write). These can be any level between 0 (lowest) and 14 (highest). Similarly each field and file has a security level. For access rights, the user's access level must be greater than or equal to the security level. As protection is given to the field as well as file, a user may be able to access a logical file (for example, employee), but not a particular element within it (for example, salary).

7.6   ONTOS - AN OBJECT-ORIENTED DBMS

Ontos (Andrews, Harris and Sinkel, 1991) is a successor product to Vbase (Andrews

& Harris, 1987 and Elmasri & Navathe, 1989). It is an object-oriented DBMS which is available commercially. As would be expected from such a product, the data management and programming language aspects are integrated: all data is represented as objects and the programming language manipulates objects. The Ontos DBMS supports complex objects, object identity and inheritance, features which we identified as important for object-oriented systems in Section 4.9. Each object is defined by a unique identifier (UID), described as object identity in that section, which enables different versions and different logical identifiers for any given object.

The DBMS also has the general features expected in any DBMS, such as the ability for users to share data (but with concurrency control). For example, users may share data using a local area network, on a variety of hardware platforms. Although a database may be held on a single node, Ontos is a distributed database (Chapter 10). Security features, such as the ability to make back-ups and recover from a system failure, are available. The aim is to produce vastly improved performance over relational databases for suitable application types, such as computer-aided design (CAD). The user has control over memory use and other physical aspects to help achieve this aim.

The first version of Ontos supports C++ as the application program interface, but other interfaces are expected in later versions. It is an extension to C++, the class library, which facilitates aggregates and classes for schema definition as well as support for versions. Aggregate classes include dictionaries, sets, arrays and lists. Vbase, its predecessor, used another extension of the C programming language called C object processor (COP). This argues for the status of C++ as a possible standard object language. As well as an applications language, C++ is used as the schema definition language.

A variation of SQL, called object SQL, is also supported by Ontos, and SELECT queries of the type discussed in Chapter 8 (having the structure SELECT ... FROM ... WHERE) are used to generate various reports as well as creating *ad hoc* queries. The concept of a table in SQL includes collections of objects such as classes and aggregates. The extensions to SQL have enabled one-to-many relationships to be expressed via aggregate objects, rather than join operations, through extensions to the WHERE clause. The SQL interface can be accessed from applications programs or as an interactive query facility.

In this section we have provided a brief overview of Ontos. These are early days in object-oriented databases, but Ontos does provide a possible direction and such databases are likely to have considerable impact on the database scene in the next few years.

7.7 FURTHER READING

Date, C. J (1990) *An Introduction to Database Systems, Volume 1,* 5th ed, Addison-Wesley, London.

Elmasri, R & Navathe, S. B (1989) *Fundamentals of Database Systems,* Benjamin/Cummings, Redwood City, Ca.

McFadden, F. R & Hoffer, J. A (1991) *Database Management,* 3rd ed, Benjamin/Cummings, Redwood City, Ca.

Pratt, C. J (1987) *Database Systems: Management and Design,* Boyd & Fraser, Boston.

There are a number of excellent texts which include a detailed description of various DBMS, and the above are among that list.

Chapter 8
SQL

8.1 INTRODUCTION

In Chapter 3 we considered the advantages of relational modelling and normalisation and in Chapter 4 we looked at the relational algebra operations, including union, intersection, difference, product, project, select and join, which are the basic operations for manipulating relations in a relational database. Any data manipulation can be performed on a relational database using this language; it is relationally complete, but the language itself is not easy to use and few commercial DBMS languages are based on the relational algebra. The major disadvantage of the relational algebra is that it is necessary to specify exactly how to execute the query operations, including their sequencing.

In Chapter 4 we also looked at the relational calculus and Codd's data sub language DSL ALPHA which is also relationally complete, but which is more oriented towards expressing user requests in a way that the user might construct, that is, specifying what is required, rather than how the result will be obtained. It is a development of this relational calculus that has become the standard language on relational DBMS. This language is SQL (Structured Query Language), and is used on many DBMS, both on small and large computers, including DB2, SQL/DS, Oracle and Unify. The relational DBMS discussed in this text, DB2 (Chapter 7) and Oracle (in the context of a 4GL and Case tool, in Chapter 11), use SQL as the main data language, and the language of Ingres, Quel, is not too dissimilar (see Chapter 14). Further, because of user demand for the standard language, it is possible to obtain an SQL 'add-on' for the Ingres DBMS. dBaseIV, discussed in Chapter 9 in the context of a microcomputer DBMS, now also has an SQL interface.

Although 'Structured Query Language' would suggest it is only suitable for query processing, the language is now comprehensive, having statements for data definition, query and update. It is therefore both a data manipulation language and a data definition language (Section 4.1). However, for complex processing it is usual to embed SQL statements in a host language such as Cobol, PL/1 and Pascal. This is called embedded SQL.

Unfortunately, though SQL is commonly used on relational DBMS, and is a standard in that sense, there are many versions; indeed there seems to be a different version for each DBMS. There have been attempts to standardise SQL, for example,

ISO, 1987. The standard was to:

- Specify the syntax and semantics of SQL data definition language and data manipulation language
- Define the data structures and operations for designing, accessing, maintaining, controlling and protecting an SQL database
- Enable modules containing SQL definitions to be portable across DBMSs with SQL interfaces
- Specify a minimum and complete standard so that different products (those capable of being run on micros or mainframes) could conform to either a minimum or complete SQL product.

These are all laudable aims. Unfortunately, however, commercial interests have so far prevented an SQL standard from being adopted by all DBMS that have an SQL interface. This is a case of history repeating itself as there have been many versions of Cobol and other third generation languages, despite the ANSI standard, as each supplier produces a version that is 'better than the standard'. However, using the short introduction to SQL presented in this book, which is based on the DB2 dialect, it is to be hoped that users will be able to get started using their relational DBMS by setting up data definitions, entering the data and processing queries. This chapter is not, of course, a replacement for the particular user manual, nor is it a complete course on SQL!

8.2   DATA DEFINITION

There are three basic commands for data definition: CREATE TABLE, ALTER TABLE and DROP TABLE (SQL uses the more inexact but more popular language of table, row and column, rather than relation, tuple and attribute). The CREATE TABLE command specifies a new relation; the ALTER TABLE command is used to add attributes to a relation: and DROP TABLE is used for deleting a relation. Some implementations of SQL permit specification of key fields using a variant of the CREATE TABLE command. Others, such as DB2, have a separate CREATE INDEX command and we will describe this alternative. Some have both.

The CREATE TABLE command sets up a new relation by giving it a name and detailing its attributes. In turn, each attribute is given a name, a data type and sometimes some constraints on possible values. The data type can be numeric (INTEGER, FLOAT (floating point) or DECIMAL (i,j) where i is the number of digits and j is the number following the decimal point). Character fields are specified by CHAR (n) where n is the number of characters or VARCHAR (n) for fields of varying length but not exceeding n characters and there are others, such as DATE (used to store calendar dates), SMALLINT

LECTURER-MODULE

MODULE	LECTURER-NAME	N0-OF-WEEKS
1	Clarke	10
1a	Goodwin	10
1b	Goodwin	10
2	Knight	10
2a	Collins	10
2b	Baker	10
2c	Jagger	10
3	Fisher	10
3a	Oldham	10
4	Glenn	20

ATTENDANCE

STUDENT-NAME	MODULE	LECTURER-NAME
Ashworth	1	Clarke
Ashworth	1b	Goodwin
Ashworth	2	Knight
Ashworth	2a	Collins
Ashworth	3	Fisher
Ashworth	3a	Oldham
Ashworth	4	Glenn
Atkins	1	Clarke
Atkins	1a	Goodwin
Atkins	2	Knight
Atkins	2b	Baker
Atkins	3	Fisher
Atkins	3a	Oldham
Atkins	4	Glenn
Johnson	1	Clarke
Johnson	1a	Goodwin
Johnson	2	Knight
Johnson	2c	Jagger
Smith	1	Clarke
Smith	1b	Goodwin
Smith	2a	Collins
Smith	3	Fisher
Smith	3a	Oldham
Smith	4	Glenn
Perkins	3	Fisher
Perkins	3a	Oldham
Perkins	4	Glenn

STUDENT

STUDENT NAME	YEAR-OF-COURSE
Ashworth	1
Atkins	1
Johnson	1
Smith	1
Perkins	3

Fig. 8.1 The relations associated with an MSc course

(SMALL INTEGER), and LONGVAR CHAR (LONG, VARIABLE LENGTH, CHARACTER).
Constraints, such as NOT NULL and UNIQUE, may be specified (for example, for key
attributes). The CREATE TABLE command sets up the relation definitions on the DBMS

CREATE TABLE STUDENT	(STUDENT_NAME	VARCHAR(40)
	NOT NULL	
	YEAR_OF_COURSE	INTEGER);

CREATE TABLE LECTURER_MODULE		
	(MODULE	VARCHAR(3)
	NOT NULL	
	LECTURER_NAME	VARCHAR(40)
	NOT NULL	
	NO_OF_WEEKS	INTEGER);

CREATE TABLE ATTENDANCE	(STUDENT_NAME	VARCHAR(40)
	NOT NULL	
	MODULE	VARCHAR(3)
	NOT NULL	
	LECTURER_NAME	VARCHAR(40)
	NOT NULL);	

Fig. 8.2 Creating the SQL relation definitions associated with an MSc course

and these are called **base tables**. Figure 8.2 shows the SQL statement to set up the relations shown as Figure 8.1 (we will show later how the data is input). Two of these relations were used in the explanation of the logical schema (Chapter 4).

The ALTER TABLE command is used to add an attribute to the relation, for example,

ALTER TABLE STUDENT ADD A_LEVEL_SCORE INTEGER

will add a new attribute for the qualification to the relation called STUDENT and

ALTER TABLE LECTURER_MODULE ADD MIN_A_LEVEL_SCORE
INTEGER

will add a new attribute laying down minimum qualifications for a particular module in the relation LECTURER_MODULE. This ability to add an attribute to a relation already containing data is not found in all database systems (though very welcome and useful). With some DBMS, such a requirement would mean redefining the schema and reloading the database (which requires shutting down the system to applications whilst this is carried out).

The DROP TABLE command deletes the relation, for example,

DROP TABLE ATTENDANCE

will delete the relation called ATTENDANCE.

Relations are usually accessed either sequentially or through the use of indexes. The

CREATE INDEX command is used to specify one or more attributes in a relation which we want to index. The value(s) of the attribute(s) may or may not be unique. When data updates lead to changes in the relation, SQL will automatically update the corresponding data in the indexes. An index makes accesses based on the value of the attribute which is indexed much faster, particularly for large relations, but they can be expensive to maintain when updating and require additional storage. Thus:

CREATE INDEX STUDENT

ON STUDENT_NAME

will create an index for the STUDENT relation using the attribute STUDENT_NAME. If the attribute is a key, then the following version of the command will be used:

CREATE UNIQUE INDEX STUDENT

ON STUDENT_NAME

Indexes can be dropped using:

DROP INDEX STUDENT

although indexes of key attributes should not be dropped. SQL also enables the user to add COMMENTS, specify synonyms through the CREATE SYNONYM, and other features for documentation.

8.3   DATA RETRIEVAL

The SELECT command is the only command for querying the database, but it has many variants. The command has three clauses as follows:

SELECT attribute list

FROM table list

WHERE condition

The attribute list contains the names of those attributes whose values are to be retrieved; the table list is a list of the relation names required to process the query; and condition is a Boolean expression which identifies the tuples to be retrieved.

Thus, in order to find the name of the lecturer who teaches module 1, the SELECT statement will be:

SELECT LECTURER_NAME

FROM LECTURER_MODULE

WHERE MODULE='1'

This would require a SELECT and a PROJECT if we were using the relational algebra discussed in Section 4.3. Thus the SQL SELECT and the relational algebra SELECT statements should not be confused.

A test to ensure that a student called Atkins has the minimum qualifications for module 3a would require the two ALTER statements made earlier:

ALTER TABLE STUDENT ADD A_LEVEL_SCORE INTEGER

ALTER TABLE ATTENDANCE ADD MIN_A_LEVEL_SCORE INTEGER

and the following SELECT statement

SELECT A_LEVEL_SCORE, MIN_A_LEVEL_SCORE

FROM STUDENT, ATTENDANCE

WHERE STUDENT_NAME='ATKINS' AND MODULE='3A'

This would require a SELECT, PROJECT and JOIN in the relational algebra because the STUDENT and ATTENDANCE relations would need to be joined on student name, then the tuple containing Atkins and the required module would be selected, and finally the two attributes containing the minimum qualification for the module and Atkins' qualification would be projected for the user to compare. The SQL system effectively translates the SQL SELECT into the relational algebra equivalent. The join aspect needs to be carried out on a common attribute of both relations (perhaps a primary key on one and a foreign key of the other). A foreign key is an attribute of one relation which is not a key, but this particular attribute is a primary key of another relation.

There are a large number of variants to this statement, for example those requiring complex Boolean expressions in the WHERE statement consisting of combinations of ANDs, ORs, =, + and - and even BETWEEN and LIKE in some implementations where BETWEEN gives a range of values and LIKE helps the searcher where the exact value is not known; or those requiring some computation on the SELECT expression, so that fields are added using SUM or the minimum, maximum or average values of an attribute are obtained using MAX, MIN or AVG; and those requiring large numbers of relations to obtain all the information. Thus, the following would obtain the average and total number of weeks of modules that the students Goodwin and Knight take:

SELECT AVG (NO_OF_WEEKS), SUM (NO_OF_WEEKS)

FROM LECTURER_MODULE

WHERE STUDENT_NAME='GOODWIN' OR STUDENT_NAME='KNIGHT'

and the following will obtain the names of students taking modules 1, 1a or 1b and report on them in alphabetical order of the student names:

SELECT STUDENT_NAME

FROM ATTENDANCE

WHERE MODULE IN (1,1A,1B)

ORDER BY STUDENT_NAME

Some queries require nested SELECT statements which are complex to write correctly.

One variation enables retrieval where the user is not sure of the exact content of an index field, for example:

WHERE (STUDENT_NAME LIKE SMI%)

In this example, the % represents zero or more characters, and this would retrieve

Smith and Smithson and others (if they exist in the database). The unknown character % can be placed in the beginning, amongst or at the end of a character string. This can also be represented by the underline character _, rather than the %, but in this case the exact number of missing characters has to be known and represented by the exact number of underline characters. Thus Smi_ _ would retrieve Smith but not Smithson.

A further two related clauses can be present in the SELECT statement. These are GROUP BY and HAVING which are related:

GROUP BY grouping attribute(s)

HAVING group condition.

The GROUP BY extension places the tuples of a relation into groups (based on the value of an attribute or attributes). Thus,

SELECT LECTURER_NAME, SUM (NO_OF_WEEKS)

FROM LECTURER_MODULE

GROUP BY LECTURER_NAME

will divide the lecturer_module tuples into groups - each group having a different lecturer and give the total number of weeks that the lecturer teaches. Figure 8.3 shows how the two tuples of Goodwin (the only lecturer apparently taking more than one course) have been combined with the total number of weeks calculated.

LECTURER-MODULE

MODULE	LECTURER-NAME	N0-OF-WEEKS
1	Clarke	10
1a	Goodwin	10
1b	Goodwin	10
2	Knight	10
2a	Collins	10
2b	Baker	10
2c	Jagger	10
3	Fisher	10
3a	Oldham	10
4	Glenn	20

LECTURER-NAME	SUM (NO-OF-WEEKS)
Clarke	10
Goodwin	20
Knight	10
Collins	10
Baker	10
Jagger	10
Fisher	10
Oldham	10
Glenn	20

Fig. 8.3 The use of the SQL GROUP BY statement

The HAVING clause:

HAVING GROUP CONDITION

which only appears with a GROUP BY clause provides a particular condition on the group of tuples associated with each value of the grouping attributes, and only groups which satisfy the condition are retrieved. Thus, if we were only interested in lecturers who teach more than one course, then the following will produce only one tuple (the COUNT option with (*) will add the number of tuples in each group), that of Goodwin:

SELECT LECTURER_NAME, SUM (NO_OF_WEEKS), COUNT (*)
FROM LECTURER_MODULE
GROUP BY LECTURER_NAME
HAVING COUNT (*) > 1

A query in SQL can have up to six clauses: SELECT, FROM, WHERE, GROUP BY, HAVING and ORDER, but only the first two are mandatory. As has been demonstrated in this very brief overview, it is a very powerful statement. On the other hand, complex queries are likely to require a complex, and sometimes. nested statement, which can be difficult to construct.

8.4   DATA UPDATE

There are three commands to modify the database: INSERT, DELETE and UPDATE. The INSERT command is used to add tuples to a relation; the DELETE command is used to delete tuples from a relation; and UPDATE is used to modify attribute values in one or more tuples.

The INSERT command takes a number of forms. To add a tuple to a relation the values should be in the same order as the attributes in the relation. For example, to add a tuple to the STUDENT relation for a new student called Jones, who is in the third year of her course, the following is required:

INSERT INTO STUDENT
VALUES ('Jones','3')

whereas in a second form of the command, the attributes are named but null values left out. Say, we did not know the year of Jones' course, then this could be specified by:

INSERT INTO STUDENT (STUDENT_NAME)
VALUES ('Jones')

the command would have been rejected if we had specified NOT NULL for the attribute YEAR_OF_COURSE.

The above are useful where only one or two tuples are added to the relation. For inserting multiple tuples in a relation, we use the CREATE command followed by a variation of the INSERT command which loads the data with the result of a SELECT. Thus we can create a temporary relation called MODULES_TAKEN and INSERT data coming from other relations in the database. Thus:

CREATE TABLE MODULES_TAKEN   (STUDENT_NAME
VARCHAR(40) NOT NULL
NO_OF_MODULES INTEGER);
INSERT INTO MODULES_TAKEN (STUDENT_NAME, NO_OF_MODULES)

        SELECT STUDENT_NAME, COUNT (*)
        FROM ATTENDANCE
        GROUP BY STUDENT_NAME

will insert into the temporary relation one tuple for each student with the number of modules taken (effectively a count of the number of tuples for that student in the ATTENDANCE relation) so that NO_OF_MODULES will be 7 for Ashworth, 7 for Atkins, 4 for Johnson, 6 for Smith and 3 for Perkins.

Some implementations of SQL have an INPUT command which enables new tuples to be added to the relation interactively. Some also have CHANGE and RECALL commands. The former is used to change the most recent command entered and RECALL is used to display it. Users often follow a CHANGE with a RECALL to check that a modification was carried out in the way anticipated.

The DELETE command removes tuples from a relation, for example:

        DELETE FROM STUDENT (STUDENT_NAME)
        WHERE STUDENT_NAME='Jones'

will delete all tuples of that particular student, whereas

        DELETE FROM STUDENT

will delete all tuples in the STUDENT relation, but this will create an empty relation, it will not delete reference to the relation in the database (which will require the DROP command).

The UPDATE command is used to modify attribute values of one or more selected tuples, with their values being altered by the SET clause. Thus:

        UPDATE LECTURER_MODULE
        SET NO_OF_WEEKS = NO_OF_WEEKS * 2
        WHERE MODULE='4'

will set the NO_OF_WEEKS attribute to 4 from 2 for MODULE 4. It is also possible to update a number of tuples by selecting a number of tuples using the SELECT, and applying an operation using the SET clause.

8.5   VIEWS IN SQL

A view in SQL is a single relation which is derived from other relations, which could be base tables or other views. It does not necessarily exist on the database (it is the external view in ANSI/X3/SPARC terms), but appears to exist to the user and its purpose is to simplify the users' use of the database. In other words, tuples in base tables are stored on the database, those in views might appear on the screen, constructed from data which is stored physically. A view may be referenced frequently, but as it is derived from other relations may not be stored physically. In other words, it is the way in which SQL achieves data independence. A view is created using the CREATE VIEW command which specifies the name of the view and the tuples it contains using a SELECT command. Thus we may create a view having attributes coming from the LECTURER_MODULE and ATTENDANCE relations as follows:

CREATE VIEW LECTURER_MODULE_ATTENDANCE

AS   SELECT MODULE, NO_OF_WEEKS, STUDENT_NAME

FROM LECTURER_MODULE, ATTENDANCE

WHERE MODULE=MODULE

and because the attribute names for the view are not specified, LECTURER_MODULE_ATTENDANCE will inherit the attribute names of the two base tables. Having created the view, it is possible to specify queries using the SELECT command on the relation. Such commands will be simpler than achieving the same results using the original relations. To delete the view the command DROP VIEW is used, for example,

DROP VIEW LECTURER_MODULE_ATTENDANCE

8.6   EMBEDDED SQL

SQL can be embedded into a host language, such as Cobol or Pascal. There are many reasons for going along this route. For example, successful programs which used file processing can be modified to run against the database without changing the basic processing functionality. Another reason is that some logic sets available in conventional programs do not have an SQL equivalent, an obvious one being the IF...THEN.... ELSE construct.

Any SQL statement - all the ones discussed above - can be embedded in the program. The full power of the SQL data manipulation statements discussed above, such as the SELECT statement, is maintained in the host language version. Such statements will be prefixed with a special character or characters which enable identification by the precompiler as being SQL and not Cobol (or whatever). The statements are checked for correct SQL syntax and translated into call statements of the host language.

The database files will not be described by the user. File operations will be handled by the SQL program, so the user does not need to know anything about the structure of the files and this provides data independence and makes programming easier. The precompiler generates the data structure definitions according to the syntax of the host language. The precompiler also defines areas so that database contents can be handled by the program along with any messages relating to the use of the database, successful or otherwise.

8.7   CONCLUSION

In this chapter, we have attempted to provide enough of the flavour of SQL to enable the user to use the language on the many relational DBMS that have an SQL query language, and these include many of the popular DBMS such as DB2, Oracle, Unify, Informix and Ingres. Many features and commands, and the detail of those covered, for example, nested queries and many of their variants, have been omitted. A full description would require a whole text book. Further, such aspects as data integrity controls, security controls, have not been covered at all nor have the query optimiser facilities (the way in which SQL attempts to work out the most efficient way of fulfilling a query).

The popularity of the language and the move towards a standard have led more and more DBMS suppliers to include an SQL interface to their products. However, it does have limitations. For example, although easier to use than a conventional programming language, it is not ideal as a 'user friendly' interface and, in any case, many users require host language facilities as well. Further, it has been criticised in that a particular requirement may be fulfilled in a number of ways. In other words, the language itself is partially redundant.

However, it is the most widely used DBMS language, is relationally complete, provides physical data independence and can be used as a separate language or embedded in a host language. It is likely to be a standard language for many years to come.

8.8   FURTHER READING

Date, C. J (1984) A critique of the SQL database language, *ACM Sigmod Record,* **14,** 3.

Date, C. J & White, C (1988) *A guide to DB2,* 2nd ed, Addison-Wesley, Reading, Mass.

The above are devoted to DB2 and are recommended. General database texts recommended in previous chapters all cover SQL to an extent.

Chapter 9
Microcomputer Databases and Database Machines

9.1   THE DEVELOPMENT OF DATABASES ON MICROCOMPUTERS

The history of databases on microcomputers has been one of very rapid development. The 8-bit microcomputers with 64k memory running under the CP/M operating system using low capacity floppy disks of the early 1980s were capable of running file management systems, and such systems were frequently one of three packages used on microcomputers (the others being spreadsheet and word processor). However, these file management systems were somewhat limited. They represented the computer equivalent of a card index (containing, for example, the patient records of a dentist). Usually, they would only permit the processing of one file at a time, there would be limited data independence so that users were not cushioned from changes in data storage, they might be restricted to about a thousand records per file and they might be limited in other ways such as in their retrieval, update and sorting capabilities.

A typical file management system was dBaseII (which has grown in its dBaseIV version to be a popular and, by comparison, advanced DBMS for microcomputers). In its early form, only two files could be open at any one time. It could not handle arrays of data, which made the handling of all but the most trivial sets of data difficult. The maximum number of characters per file was 255; the maximum number of fields per record was 32; and the maximum number of records was 1000. These points should not be read as criticisms of the package, more as an illustration of the limitations of DBMS running on previous generations of microcomputers.

Since the advent of 16 bit microcomputers in 1983, in particular the IBM PC and 'look-alikes', it has been possible to use rather more sophisticated database packages. These microcomputers had increased internal memory capacity and faster processors. The basic internal memory was 256k for most 16 bit microcomputers, although they were expanded to many times this size. Disk storage technology also became more sophisticated, the floppy disks on these micros being designed to have four times the storage capacity of the previous 'generation' (microcomputer generations are usually separated by about four years). Some systems used a high density flexible disk having a capacity of half a megabyte (half a million characters) or more. More important from the database viewpoint was that hard disks, having a capacity of 10 or 20 megabytes and upwards, became available with these computers. Along with the improved hardware, operating systems such as MS-DOS have made genuine database management much more feasible.

In the mid 1980s came the Apple Macintosh, with its operating system having a WIMP interface (windows, icons, mice and pull-down menus). This provided the following features:

- *Windows:* these split the screen into sections, each running an application, so that many applications and files can be on the computer 'desk top' simultaneously
- *Icons:* these are picture representations of items, such as files, using the graphics (sometimes colour graphics) features of a modern microcomputer
- *Mice:* these are hand held pointing devices which can point to an item on the screen, such as a file, and are activated by pressing a button on the mouse
- *Pull-down menus:* these are lists of options that the user can pick, using a mouse.

These features have made computer systems more attractive to the user and made applications much easier to use, being more natural, simulating a desk top. The MS-Windows interface, similar in style, came later on the IBM PC computers and may eventually replace the more conventional MS-DOS operating system on PCs. Whereas mainframe DBMS are associated with specialist design and use, because of these improvements in the user interface, the end-users are using microcomputer databases to a far greater extent.

Very powerful workstations or 'supermicros', such as the products of Sun, Compaq and Apollo also became widely available having an internal memory of a megabyte or more. Hard discs with a capacity of over 100 megabytes can be attached to them. Some of these systems provide very powerful facilities for the single user, others are multi-user. The operating system, most frequently Unix, can run powerful DBMS as efficiently as many minicomputers. Again there are WIMP interfaces to these systems, such as X-Windows. The Ingres application discussed in Chapter 14 was implemented on such a supermicro. It is therefore not now incongruous to discuss 'real' database management in a microcomputer environment.

By the turn of the 1990s, the standard IBM PC or 'look-alike' is a 32-bit computer based on an Intel 80486 chip. On such computers, there are several megabytes of memory and they have much faster processing speeds. Large capacity hard disks (of sometimes several hundred megabytes) with very fast access speeds can be used and floppies capable themselves of storing several megabytes also make medium-scale database applications feasible. Such a computer could be used stand-alone or it could be used as a central database for a number of users using microcomputers connected to it via a local area network. The MS-Windows operating system, of the WIMP type, is becoming more common on these systems because the capacity of the computer system enables the user to take advantage of the facilities provided by the Windows environment. The graphical user interface of Windows (and the similar interface on the

Apple Macintosh) is attractive for users. DBMS packages are available that are very sophisticated when compared to the early file management systems, and popular ones at the time of writing are Paradox, dBaseIV, Foxbase and Omnis. There are also PC versions of popular minicomputer and mainframe DBMS, such as PC Oracle and PC Informix, which have most of the features of their mainframe equivalents. Many users develop a prototype version of the database application using the PC version and implement the operational version on their mainframe.

In view of these developments, the reader may ask how these database environments may differ from the mainframe counterparts. As we have said, the user may see few differences in functionality, though aspects such as back-up and recovery may be less sophisticated. But there may be differences in how they are used (because microcomputers *are* smaller and less powerful than mainframes). For example, many microcomputer DBMS are expected to be used in a single user mode. The microcomputer is dedicated to that user's processing and the database is set up and used only by that one user. Sometimes the microcomputer database is shared by a number of users who each have access to the microcomputer itself or they share the database by being connected in a local area network. In the microcomputer environment, the number of uses sharing the database may be limited to make speeds of access reasonable or the system to handle concurrent access may be less watertight than in a mainframe environment. Recently the possibility of a distributed database is more real (Chapter 10 is devoted to distributed database systems). Another possibility, mentioned in the previous paragraph, is to link the microcomputer to the mainframe. Parts of the database could be copied onto the microcomputer database and the user could manipulate the data on the microcomputer system.

It is noticeable that whereas most of the original DBMS on mainframes were hierarchical or network because these systems developed in the mid-1960s and 1970s when relational databases were only in the realm of the researcher, most microcomputer database systems are relational and have been from the start. As we have seen, relational systems are now usual on mainframe computers as well.

Frequently, microcomputer databases have query languages far more 'user friendly' than the equivalent mainframe system. Microcomputers have been sold to the general business user rather than to computer professionals, and so this is perhaps not surprising. Data can be input using a question-and-answer session with the user. Alternatively, data can be entered by means of setting up a table or filling a 'soft form' on the screen. Query-by-example (QBE) which was introduced in Section 4.4 is a common query interface in many systems and most provide an SQL interface. Rarely is the user required to have an in-depth knowledge of computers or any knowledge of a conventional programming language.

Of course a major advantage of microcomputer DBMS is their portability. The database can be carried on a number of floppy disks. The same microcomputer DBMS can run on a number of computers of the same type and supplier, even when they are of different size and capability. Many DBMS can run on different computers altogether.

In this section, I have tried to show how the rapid development of microcomputers has made DBMS applications feasible. My fear is that this section will be out of date very quickly! In Sections 9.2 and 9.3, we look briefly at the basic features of two commercial microcomputer DBMS: dBaseIV, which is a popular system on IBM PCs, and OmnisV, a popular package used on Apple Macintosh computers. Paradox, another popular package on PCs, uses a QBE-style interface, and therefore is similar to the QBE interface on DB2 which was described in Section 7.4. In each case we introduce a small example of its use. In Section 9.4 we look at database machines, that is, computers dedicated to database use.

9.2   DBASEIV

dBaseIV is the latest (at the time of writing) version of the dBase product which has been for some time one of the top selling microcomputer DBMS. We will look first at a simple example creating a record description, adding data and querying the database thus formed.

On entering dBaseIV, the user sees a screen called the 'control center'. This has six headings to enable the creation of data, queries, forms, reports, labels and applications. The 'data' option enables the user to create and change table definitions; 'queries' enables the user to create, change and use queries; 'forms' enables the user to create, change and process data using the screen formats supplied in the system; 'reports' enables the user to create, change and print user-created reports; 'labels' enables the user to create, change and produce mailing lists; and, finally, 'applications' enables the user to design and run applications which have previously been coded and stored.

By choosing the data option, it is possible to describe the file. For each field (attribute) in the file (relation), the user has to enter its title, type, width, decimal places and index. In Figure 9.1, we have entered data descriptions for a file of data relating to text books. The fields are author, title, publisher, number of pages and date of publication. The system helps the user by filling in data automatically where this is appropriate. For example, if the field type is date, then the width will automatically be 8 characters.

Once the records have been defined, dBaseIV responds: 'Input data records now? (Y/N)' and if the user keys in Y for yes, the basic form is displayed and the user keys in the information for each record. There is a line for each attribute, headed by the

Num	Field Name	Field Type	Width	Dec	Index
1	AUTHOR	Character	25		N
2	TITLE	Character	45		N
3	PUBLISHER	Character	25		N
4	NO. OF PAGES	Numeric	4	0	N
5	DATE OF PUBLICATION	Date	8		N

Fig. 9.1 dBaseIV - defining the data

attribute name, followed by a block and the user enters the attribute details by filling in the blanks. Figure 9.2 shows the general format.

There will be a form to be completed for each record (tuple). Once this is completed, it is possible to make a query. This is achieved through returning to the 'Control Center' but this time choosing create queries. The system requires the user to choose those attributes that are required, for example, author, title and number of pages, and once this query has been created, it is possible to list the books on the file. This follows the principles of query-by-example. From the display of all the fields on a file, the user chooses the attributes. This 'view', a subset of all attributes, is displayed underneath.

AUTHOR	David Benyon
TITLE	Information and Data Modelling
PUBLISHER	Blackwell Scientific
NO OF PAGES	254
DATE OF PUBLICATION	30/7/90

Fig. 9.2 Completing the form

Conditions can be added to any field. For example, by adding conditions to the query, it is possible to select only those texts that are published by a specific publisher:

PUBLISHER = BLACKWELL SCIENTIFIC

or published later than a particular date

DATE > 01/01/89

(as in Figure 9.3). Views can also be set up which summarise data and perform simple statistics such as sums, counts and averages. It is also possible to sort the records

Books.dbf	AUTHOR	TITLE
	PR	PR

PUBLISHER	NO OF PAGES	DATE OF PUBLICATION
PR		Condition > 01/01/89

View

<VIEW1>	AUTHOR	TITLE	PUBLISHER

Fig. 9.3 A query view in dBaseIV

selected. This will be carried out on a specified index field. Records can be added, deleted and altered and the relations printed out as well as displayed on the screen.

These basic operations can be achieved through a menu system which is easy to follow. More sophisticated and specialised reports will probably need to be written in the dBaseIV command language. It is a full programming language having 440 commands and functions. To use these facilities fully requires some programming skills. However, the basic functions are also provided, such as the ability to use an equivalent of the project operation in relational algebra. The command:

LIST AUTHOR, TITLE

will list these two attributes for all records on the file. Conditions can be added so that, for example, the list will contain only those texts where date of publication is greater than 21/12/89. There is a command to join relations, though the SQL operators are usually chosen for such tasks. To use the command language, the user needs to change from menu mode to command mode by asking for the 'dot prompt' (the DBMS returns a full stop before each command).

dBaseIV has an SQL interface. There is also an applications generator available which will enable the 'professional' user to set up menus and other application structures for end-user applications. In other words, dBaseIV provides a very easy to use interface for simple applications, but also has the sophistication to enable more complex microcomputer applications to be designed.

9.3 OMNISV

OmnisV is the latest version (at the time of writing) of the Omnis package, supplied by Blythe Software, which runs on the Apple Macintosh and takes advantage of the WIMP interface. There is also a version of the product which runs on PCs. We will illustrate the use of Omnis by looking at an application designed for the editor of a journal who has to keep track of manuscripts submitted, as they are read by referees, rejected or accepted, and published in the journal.

There are five main components which make up an OmnisV application. These are file formats, window formats, search formats, menu formats and report formats. All these are important features of any OmnisV application, and must be created by the user before any data entry. Selecting the formats option from the main design menu opens the format tool box and the type of format is selected from the format selection box by double clicking the mouse after pointing to the required format. Figure 9.4 shows the window format highlighted, and the main panel shows the names of all the windows that were eventually designed in the application. There are also a number of 'buttons' which can be pressed (using the mouse) for opening, closing, modifying and renaming the designs (amongst other possibilities).

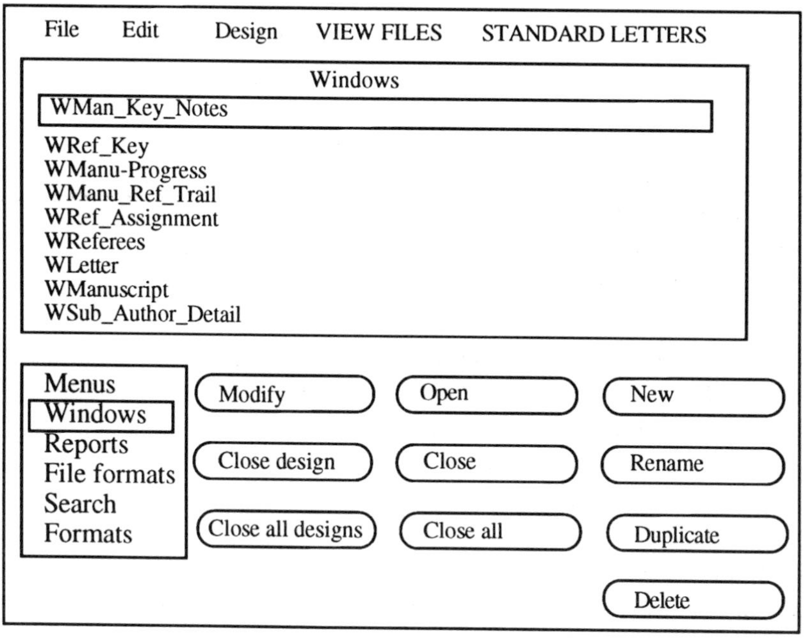

Fig. 9.4 The format tool box for windows in OmnisV

When an application is being designed, the various file (relation) structures need to be set up. The file formats option in the format tool box will be selected and the 'new' button chosen. A name box will appear and the user keys in the name and description which will open a design window so that the relation can be defined (Figure 9.5). The files can be updated (modified) and new fields added at a later date.

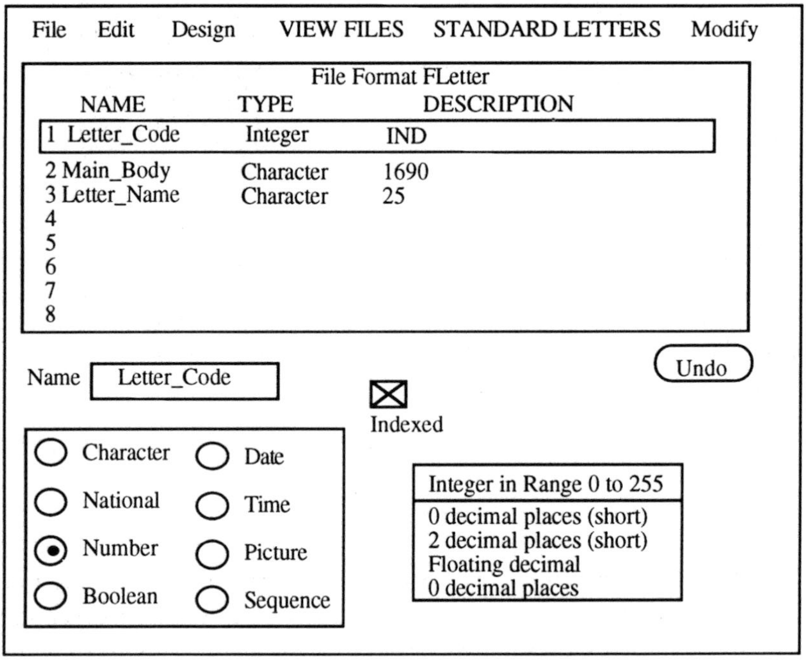

Fig. 9.5 The file formats design window

There are eight field types. The Letter_Code field has been defined as numeric and a list has appeared so that the user can specify that this number is an integer in the range 0 to 255. This field has also been chosen as an index so that a particular value can be located quickly. Up to twelve fields in a file can be indexed in this way.

Once the structures have been created, data can be entered. This is achieved through the use of OmnisV windows which are designed by the user. The format design window consists of a palette and a single large window on which the design is 'painted'. By choosing the text option, text can be placed in the window. A field is placed in the window by selecting the field option, defining its position and naming the field. Figure 9.6 shows part of the screen design to enable the user to key in information about a referee.

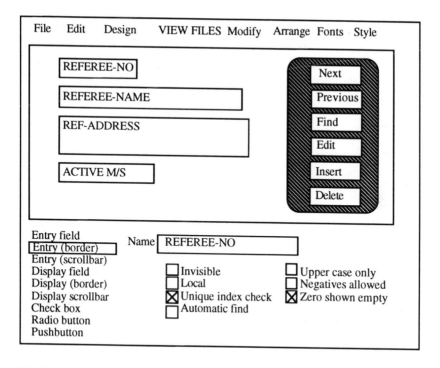

Fig. 9.6 Designing windows for data entry

The options on the bottom left enable the user to specify such format as radio buttons (the circles on the bottom left of the screen design shown as Figure 9.5), buttons (shown in the top right of Figure 9.6) as well as more conventional data entry. The user may wish to specify a number of reports and menu designs which also use the WIMP interface to advantage. This makes OmnisV score well on usability criteria.

9.4   DATABASE MACHINES

In this chapter, we have so far considered the rapid improvement of microcomputer database management systems and looked in brief at two commercial DBMS, dBaseIV and OmnisV, which are popular systems running on PCs and Apple Macintosh machines respectively. In this section we look at another aspect of the database field, that of database machines.

Most database systems are implemented on general-purpose computers which are used for many applications, some of which use the database and others which do not. An alternative scenario is to locate the DBMS on a separate computer from the applications, a computer dedicated to database work. This is the database machine. There are computers specifically designed for this purpose, and they include the Britton-Lee IDM500 and the Teradata DBC/1012. The specialised hardware is capable of executing functions which would normally be carried out by the DBMS software. Such an environment can increase overall efficiency - whilst the database machine is searching the database, the applications computer can be executing application programs. A typical architecture is as shown in Figure 9.7, with the database machine being a 'back-end computer'. Some installations have a dedicated database machine connected to a number of general-purpose computers. This may cause a bottle-neck, however, and some organisations have opted for several computers of each type. Where there are several database machines, the architecture is like a distributed database system (Chapter 10).

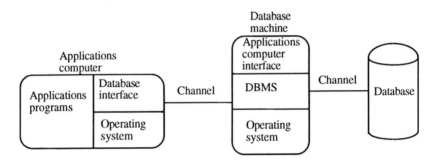

Fig. 9.7 The database machine - a possible architecture

If the general-purpose machine (applications computer or host machine) is running a program waiting for data from the database machine, it can run another applications program until the data has been received. Overall speed is also increased because the database machine can hold indexes to the data in main memory, indeed such computers are designed for efficient database processing and can be free of non-database processing responsibilities and facilities. Likewise, the applications computer is free of database processing responsibilities. Most database machines now use a relational DBMS (earlier ones did not and were not very successful in the market place).

With a dedicated database machine, security of the database may be easier, and there may be cost advantages as well. On the other hand, the organisation will be vulnerable if the database machine fails. Back-up is at least as important as in a conventional computer database and this may sometimes necessitate a second database machine.

9.5 FURTHER READING

McFadden, F. R & Hoffer, J. A (1991) *Database Management*, 3rd ed, Benjamin/Cummings, Redwood City, Ca.

This text, unusually for database books, looks at microcomputer DBMS (in particular, dBaseIV), and also has a section on database machines.

Chapter 10
Distributed Databases

10.1 INTRODUCTION

As we have seen, centralised databases originated in the late 1960s and they have been in a state of continuing development ever since. During the latter part of their development at least, they have been successfully used in many organisations. With the exception of the discussions in Chapter 9, the assumption in this text has been that the database will eventually rest on one large mainframe computer and be used by the many users who have access to it. In some organisations, however, users are asking for 'their' part of the database to be on their departmental microcomputer or minicomputer system. There may be good reasons for this and as we saw in Chapter 9 the technology is available. However, it may lead to a state where the strategy for information systems in an organisation disintegrates into a large number of different systems with no other user having access to another's database. Effectively, each group of users has set up their own databases, each of which can be shared by other users in that group, but not by other groups. Depending on the particular circumstances of the organisation, many advantages of the database approach could be lost.

The alternative strategy is to enable a planned geographic distribution of the database where the several computers holding parts of the database are interconnected by a communications network. This is a distributed database system. In this situation, each group of users (or individuals) can have 'their' part of the database held on their local computer, but this data can be used by all other users who have rights of access to that part of the database. Data can therefore be held where it is collected and validated or where it is used most (but not necessarily used exclusively). A distributed database can be seen as a 'virtual' database, the component parts of which are stored in several physical sites (sometimes called nodes). There must be some kind of computer network between these nodes. However, if data is held where it is used most, then data transfers are minimised.

Such a strategy may be particularly suitable to organisations which are themselves dispersed and therefore a distributed database system is more natural. The management of each part of those organisations may need their independence. It may also be suitable for organisations where the use of microcomputers has led to a number of existing independent databases which need to be integrated somehow (for the reasons given in support of any database), but where it would be politically or otherwise impractical to expect these users to move to a mainframe corporate database. A distributed database approach also supports an organisation which tends to grow incrementally, for example, by buying out its competitors or suppliers or by the addition of new branches or warehouses.

Pactel (1979) suggests eight key factors which will together determine the appropriateness or otherwise of distributed database systems to any particular organisation. Distributed database systems might be appropriate depending on the degree of:

- Decentralisation of the organisation
- Central control exercised by the administration
- Autonomy afforded to local units
- Interaction between sites, particularly in respect of data
- Integration required
- Ease with which data can be distributed
- Natural clustering of the data
- Locally held data needing to be referenced from other sites.

Pactel (1979) adds that distributed database systems will enable distributed computer systems to be seen as an integrated operational whole; the retention of corporate control over systems development and data administration; support for the growing functions of corporate information management; the flow of data and information between systems; intercommunication between systems on an ad-hoc basis; and automatic extraction of consolidated management information from different operating systems.

Langham (1989) adds that they may be used to link operational and management information systems databases; link microcomputer users into the corporate database strategy; bridge heterogeneous databases held on different computers; bridge old and new databases on different computers; and support a true integrated computer aided software engineering environment.

There are many possible bases on which to compare conventional and distributed databases (see Ceri & Pelagatti, 1984). Consideration of only three of these shows the potential for differences between the two types of database design:

- *Centralised control:* As we will see in Chapter 13, in conventional databases it is feasible to have a database administrator (or data administrator) who exercises control over the information resources of the organisation. In distributed database systems control is less centralised. A global database administrator may be given central responsibility, and the communications network which is essential to a distributed system, represents a major security problem, but there is also a need for local database administrators at each site who have 'site autonomy', thus giving a hierarchical structure to control aspects.

- *Data independence:* It is important in either database design to make the actual organisation of data on disk transparent to the user so that programs and applications are not affected by changes related to data storage. With distributed database systems, as we will see in Section 10.2, distribution transparency is also important. Users should not be aware that any data on the database is distributed so that, for example, programs will not be affected if data is moved from one site to another.

- *Reduction in redundancy:* The reduction in duplication is seen as desirable in conventional databases to avoid inconsistency between versions of the 'same' piece of information and to save storage space. However, controlled data redundancy is a desirable feature of distributed systems. The main reason is to increase system availability, since site failure will not prevent access to any data at other sites. Further, it is often more efficient to store the data at those sites that need frequent access to that data. Such data replication means that regard to consistency is essential so that updates are performed consistently on all sites.

In Section 10.2, we look in more detail at some of the principles of distributed database systems and in Section 10.3 at possible design considerations. Finally, in Section 10.4 we will debate some issues associated with the implementation of distributed database systems.

10.2 PRINCIPLES AND REQUIREMENTS OF DISTRIBUTED DATABASE SYSTEMS

The purpose of this section is to elaborate further about what is required in a distributed database system. Date (1987a and 1987b) puts together twelve rules plus a fundamental principle in an attempt to explain the essentials of an ideal distributed database system. He suggests that these 'are intended to constitute a list of features that might reasonably be required of distributed database systems, as those systems evolve over the next several years'. Added to these twelve rules there is one fundamental principle:

- To the user, a distributed database system should look exactly like a non-distributed database system, that is, users performing data manipulation in a distributed database system should behave exactly as if the system were non distributed.

  In fact, this principle leads on to the twelve rules summarised below:

- *Local autonomy:* Local data should be owned and managed locally, with local accountability and security. Local operations should remain local and no site must depend on another for successful functioning. This means that each site must store all data dictionary information (Chapter 12) necessary to be independent.

- *No reliance on a central site:* There should not be any reliance on a master site for some central service for at least two reasons. First, the central site might be a bottleneck. Second, the whole system would be vulnerable as if this central site's computer system went down, the whole distributed database system would go down.

- *Continuous operation:* There should never be a need for a planned system shutdown. For example, if a new site should be incorporated into an existing distributed system, no changes to existing user programs or terminal activities should be required for operation at the new site nor should the service at any other site be disturbed. It should also be possible to upgrade the software (for example, the DBMS) at any site without disrupting the general service.

- *Local independence:* Users should not need to know where data is physically stored, indeed they will act as if the data were stored locally.

- *Fragmentation independence:* Any part of the database (a relation, for example, if a relational system - and Date assumes such a DBMS) should be capable of being divided up into fragments for physical storage purposes.

- *Replication independence:* A given relation (or fragment of a relation) should be capable of being represented at the physical level by many distinct stored copies (or replicas) at many sites.

- *Distributed query processing:* Local processor and input/output activity should be capable of being carried out at multiple sites. Both local and global optimisation of query processing should occur.

- *Distributed transaction management:* Single transactions should execute code at multiple sites, causing updates at these multiple sites.

- *Hardware independence:* Distributed databases should be able to run on different kinds of hardware, with all machines participating as equal partners where appropriate.

- *Operating system independence:* The same DBMS should be able to run on different operating systems.

- *Network independence:* The system should support local area networks, such as Ethernet, or long-haul networks, such as the system of telephone lines, and a wide range of differing network architectures.

- *DBMS independence:* Distributed databases should be able to run using different kinds of DBMS, provided that they have the same interfaces.

In addition to these rules, Stonebraker proposed a set of six rules that create a model for distributed database systems. These were later modified and extended (Yalonis, 1988). In effect, these rules again elaborate Date's fundamental principle with respect to the types of transparency that a fully distributed database system should support. By transparency is meant the invisibility of a process to a user or full simultaneous distribution of functionality to all nodes. The types of transparency that should be provided are:

- *Retrieval transparency:* Data can be retrieved from any site, regardless of where the transaction originates, and the results received should be the same for all sites.
- *Update transparency:* Data should be updated at any site, no matter where the update originates from, with the same effect as an update from any other site.
- *Schema transparency:* The user should be able to make data definition schema changes from any site, and those changes will be visible throughout the network.
- *Performance transparency:* A command made at any site performs as the same command from any other site. For a comparable performance, a distributed DBMS should have a query optimiser that views the whole network and constructs an access plan to reach a processor best suited to process the query.
- *Transaction dependency:* A distributed DBMS should organise transactions to provide efficient concurrent access, whilst minimising the vulnerability of the update process to disruption from site crashes or simultaneous access.
- *Copy transparency:* The loss of one site (even a site with the original copy of data) should not lead to the loss of any data on the network. Even with the loss of several nodes, the system should maintain high availability of data with redundant copies. This may not degrade performance as needed data is close to many user groups and it may also reduce communication costs.
- *Tool transparency:* All tools should be applicable to all sites.

The ideal distributed database system suggested in the lists provided may not be feasible at present because of technological capability and cost. However, systems available are conforming to more and more of these rules and it is likely that distributed database systems will be available which fully conform to any agreed standard. Having looked at a number of principles to which a distributed database system should conform, we look at the services that such a system should provide. The following have been proposed by Codd (1987):

- Data storage, retrieval and update facilities, both locally and remotely over different nodes on the network
- Data dictionary, which is a user-accessible catalogue present at each node to describe the local data of every node
- Transaction support to ensure that all (or, if not, none) of a sequence of database changes are reflected in the database (whether the changes happen locally or over the network)
- Recovery services in case of failure for both local and distributed transactions

- Concurrency control services to ensure that concurrent transactions (both local and distributed) behave in the same way as if they had been run in some sequential order
- Authorisation services to ensure that all access to and manipulation of data be in accordance with specified constraints on users and programs
- Integration between different DBMS and between applications and DBMS
- Local integrity services ensuring that database states and changes of state at each node conform to specified rules
- Communications network directory services which drive the internal DBMS programs and the mapping information between one level of schema and another
- Some degree of transparency (the seven points above) which will be supported to a different extent by different systems because there is a strong trade-off between distribution transparency and performance.

10.3 DISTRIBUTED DATABASE DESIGN

As we have said, the ideal distributed database system suggested in Section 10.2 may not be feasible at present, but in many organisations the ideal (assuming it is attainable) may not be necessary nor appropriate. A distributed database system should model the structure of the organisation to some extent, and this would suggest that different configurations are required in different situations. Although most organisations are at least logically distributed and, most likely, physically distributed as well, other businesses are centralised physically and controlled from the centre, and therefore a distributed database system would not be suitable.

However, assuming that some sort of distributed database system is envisaged, decisions have to be made by information systems managers related to how many sites should be connected to the distributed database system, what performance is required, where each part of the database should be located and where it should be used, and what hardware and software are needed. Another factor is cost: there should be some desired mid-point between total centralisation and total decentralisation which supports user needs and yet minimises costs (Figure 10.1).

Reinsch (1988) defined five distinct levels of distribution:

- *User assisted distribution:* At this most basic level, the user interacts with one system to extract the data needed. The data is then taken by the user physically to the system where the data is required. If this external data need occurs rarely, then this arrangement may be adequate.
- *Remote requests:* When the user requires data, the user interacts with an application

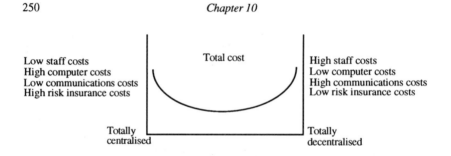

Low staff costs   Total cost   High staff costs
High computer costs   Low computer costs
Low communications costs   High communications costs
High risk insurance costs   Low risk insurance costs

Totally   Totally
centralised   decentralised

Fig. 10.1 Costs of centralised versus decentralised systems (after Lawson, 1988)

running on the local machine to extract the data. It is therefore similar to the above, except that the operation is automated.

- *Remote unit of work:* When an application program executes on one machine, it can use a remote application program interface provided by another system. This enables any local DBMS facilities to be available to applications running on remote systems.
- *Distributed unit of work:* There are two key extensions provided by distributed unit of work or distributed transaction processing over remote unit of work. First, the DBMS knows or finds out which system manages the data to be read or changed by each request. Second, the DBMS coordinates updates at several locations in a single transaction.
- *Distributed request:* Here, all data location restrictions are removed. Whatever would be possible with all local data is now possible with the distributed environment. The distributed database looks like one very large single database.

The distributed database system environment might be arranged as shown in Figure 10.2.

Within this overall framework there are many alternatives. For example, the computer sites might be *homogeneous* (same computer configuration at each site) or *heterogeneous* (different computer configurations at a number of the sites) and the data partitioning might be arranged *vertically* where specified domains of relations (columns) are stored at specified locations and where each column is found at only one location (excluding the key column which needs to be kept at all locations to enable table reconstruction), or *horizontally* where specified tuples (rows) are stored at locations based on specified values of the key data items.

There are also many technological issues which must be decided. Many apply to conventional database systems, but can be more difficult in a distributed system because of the added complexity of some routines. Although the detail of these aspects is considered outside the scope of this book, they are important because they affect the speed, accuracy and reliability of the service provided. The distributed database world

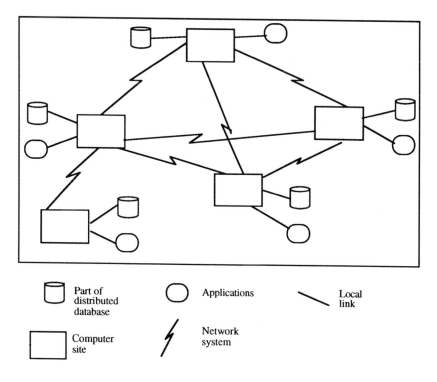

⬭ Part of distributed database	◯ Applications	⬋ Local link
▭ Computer site	⚡ Network system	

Fig. 10.2 Architecture of a distributed database environment

is complex and therefore efficiency is particularly important. Such technological considerations include query decomposition and optimisation, consistency and synchronisation, and fault tolerance and recovery.

Query decomposition is necessary because processing a query often requires access to many nodes. The optimisation of this process is desirable in order to ensure that this process is carried out efficiently (according to loading on the various computers, their underlying speed, resource utilisation, traffic on the network, and so on).

To improve the availability and response times, multiple copies of data may be stored in the system and as a result of this replication the loss of a processor, for example, will not result in the loss of the data held there for other users. However, these different copies must be kept consistent and updates need to be synchronised. This is also technically complex with many alternative ways of achieving this result.

Fault tolerance and recovery is another important technological issue. The database must preserve its consistency and integrity even if one or more nodes is not working. Son & Choe (1988) suggest a number of types of failure, such as transaction failure (caused by erroneous data values or processing), system failure (caused by errors in the hardware or software), malicious failure (caused by an unhappy employee, for example) and media failure (caused by a damaged disk, for example). All these risks apply to conventional databases, but recovery and also security may well be more difficult in a distributed environment. It is important both to minimise these risks and to ensure that it is possible to recover from such failure.

Whereas the components of a conventional database system are threefold:

1) *Database:* where the data is stored
2) *DBMS:* which enables the creation and maintenance of the database and execution of programs using the database
3) *User program:* which may be an application program or consist of requests to the database

a distributed database system is spread over several nodes on a computer network, and requires a further three components:

1) *Distributed executive (network DBMS)* which intercepts a user request and determines where to send it or what nodes need to be accessed to satisfy the request; coordinates the processing of complex transactions which require access to several nodes; and accesses the communications network directory in order to provide translation services between DBMSs on different nodes on the network
2) *Global schema catalogue (communications network directory)* which is the means by which distributed DBMS determine which storage nodes need to be accessed (normally combined with the more conventional data dictionary)
3) *Adaptation module* whose primary function is to connect the local DBMS to the communications subsystem and to carry out any data or process translation that might be necessary.

Figure 10.3 shows how the six components of a distributed DBMS are connected.

There are now a number of distributed database systems in existence. Some were custom-made for a specific application, such as those for military applications which include the System for Distributed Databases (SDD-1) of the Computer Corporation of America; others research prototypes, such as the Japanese system Interoperable Database System, the UK project PROTEUS and the IBM developed System R*; and there are many commercial products, such as Oracle's SQL*Star, Relational Technology's INGRES/STAR and Sybase's SYBASE. Ceri & Pelagatti (1984) and Gretton-Watson (1988) provide detailed information on particular products.

It should be noted that, at least at the time of writing, none of these products conform to all the requirements listed in Section 10.2 for a distributed database system. Gretton-Watson (1988) analysed products according to Date's rules and found that they tended to rely on a central site, did not provide full fragmentation independence, were not hardware or software independent, and most were dependent on a particular

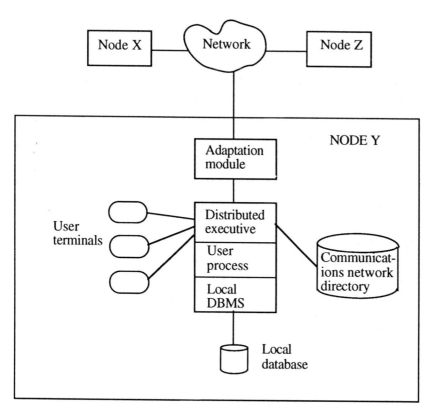

Fig. 10.3 A complete node in a distributed database system, adapted from Draffan & Poole (1980)

DBMS. Some of these failures may be due in part at least to commercial considerations, but many were due to the difficulties of achieving the objective.

At present, distributed DBMS are relational because:

- Fragmentation independence is feasible as relations can be divided up into fragments for physical storage purposes
- Fragmentation support is feasible as relations can be decomposed into row or column fragments and recomposed easily without the need for pointers
- Relational requests have a high semantic content through the powerful data manipulation languages
- Relational responses are multiple-record responses
- Relational requests are optimisable, that is, it is possible to derive an optimum path to follow as a response to a request.

As a result, relational DBMSs separate the user data view from its physical representation and the users do not see any differences in accessing data, so that the illusion created is that the distributed database is a centralised database, the major prerequisite for any distributed system (Section 10.2).

Another factor which promotes relational DBMS is the growing stature of SQL as a standard language for database processing. Although, as we have seen, SQL does not conform to an 'ideal' database language, the fact that there are internationally agreed standards is crucial to it becoming a potential common interface between heterogeneous systems. However, as was made clear in Chapter 8, at the time of writing there are many versions of SQL in use; indeed, there do not seem to be many commercial implementations of SQL that conform exactly to any agreed standard.

We will look briefly at one distributed DBMS, SQL*Star from Oracle (we will look further into Oracle in Chapter 11 in the context of tool support). The SQL*Star products SQL*Net and SQL*Connect support the network protocols and interfacing. SQL*Net can be used to bring together parts of physically separate databases, and SQL statements can be used which will join relations from different sites or answer queries which require data from more than one site. In doing so, there is no reference to any network address: relations are identified by name. Further, it is possible to update several databases within one application program.

Another area where the product matches the requirements of a distributed database is in terms of local support for a local data administrator. However, although the location of tables is transparent to the users, it is not to the database administrator. Each system operating in distributed mode has a local directory/dictionary which specifies the location and method of communication for reaching remote tables. This decentralisation of the directory/dictionary enables each site to be autonomous and as a result the failure at one site will not bring the whole system down. However, the database administrator has to keep all the directories and dictionaries up-to-date manually.

As needs change, it is feasible to reconfigure the network (for example, by adding sites to the network and redistributing some of the data across the network) and the users need not be aware of the changes that have taken place. SQL*Connect is the product that provides gateways linking the databases and these may be heterogeneous. For example, a mix of Oracle and DB/2 databases is feasible, running on different operating systems. Databases may also be held on computers of different manufacturer and type. As Dowgiallo (1989) points out, there is some optimising algorithm applied by the SQL*Star system, but it is not ideal. Nevertheless, the product conforms to many of the requirements of distributed database systems and, one assumes, with time will meet many of the others as well.

10.4 IMPLEMENTATION ISSUES

In this section we look at some of the complicated and often interrelated issues involved in the implementation of a distributed database system. Such systems are complex because relations in the same database can reside at a number of sites and can be fragmented and replicated making data dictionary management and query processing difficult; user transactions involving data resident at several sites will require much processing at these different sites with added difficulties of concurrency control and synchronisation among the sites; as data copies may continue to be updated at a number of sites even when a site is down, its recovery requires information from these other sites to ensure consistency; and, finally, the support of the various forms of transparency adds another translation mechanism which will be costly to maintain. Following Pactel (1979) and Kassapis (1989), these will be considered under the headings: key decisions, organisational issues, economic issues, technical issues and legislative issues.

Key decisions

- *How should the problem be approached:* If the approach is to start from scratch, then the latest hardware and software technology can be used, whereas creating a distributed database system from an existing centralised system would require restructuring which is likely to be very expensive, time-consuming and error-prone. However, a 'green-field' approach is not always practicable as there is an investment in the present systems. In this case it could be best to attempt to integrate the heterogeneous databases, replacing some hardware and software (where inappropriate) by a preferred 'standard'.
- *Data and data directory/dictionary allocation:* Decisions about where to locate the data itself and the directory/dictionary and whether to replicate them will have major repercussions on the speed of the system. A rule of thumb is that things should reside where they are used most. But associated questions complicate the issue, for example, should data files and/or the directory/dictionary be fragmented (and if so, horizontally or vertically)?, how much redundancy is needed and which fragments need to be replicated?
- *Control allocation:* Control mechanisms, which relate to recovery, concurrency and synchronisation, amongst others, can be centralised, distributed or both in a distributed database system. Distributed control, in principle, increases efficiency and survivability of a system. However, there will be a trade-off with other issues when paying regard to whether ultimate authority over data definition and access is handled locally, who should be able to read and/or update data, how frequently data

is updated and whether this is always done across the network and who is responsible for data integrity and security.

• *Performance:* This is an issue which is very important, is probably most at risk from poor design decisions and is very susceptible to trade-offs with other objectives. The crucial aspects of performance include speed of processing (response times) and the ability to provide accurate and up-to-date information. Decisions about fragmentation and redundancy are also very relevant here as are decisions about the hardware (including communication facilities) and software (including the provision of optimising mechanisms).

• *Reliability and data integrity:* One of the 'selling points' of a distributed database system is its reliability, but this can only be provided at the cost of frequent back-up and complex recovery and restart mechanisms which have to cope with synchronisation of multiple updates (including that of replicated data).

• *User interface and transparency to the user:* As we have seen in Section 10.2, there are different degrees of transparency. The higher the level of transparency, then the greater likelihood of a user-friendly system. However, systems offering higher transparency may be less user-friendly from the point-of-view of query language provided or user interface (menu or command). The different users at each node may suggest different choices at each node, and this will also have technical and cost trade-offs.

Organisational issues

• *Suitability of distributed database systems for the organisation:* This issue comprises a number of aspects. The first relates to the amount of potential and actual interaction between sites in terms of the information flows and also how operations carried out or decisions taken at one site affect others. The second relates to the degree of decentralisation of management authority and control. We have already mentioned these points. The third relates to how much the data needs to be accessed from more than one site. If most data needs to be accessed by most people, then a centralised DBMS may be a better solution. Finally, it concerns how up-to-date the data must be. Again, if it has to be completely up-to-date, then, a centralised DBMS may be a better solution. As with conventional databases, it is essential that top management perceives its value and that this in turn is seen by the rest of the organisation through top management commitment and involvement in the distributed database project.

• *Administration and organisational control:* A distributed database system is likely to have more impact on the organisation than either traditional batch processing or terminal-based central database systems. As well as the data administrator and database administrator teams of centralised systems, there need to be local database administrators at each site (indeed, if there is total autonomy, a global data*base* administrator may not be necessary). Implementing such a system also requires people who do not normally work together to cooperate. There may also be conflict of interests over the ownership of data in a distributed database system.

- *User acceptance and education:* Again, this is also vital in a conventional database system, but there may be even greater pressures in a distributed database system environment such as the resentment felt by users who see their data being used by other companies in the organisation remote from their site.

- *Procurement policy:* Although distributed database systems do permit greater freedom to local management, it is essential that they are restricted to hardware and software from an approved list of well-tried systems and are tested on the distributed network.

- *Implementation risks:* There will be a number of risks as with any new venture, for example, that the distributed database systems will not perform properly, there will be delays or unbudgeted expenditure, the benefits are exceeded by increased complexity and technical demands or non-compliance with government or other requirements.

- *Security:* This will also require new management procedures. Physical security, for example, simpler in a central system, becomes more complex as there are a number of locations. The opportunity for users to access 'remote databases' has its dangers as it enables remote access to systems which may contain data not for public use.

- *Dispersal of expertise:* The distributed nature of the system may also lead data processing professionals to disperse with a resultant loss of the concentration of knowledge and experience of computing and the synergy that can result from a well recruited and well managed data processing department.

Economic issues

- The main costs in running the system will be communication costs, hardware and software maintenance costs, technical support costs and personnel training costs. However, distributed database systems are frequently implemented on smaller systems which will lead to cost savings compared to a large and powerful centralised mainframe system.

Technical issues

- The need for standards for communications protocols and interfaces in open systems architecture (OSA) is immediately apparent, otherwise organisations will be tied to a particular supplier. However, there are now a number of relevant and acceptable standards, such as, manufacturing automation protocols and technical and office protocols for OSA, the broadband integrated services digital networks for wide area networks and the ANSI/ISO standards for SQL.

Legislative issues
- Two main issues are involved here. The first includes any privacy legislation, such as the Data Protection Act in the United Kingdom which has very specific requirements concerning personal data, and the second concerns licensing of software which will involve the exact form of agreement between the user organisation and the supplier. With multiple sites, this agreement can be complex.

10.5 FURTHER READING

Ceri, S & Pelagatti, G (1984) *Distributed databases,* McGraw-Hill, New York.

Codd, E. F (1987) Codd's 12 rules for relational DBMS, *Relational Journal,* **1**, 1.

Date, C. J (1987a) What is a distributed database system? (part I), *Relational Journal,* **1**, 1.

Date, C. J (1987b) What is a distributed database system? (part II), *Relational Journal,* **1**, 2.

Dowgiallo, E (1989) The art of distribution, *DBMS,* **2**, March.

Pactel (1979) *Distributed database technology,* Wiley, Chichester.

The above texts and papers give a good introduction to the subject. Further references are provided in the general reference list.

Chapter 11
Tool Support: Fourth Generation, Workbench, Case and Multi-Media Systems

---

11.1 FOURTH GENERATION SYSTEMS

There is no generally agreed definition on what constitutes a fourth generation system, a workbench and a Case system. It is often argued that development work should be carried out by people who are not programmers, and this, perhaps, lies at the heart of the tools which are collectively known as fourth generation systems. Case systems are designed for the specialist, the computer programmer and analyst. But fourth generation systems can also be useful to professional computer people developing information systems. Indeed, Martin (1982b and 1983) distinguishes between end user and professional fourth generation systems. Further, some Case tools are used by end-users. Case and fourth generation systems are therefore not easily distinguished.

The basic aim of fourth generation systems is to speed up the work of developing new systems and hence reduce any applications backlog - a queue of users' applications waiting to be developed. This queue is long in most data processing installations. Surveys show that it commonly varies between three and five years in most organisations. It might be significantly longer if one considers the 'invisible backlog' of applications which are not on the list because users do not think it worthwhile to join the queue. A further benefit accrues to applications developed using fourth generation systems, for they are not just developed more quickly but, when they require changing, as they inevitably will, the changes can usually be made speedily. Thus maintenance time and effort is reduced as well as the time and effort spent developing the original applications.

According to Watt (1987) the principles of fourth generation systems are to minimise:
- Work
- Skill
- Complexity
- Time
- Error
- Maintenance.

As stated above, these tools are usually designed for use by users themselves, but they are sometimes also used by professionals in association with users. In principle there is no difference, but we would expect the systems for users to be simpler, although probably more limited in their facilities. Their simplicity is exemplified by the the various fourth generation system languages which are normally very different from conventional programming languages and require far fewer lines of code to generate the same processes.

The term **fourth generation languages** is also used to describe these systems, but the use of 'language' is narrow, even though the non-procedural (compared to high level languages) form of languages used in these systems is a particularly important feature. The term fourth generation language (4GL) inevitably arouses interest in the earlier generations of programming languages. These are:

- *Machine code* (first generation): this is the language of computers, a pattern of ones and zeros (for on and off states) and therefore very difficult and tedious to use, prone to error and difficult to debug and modify. Such programming requires an intimate knowledge of the physical hardware. This binary coding largely disappeared when assembly languages were developed.

- *Assembler* (second generation): this is one step away from machine code and appeared in the mid 1950s. Although there is a one-to-one relationship between the two sets of instructions, assembler represented the instructions using mnemonics (such as MPX for multiply) and symbols for particular items. This language is therefore slightly easier to use and produced code more quickly with fewer errors. However, the programmer still needs to know about the specific hardware on which the program is being developed.

- *High level procedural* (third generation): these are procedural languages which started to appear in the 1960s and were designed to be used for different types of application. Examples include Cobol and PL/1 (for business applications) and Fortran and Pascal (for scientific applications). One high level language statement can be compiled into several machine code instructions. Programs written in one high level language should in theory be usable on different machines with few changes being necessary, a feature called software *portability*. These languages are easier to use (when compared to their forerunners), though still designed for computer professionals. These languages have contributed greatly to the expansion of computing. However, they are still difficult to learn and use, requiring considerable training. Although natural language words are used in some of these programming languages, they are far removed from natural languages. Indeed the English words are likely to mislead the naive user. Most importantly, third generation programs are slow to use, requiring considerable time to design, code, debug and maintain.

- *Non procedural* (fourth generation): in these systems procedures are not designed by the programmer but by the fourth generation software itself, in the form of previously constructed, parameterised algorithms. Each user request is one for a result rather than a procedure to obtain this result. Compared to third generation languages, they require fewer lines of coding, and programs are quicker to write and test and easier to maintain. Fourth generation systems are designed for interactive use and the dialogue between user and software enables errors to be corrected as the application is being developed. Mnemonics, which require learning and remembering, are replaced by menus, semi-natural language, and other easy-to-use facilities. The language is designed so that non-computing people can develop their own applications. This results in more projects being completed more speedily and therefore a smaller applications backlog as well as, in the long term, alleviating the problem of trained programmer shortage.

Most fourth generation systems use a mixture of graphics and text which eases the specification of user requirements. Some use a technique whereby the user 'fills in the blanks' and rapid development is further helped through the sensible setting of default options, which are followed if the user does not specify otherwise. 'Intelligent' defaults, might include, for example, the place and format of the date on a report. If the users specify and implement the fourth generation solution, they can also maintain it without involving the data processing professionals and thereby reduce the large maintenance costs of traditional computing.

The tools that make up a fourth generation system often have a WIMP computer-user interface. As we saw in Chapter 9, WIMP stands for:

- Windows
- Icons
- Mouse, and
- Pull-down (or pull-up or pop-up) menus,

(or, sometimes, Windows, Icons, Menus and Pointers!).

Windows allow users to work on parts of a number of application areas (for example, different parts of a fourth generation system) at the same time. Each window represents a compartment on the screen and can be moved up and down and the size changed. Thus, whilst the user is working on one part of the system, other parts can be kept in view. The icons represent graphical ways of representing different aspects of the system (filing cabinets, waste-paper baskets, 'in' and 'out' trays, and so on) the meaning of which are easily understood as the represent the **desk top** or whatever the real-world metaphor happens to be. The mouse is a physical box which can be moved around on the desk top and this movement is tracked on the screen. The user moves the mouse as a kind of pointer to arrive at a point on the screen and clicks a switch on the mouse to execute that function. Usually these functions or options are listed in a menu or set of menus. Normally, the name of the menu is given at the top (or bottom) of the screen and the mouse is used to point to that name and then, by dragging the mouse downwards (or pulling up), the full list of options on the menu is displayed.

One obvious advantage with the users developing their own applications is that it avoids some of the communication problems that arose in the past between users and developers. A major criticism that users make of data processing professionals is that they have little understanding of the business and do not pay enough attention to users' requirements. Further, if the development is speeded up, the likelihood of the user requirements changing during the development process is reduced. In addition, programming and systems analysis expertise is a scarce resource in most organisations and due to the demand there is frequently a long lead time before projects are implemented. However, fourth generation systems can have a major disadvantage, that is they usually need increased computer resources, and application programs usually have longer running times. This is a real problem where applications require complex processing and such fourth generation systems may be more suited to small and medium-sized applications.

Fourth generation systems are designed for 'self help' and the use of these systems has also coincided with the spread of the information centre (discussed in Section 6.4) where professional expertise is available to encourage users to help themselves, frequently using their 'private' facilities, usually personal computers in their office. Should more powerful facilities be required, these personal computers might be linked to the organisation's mainframe computer, giving an opportunity to use its facilities. An important justification for the information centre is to ensure *some* control over user development. For example, it should prevent a number of users attempting to solve the same problem or purchasing incompatible machines and software. The information centre should help in initiating application development, training users, encouraging efficiency, and encouraging the sharing of data (and ensuring its shareability by helping to establish thorough validation routines and security provisions). This should also ensure that professional computing staff are also committed to the fourth generation environment as they are recognised in the organisation as facilitators, important cogs in the wheel.

There are a number of characteristics of a system orientated towards the user to which fourth generation systems would be expected to conform (see also Nelson, 1985):

- They should be easy to learn and use effectively. As well as good written documentation, there should be on-line 'help' facilities that users can call on when unsure of the next step, also useful and relevant debugging aids should be available to help users when an error has been made.

- They should be available for use interactively on a terminal connected to a mainframe computer or using a microcomputer. Many fourth generation systems have microcomputer and mainframe versions. Whereas the programmer writing programs in conventional languages wrote the programs which were then compiled and tested, the user and system build the application 'together', with each user request producing a system response.
- They should be robust, so that they do not 'crash'. Such systems should be designed to be 'tolerant' of mistakes in data entry. However, any errors should be detected by the system and reported to the user in a readily understandable way. Many third generation compilers give an error number and the programmer has to look up its meaning in a handbook. This may provide a very technical explanation. This would be inappropriate to fourth generation systems.
- They should self-document any work produced, so that the operational systems are easy to maintain.

As well as producing final applications, fourth generation systems can also be used to generate prototypes (Section 6.5). Performance criteria are less consequential when developing a prototype, which can be looked on as a working model, a means of refining the exact form of a working model, of the operational system. The system may produce skeletal programs and the user can experiment with various options. Principles and user requirements can be tested for viability so that costly mistakes in solving a complex data processing problem can be avoided. Fourth generation systems can produce fairly cheap and effective prototypes.

11.2 COMPONENTS OF A FOURTH GENERATION SYSTEM

We will look at the various parts of a fourth generation system separately. Stand-alone DBMS and query languages have already been discussed and data dictionary systems will be discussed in detail in Chapter 12, and therefore those aspects particularly relevant to fourth generation systems are discussed here in overview form.

Database management system
Most fourth generation systems will support their own database. Some will also support an external database, not formed using the fourth generation environment. This is useful as the users can draw on whatever data exists in the computer system already. Most fourth generation database systems are relational. These allow users to perform operations on the data without knowing its structure, an important feature as users then need only know what is to be done, not how it is achieved. As we saw in Chapter 4,

this feature of relational databases, structure independence, means that data relationships implied by user requests are set up dynamically by the system itself. However, the relational database can be slow and so some fourth generation systems offer the facility to set up hierarchies and networks, where the links between data structures are established when setting up the database.

The facilities of a fourth generation DBMS should not be dissimilar from any good stand-alone DBMS, although it is likely to be designed to include an interface that can be used by untrained users. There must also be good security and integrity features so that there is protection from errors that may be made by inexperienced users. Some operations may be effected by filling in a form or by the use of question-and-answer dialogues. Again, defaults will be used wherever possible to minimise this work. Usually the data dictionary information will be held in a specially protected part of the database.

Data dictionary

The data dictionary is an important element of developing applications in a fourth generation environment. It acts as a reference point for data held in the database, and also describes validation routines. In fact, it can be used to hold details about the applications as well as the data, so that it can represent total system documentation. Many fourth generation data dictionary systems are what is termed active systems (see Chapter 12), that is the data dictionary is automatically updated when relations are created, amended or deleted from the database.

Query language

The query language is used primarily to interrogate data in the database, normally interactively. Originally the query language could only be used in retrieval mode allowing one-off queries to the database, but now, more commonly, simple update facilities are also provided. Frequently the language used is SQL (Chapter 8) as this is becoming a standard for relational databases (though there are many versions of SQL). Some systems offer alternatives, such as Query-by-Example (Section 7.4) or query by forms, whereby users state their requirements by filling in a soft copy form. These enable efficient use by inexperienced users who may also have little knowledge of the underlying data structures. A security mechanism to allow different levels of access to different users is normally provided.

Most systems support a set of standard queries which are stored for regular use, and easily included in particular applications. Results may be displayed in tabular form on a screen or as a number of windows on a screen. *Ad hoc* queries are also supported. Much fourth generation dialogue can be of the question-and-answer type, such as:

System   WHICH CUSTOMER RECORD DO YOU WANT TO SEE?
User   PARKES HOLDINGS

This dialogue may be computer initiated (as above) or user initiated.

Report generator

Report generators retrieve data that is held in the database and format it into reports requested by the users. Again, users specify their requirements in some form of non-procedural language or by filling in a form; they do not program the logic to produce these results. The report generator will set up the page headings, subheadings, totals and detail lines after sorting the information as requested. Most will also carry out arithmetic and logical operations such as working out percentages or maximum and minimum values. For example, customer details in a sales analysis report might only be printed if the total of purchases exceeds a certain amount. Some systems use high resolution graphics to generate reports.

The report writer will normally be used for setting up standard formal reports and is mainly intended for end users. A report lay-out might be 'suggested' by the system and, through a process of refinement, the prototype frames are established. Totals, subtotals, headings and row and column placement may all have default values for the easy creation of standard forms, but can usually be changed easily where required.

Screen painter

Screen painters or generators are used to set up screen displays quickly and easily. The required design is drawn on screen and the system produces the code to generate the screen as required. This is normally done interactively. Screens can be set up from scratch or by modifying ones already created, and held in the database as necessary to suit user needs. Screens can be set up which have titles, sets of menus, boxes (for users to fill in) and some of these can be defined through the data dictionary. Once a number of screens have been set up on the database, they can be re-displayed regularly in a pre-defined sequence. They can also be used as prototyping tools.

Program generator

It is frequently possible to purchase application packages which are systems bought 'off the shelf' to do a particular job. Some applications, however, are particular to the firm and do not have suitable application packages readily available. The use of the company's computer department - if there is one - may result in a long wait, a large cost, or a system that is not exactly what is required. Program generators, designed for users, can assist in the development of these 'tailored' computer applications.

Program or application generators automate the production of code using information held in the data dictionary. They are therefore a development from report generators, producing code for data definition, validation, security, as well as reports. Much time is taken up in conventional programming to screen and report design and data validation routines. Using program generators, generating a program may involve simply naming the files to be used and specifying which screen definitions and report layouts are to be output. In other words, they are largely non-procedural, being concerned with what the requirements are, not how to achieve these. A more general purpose program might require a menu to be designed so that the users can choose which options they require at run time. Fourth generation systems therefore normally have menu creating facilities.

It may not be possible to generate all code using fourth generation systems, however, and some enable program statements from a conventional (third generation) programming language to be incorporated into generated code. Alternatively, some third generation languages include the added facilities of a program generator. Where object code is produced in a third generation language like Cobol, the trained programmer can pick this up and add to it or amend it as required. It is not always easy to follow the logic of these programs (just as it is not always easy to follow someone else's programs). This obviously needs to be taken into account when time estimates are made for developing fourth generation applications, and it must be remembered that any subsequent changes cannot be so easily handled as with 'pure' fourth generation developed programs.

The data for the reports will be either created especially for the new application program (defined, entered, validated and stored) or generated from another subset of the fourth generation system, the database and/or data dictionary. There will be facilities to specify how files are updated on the database and what calculations or logic functions are to be performed.

Most program generators facilitate the development of programs on-line, and this speeds up the process. Of course the specification of the user requirements must also be thorough and the code generated by a program generator must still be tested thoroughly.

Fourth generation systems may include a specification language that helps enforce rigour when specifying requirements and it is this language that is the input to the program generator. This could be similar to structured English (Section 6.3). There is no coding phase as there is when using third generation languages: the specification is converted directly into executable programs.

Other facilities of a fourth generation system
Most fourth generation systems incorporate other facilities such as graphics (to produce

bar charts, pie charts, and scatter diagrams), spreadsheet (for financial analysis), statistical analysis (to calculate averages, variances, standard deviation, linear regression and perform various statistical tests), and may include word processing and mailing facilities. Some systems may also have tools for specific applications, such as investment analysis. Indeed, a fourth generation system is likely to give the user a comprehensive 'toolkit'. Finally, most systems will have a data communications interface which will enable the easy transfer of the application from any development system (such as a workstation) to the target computer (frequently a mainframe computer).

11.3 FOCUS

Focus is a fourth generation product of Information Builders and it is classified as being suitable for end users to develop their own systems, as well as professionals. There exist both mainframe and microcomputer versions of Focus, which is a family of products that can be purchased in different combinations. The core of the product is the Focus database, which is relational, the Report Generator and Dialogue Manager. In addition there exist a number of optional modules for generating screens, for entering data, for performing various standard statistical functions, for producing graphs, for querying data, for performing financial modelling, for integrating files from non-Focus databases, and so on.

Information Builders claim possible improvements in productivity of over 10:1 by using Focus rather than developing systems using a third generation language. They also state that Focus enables the data processing professional and the end user to perform *ad hoc* queries and create reports in a fraction of the time required with traditional programming languages. 'A few simple English statements replace thousands of lines of equivalent COBOL or PL/1 program code'! Of course, such claims might be appropriate if the application lends itself to this standard approach. As with any tool, it will be costly if used inappropriately.

As a small illustration of its use, examine the two database files in Figure 11.1 and suppose a report is required that is sorted by store code, within region, for all order amounts over 1,000. Figure 11.2 shows the Focus request to achieve this and Figure 11.3 the result. Any details not specified in the request have automatic default values assigned.

A more complicated example would be a request to know if there are any shortages that will cause problems in supplying products to unfilled orders (an unfilled order has a shipment code of anything other than 'Y'). This requires data from both the Sales file

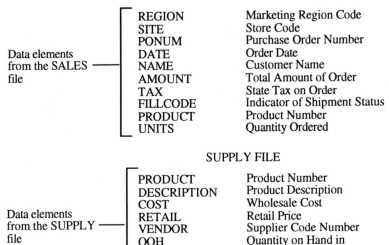

Fig.11.1 Focus database files

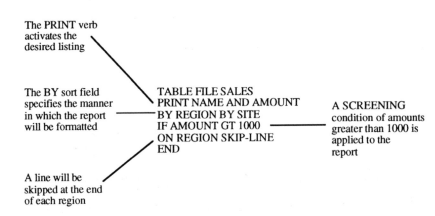

Fig. 11.2 Focus statements (courtesy of Information Builders)

and the Supply file. The JOIN command is used to combine the two files which can then be used as if they were one. The request to achieve this is shown in Figure 11.4 and the result in Figure 11.5.

The report is sorted by site within region			All quantities are greater than $1000.

PAGE 1

REGION	SITE	NAME	AMOUNT
MA	NEWK	ELIZABETH GAS	$2,877.30
	NEWY	KOCH RECONSTRUCTION	$6,086.23
	PHIL	ROSS INC	$3,890.22
		LASSITER CONSTRUCTION	$1,120.22
MW	CHIC	BAKESHORE INC.	$5,678.23
		ROPERS BROTHERS	$2,789.20
	CLEV	BOVEY PARTS	$6,769.22
		ERIE INC	$1,556.78
NE	ALBN	ROCK CITY BUILDER	$1,722.30
	BOST	HANCOCK RESTORERS	$8,246.20
		WANKEL CONSTRUCTION	$2,345.25
		WARNER INDUSTRIES	$3.155.25
	STAM	ACORN INC	$2,006.20
		KANGERS CONSTRUCTION	$2,790.50
		DART INDUSTRIES	$7,780.22
		ARISTA MANUFACTURING	$4,295.90
SE	ATL	RICHS STORES	$1,345.17
	WASH	CAPITOL WHOLESALE	$3,789.00
		FEDERAL DEPOT	$2,195.25

Report lists names, amounts and a line is skipped between each region.

Fig. 11.3 The Focus report (courtesy of Information Builders)

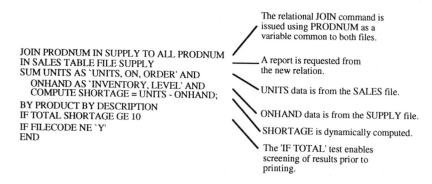

The relational JOIN command is issued using PRODNUM as a variable common to both files.

```
JOIN PRODNUM IN SUPPLY TO ALL PRODNUM
IN SALES TABLE FILE SUPPLY
SUM UNITS AS 'UNITS, ON, ORDER' AND
   ONHAND AS 'INVENTORY, LEVEL' AND
   COMPUTE SHORTAGE = UNITS - ONHAND;
BY PRODUCT BY DESCRIPTION
IF TOTAL SHORTAGE GE 10
IF FILECODE NE 'Y'
END
```

A report is requested from the new relation.

UNITS data is from the SALES file.

ONHAND data is from the SUPPLY file.

SHORTAGE is dynamically computed.

The 'IF TOTAL' test enables screening of results prior to printing.

Fig. 11.4 Focus report request (courtesy of Information Builders)

Unit on order minus inventory levels equals shortage. Only shortages of 10 or more will print on the report.

PRODNUM	DESCRIPTION	UNITS ON ORDER	INVENTORY LEVEL	SHORTAGE
11275	RADIAL ARM SAW (10 INCH)	570	489	81.00
13938	LATHE	735	689	46.00
14156	ENGINE ANALYZER	797	450	347.00
16394	ALTERNATOR (3000 WATT)	533	367	166.00
17905	PAINT SPRAYER	421	344	77.00
56267	ARC WELDER	1251	244	1,007.00

Fig. 11.5 Focus report derived from request (courtesy of Information Builders)

All these requests can be saved in Focus as procedures so that they can be executed in the future with a single command. These procedures can call other procedures so that entire applications can be constructed. Additionally the procedure can be interactive so that users can supply run time information to guide the operation of the application. The responses from the users are automatically validated according to a list of acceptable responses. Figure 11.6 is such a procedure and Figure 11.7 is the resultant interactive dialogue.

Hopefully this illustrates some of the power of a Fourth Generation Language it would certainly take considerably more code to achieve this in traditional programming language.

11.4 FOURTH GENERATION SYSTEMS - A CONCLUSION

In view of the claims made by vendors of fourth generation systems regarding their benefits, it is interesting to ask why they have not currently made a great impact on reducing the application backlog. We suggest possible reasons:

- They are comparatively new and still in the early development stage
- They require a considerable change in the systems development culture of an organisation, and not all organisations are yet ready to make this change
- The type of application that successfully used fourth generation system developments has been limited to fairly small, one-off type developments
- Fourth generation systems are often less efficient in operation than code produced by third generation programming, but any inefficiency, in terms of excess running time and memory required, must be traded off against increased productivity. Some attention is now being paid to efficiency considerations - the final version of the system being converted to fast object code modules by the system optimisers.

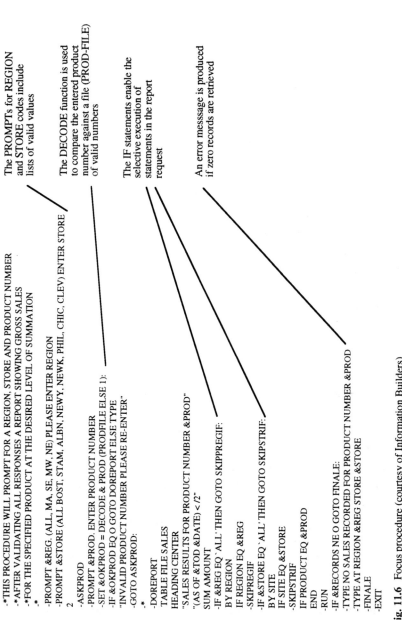

The PROMPTs for REGION and STORE codes include lists of valid values

The DECODE function is used to compare the entered product number against a file (PROD-FILE) of valid numbers

The IF statements enable the selective execution of statements in the report request

An error message is produced if zero records are retrieved

```
-*THIS PROCEDURE WILL PROMPT FOR A REGION, STORE AND PRODUCT NUMBER
-*AFTER VALIDATING ALL RESPONSES A REPORT SHOWING GROSS SALES
-*FOR THE SPECIFIED PRODUCT AT THE DESIRED LEVEL OF SUMMATION
-*
-PROMPT &REG. (ALL, MA, SE, MW, NE) PLEASE ENTER REGION
-PROMPT &STORE (ALL BOST, STAM, ALBN, NEWY, NEWK, PHIL, CHIC, CLEV) ENTER STORE
2
-ASKPROD
-PROMPT &PROD. ENTER PRODUCT NUMBER
-SET &OKPROD = DECODE & PROD (PRODFILE ELSE 1):
-IF &OKPROD EQ O GOTO DOREPORT ELSE TYPE
"INVALID PRODUCT NUMBER PLEASE RE-ENTER"
-GOTO ASKPROD:
-*
-DOREPORT
TABLE FILE SALES
HEADING CENTER
"SALES RESULTS FOR PRODUCT NUMBER &PROD"
"(AS OF &TOD &DATE) </2"
SUM AMOUNT
-IF &REG EQ 'ALL' THEN GOTO SKIPPREGIF:
BY REGION
IF REGION EQ &REG
-SKIPREGIF
-IF &STORE EQ 'ALL' THEN GOTO SKIPSTRIF:
BY SITE
IF SITE EQ &STORE
-SKIPSTRIF
IF PRODUCT EQ &PROD
END
-RUN
-IF &RECORDS NE O GOTO FINALE:
-TYPE NO SALES RECORDED FOR PRODUCT NUMBER &PROD
-TYPE AT REGION &REG STORE &STORE
-FINALE
-EXIT
```

Fig. 11.6 Focus procedure (courtesy of Information Builders)

A   Procedure is executed.   EX CAFDMI
        All prompts are in   ──── **PLEASE ENTER REGION**
        bold face.   MA
                                  ENTER STORE
B   Reply validation   ┌─ NEWD
        detects an incorrect │   **PLEASE CHOOSE ONE OF THE FOLLOWING:**
        store code (NEWD)   ─┤   **ALL, BOST, STAM, ALBN, NEWY, NEWK, PHIL, CHIC, CLEV**
        and re-prompts   │   **ENTER STORE**
        for a valid value.   └─ NEWY
                                  ENTER PRODUCT NUMBER
                                  14156

                              ┌─ NUMBER OF RECORDS IN TABLE = 7,345 LINES = 1
                              │
C   Report executes   │   PAGE 1
        based on   │
        specified values,   ─┤   SALES RESULTS FOR PRODUCT NUMBER 14156
        producing the   │   (AS OF 12.39.02 10/07/82)
        desired results.   │
                              │   REGION   SITE   AMOUNT
                              └─ MA   NEWY $96,814.00

Fig. 11.7 Focus report derived from request (courtesy of Information Builders)

However, with advances in hardware development (for example, in very large scale integration and faster logic), these considerations might become less important.

Thus, most large transaction processing systems are still developed in traditional ways. Nevertheless the impact of fourth generation systems will increase, particularly on smaller systems for less complex applications, but whether they are ever used for all developments seems unlikely. Indeed, it is somewhat an irrelevant debate because as long as a significant number of developments are undertaken using fourth generation systems, then most objectives will have been achieved.

11.5 WORKBENCHES

We will now look at systems described as **methodology workbenches**. The relationship of methodology workbenches to fourth generation systems and Case often causes confusion. This is because some aspects of a fourth generation system may in fact be included in a methodology workbench and vice versa. The methodology workbench is usually aimed at the technologist rather than the user. In this regard they are nearer Case tools than fourth generation systems. However, they are usually designed to support a particular information systems development methodology (Avison & Fitzgerald, 1988), such as Information Engineering, STRADIS and SSADM, although some are more general purpose. The methodology workbench usually covers a wider range of activities than simply the generation of code for an application: it may support information and process modelling, database design, even strategy planning, as well as the programming or construction of an application which may include support for fourth generation tools. Some methodology workbenches also support the management and control of project development.

Methodology workbenches are sometimes separated into two parts and termed analyst workbenches or programmer workbenches. **Programmer workbenches** support the design and construction of programs. The objective is to provide an environment in which software which adheres to the principles of software engineering can be speedily developed. Within this framework there are usually two distinct support features, a code generation facility and a facility to provide sub-programs. A code generation facility generates source code in a traditional third generation language from a high level specification language, such as pseudo code. The second support feature is the provision of building blocks of code that have been pre-written for functions and processes which are frequently required and can be incorporated into a final application.

A workbench is likely to include test tools and diagnostic aids. A subroutine or program can be tested independently of other subroutines or programs. These facilities might be used to trace the execution of the subroutines or programs so that intermediate results can be validated. For this reason, the workbench can also be used to maintain programs and systems as well as creating new ones. Workbenches aim to attack the applications backlog by reducing maintenance time as well as development time.

Analyst workbenches support the systems analysis and design tasks. In particular, they usually support the logical data modelling processes by automating the construction and maintenance of entity models, and the conversion to a variety of target DBMS schema designs (including normalised data). On the process modelling side they usually support the construction and maintenance of data flow diagrams and function hierarchy charts of some kind. There may well also be support for screen and report designs and a menu and dialogue design facility. Analyst workbenches will have some kind of data dictionary or system encyclopedia as the central core of the facility.

11.6 INFORMATION ENGINEERING WORKBENCH (IEW)

Inevitably analyst and programmer workbenches have been combined to form integrated project workbenches which address the whole of the development of a project from analysis through to construction, using a common set of tools and user interfaces.

An example of such a workbench product is the Information Engineering Workbench (IEW) jointly developed by Arthur Young and Knowledgeware. The core of the IEW is the Encyclopedia, which contains information about all the objects in the development project, be these entities, processes, relationships, attributes or whatever. The Encyclopedia is in two parts, one dealing with the organisation's information and data, and the other with the organisation's functions or activities. Information is also kept that relates one part to the other, for example, which data is used by what function.

IEW provides access to a series of diagramming support tools for drawing data flow diagrams, entity models and functional decomposition diagrams. Sitting between these diagramming support tools and the Encyclopedia is something called the Knowledge Co-ordinator. This is an 'expert system', enforcing the correct standards for completeness, consistency, and accuracy of the diagram content. The repository of the IBM AD Cycle product, which includes organisation models, data models and process models, is derived from the Knowledge Co-ordinator of IEW (Martin 1991).

IEW adopts an interesting approach to the storage of the various diagrams, and unlike most other workbenches it does not store them as diagrams, for example, as DFDs, but as a series of definitions about the objects in the diagrams. This means that objects that appear in more than one diagram are only stored once and that diagrams are generated from the current information in the Encyclopedia, as and when they are needed. When changes are made to one diagram, the effects of that change are automatically reflected when other diagrams in which the object appears are generated. It is the Knowledge Co-ordinator that translates the Encyclopedia information into diagrams and displays, and vice versa. This enables the basic Encyclopedia information to be displayed in a number of ways according to needs. For example, an object may feature in an entity model, a data flow diagram, and an action diagram (another type of diagram used in the Information Engineering methodology).

IEW is still in the process of development and features being tested currently include modules for producing physical designs for programs and databases. Ultimately it is hoped that the product will be a full system development environment for the Information Engineering methodology. Other systems of this type include Excelerator (Index Technologies), Information Engineering Facility (IEF) (James Martin Associates and Texas Instruments) and Application Factory (Cortext/Corvision).

As stated earlier, the facilities of workbenches are usually included in Case systems which have grown in number at the expense of workbenches. Many workbenches have grown into full Case tools, and products such as Excelerator, Auto-Mate Plus and Information Engineering Workbench are now usually listed as Case tools. The distinguishing characteristic, workbenches being, in general, methodology specific and Case tools being general purpose, is still true to some extent. Nevertheless it is now possible to purchase versions of Case tools and whole Case products which are methodology specific.

11.7 CASE (COMPUTER-AIDED SOFTWARE ENGINEERING)

Case represents a growing family of software tools whose main aim is to automate much of the software development process. Early tools were developed around the needs of computer programmers in producing software in a well-disciplined, formal manner, adhering to the principles of software engineering. These are now sometimes referred to as 'Lower Case' products. Most Case products emphasise the importance of producing 'quality software'. Many Case products have developed further to provide more general facilities for analysts as well as programmers, and these 'Upper Case' tools may be run on mainframes and microcomputers:

- Mainframe-based: enabling models to be produced in third normal form and/or entity-relationship models displayed in graphical form using different information, such as input forms, computer listings, file structures and clerical records.
- PC-based: using the more recent, powerful microcomputers or workstations, combining data dictionary and computer-aided design systems to enable interactive modelling and data dictionary creation and modification.

Such tools are designed to achieve productivity gains and improved quality and control by supporting all the formal aspects of systems development and not only the software development aspects.

The core Case facilities include:

- Graphical facilities for modelling and design
- Data dictionary
- Automated documentation
- Analysis of the problem areas

and all Case tools should contain these facilities, whilst advanced Case features include:

- Code generation from systems specification or from the models designed using the tool
- Automatic audit trail of all changes
- Critical path scheduling with resource availability (that is, project control)
- Automatic enforcement of the standards of a chosen software development methodology.

It is important that these facilities are completely integrated so that they provide a consistency for analysis and design.

Sometimes Case tools are categorised into three main types:

- CaseI - automates the conceptual and logical modelling stages of database design (Excelerator, DesignAid and Stradis/Draw)
- CaseII - includes also prototyping tools and a DBMS (GoldenGate, PC-Oracle and TAB)

- CaseIII - includes also project management and control tools (Oracle, CASE2000)

Excellent graphics facilities can be expected with a modern Case tool, with the more commonly used symbols (of data flow diagrams and entity-relationship diagrams, for example) being included in a pre-defined set. Frequently there are alternatives provided (for example, the symbols for Gane & Sarson and Yourdon data flow diagrams differ). There should be a simple method for the deletion of items, including facilities for removal of those references in the data dictionary, ensuring that inconsistencies do not accrue. According to Martin (1991), second generation Case graphics should be able to diagram automatically from the underlying data in the data dictionary. Correspondingly, entries in the data dictionary should be checked and updated as the entity-relationship model is being drawn. In some systems, access to the data dictionary record can be achieved by clicking on the required object using a mouse. Good word processing facilities are sometimes provided for narrative sections on diagrams and for entries into the data dictionary. Indeed, automatic production of much of the documentation necessary to support an application would be expected. This includes system specifications, project management documentation (particularly sophisticated developments in CaseIII products) and technical and training documentation.

The data dictionary is another vital part of the Case tool, and features are usually comprehensive being integrated with all aspects of the development process so that consistency checking can be carried out. According to Misra (1990), it should classify the various objects, such as data elements, external entities on data flows, data stores, processes and program design modules and group them in some defined order. This should be done automatically.

Although many Case tools neglect the early planning phases of the life cycle, concentrating on design and implementation phases, some Case tools cover all the stages of the systems life cycle. They enable the workload to be split between several members of the team. This is feasible because of the Case tool's multi-user facility as well as the integrated data dictionary, which will include information about the proposed system.

Although all users in the organisation will see the benefits of Case by software which is quicker to develop, efficient and easier to maintain, it is the technical staff who are most directly affected. This provides the main distinction between Case and fourth generation systems (but, as we have seen, it is not a fool-proof distinction because of confusion in the market-place).

Through the use of high-resolution graphics, analysts are able to clearly define the application system using the various diagramming techniques provided (such as entity-relationship diagrams, function diagrams, data flow diagrams, and the like) and these can be changed, rearranged and scaled, with the software carrying out consistency and completeness checks and automatically updating the data dictionary.

The main problem encountered when implementing Case is the change necessary in the culture of the organisation, particularly of data processing staff, and this requires training. Users have also found that the promised productivity increases have not always materialised!

11.8 ORACLE

The components of Oracle's system include:
- Oracle relational DBMS
- SQL*Menu
- SQL*Forms
- SQL*ReportWriter
- Easy*SQL
- SQL*Calc
- SQL*Star.

Oracle DBMS is a relational DBMS offering a full version of SQL as well as embedded SQL (in ADA, C, Cobol, Fortran, Pascal and PL/1). It is a very portable system, being available on mainframes, minicomputers, workstations and microcomputers running different operating systems. SQL*Menu provides a common front-end to Oracle and other related applications so that the user need learn only one common interface to all applications. SQL*Forms allows the creation of a form-based transaction processing application without the user having to write code. SQL*ReportWriter enables the user to set up a number of types of report using the data held in the DBMS. The user can specify the requirements by filling in a form. Easy*SQL is aimed at the end-user who wishes to access the organisation database without having to learn full SQL which is more appropriate to regular users. By following a series of menus, the users are guided into stating their requirements (including a query-by-example forms management) and the equivalent SQL statements are constructed by the system. SQL*Calc is a spreadsheet facility and can interface with other spreadsheets such as Lotus 1-2-3. SQL*Star is a distributed database system (which we discussed in Chapter 10) that ties the local databases into a single logical database, even if they are on dissimilar computer systems. There are other add-ons, such as a graphics capability, an accounting module and a mailing system.

Up to now, we could sensibly classify Oracle as a fourth generation product, having 4GL extensions to the DBMS. However, there are now Case extensions to Oracle which provide Case as well as fourth generation and basic DBMS facilities. The latest version of Oracle provides all three category III Case facilities, running on powerful workstations. It has the following components:

- *Case*Designer:* which is a mouse-driven diagramming tool allowing rapid development of models, such as entity-relationship diagrams, function hierarchies, data flow diagrams and matrix diagrams and covers most of the main techniques of systems analysis and design in a database environment. There is immediate entry to the data dictionary, so that the dictionary is always consistent with the designer. Reporting, cross-references and consistency checking are also part of this tool. Automatic database design and sizing, impact analysis, version control and database generation using SQL and program code generation (for prototyping) is also featured.

- *Case*Method:* this provides support for Oracle's system development approach which is a top-down structured approach to systems development, involving managers and users gathering business objectives, requirements and determining priorities. It uses such methods as functional decomposition, entity diagramming and data flow diagramming. Much of the documentation is output automatically. It supports the separation of logical and physical designs. Applications are expected to be prototyped.

- *Case*Dictionary:* an automated data dictionary, being the central repository of the organisation's data. Over seventy reports are generated by the system including cross references, impact analyses and exception reports. The tool can be used to generate a set of normalised relations and then to create the database itself. Information about the relationships, attributes, identifiers and synonyms on the entity relationship side, will be kept alongside information about the functions, events, data flows and module definitions on the function side, along with data relating to the physical data model such as database tables, index definitions and file and record layouts. There are also a number of utilities and reports generated to help the database administrator.

11.9 MULTI-MEDIA SYSTEMS

Multi-media systems extend the concept of a *data*base to include graphics, images, video, sound as well as numeric and character sets and text. This is very challenging because of the diverse characteristics of these categories of data. Traditional data is record-based, discrete and requires search and retrieval methods to support the user. Text has no naturally discrete fields or records, it has a 'meaning and context' element, and most searches ignore the meaning element but rely on keywords.

Graphics, on the other hand, is stored as a bit-map, is slow and difficult to retrieve and requires indexing either by manual input or by incorporating a partial identifier on a graph which is to be scanned. Images, such as photographs, are also bit-mapped and require an even larger storage capacity and processing power. Video is not static and requires a huge storage capacity. Sound is also not static and requires more storage than that required by text.

Technology improvements, such as optical storage, have enabled the online storage of large amounts of data. CD-ROM and WORM (write-once, read-many) are optical online storage methods which are comparatively low priced. Hardware and software support is now available for multi-media systems. In time, they are likely to enable new ways of analysing and presenting information, which has been limited in the past largely to text and conventional data, or to specific and separate packages for graphics, video and speech which were not integrated in any way. With hypermedia systems, users can link all types of data, creating paths through different types of material so that mixed media documents can be produced. The potential of such systems is great because 'real life' is made up of visual, audio and text material.

11.10 USE OF TOOLS IN THE DATABASE APPROACH

This text has suggested five stages to the development of a database system and its applications:
* Business analysis
* Conceptual modelling
* Logical modelling
* Physical modelling
* Applications development.

In this section we examine the ways in which we could use software tools to help the process.
* Business analysis (Chapter 2): This is the stage in which there is a detailed examination of the organisation. It is a phase where tools are of least help (or at least the right kind of tools are not available) as information is gained through interaction with users and management and by looking through existing documentation. However the data dictionary system will be used as a repository of some of the information gathered and will be of value to the next phases in the system. Some Case tools provide assistance in drawing up and verifying users needs, for example, by providing templates for consistent and complete documentation. Further, efforts are being made, at least in the research arena, to develop tools to support rich picture diagramming and root definitions (Avison &

Golder, 1991). Multi-media systems are also potentially helpful as they can store photographs, rough sketches, annotated notes and forms: no longer are we restricted to the storage of pure text on computer files.

- Conceptual modelling (Chapter 3): The process of data modelling using entity-relationship diagrams and the normalisation of relations can be greatly aided by Case tools. The information from business analysis, stored in the data dictionary, can be used as a basis for some of the information on the diagrams and the tedious task of drawing the diagrams, and amending them, is greatly eased by the graphics facilities of a modern Case tool. Very often the analyst will use such a tool on a PC, only transferring it to the mainframe for documentation of the live system. The process of normalisation is also helped by tool support, the analyst prompted to provide information about the dependencies and the system producing the final relations, checking for errors, and reconciling the information with that on the E-R diagrams. Some algorithms for normalisation, along with their sources, are given in Maciaszek (1990).

- Logical modelling (Chapter 4): The results of the conceptual modelling stage, held in the data dictionary, can be used to produce the required data structures for the DBMS (usually relational, hierarchical or network). With most modern DBMS being relational, it is easy to map the conceptual model to the logical model, however the mapping to a hierarchical or network system is also rule-based and therefore subject to automation. Quang and Chartier-Kastler (1991) detail many of these basic rules.

- Physical modelling (Chapter 5): The way that data is stored on the database will be largely automated by the DBMS using the data dictionary with help from the database administrator, who may be asked by the system to make some decisions. This role will be eased by the simulation facilities of most DBMS which will give the timings, for example, of various access strategies.

- Applications development (Chapter 6): It is at this stage that tools can be of particular benefit to the analysts, users and the organisation as they enable more thorough analysis, facilitate prototyping, which will help clear up misunderstandings, and inconsistencies and speed up development. Case tools, workbenches and fourth generation systems can all be used here. The diagramming facilities of Case tools can be used to help draw the data flow diagrams, function diagrams and frequently draw up decision trees and decision tables as well. The production of program specifications can be automated and the programs themselves generated from formalised specifications, such as those in structured English. Where prototypes are developed with the user or by the user, the 'fill-in-the-form' interface of many fourth generation systems is usually more helpful than those of Case tools which are designed for computer specialists. The prototype may be used as the basis of the operational system or as a method of improved requirements analysis for the application. Some Case tools include performance-tuning frames that can specify the most effective design from the technical point of view and therefore help to generate applications which are reasonably efficient. Fourth generation system generated programs tend to be inefficient, sometimes incomplete, and therefore may require modification by a programmer experienced in a third generation language. Case tools can also generate sample programs at minimal cost, thus helping the evaluation of technical alternatives. Another area where tools can be used is in testing as they can use test data stored in the data dictionary (or generate their own) to run through the application programs. Finally, Case tools can be particularly valuable at the maintenance stage, generating new code to satisfy new needs which can be added to existing programs.

11.11 EVALUATING TOOLS

Automated development tools are now a very important part of database design, implementation and the development of applications using the database. The costs of purchasing and using such systems are high and therefore the choice of system needs to be a strategic decision with user and database administrator involvement. Once the system has been purchased and used, the cost of change will be particularly high. Yet these systems are constantly changing and developing.

Case tools seem to be overtaking fourth generation systems in terms of sales in the market place as they become more sophisticated and more general in their application and relevance to the various people involved in the development of database applications.

When assessing a particular tool product, the following list of considerations, amongst others, will be useful:
* Number of sites the tool has been installed
* Number of workstations installed
* Cost of product
* Cost of maintenance
* Programming language in which the tool was written
* Software environment necessary for the tool to function
* Year of design of the tool
* Methodology(ies) supported
* Stages of the methodology supported

- User interface (for example, graphical, WIMP or command language)
- Help facilities provided
- Logical model supported by the tool (hierarchical, network or relational)
- Security facilities provided
- Documentation provided
- Training necessary
- Maintenance and after-sales service.

The claims of suppliers (and many writers in the field) should be looked at carefully. Dramatic increases of programmer productivity, decreases in development time, reductions in maintenance effort, reductions in errors (bugs in programs, failure to meet requirements and so on) and increases in the level of user satisfaction, have certainly not been found everywhere. For example, the phrase 'automation of the normalisation process' sounds very promising, but it may be in the form of a dialogue leading the user through the various documentation, asking for the identification of functional dependencies and repeating groups, a tedious and limiting task. Case tools are still in the early stages of development: many products have expected facilities missing (the next release!) and some of the facilities provided are sometimes incomplete or difficult or tedious to use. For example, excellent graphics facilities may be offset by poor facilities for document production. They should not be regarded as 'total solutions': the methods that they automate (or partly automate) need to be selected carefully as suitable for the organisation: sometimes a claim for methodology support is in truth support for only some aspects of a methodology. The use of software tools does not imply that the role of people: users, programmers, systems analysts, database administrators and managers are any less important. Even good tools will produce poor results if the people side of systems is neglected.

11.12 FURTHER READING

Chen, M, Nunamaker, J. F & Weber, E. S (1989) Computer-aided software engineering: present status and future directions, *Data Base*, Spring.

Holloway, S (Ed) (1990) *Fourth generation systems - their scope, applications and methods of evaluation*, Chapman and Hall, London.

Horowitz, E (1985) A Survey of Application Generators, *IEEE Software*, January 1985

Martin, C. F (1988) Second generation CASE tools: a challenge to vendors, *IEEE Software*, March.

Martin, J (1982) *Fourth Generation Languages, Vol 1*, Prentice-Hall, Englewood Cliffs.

Martin, J (1983) *Fourth Generation Languages, Vol 2*, Prentice-Hall, Englewood Cliffs.

Misra, S. K (1990) Analyzing CASE system characteristics: evaluative framework, *Information and Software Technology*, **32**, 6.

Tozer, E (Ed) (1984) *Applications Development Tools - A State of the Art Report*, Pergamon-Infotech.

Watt, J (1987) *Applied fourth generation languages*, Sigma Press, Wilmslow.

These texts and papers cover fourth generation systems, workbenches and Case tools. Further references are found in the bibliography. The pace of change is so fast in this area that computer journals and magazines are useful sources of information about the various products available.

Chapter 12
Data Dictionary Systems

12.1 INTRODUCTION

There has recently been a significant increase in the use of data dictionary systems (DDS). This is mainly due to the corresponding growth in the use of data analysis techniques, DBMS and fourth generation and Case products. Organisations frequently purchase a DDS along with a DBMS in order to record details of the data which will be held in the database. Many DDS are integrated with a particular DBMS or offered as a possible 'extra' to a DBMS.

A DDS is a software tool for managing the data resource. It enables the recording and processing of data about the data (meta data) that an organisation uses. Originally DDS were designed as documentation tools, ensuring standard terminology for data items (and sometimes programs) and providing a cross-reference capability. They have now evolved as an essential feature of the information systems environment and are of particular importance to the database administrator who will use the DDS to control the computer and manual systems and their uses of data. This helps to minimise maintenance and development costs. Any tools used should interface with the data dictionary, indeed, as we have seen, it may well be an integral part of the tool.

There are many data dictionary products available, but despite the setting up of a Codasyl committee on Data Dictionaries in 1980 and the UK equivalents (for example a British Computer Society working group), there is no industry-wide standard for data dictionaries. Most are integrated with a specific DBMS, but a few are stand-alone and can be used with a number of DBMS.

A DDS is a central catalogue of the definitions and usage of the data within an organisation. This can ease the sharing of data among applications. If used alongside a DBMS it could be said to be a directory of the database, 'a database of the database', although this relationship might be better expressed as an 'information source about the database'. Most DDS are used chiefly as a documentation aid and as a control point for referencing data. A DDS will hold definitions of all data items, which may be any objects of interest, and their characteristics. It will hold information on how this data is used as well as how it is stored.

A DDS may play an active role in systems design, programming and in running systems. It could be used to provide the data structures to the program at compile time or validate data at execution time. It can be used as a storage base of programming code (subprograms) and these subprograms may be used in a number of programs. Many DDS are therefore more than mere points of reference and they hold information about processes as well as data.

However, the major benefit of most DDS stems from it being the central store of information about the database. The DDS pervades all aspects of systems work and its use could lead to:

- Improved documentation and control
- Consistency in data use
- Easier data analysis
- Reduced data redundancy
- Increased data integrity
- Increased data security
- Simpler programming
- Greater enforcement of standards
- Better means of estimating the effect of change
- More flexible reporting.

Of course some of these advantages could be equally said to be the result of using a database with a DBMS and an effective database administration team. Indeed, they all contribute to an effective data processing environment.

The influence of the DDS, as shown in Figure 12.1, can pervade all areas of data processing: to users, managers and auditors, as well as to data processing professionals and the database administrator. However, they will only be truly effective if they are on-line, otherwise they will not be complete, accurate and up-to-date.

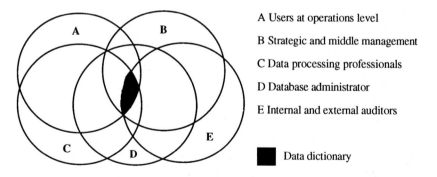

A Users at operations level

B Strategic and middle management

C Data processing professionals

D Database administrator

E Internal and external auditors

■ Data dictionary

Fig. 12.1 Influence and users of the data dictionary

From the point of view of the organisation, management is now becoming more aware that the data of the enterprise is a valuable and important resource which must be properly managed. There must therefore be a knowledge of what data exists and how it is used. There must be control over modifications to the database and the processes that use it. There must also be control over plans for new uses of data and over the acquisition of data. The DBMS may well achieve some of these objectives itself, but in order to gain full control over the data resource, it is necessary to collect and store information about the data.

The British Computer Society set up a working party (referred to hereafter as the BCSWP) to suggest a standard for data dictionary systems. Their report was published in 1976 and has proved influential. The BCSWP suggested that a DDS should provide two sets of facilities:

- To record and analyse data requirements independently of how they are going to be met.
- To record design decisions in terms of database or file structures implemented and the programs which access them.

These two sets of facilities are referred to as the **conceptual data model** and the **implementation data structure** respectively, some writers referring to these as management use mode and computer use mode.

The conceptual view shows a model of the organisation, that is, the entities, their attributes, and the relationships between these entities. This model is the result of the data analysis process and is therefore independent of any data processing implications. The conceptual view can also include details of the events and operations that occur in the organisation. It represents therefore the conceptual schema - the end result of the data analysis exercise described in Chapter 3. The forms that were used to document the entities, attributes, relationships, events and operations, that were shown in Chapter 3 as Figures 3.12 to 3.16, can be used to input the data into the data dictionary.

The implementation view gives information about the data processing applications in computing terms. The processes are therefore described as systems, programs and subprograms (modules), and the data is described in terms of files, records, and fields, or in the terminology of the DBMS used (for example, segments, sets and data items). Some systems also include an operations view as part of the implementation level. This will include information relating to the operation of the system, such as the schedule for running the system and its hardware requirements.

The BCSWP argued that one of the main functions of a DDS should be to show the relationship between the conceptual and implementation views. One view should map on to the other view. Any inconsistencies between the two should be detected. It should be noted, however, that many DDS currently available only support the implementation view and those which hold a conceptual as well as implementation view do not always map one to the other automatically nor carry out any checks to ensure their consistency.

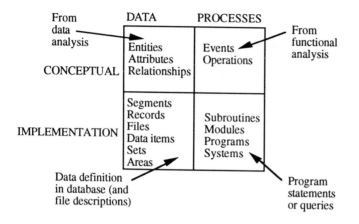

Fig. 12.2 The four quadrants of a data dictionary system

The conceptual and implementation views for data and processes are shown in Figure 12.2. The four quadrants represent the components of the DDS. There is a fifth component, mentioned before, which indicates the cross-referencing between the components. Indexes can be used to identify entities, functions, and programs and this simple referencing system will be an effective tool in maintenance.

Of increasing importance when assessing DDS is the distinction between active and passive systems. A **passive** DDS is one used for documentation. **Active** DDS will do more. For example, they might liaise with the DBMS and applications so that data is picked up from the database and entered into the application when it is running using data descriptions in the data dictionary. The DDS might first check security information in the data dictionary to ensure that the application has the right to access the information. In an active DDS, these types of activities will be performed without human intervention.

12.2 FACILITIES OF A DATA DICTIONARY SYSTEM

For each data element, the DDS will contain amongst other things, the following:
- The names associated with that element - there may be different names used by the various users and computer programs to refer to one element
- A description of the data element in natural language
- Details of ownership (normally the department which creates the data)
- Details of the users who refer to the element
- Details of the systems and programs which refer to or update the element
- Details on any privacy constraints that should be associated with the item

- Details about the data element in data processing systems, such as the length of the data item in characters, whether it is numeric, alphabetic or another data type and what logical files include the data item
- The security level attached to the element in order to restrict access to it
- The total storage requirement
- The validation rules for each element, for example, the range of acceptable values
- Details of the relationship between the data items.

The data dictionary is likely to record information about elements other than data, for example, reports output by the various applications. Information about them could include the report name, who gets copies, when the report is produced, special forms required, formatting instructions, and details of the application and program which produce the report.

With so much detail needed to be held on the data dictionary, it is essential that an indexing and cross-referencing facility is provided by the DDS.

Earlier DDS concentrated on documentation and on producing reports about the data on the database to the database administrator or other 'professional' user of the DDS. In installations where there is no DDS, computer systems can become entangled in a confusion of data. Data dictionaries are used to ensure greater discipline. Reports produced by the DDS are of use in particular to the data administration staff who will attempt to improve the efficiency of use and storage of the data.

So that the user can request these facilities and to input data into the system, a pre-printed form usually in fixed format is provided by many DDS. There will also be some form of enquiry language. Where a DDS is associated with a particular DBMS, then this will use any query language provided by the DBMS. The DBMS may assist in managing the data dictionary, indeed the data dictionary will be held on the database, just like any other database file.

Most commercially available DDS go beyond these basic facilities so that the DDS is a tool with a number of objectives:

- To provide facilities for documenting information collected during all stages of a computer project, according to the standards of the organisation
- To provide details of applications usage and their data usage once a system has been implemented, so that analysis and redesign may be facilitated as the environment changes
- To make access required for the above easier by providing cross-referencing and indexing facilities
- To make extension of the DDS easy
- To encourage systems analysts to follow the information systems development methodology of the organisation.

This last objective could point, for example, to data dictionaries holding details of the contents of the sources and destinations (sinks) of data flows. In other words, data dictionaries are a tool of process definition as well as data definition. The scope of a DDS is therefore broad. It is not merely a documenting aid: it is a support to all stages in the development and maintenance of an application and the control of the database.

A more sophisticated DDS will have a number of extra facilities such as the following:

- Automatic input of data definitions from source code. These can be copied in the program at compilation time
- The generation of source code relating to items in the data dictionary to a sort program or applications program
- The recognition that several versions of the same programs or data structures may exist at the same time. The different versions could represent:
    * live and test states of the programs or data
    * programs and data structures which may be used at different sites
    * data set up under different software or validation routines.
- The coordination and communication between development activities, and avoidance of potential problems such as version management or poor communications between development staff
- Impact analysis, whereby the implications of any changes can be seen, such as 'which programs will be affected by changing the description of a data object'
- The automatic verification of designs according to standards laid down, frequently by interacting with a Case product or other tool
- The provision of on-line facilities to aid the interrogation of the database. Here, an interactive query language needs to be provided as part of the DDS.
- The provision of an interface with a DBMS
- The provision of security features, such as password systems. These may be built in to restrict access to the DDS. For example, users should only gain access to that part of the data dictionary which is relevant to the job in hand
- The ability to restrict the type of access, such as read, delete, write, and update, is as important to the DDS as it is to the database
- The provision of facilities to generate application programs and produce reports and validation routines.

A particularly useful facility for the database administrator is the help provided by most DDS in the initial creation of the data dictionary. They frequently provide a default data structure for modelling the meta data and this will be suitable for most applications. This speeds up the laborious and sometimes difficult early work.

12.3 ADVANTAGES AND COSTS OF USING A DATA DICTIONARY SYSTEM

A number of possible benefits may come from using a DDS:

- A DDS can improve the ability of management to control and know about the data resource of the enterprise. It can also show all the programs, files and reports that may be affected by any change to the definition or usage of data elements. It may be used to generate code which reflects that change. It may also be possible to assess accurately the cost and time scale to effect any change. A DDS also enables management to enforce data definition standards and detect unauthorised use.

- A DDS reduces the clerical load of database administration. The form, meaning, and usage of data can be more easily documented. It also gives the database administrator more control over the design and use of the database. Accurate data definitions can be provided directly to programs. Sensitive data can be made available only to particular users. Test and production versions of files and programs can be checked and the database administrator can ensure that standards are being followed.

- A DDS can aid the recording, processing, storage and destruction of data along with associated documents flowing through an organisation.

- A DDS can help systems development by generating test files and providing documentation.

- A DDS provides application programs with data definitions and subroutines and therefore enforces some standards on programming, making programs more readable and consistent, removing much of the tedium associated with application program development and helping to eliminate misunderstandings that might otherwise occur.

- A DDS aids application program maintenance because changes to the data and the data structures can be made where appropriate to all programs using the data. The DDS may itself automatically document the change.

- A DDS aids the operations side of computing by holding details of storage and recovery procedures, and archiving information. Some DDS provide job control parameters to run the applications.

- A DDS may provide an estimate of costs of any proposed change of use of the data and estimate a time scale for making such changes. It may also be used to assess the impact of change on operational programs and modules.

- A DDS can provide effective security features, such as passwords, to assist in the protection of the data resource.

- A DDS can be an aid to communication by providing information about the data and applications in the required forms for users, analysts, programmers and database specialists.

- A DDS can support an increase in the commitment of the users to the system and, in general, can improve standards of computer applications in the organisation. Such standards will include those relating to data usage and responsibility and other attributes such as format, meaning and validity criteria.
- A DDS can be helpful in providing the continuity of information about applications where hardware, software, applications and personnel in the organisation change.
- A DDS can help in auditing so that, for example, the use of a given data entity to the applications can be identified and therefore enable a cost-efficiency study of the database and applications to be carried out
- A DDS can encourage the employment of a database administrator, and once installed, help that person carry out the role. Indeed, in view of the necessity of administrating the use of thousands of frequently changing program and data facilities, it can make such a task feasible.
- A DDS can make the DBMS effective. This might be achieved, for example, by controlling redundancy (it is the information base by which duplicated data can be identified)
- A DDS should provide a body of information, being centrally maintained and conforming to standards, which can be trusted by all its users.

Although, as we have seen, the DDS is a very useful management tool, there is a price to pay. The DDS 'project' may itself take two or three years. It needs careful planning, and defining the exact requirements, designing its contents, testing, implementation and evaluation will all require time and effort. This may take as long as the DBMS development project itself. The cost of a DDS includes not only the initial price of its installation and any hardware requirements, but also the cost of collecting the information, entering it into the DDS, keeping it up-to-date and enforcing standards.

Just as the use of a DBMS requires management commitment, so does a DDS. This is not always easy to achieve, particularly where the benefits are intangible and long term. Users have to accept that 'their' data can be shared and that they cannot be permitted to ignore the requirements of the organisation as a whole when wishing to reformat data, use different validation routines, or make any other move which might affect other users. Some users find conforming to the requirements of a DDS a 'nuisance' at best. This requires commitment by management to the database administrator function, because the DBA is the focal point for setting good standards and enforcing them.

Unless a management decision is made to commit the organisation to the DDS route and accept these costs, the overall database project will be threatened. It has to be well planned. Usually the applications which are presently being developed are installed in the data dictionary first - documentation is convenient and it will usually be these applications that will have the longest life. In summary, then, the DDS is likely to save development and operating time and reduce costs of the computing facilities.

So far in this chapter we have looked at the possible features of a DDS, both the minimum features that would be expected and those of a more sophisticated system. The following sections consider two prominent commercial DDS which are widely used.

12.4 ICL DATA DICTIONARY SYSTEM

The ICL DDS is designed to take into account the conceptual as well as the implementation level. It therefore attempts to describe the business and the computer representation of data. It is modelled on the recommendations of the BCSWP discussed in Section 12.1. Further, the DDS is an important part of the ICL data analysis methodology. Many forms which are completed as part of data analysis are used as source documents for the ICL DDS. It is therefore used as a design aid as well as a documentation tool. The conceptual view which will be held on the data dictionary will include the entities, attributes, relationships, operations and events which define the data model. There is one form type to document each of these aspects of data modelling.

At the implementation level, the view is represented by systems, programs and modules. ICL DDS is expected to be run with IDMS which is the Codasyl-based DBMS discussed in Section 7.3. The terminology and concepts for the data are associated with this type of DBMS. In the terminology of the DDS, a schema is a description of the complete model; the sub-schema represents the various user views of the database (subsets of the schema); a file is a collection of records; an area a collection of IDMS pages (the unit of filestore for transfer purposes); a record is a collection of logically related items (usually referred to as group items) and items are the basic unit of data.

Every element is described in the DDS by its properties, including those which identify and describe the item, those which establish and describe links between items, administrative properties such as those which describe the various privacy levels required, and statistical properties such as the various access levels (peak and average frequency of access) to that particular item.

As well as having a command language (the Data Dictionary Command Language) to describe the data and processes, the system has powerful query facilities. The DDS allows interrogation through DISPLAY, ENQUIRY, LIST and PRINT commands.

The DISPLAY statement can be used to give details of an element. Thus:

DISPLAY ENTITY STUDENT-TYPE ALL PROPERTIES

will give full details of a particular entity.

LIST EVENTS * DESCRIPTION

will list all events with their descriptions as contained in the DDS. The LIST command generates a list of all elements of a given type.

PRINT ALL ALL

prints the contents of the whole data dictionary.

ENQUIRY ENTITY STUDENT

will give details of entities, operations and attributes which use the entity 'student'. The ENQUIRY command is usually used to check on references, between two specific elements, of a particular type or which conform to a particular search key.

The ICL DDS also has a free format command language which can be used to insert and edit items, and to update and interrogate the data dictionary. The description of the data and information about its use are held on the DDS database which is part of the IDMS database. It therefore has the security and other features of IDMS.

Overall, the ICL DDS is a fairly sophisticated DDS and commands can be entered via a terminal and in batch mode. Its particular strong points are that it is part of the data analysis methodology as well as close to the recommendations of the BCSWP. A number of packages have been developed by ICL to interface with the ICL DDS. They include Report Master and Query Master (for reports and user enquiries) designed for general users, there is a package Masterbuild (to develop the DDS) and Quickbuild (similar to Masterbuild, but containing streamlining facilities for quick set-up of small to medium systems). Thus the DDS, with IDMS, works alongside a number of fourth generation system tools.

12.5 DB2 DATA DICTIONARY

The DB2 data dictionary is called a **catalog** and is an active system but limited in many other respects. The catalog consists of SQL tables (relations). There may be about 25 in all. They can be queried by SQL commands, such as the SELECT statement. However, the UPDATE, DELETE and INSERT commands are not permitted because of their potentially damaging effect. The COMMENT statement can be used to add remarks which may well help the user of the catalog. Tables which are particularly important include:

- *Systables:* which contains one row for every table and view on the database. Attributes include its name, creator, number of columns, key and record length.
- *Systabauth:* which indicates the operations that users are authorised to perform on

tables and views. Attributes include user identification, table name, type of operations authorised and information about the authoriser.

- *Syscolumns:* which contains one row for every column of both tables and views. Attributes include the attribute name, table name, column type and length.
- *Sysindexes:* which contains one row for every index. Attributes include index name, its creator and the table name which it indexes.

The DB2 catalogue contains comprehensive information about the data in the database, but, compared to the ICL DDS discussed in Section 12.4, much less about people and processes. Another difference with some data dictionary systems is that the catalog is meant to be used by end users as well as database administrators and other 'professionals'. Many data dictionaries are regarded as system databases for systems people and they record the decisions of designers.

12.6 FURTHER READING

British Computer Society (1977), Data Dictionary Systems Working Party Report, *ACM SIGMOD Record*, **9**, 4.

Gillenson, M. L (1990) *Database: step-by-step*, Wiley, New York.

Van Duyn, J (1982) *Developing a Data Dictionary System*, Prentice-Hall, Englewood Cliffs.

Chapter 13
Database Administration and Database Management

13.1 INTRODUCTION

The success of the database project does *not* lie solely on the technical aspects. It lies at least as much on management and people aspects. Sherif (1988) in his book quotes Bachman (1969) and I will repeat the quote in full:

'The effectiveness of a large corporation and the ultimate limit to its size depend on how well it can store and process the data relevant to its operations and how well it can communicate between its components. The real database of an organisation is large. I don't know what large really means, but it is not 10 million or 20 million characters; 10 billion characters is more like it. This quantity at the moment is almost incomprehensible, yet we have the technical capability today to process that amount of data and we have the hardware to support it. But I am not sure whether we have the management organisation capability to collect the data, support it or train the people to use it properly'.

This sentiment is even more true 22 years later. 'People problems' have not decreased in importance, indeed they seem comparatively greater, as many of the technical problems are solved.

The role of the Database Administrator (DBA) is crucial to the success of the database project. The 'ideals' discussed in Chapter 2 of this text, such as organisation-wide planning and matching the goals of the organisation with the database project, will not be achieved without successful database administration. The DBA should be involved in the planning of the organisation's data resource and in setting up the database, as well as ensuring data availability and the maintenance of its integrity once the database has been implemented. Indeed the DBA ought to be involved in the evaluation of the basic hardware and software and ought to be an important member of the systems planning team as well as play an important part in the development of the database and its use. But the importance of the role lies as much in having a feel for the needs of the people working on the project and on management and user needs than on any technical aspects.

One of the main objectives of the database approach is to facilitate the sharing of data between many users. But users may well resist both the DBA taking control of 'their' data and other users having access to it. This may lead to conflict. The DBA needs to have the necessary status and tact to apply an organisation-wide perspective to mediate in such a conflict. Hopefully this will be achieved by facilitating communication between departments rather than by 'rule of law'. The DBA is likely to play a large part in decisions relating to rival application candidates according to some priority which reflects the objectives of management. The DBA will need the strong backing of management to succeed in this task. Otherwise, there will be no authority to back up the decisions. In order to make recommendations, the DBA also needs to have good communications with user groups.

We have seen that there are a number of problems that may arise from the sharing of data. The balancing of conflicting interests requires a managerial perspective and a good knowledge of the business. Other problems require technical knowledge. The DBA will have to deal with complaints about usage of the database and to provide technical training. These different aspects of the role of the DBA - the technical and the organisational - will be a constant theme in this chapter.

In practice, the DBA function needs to be carried out by a **DBA team**. The director of this team should have sufficient standing in the organisation to remain independent of 'pressure groups' of database users. As we have seen, the DBA is expected to be a good communicator and has to discuss aspects of data use and storage with managers, user staff, operations staff and application developers. The DBA team also needs to have technically experienced people who have the responsibility for the control and monitoring of the database, a function that includes the responsibility for:

- Defining the data needs of the organisation
- Establishing technical standards and guide-lines
- Application support through internal schema (user view) definition
- Physical and logical database definitions
- Implementing access rights
- Setting up back-up and security procedures
- Investigating known security breaches
- Optimising performance levels
- Maintaining the integrity of the database
- General maintenance of the database, the software supporting it and its use.

The software will include the DBMS, the DDS and possibly some fourth generation or Case tools as well. The team will also include people whose role is to help train the users and help them with technical difficulties. Users will require this help no matter how 'user friendly' the system is supposed to be. Some members of the team will need to have a strong applications background to fulfil some user demands.

It could be said that part of the DBA's role is that of 'public relations officer' for the database. The problems relating to conventional systems need to be pointed out along with a description of the ways in which a database environment might solve some of these problems. This education role may be followed by a training role, because should users wish to make use of these opportunities they will need more detailed help. The users may need assistance in understanding the database structures and to derive a suitable subset which will provide for their data needs. Furthermore, this subset may need to be restructured for that particular application. In this administrative and managerial role, the database administrator has to ensure that the policies and conventions of management are followed.

13.2 FUNCTIONS OF A DATABASE ADMINISTRATOR

The planning, designing and loading of the database
One of the main tasks of the DBA will be to help plan the database project and design and load the initial database following the approach adopted in this book (described in Chapters 2 to 6 inclusive). This will involve deciding on the methodology to develop the database project and in planning its development through to implementation. This whole process requires considerable computer and people time and also requires audit procedures which will be used to verify its success. Although much of the data will come from existing master files, there may be considerable re-structuring and re-naming. Some of the data will be newly held on computer. The database should be designed to reflect users' requirements now and in the future and this will involve:
- Defining, creating, redefining and deleting data
- Setting up access paths to the database
- Arranging physical storage for the database
- Developing the data dictionary.

Each of these is a non-trivial task. They require technical knowledge and experience of the DBMS and DDS, as well as knowledge of the prospective and actual applications.

But there are also organisational aspects to this role. Deciding on data retention standards requires a knowledge of the organisation (and in some cases, the law). There will need to be liaison with management , users, auditors, application development staff and operations staff. In these early stages, planning is essential, and database standards have to be agreed and documentation and publicity will require considerable resourcing, as will the training and education role. The support of strategic management is often neglected but it is crucial, and not only because of its financial support. It is important because top management must be seen to be committed to the database project. Further, this involvement is necessary to glean information about business plans, priorities and constraints.

Control of the database

This is fundamental to the success of the DBMS project because the data is shared and this cannot be successful without good control procedures. Control of the database in operation is a complex technical task as it involves:

- Effecting physical access restrictions (not usually the responsibility of DBA)
- Ensuring effective back-up and security procedures
- Verifying data validation procedures to maintain integrity
- Authorising users to update parts of the database
- Ensuring effective concurrency controls (so that two users cannot be attempting to update the same data at the same time)
- Preventing unauthorised access
- Deciding on permissible extensions to or extra services provided by the database.

The issues of privacy, security and integrity are fundamental to the success of the database project. Privacy is the right of individuals to control who can have access to personal information. Security is the protection of the database from accidental or intentional destruction, modification and disclosure. Integrity concerns the accuracy, timeliness, completeness and adherence to specification of data on the database. Many of the standards associated with these issues will be determined by management and groups of users, but the DBA will have the overall responsibility of applying these standards.

It is essential to protect stored data from unauthorised access. Data may be of a personal nature and subject to legislation (as well as a moral law) and some data may be sensitive from the point of view of the business. Prevention from unauthorised access includes physical security (to the computer room and computer), so that the user passes video surveillance and needs keys or cards to gain access, as well as identification procedures and series of passwords (to the software). The use of finger and voice prints is becoming more common to prevent access to highly sensitive areas. Most DBMS and DDS provide a whole range of security facilities and the DBA needs to use them and advise users to take advantage of them. The DBA also needs to monitor the security situation regularly and, in particular, assess unauthorised attempts to break into the system.

Whatever procedures are effected, there will be some risk involved and the task of the DBA is to balance the levels of risk with the protection given according to the nature of the data. For example, financial and product data will normally have high security because such data would be particularly valuable to competitors and loss could cause major problems to the business (the company may be forced to close down). The DBA has to be aware of different kinds of risk: environmental (such as fire), mechanical failure (such as disk head crashes), operator errors (for example, mounting the wrong tapes), program errors, theft, fraud and sabotage. Failures due to accidents are far more likely than those due to deliberate security breach. It should be noted that many risks are not normally covered by insurance.

The protection of data on the database is normally the responsibility of the DBA (with the exception of physical security, which is normally the responsibility of the data processing manager - though even here the DBA will be influential in setting standards). On liaising with the user, the DBA may implement privacy locks, such as passwords, at the logical file, record or item level. For example, salary data on an employee record is particularly sensitive and there may be access restrictions on that item above those on the rest of the record. Such measures should ensure that the data is not accessed by unauthorised users. From the point of view of the DBA, the ideal password is machine generated, changed regularly and long. Being machine generated they will be difficult to guess. On the other hand they will be difficult for the authorised user to learn.

The DBA needs to be aware of the danger of viruses, and the regular running of virus detection programs is advised as well as prevention measures, such as accepting only sealed original copies of programs from reputable software houses. The DBA may be regarded as the custodian of personal data, as required by government legislation relating to privacy and databases. Privacy locks may also be included to protect the organisation from unwarranted access of the database by competitors. The encryption of sensitive data may be necessary, and this will limit the ability of a thief to interpret data, even where a copy of a file has been obtained. The data will be coded before storage and decoded for valid users. Another way of reducing risk is to partition or physically separate areas of the database over several devices.

The DBA may set standards for copying files. Rapid recovery from failure is essential where a number of users need access to the database. Failure could occur because of system breakdown or transaction failure. It is necessary to keep regular copies of the whole database and a log (or journal file) giving details of any transactions effected since the last copy was made.

Recovery is usually made by 'roll forward' techniques, where the copy is loaded (ensuring a further copy is retained) and the log used to bring the database back to its state immediately preceding the failure. If the failure affected only a few items on the database, recovery can be made by 'roll back'. Here the log is used to copy the 'before images' (the values of the affected items before the system failed). In either case, steps will have to be made to ensure that the failure will not be repeated.

In particularly sensitive areas, where failure of the system could not be tolerated, the whole computer configuration is duplicated so that if one system fails all operations can be immediately transferred to a second computer system.

As for integrity, the DBA must be satisfied that any application programs are fully tested and corrected before a system is integrated into the database environment. This also requires regular auditing to check that procedures are working. Although some writers argue that it is the users' job to ensure the accuracy of any data admitted on the database, and that the DBA team need only concern themselves with its security, it is more usual for the DBA to set standards for data validation which will help to maintain the integrity of the database. This is reasonable because data created by one user may be used by others. Without the DBA, there will be no incentive, or security net, to ensure that the data is correctly validated.

One cause of failure, inadequate skills of the users, should have been prevented as much as possible through the education and training process discussed earlier in this section. But this needs to be continually monitored as new users wish to access the database.

The DBA needs to ensure that the concurrency problem is solved (two or more users attempting to update the same data) and this is usually achieved by locking out other attempts to access the data whilst any updating process is in operation. Most DBMS implement locks at the logical level of the whole database, relation, record and field levels, and also implement it at the physical level of the block or page. Some systems will enable other users to access the data but not update it.

Much of the information about the database, the data dictionary, and the activities of their users will be documented by the DBA. Even though documentation is not a popular task, it is essential that it is done, and it is done well. It must be up-to-date, so that changes are reflected in the documentation. Some documentation will be aimed at the user departments, others at the programmers, and others at the DBA team. The DDS can be particularly helpful in this aspect because most produce reports for this purpose. Further, there are packages available, for example, ACF2, Top Secret and RACF, which address some aspects of security in computer systems.

Maintenance of the database

The logical data structures will need to be changed over time according to the changing needs of the users. The DBA has to be aware of present and future needs and be aware of any advances in the hardware and software. The DBA could be looked upon as a forward planner, as the database can expand or be reorganised according to future needs, and this has to be done with as little disruption to the present users as possible. It may be necessary to alter the way in which the data is physically stored on the database. In this case the DBA will be involved so that the changes are carried out efficiently. This means efficient use of storage space, good access times and reduced maintenance overheads.

Efficiency of the database is not a simple matter. There are a number of criteria which may conflict. Speed of access may conflict with efficient use of storage space. The DBA may therefore aim towards 'satisficing' on a wide range of criteria, rather than optimise on any one criterion, in other words ensure that the performance of the database on a wide range of issues is satisfactory.

Evaluating the performance of a database is also difficult: is speed of access 'good' and backing storage requirements and main memory requirements 'reasonable'? The DBA needs to carry out an audit of the database so that security procedures, back-up and recovery, and concurrency procedures can be assessed along with an analysis of usage: who is using the database and what are they doing (what is accessed and the kind of access). A DBMS should help the DBA in this work by providing reports which detail disk activity, memory utilisation, data usage, and response times, and identify attempts at breaches of security, program 'crashes', and the use of any restart/recovery routines.

The DBA may have to carry out major restructuring or reorganisation of the database as a result of monitoring the situation and as a result of changes affecting the organisation, such as the incorporation into the DBMS of new areas of business or greater activity. Thus new relations (or their equivalent in other logical models), for example, may be added to the database (logical model) as a result of changes to the conceptual model or items might be stored in a different way (physical model) to enable more efficient access. Some of these tasks may be described as 'tuning' the system, whereas other tasks are more fundamental. Such changes may require users to be locked out of the system until the changes are made.

In judging a DBMS, the purchaser should bear in mind the requirements of the DBA, as much as the user. It is important that the users' expectations are not dashed. User expectations should be realistic and for this reason the training and education role of the DBA has been stressed. Users and potential users of the database need to know something of the terminology, concepts and technology that surround databases and computing. This 'education' is as important as the 'training' function: how to use the database system and comply with the standards of the organisation. Users may not see the necessity of moving to database techniques which may well involve them in a lot of work (some of which may not pay dividends to them but to other members of the organisation). It is frequently difficult for people in one department to have an organisation-wide perspective.

13.3 BENEFITS OF DATABASE ADMINISTRATION

Should the many roles of the database administrator discussed in Section 13.2 be fulfilled, then a number of benefits should result to the organisation:

- Data can be seen as a shared organisation-wide resource. This is made technically feasible by a DBMS, but made practicable by the DBA function.
- Decisions relating to the database are made by people with an organisational perspective rather than a low-level and narrow perspective (which would be the case if these decisions were made by technologists or by individual users).
- New applications will be easier to integrate into the database. As a consequence, program development time will be reduced.
- The DBA will be expected to keep abreast of advances in the technology. New technology can be implemented with minimum disturbance to the users. Faster disks or new software may sometimes be implemented without the users knowing (though they may detect better access times).
- Information on database contents and use will be easier to obtain. Reports on these aspects of the database can be standardised.
- Communication between departments can be improved as terminology relating to database use becomes familiar to all users.
- The user and applications programmers need only concern themselves with logical data structures. The DBA will ensure the accuracy and appropriateness of the physical data structures.
- As the many users of the database use the same physical database, the overheads concerned with maintaining the data will be reduced.
- The DBA may act as representative of the government and society at large, ensuring that privacy requirements attached to personal data are adhered to, including privacy legislation.

Of course many of these advantages are associated with the use of the database management system and the data dictionary system as well as the database administrator. The full gains of a database environment can only be attained where all three elements of the infrastructure exist.

The preceding discussion on the benefits of a DBA has been somewhat idealistic. It would be difficult and expensive for organisations to recruit a DBA team which successfully performed all the roles covered. Most installations compromise.

13.4 THE POSITION OF THE DATABASE ADMINISTRATOR IN THE ORGANISATION

According to Gillenson (1982), about three-quarters of DBMS installations bought a DBMS before employing a DBA. Yet we have argued that the DBA should play a major part in the acquisition of a DBMS. Further, in some organisations the DBA role is carried out by one person. In these circumstances only a few aspects of the role described in the previous sections could be carried out reasonably well. In more enlightened organisations, however, the function is carried out by a group of people, sometimes forming a separate department.

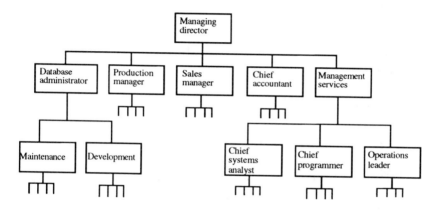

Fig. 13.1 The position of the database administrator

In some organisations the position of the DBA team in the organisation is that shown in Figure 13.1. The DBA function is seen as separate from the Data Processing Department. In view of the managerial aspects of the role, this is certainly desirable. The DBA function should not be perceived as purely the concern of the technical and computer area.

More commonly, however, the DBA function is carried out as part of the Data Processing (or Management Services) Department. The DBA may be given managerial-level responsibilities without the status to carry them out. This frequently results in the DBA reacting to events, for example, poor performance or lost data, rather than formulating and carrying out policy. Many organisations do not expect the DBA to have managerial-level responsibilities. They limit the role of the DBA to technically-oriented maintenance and innovation associated with the database. This is likely to lead to problems, because there is no-one of sufficient status to enforce standards on users.

We have also argued for a DBA team with people having a wide range of expertise. However, the size of the DBA group in most organisations is small when compared to the data processing group, frequently of the ratio of around 1:10. Worse, DBA staff are usually appointed late in the implementation of the database, perhaps when difficulties are encountered, when it is impossible to re-design the system, though re-planning with DBA expertise might be desirable.

The concentration on technical aspects and the low status of the DBA may be due to the early stage of database experience of many organisations. A DBA group fulfilling the roles suggested in this chapter will be costly. As more and more applications are added to the database, the status of the DBA will rise and the administrative role will rise in proportion to the technical role.

At this stage a distinction may be made between database administrators and data administrators, which is now being made in a number of organisations. The **Database Administrators** perform essentially a technical function and have a technical background. They are mainly responsible for the efficient design and operation of the computer database and are members of the Data Processing Department. They will be responsible for technical issues, such as, security, performance, reorganisation, back-up and recovery. The **Data Administrators** are placed at corporate management level, and perform an administrative function. They are responsible for the development and co-ordination of the policies and procedures relating to the 'data resource of the organisation' and therefore for setting up the organisational data model and maintaining organisation-wide standards. Each member of the Data Administrator team may have responsibility for a particular user area and 'represents' the user area.

An alternative scenario is for the DBA team to report to the data administrator rather than the data processing manager. This distinction, once found in very few enlightened pockets, is now a feature of a number of organisations which use large databases.

McFadden & Hoffer (1991) also identify the need for a **data steward** who manages a specific logical data resource or entity. This could be, for example, a customer, product or employee file. This role also includes management of all applications that create or use this data. The data steward will co-ordinate data definitions, quality controls and access authorisation for that particular data resource. Here, then, we have an arrangement of three roles: the data administrator, responsible for the organisation's data resource; the data steward, responsible for logical elements of that resource; and the database administrator, responsible for the technically-oriented aspects of the computer database.

The separation of the various functions is shown in Figure 13.2. In this situation, the database administrator reports to both the data administrator and management services manager: a network rather than hierarchical structure. This is feasible with the data administrator ensuring that the requirements of the organisation are being carried out and the management services manager ensuring that the technical aspects are being carried out. However, though the DBA will communicate with both, it is common for the DBA to be responsible to one or the other.

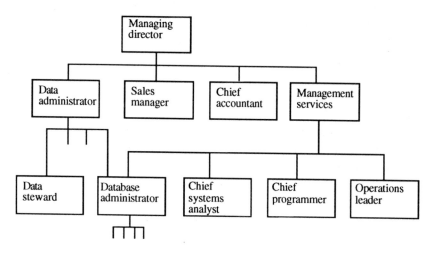

Fig. 13.2 The position of the data administration functions

The DBA function or department therefore evolves to an important part of the organisation from a subordinate responsibility within a data processing department. With this increase in status is likely to come a corresponding increase in the numbers involved with database administration. The role of the DBA may well be evolutionary and its importance becomes greater as use of the database increases.

13.5 FURTHER READING

Gillenson, M. L (1990), *Database: step-by-step,* 2nd ed, Wiley, New York.

Holloway, S (1988) *Data administration,* Gower Technical Press, Aldershot.

Lyon, J.K (1976) *The Database Administrator,* Wiley, New York.

McCririck, I. B & Goldstein, R. C (1980) What do Data Administrators do?, *Datamation,* **26,** 8.

Weldon, J-L (1981) *Database Administration,* Plenum Press, New York.

These texts contain good chapters on database and data administration.

Sherif, M. A (1988) *Database Projects: a framework for effective management,* Ellis
    Horwood, Chichester.
This text uses survey data to analyse organisation's experiences of database
administration.

Baskerville, R (1988) *Designing Information Systems Security,* Wiley, New York.
A thorough review of security aspects.

PART FOUR

THE APPROACH IN ACTION

Chapter 14
An Application of the Database Approach

14.1 INTRODUCTION

This chapter describes an application of the approach carried out by Aston University students in the Systems Development Division of Comshare Limited. I would like to express my gratitude to Comshare for permission to publish these details and to the students working on this and related projects: Andrew Baker, Michelle Chan, Stanley Ho, Kelvin Lam, and Richard Abbot, Sally Beer and Caryn Lewis. It should be noted that since the time when the work was carried out, aspects of the application area described may well have changed. The report submitted by the students was 250 pages long, and so it is only possible here to represent the 'flavour' of their work. The DBMS used, Ingres, is described in this chapter because it was not described in Chapter 7 (DB2 being the relational database system discussed there).

Comshare Ltd. is a computer service company. It provides a computer timesharing service (Commander II), software for in-house computers (which could be mainframe, minis and micros), consultancy and systems development facilities. The software packages include data management, financial modelling and decision-support systems. The Systems Development Division (SDD) is largely engaged in developing information systems using Comshare products, which can be transferred to either Comshare's Bureau machine or the customer's machine, once the system is developed.

The project involved the following:

- The analysis of the SDD using the entity-relationship approach to derive a conceptual model
- The mapping of the conceptual model derived onto a hierarchical, network and relational design (logical model)
- The implementation of the system using several DBMS/computer combinations (physical model)
- The implementation of some application systems in order to test the appropriateness of the designs.

Obviously, if this was carried out for commercial considerations, only one logical design and one DBMS would be used. The purpose of the project was foremost to enable students on an information systems course to gain experience of the various options when developing information systems using a database approach.

14.2 ENTITY-RELATIONSHIP MODELLING

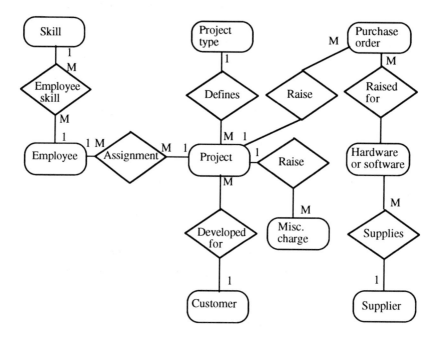

Fig. 14.1 Preliminary E-R model

In order to derive a satisfactory E-R model, a number of E-R type diagrams (see Chapter 3) are sketched from information gained from a requirements specification and from interviews with management. Initially they are more akin to doodles which are then tidied up to use as a basis for discussion. One of the first of these is shown as Figure 14.1. Entities are also listed by name with key attribute(s) but little else at this stage:

    EMPLOYEE(employee-no,....)
    EMPLOYEE-SKILL(employee-no,skill-no,....)
    SKILL(skill-no,skill-desc,....)
    PROJECT(project-no,....)
    ASSIGNMENT(employee-no,project-no,....)
    PROJECT-TYPE(proj-type,....)
    CUSTOMER(customer-no,....)
    MISC-CHARGE(charge-no,....)
    PURCH-ORD(purchord-no,....)
    SUPPLIER(supplier-no,....)

Let us see how the E-R model shown in Figure 14.1 was drawn and can be interpreted. The SDD is essentially 'project driven'. EMPLOYEES are assigned to PROJECTS and many EMPLOYEES may be assigned to a PROJECT. PROJECTS are developed for CUSTOMERS. PRODUCTS are not included in the diagram as these are produced by Comshare's Research and Development Group. More than one PROJECT may be carried out for a particular CUSTOMER, but more than one CUSTOMER will not be involved in any particular PROJECT. This suggests the three entities EMPLOYEE, PROJECT and CUSTOMER with their relationships being the assignment of EMPLOYEES to PROJECTS and development of PROJECTS for CUSTOMERS.

Developing the model further, we see that there are different types of PROJECTS such as consultancy, project management, new applications and maintenance. Hence the PROJECT-TYPE entity. EMPLOYEES will have different skills. These will include experience on Comshare's products and experience on different hardware platforms, hence the entity EMPLOYEE-SKILL.

Further, PROJECTS may require HARDWARE-AND-SOFTWARE from a SUPPLIER. (In this environment it is not necessary to distinguish between hardware and software - they may be distinct entities in any E-R model describing groups within Comshare). Normally the CUSTOMER will buy these items direct but in certain circumstances Comshare acts as a retailer. Therefore PURCHASE-ORDERS are raised. Initially, they are raised as a MISCELLANEOUS-CHARGE, until the PURCHASE-ORDER has been sent.

After this preliminary investigation of the entities and relationships, further data analysis leads to a 'filling-in' of the detail, and then to an analysis of the possible processes that the data model must support. This was used in the project as a checking mechanism. So as to avoid the construction of a huge data model, and the consequent expense of construction and maintenance of the database, and the possibility of holding data that would never be accessed, only those data items that are used by processes were included in the model. Functional analysis, therefore, was carried out to identify events and operations and thereby ensure that the model was appropriate to current needs. This is a constraint given to the design team which limited the extent of the data analysis.

In the SDD, a project may originate from an enquiry (an 'event') to the Comshare office from a new or existing customer. Possible projects are discussed in outline with the SDD manager in order to decide whether such projects are feasible. An outline specification is written which leads to the design of the contract between the customer and Comshare, and then its signing by both parties. Each month a summary of project progress is completed by the project manager along with expense details and employees' time-sheets. These are just some of the 'operations' following the 'event'. This analysis of functions proved particularly helpful in 'discovering' attributes which

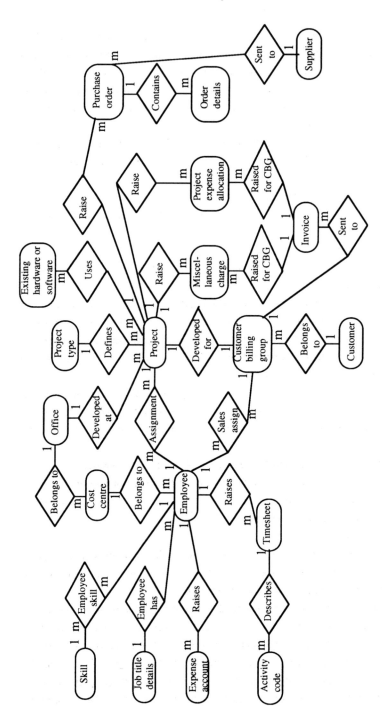

Fig. 14.2 Final systems development E-R model

had not previously been identified. A revised E-R model is presented as Figure 14.2.

Although an E-R model diagram describes many of the important features of a conceptual model, it does not show the attributes associated with the entity. This detail is represented in the relations, developed from the entities, which are then normalised to third normal form (Section 3.7). Thirty relation types, fully normalised, were identified by the group and only some of them are listed below.

EMPLOYEE(empnum, empname, empinitials, empaddress, empphone, sex, marstatus, mobility, nationality, birthdate, birthplace, entrydate, jobtitle, costcentre, salary, commission, lastrvw)

EMPLOYEE-PROJECT(empnum, projnum)

PROJECT(projnum, projdesc, projappl, projhw, projsw, costctr, custnum, projstdte, projenddte, projcost, mandays,...)

COST-CENTRE(costctr,cstctrdesc,...)

PURCHASE-ORDER(purchord, suppnum, dateorder, datereq, costctr, origempnum, authempnum, totpurchcst)

A further cross-check was made by analysing the report requirements of the SDD and performing an overview document-driven data analysis (Section 3.5). Six of a large number of reports looked at were: Project Details, Outstanding Charges for Projects, Office Profitability, Employee Availability, Ad-hoc Personnel Enquiries and Hardware and Software Availability.

At this time it is also possible to start setting up the data dictionary. For this particular exercise the data dictionary was used as a documentation tool only, since data dictionary software was not available. The data dictionary in its final form had five major components:

- The entity model, giving details of entities, attributes and relationships
- Functions that the database supports, described as events and operations
- Physical database structure
- Program documentation
- Cross-reference index.

At this stage, only the first of these can be fully built up, along with, through an analysis of functions, much of the second. The third and fourth components refer to implementation, rather than conceptual, information.

The entity model therefore gives details of entities, which include EMPLOYEE, PROJECT, COSTCENTRE, CUSTOMER, SUPPLIER, PURCHASE ORDER and INVOICE, details of their attributes, and the relationships between them, as shown in the E-R diagram. Part completed data dictionary forms are shown in Figures 14.3 to 14.6 for two attributes (employee number and sex of employee), an entity (employee) and the relationship between employee and skill. Please note that these basic forms for documenting entities, attributes, relationships, events and operations have since been modified (as shown in Chapter 3, Figures 3.12 to 3.16).

ATTRIBUTE TYPE SPECIFICATION FORM   System:

Attribute name	EMPLOYEE NUMBER	

Description A UNIQUE IDENTIFIER OF EACH EMPLOYEE
           OF COMSHARE

Synonyms	EMPNUM EMP-NO	
Date specified	7/1/85	Status (P/V/I)

Entity cross reference
                    EMPLOYEE
                    EMPLOYEE-PROJECT

Create authority   PERSONNEL

Delete authority   PERSONNEL

Access authority   ANY

Functions involved cross reference

Comments   MUST BE NUMERIC LESS THAN
            500 OCCURRENCES

            DD NAME EMPNUM
            5 CHARS NUMERIC (INGRES I2)

Fig. 14.3 Attribute documentation for employee number

ATTRIBUTE TYPE SPECIFICATION FORM	System:

Attribute name	SEX OF EMPLOYEE

Description   IDENTIFIES SEX OF EACH EMPLOYEE
OF COMSHARE
F= FEMALE, M = MALE

Synonyms	SEX

Date specified	7/1/85	Status (P/V/I)

Entity cross reference
                EMPLOYEE

Create authority	PERSONNEL

Delete authority	PERSONNEL

Access authority	ANY

Functions involved cross reference

Comments
        MUST BE 'F' OR 'M'
        ONE PER EMPLOYEE
        1 CHAR ALPHABETIC (INGRES I1)

Fig. 14.4 Attribute documentation for sex of employee

ENTITY TYPE SPECIFICATION FORM		System:	
Entity name	EMPLOYEE		
Description	GIVES DETAILS OF EMPLOYEES OF COMSHARE		
Synonyms			
Identifier(s)	EMPLOYEE NUMBER		
Date specified	7/1/85	Status (P/V/I)	
Minimum occurrences		Maximum occurrences	500
Average occurrences		Growth rate %	
Create authority			
Delete authority			
Access authority			
Relationships involved cross reference	SKILLS EXPENSE ACCOUNT COST CENTRE TIME SHEET JOB TITLE DETAILS PROJECT		
Attributes involved cross reference	EMP-NUM EMP-NAME EMP-INITIALS etc		
Functions involved cross reference			
Entity sub types			
Comments	176 CHARACTERS		

Fig. 14.5 Entity documentation for employee

RELATIONSHIP TYPE SPECIFICATION FORM		System:

Relationship name	EMPLOYEE-SKILL

Description	ASSOCIATES PARTICULAR SKILLS OF EMPLOYEES i.e. EMPLOYEE HAS SKILLS

Time state	
Synonyms	

Date specified	7/1/1985	Status (P/V/I)	

Entities involved (Owner)   EMPLOYEE

                   (Members)   SKILL

Degree (1:1, 1:m, m:n) M:N	Optional Contingent Mandatory

If contingent, state optional entity

If exclusive, state paired relationship name

If inclusive, state paired relationship name and first existence relationship name

Create authority

Delete authority

Access authority

Comments   PRIVACY LEVEL 2

Fig. 14.6 Relationship documentation for employee-skill

14.3 LOGICAL SCHEMA

The normalised relations developed in the conceptual schema stage form the basis for the relational logical schema. In the relational approach (Section 4.2), no links between relations need be specified at the logical modelling stage; they are set up as required when accessing the database. The model has been implemented on two relational DBMS, Ingres and Questor (from Comshare).

For the hierarchical model (Section 4.5), the system ran on IMS (Section 7.2). The overall model is represented as a number of connected physical databases, defined in a database description. In IMS the DBD includes part of the specifications for the mapping of the database into storage and access method specifications. These physical model considerations ought to be separate from the logical schema. This overall DBD is split up into subsets which each application program sees, as described in Section 7.2.

Sample EMPLOYEE database definition statements are:

DBD NAME=EMPLOYEEDB,ACCESS=HISAM
SEGM NAME=EMPLOYEE,PARENET=0,BYTES=176
FIELD NAME=(EMPNUM,SEQ,U),BYTES=5,START=1,TYPE=C
FIELD NAME=EMPNAME,BYTES=30,START=6,TYPE=C
FIELD NAME=EMPINITIALS,BYTES=4,START=36,TYPE=C
FIELD NAME=EMPADDRESS,BYTES=70,START=41,TYPE=C

Pointers have to be predefined in a hierarchical database to link the files (called segments in IMS). Although this means that the database loses in flexibility, the definition of the access paths implied by the structure means that the paths do not have to be created during query and update processing. The advantage of such early 'binding' is a considerable gain in processing speed and a simplification of query formulation.

The hierarchical data model for Comshare SDD is shown as Figure 14.7. You may note that some entities have had to be duplicated, for example, EMPLOYEE and MISCELLANEOUS-CHARGE. As we saw in Section 7.2, this is a consequence of the hierarchical approach.

The network approach (Section 4.6) consists of relations linked together in a series of closed loops, called sets. This is a more general structure than a hierarchy. A number of sets are shown in Figure 14.8. The relationship between PROJECT and EMPLOYEE, being a many-to-many relationship is connected by the link record assignment.

An example from an IDMS data definition (Section 7.3) is:

SCHEMA NAME IS COMSHARE
AREA NAME IS EMPLOYEE-AREA
RECORD NAME IS EMPLOYEE
    LOCATION MODE IS DIRECT EMPNUM

DUPLICATES ARE NOT ALLOWED
WITHIN EMPLOYEE-AREA.

02	EMPNUM	PIC 9(5).
02	EMPNAME	PIC X(30).
02	EMPINITIALS	PIC X(4).
02	EMPADDRESS	PIC X(70).

SET NAME IS EMPSKILL
    ORDER IS SORTED BY DEFINED KEYS
    OWNER IS EMPLOYEE
    MEMBER IS EMP-SKILL
        MANDATORY AUTOMATIC
    KEY IS ASCENDING EMPNUM IN EMPLOYEE

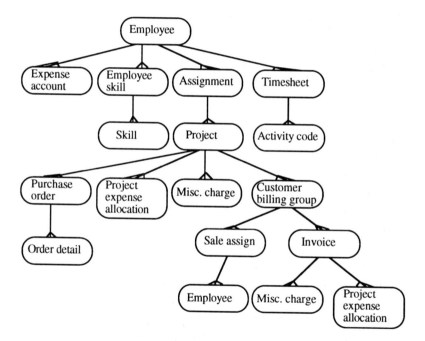

Fig. 14.7 Hierarchical data model

14.4 PHYSICAL SCHEMA

We describe the implementation using the Ingres DBMS. This is a relational DBMS designed to run under the Unix operating system. The data manipulation language on Ingres is QUEL, not too dissimilar to SQL, and firmly based on the relational calculus.

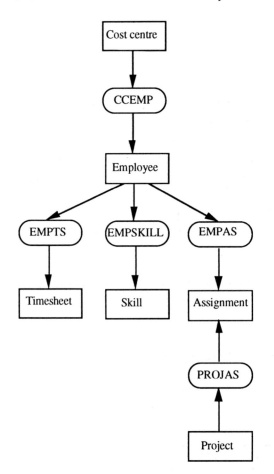

Fig. 14.8 Network data model

Ingres also has a report writer and query-by-forms facilities. The database is implemented on a 'supermicro' system (Section 9.1). After following the protocols to use the computer system, the database is created by:

CREATEDB Baker

This command allocates memory, and files are organised in a hierarchical fashion with a root file and a number of other files in that subdirectory.

Once the database has been set up, Ingres is invoked by keying-in 'Ingres' followed by the name of the database, thus:

INGRES Baker

Ingres is then loaded and, when ready, the user receives the message 'GO' followed by the Ingres prompt '*', which indicates that Ingres is awaiting user commands:

GO

*

The relations are set up using the CREATE command:

* CREATE TIMESHEET (EMPNUM=I2,MONTH=C3,ACTCODE=I1,
                          PROJNUM=I2)
* CREATE ACTCODE (ACTCODE=I1,ACTDESCR=C50)

where 'I' means that the data in that field is integer (numeric data) and 'C' for character. A third possibility is 'F' for floating point. This information should be added to the data dictionary.

There are also commands to create an index and a view (INDEX and DEFINE VIEW respectively), commands to delete a relation, index or view (DESTROY) and change a relation (REPLACE).

The APPEND command can be used to enter data:

* APPEND TO TIMESHEET (EMPNUM=1105,MONTH='AUG',ACTCODE=10
                          PROJNUM=551)

Thus the TIMESHEET RELATION:

EMPNUM	MONTH	ACTCODE	PROJNUM

becomes:

EMPNUM	MONTH	ACTCODE	PROJNUM
1105	AUG	10	551

Only one tuple at a time can be entered in this way. Data can also be entered using soft copy forms on the terminal, but the COPY command is best for larger files. The use of the COPY command for building up the database is less tedious as the data is read line by line into tuples until the end of file indicator is reached. The COPY command has the format:

COPY relationname(domainname=format,....)FROM datafile

Thus, if we had created the records on a datafile, we would copy them on to the Ingres file by the following command:

COPY TIMESHEET(EMPNUM=I,MONTH=C,ACTCODE=I, PROJNUM=I)
FROM DATAFILE

The QUEL commands are set up in a user workspace until the user passes the request to Ingres with the command '\g'.

The PRINT command can be used to check that the data has been entered correctly:

* PRINT TIMESHEET \g

Executing...

timesheet relation

EMPNUM	MONTH	ACTCODE	PROJNUM
1105	JAN	10	551
1190	FEB	10	551
7134	FEB	10	712
5765	FEB	10	551

continue...

Ingres replies 'executing' to say that the request is legal and the system is obtaining the data requested, and 'continue' means that the system has finished the request. A number of relations can be printed off by using the print command and separating the relation names with commas.

When Ingres receives '\g', it executes the QUEL command or commands. It is frequently useful to store a series of commands as a file to be executed when appropriate. This avoids setting up the same set of commands on each run. One QUEL command has already been used, the PRINT command, which lists relations on the screen. By attaching a printer to the terminal, this can be used to echo that 'printed' on the terminal to print on paper. Perhaps the most important QUEL command is the RETRIEVE (the SQL SELECT command is similar in effect) which enables data to be retrieved from the database in the form of a relation. It permits a full range of arithmetic and boolean operators. The RETRIEVE statement has the general format:

RETRIEVE attribute list

WHERE condition

SORT BY attribute list

and an example of the statement is:

RETRIEVE (TIMESHEET.MONTH) WHERE TIMESHEET.EMPNUM=1105

MONTH
JAN

We have already looked at the APPEND command which is used to add tuples to a relation. The other two update operations are REPLACE and DELETE. The DELETE operation is used to delete tuples, for example:

DELETE TIMESHEET WHERE TIMESHEET.EMPNUM = 1105

will delete the tuple that we earlier appended to the relation TIMESHEET. The statement:

REPLACE TIMESHEET (ACTCODE=TIMESHEET.ACTCODE+10)

WHERE TIMESHEET.EMPNUM = 1105

will change the value of ACTCODE from 10 to 20 for that employee.

Details about relations can also be obtained using:

HELP

\g

which will list the relation names and the 'owner' (creator). If the HELP is used along with the particular relation name, such as:

HELP PRODUCT (or HELP P)

\g

the system will give the user information about the relation. Descriptions provided by Ingres of some of the relations in the application follow. You will note that the information provided follows conventional relational terminology such as tuple, attribute and relation. Some relational systems have avoided the use of 'pure' relational terminology, using the more familiar, but less exact, record, field, and file or table.

Relation:	orderdetail
Owner:	baker
Tuple width:	18
Saved until:	Thu Jan 17 18:21:59 1985
Number of tuples:	0
Storage structure:	paged heap
Relation type:	user relation

Attribute name	Type	Length	Keyno.
Purchord	i	2	
Purchitem	c	10	
Quantity	i	1	
Purchnetcost	s	4	
Vat	i	1	

Relation:	invoice
Owner:	baker
Tuple width:	27
Saved until:	Thu Jan 17 18:21:58 1985
Number of tuples:	0
Storage structure:	paged heap
Relation type:	user relation

Attribute name	Type	Length	Keyno.
Invoice	i	2	
Custnum	i	4	
Cbg	i	2	
Invitemname	c	10	
Invitemcost	f	4	
Vat	i	1	
Invtotcost	s	4	

Relation: jobtitledet
Owner: baker
Tuple width: 14
Saved until: Fri Jan 18 13:30:25 1985
Number of tuples: 0
Storage structure: paged heap

Attribute name	Type	Length	Keyno.
Projapp	1	1	
Projappdesc	c	20	

Relation: proghard
Owner: baker
Tuple width :   21
Saved until: Thu Jan 17 17:55:21 1985
Number of tuples: 0
Storage structure: paged heap
Relation type: user relation

Attribute name	Type	Length	Keyno.
Projhard	i	1	
Projharddesc	c	20	

Relation: salesassign
Owner: baker
Tuple width: 8
Saved until: Thu Jan 17 18:21:47 1985
Number of tuples: 0
Storage structure: paged heap
Relation type: user relation

Attribute name	Type	Length	Keyno.
Custnum	i	4	
Cbg	i	2	
Empnum	i	2	

Relation: supplier
Owner: baker
Tuple width: 68
Saved until: Thu Jan 17 18:21:52 1985
Number of tuples: 0
Storage structure: paged heap
Relation type: user relation

Attribute name	type	Length	Keyno.
Suppnum	i	4	
Suppname	c	30	
Suppaddr	c	30	
Supptel	i	4	

The physical method of file organisation, the paged heap, is a list file (Section 5.4) in which the additions and deletions are made at the same end. The heap can be sorted on a particular attribute by the HEAPSORT command. Heap storage is suitable where the number of tuples in a relation is small. Ingres does offer alternative access methods such as hashing, where a tuple can be retrieved quickly using the key, or by using indexed sequential access method (Section 5.2).

The RETRIEVE command enables users to access the database. In the example it is preceded by the RANGE statement,

* RANGE OF A IS TIMESHEET

* RETRIEVE (A.EMPNUM,A.PROJNUM).

Other ways of using the retrieve command include:

* RETRIEVE (A.ALL)

* RETRIEVE (A.ALL) SORT BY EMPNUM:ASCENDING

* RETRIEVE (A.ACTCODE) WHERE A.PROJNUM=551

* RETRIEVE (A.EMPNUM,A.MONTH) WHERE A.PROJNUM>700.

The latter retrieval will give the following relation, using the data shown previously:

EMPNUM	MONTH
7134	FEB

1 tuple

This may be very useful to the database administrator who could also use the RESTRICT ACCESS command to prevent unauthorised access to sensitive data. As with most systems, Ingres has password control. The integrity of the database can be helped by giving a range of valid values when entering data:

INTEGRITY A.ACTCODE > 69

Ingres permits abbreviated versions of commands, such as '\g' for GO and '\p' for PRINT (the contents of the memory buffer), '\i' for INCLUDE (to be followed by the filename), '\e' for EDIT the buffer, '\r' for RESET (which clears the buffer) and, finally, '\q' to QUIT the Ingres run.

We have described the QUEL query language. Ingres also has a Query-by-Forms (QBF) interface and a report writer. QBF allows simple functions to be performed on an Ingres relation, but retrievals requiring multiple relations are not supported in QBF. It is menu driven and this enables the user to add data to the database, change the data and view the data. A form is put on the screen by the statement:

QBF database name, relation name

for example,

QBF ORDER TIMESHEET

and the system will reply with the attributes in the TIMESHEET relation:

TABLE IS TIMESHEET

empnum:

month:

actcode:

projnum:

and

RETRIEVE 7134

would fill in all the details of the employee with an employee number of 7134. A part-completed description could be used using the 'wild card' facility. For example, QBF could look for a match on

NAME="SMI*"

which would list names such as SMITH and SMITHSON.

The report writer facility gives a formatted listing from a database. It is particularly useful for summary reports.

14.5 IMPLEMENTING APPLICATIONS

The information system produced supports the loading and retrieval of the following information:

Possible and Probable Projects: This report giving this information has the following elements - Comshare Office, Customer Name, Project Description, Project Leader, and estimates of Number of Days, Cost and Start Date.

Current Projects: Comshare Office, Project Number, Project Description, Customer Name, Customer Billing Group, Project Definition, Salesman, Project Leader, Start Date, and estimates of Number of Days and Cost.

Other reports produced include Outstanding Charges for Projects and Employee details.

These reports can be set up as files in Ingres. Further, commonly utilised sets of queries can also be stored and executed on request. When reports are produced by the Ingres Report Writer, the data is retrieved, sorted, formatted according to the user's specifications (or generated as system defaults), and written to a file or listed directly to the screen and/or printer.

The Query by Form (QBF) interface is easy to use but as it only gives information on one relation in one execution, requests have to be simple.

There is a host language version of QUEL called EMBEDDED QUEL (or EQUEL). The host language can be Cobol, C, Fortran, Basic or Pascal. The characters '##' preceding the command denotes an EQUEL statement to the pre-processor.

As well as interrogating the database, data needs to be changed. Data on the database has to be modified when, for example:

- A possible project becomes an actual project or ceases to be a potential project
- A current project is completed
- An employee leaves the company.

Systems definition therefore specifies input documents and procedures for changing as well as loading the data onto the database.

Chapter 15
An Application of Multiview

This case study concerns the development of an information system for the Computer Science Department of Aston University using Multiview. The project has the long term aim of fulfilling the information requirements of staff and students of the department. It should also integrate with other systems of the university. It was carried out by groups of students over a period of four years. The department has grown considerably over the last few years, and it is of the size where communications become more difficult and the sheer weight of administrative work makes control a particular problem. But it is essential to meet target dates, such as those stated in conference 'calls for papers' or research council 'calls for proposals', and to meet examination schedules. It is also necessary to control activities in the department, such as the selection, purchase, maintenance and use of equipment.

As the early draft of the rich picture shows (Figure 15.1), there are a number of areas that warrant investigation in the problem situation. The emphasis in this diagram has been placed on the courses offered by the department. Figure 15.2 gives an alternative view of the department and emphasises the role of the head of department and senior tutor. The various intermediate rich pictures were later merged to form one which was generally acceptable. Rich pictures were also drawn for a number of areas of concern in the department, and these areas have been identified as:

- *Admissions*: The admissions process must handle enquiries, visits, student and staff presentations, ensure an adequate supply of booklets, and so on. A departmental information system (DIS) should provide useful information such as the correlation between student visits and admissions, and statistics on the qualifications of applicants.

- *Lecturer/course/student*: This subsystem needs to provide up-to-date class lists, syllabuses, reading lists and tutor lists, draw up and provide printed timetables and monitor student assessment of courses. The fact that this information is held for the community will help to ensure that the latest versions are always readily available, and there is no confusion about which *is* the latest version.

- *Examinations*: Keeping track of progress in following the examination schedule through the processes of examination paper design, writing questions, typing and checking, sending to external examiners, and holding boards of examiners meetings, is complex, and failure to keep to timetables causes many problems. This

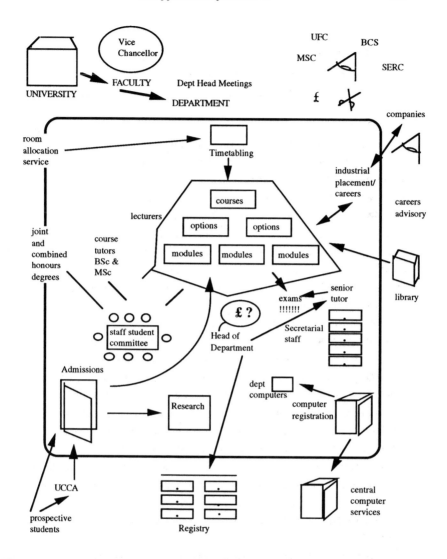

Fig. 15.1. Rich picture of academic department

subsystem is likely to inter-relate with the electronic notice-board and departmental diary subsystems.

- *Notice board*: An electronic notice board and diary can be used to hold details of department meetings, such as seminars, committee and staff meetings, and give dates related to calls for papers and research proposals. This would help to ease the process of arranging meetings when people are free.

- *Industrial placements and careers*: It is important to keep details of industrial

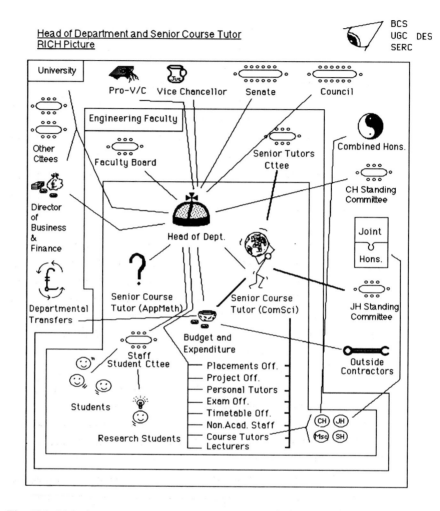

Head of Department and Senior Course Tutor
RICH Picture

BCS
UGC   DES
SERC

Fig. 15.2. Rich picture - concerns of head of department and senior tutor

placements (about half of the undergraduates opt for a 'sandwich' year). This has
been further complicated recently by a number of foreign exchanges which have
been financed by European programmes such as Erasmus. The information held
will include a record of visits and company names and contacts. It would also be
very useful to follow the careers of graduates. Present records depend on the
willingness of graduates to provide this information (which usually comes with a
request for a reference) and it would be helpful to formalise this process.

• *Research*: Many calls for research proposals require detailed information about the
  proposed project, research staff, equipment, finance required, and so on.

Completing each application individually takes much time, but the process could be speeded up considerably with a general departmental database. The details of previous research applications held in the DIS would also be useful as much of this material may be common to a number of applications.

- *Library*: The departmental library holds books, journals, technical reports, student project reports, dissertations and theses, and the library subsystem will hold details of stock, borrowings recorded, and will link to the university library and its computerised information system (GEAC). The present paper system often fails to identify easily the whereabouts of some material. The system should also manage an exchange scheme which exists between universities. The DIS could provide a satisfactory solution, for a full-time librarian for the department is not feasible at present.

- *Equipment*: Details of equipment need to be held on the database and this will include their 'owners', place held, serial numbers, costs, and maintenance record. It is true that these details, like many others discussed, *are* held presently, in this case by the computer officer given this responsibility. What is lacking is the ability to link with other aspects of the departmental system, so that, for example, equipment loaned can be tied in with coursework and project timetables, so as to make the best overall use of available equipment.

- *Computer registration*: This subsystem would register students who have rights of access to particular computer systems, and allocate paper usage and disk space. Registration and de-registration could be achieved automatically by 'liaising' with the student records on the database. Only special requests, such as those for extra disk space or for use of a new machine to carry out a project, should need significant intervention.

- *Accounting*: This subsystem could detail the financial incomings and outgoings of the department, keeping track of funds for conferences and travel, equipment, stationery, fees for seminars, and so on.

- *Decision support system*: This system would facilitate access to particular individual subsystems to deal with *ad hoc* queries and also facilitate (to appropriate users) the provision of information which might necessitate source data coming from a number of subsystems.

The overall system is to produce standard reports for regular output, provide statistical analyses, and handle *ad hoc* queries.

The entity model, shown as Figure 15.3, shows the scale of the overall project. The number of entity types approaches one hundred. This was decomposed into more manageable sections. Figure 15.4 shows the entity model for the area 'students and courses'. Each development team involved in the project tended to concentrate on one area, but as the full entity analysis had been carried out first, then the development work of each group was carried out in the knowledge that their section was part of the overall data model (and database).

The details of the entities found on Figure 15.4 are shown below. In retrospect, the attribute names should have been more helpful, this is a criticism of the database administrator (the author in this case!). We were limited to eight characters on the database management system used.

Entity :	CANDIDATE	
Description :	Person that applies to the department for place on a course	

Attribute	Description	Example
FCADDR1	Candidate address line one	24, High Street....
FCADDR2	Candidate address line two	
FCADDR3	Candidate address line three	
FCAPDAT	Application date	12/04/93
FCAPNUM	Application number	89456937
FCNAME	Name of applicant	Davy, John.
FCSEX	Sex of applicant	M
FCTEL	Contact telephone number	0855-756453 EXTN 2234

Entity :	COMPANY
Description :	General entity referring to either industrial placement or 'first-job' organisation.

Attribute	Description	Example
FCOADD1	First line of company address	162, Baker St.
FCOADD2	Second line of company address	London,
FCOADD3	Third line of company address	W1
FCOCNAM	Name of company contact	Nigel James
FCOINFO1	First line of other details	Pay around average
FCOINFO2	Second line of other details	
FCOINFO3	Third line of other details	
FCOINFO4	Fourth line of other details	
FCOINFO5	Fifth line of other details	
FCONAME	Company Name	Cobil Oil Co. Ltd.
FCOTELE	Telephone number	01-936-8245

Entity :	COURSE
Description :	A university course made up of a set of modules

Attribute	Description	Example
FCADMRE	Course admission requirements	BBC at 'A' level
FCTITLE	Course title	BSc. Computing Sc..
FCCODE	Unique course code	G500
FCOBJ	Course Objectives	Learn to ....
FCPROF	Course Profile	4 Years......
FCASSES	Part-time, full-time or both info	Full-time
FCSDATE	Course start-date	September 1986
FCEDATE	Course end-date	July 1990
FCTUTOR	Course tutor	P.C. Smith

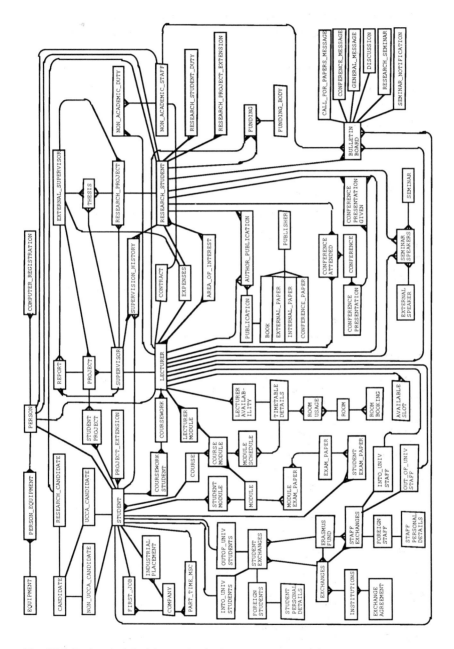

Fig. 15.3. Entity model of the academic department

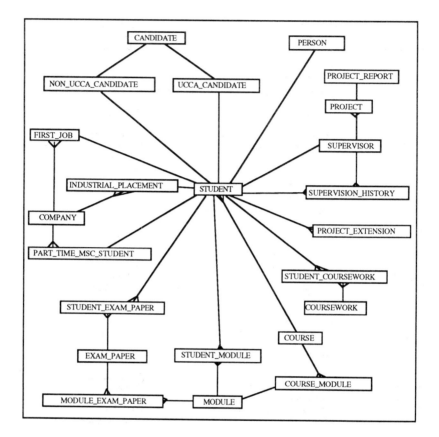

Fig.15.4. Entity model for students and courses

Entity :	COURSE_MODULE
Description :	Links COURSE and MODULE

Attribute	Description	Example
FCMASSES	Method of assessment	50% Exam....
FCMCCODE	Course code for that module	G500
FCMMCODE	Module code	CS310
FCMTEACH	Teaching method	Practical Sessions..
FCMTIME	How much time does the course involve	22 hours

Entity :	COURSEWORK
Description :	Piece of assessed work as part of a module

Attribute	Description	Example
FCWTITL	Title of the coursework	A Study...
FCWCCOD	Course code of work	G500
FCWMCOD	Module code of work	CS350
FCWABS	General description of work	Discuss...........

FCWREQ	Detailed requirements	Write a ....
FCWLDAT	Submission date	25/01/90
FCWSREQ	Submission requirements	Submit to......

Entity : EXAM_PAPER
Description : A single exam paper, from one or more modules

Attribute	Description	Example
FEPTITL	Full title of paper	Digital Systems....
FEPNUM	Unique paper identifier	CSC543
FEPDUR	Length of exam	3 Hours
FEPEQN	Equipment needed for exam	Calculator

Entity : FIRST_JOB
Description : First employment after leaving the department

Attribute	Description	Example
FFJCOMP	Company name	Joe Bloggs Ltd.
FFJID	Unique student ID number	861115703
FFJSAL	First job starting salary	£13,000
FFJTITL	First job title	Service Analyst

Entity : INDUSTRIAL_PLACEMENT
Description : Employment as part of a course

Attribute	Description	Example
FIPCOMP	Company name	Joe Bloggs Ltd.
FIPLOC	Location of placement	Reading
FIPDATE	Placement start date	01/08/88
FIPID	Unique student ID number	861115703
FIPTITL	Job title	Network Operator

Entity : MODULE
Description : Subject taken as part of a course

Attribute	Description	Example
FMCODE	Module code	CS310
FMTITL	Title of Module	Intro to Struc...
FMPREREQ	Pre-requisites to starting module	CS234/ ...
FMSYL	Syllabus of module	Intro......
FMOBJ	Module objectives	To study....
FMREAD	Indicative reading list for course	NASHELSKY...

Entity : MODULE_EXAM_PAPER
Description : One of the modules in an exam paper

Attribute	Description	Example
FMEPCODE	Module code	CS310
FMEPDUR	Time allocated to this module in paper	1.5 hours
FMEPNUM	Exam paper number	3

Entity : NON_UCCA_CANDIDATE

Description :	Course application not via UCCA	
Attribute	Description	Example
FNUCAPNUM	Application number	00768
FNUCOUR	Course code applied for	G500
FNUCINTD	Interviewed ?	Yes
FNUCINDAT	Interview date	05/03/89
FNUCOFF	Type of offer made	Unconditional
FNUCRES	Candidates response	Accept

Entity :	PART_TIME_MSC	
Description :	Job held by the part time MSc student	
Attribute	Description	Example
FPTCNAM	Name of company worked for	Tesco
FPTID	Unique ID number	853441226
FPTEL	Work telephone number	021-765-8765
FPTTITL	Job title	Store manager

Entity :	PROJECT	
Description :	Details of project undertaken by department member	
Attribute	Description	Example
FNRPID	Unique student ID number	861115703
FNRPNUM	Project number	765
FNRPTITL	Project title	A Study into...

Entity :	PERSON	
Description :	Any member of the department, student, academic etc	
Attribute	Description	Example
FPSNAME	Surname	Taylor
FPFNAME	First name	Jessica
FPONAME	Other names, not first or surname	Sally
FPID	Student unique ID number	861115703
FPDOB	Date of Birth	19/08/70
FPHAD1	Home address lines	15, Queen St.,
FPHAD2		
FPHAD3		
FPHAD4		
FPSEX	Sex	Female
FPSPDET1	Special details lines	Suffers from...
FPSPDET1		
FPSTAT	Status of student	Placement
FPINT1	Interests/hobbies lines	Football
FPINT2		Archery
FPUAD1	University address lines	Flat 3, ...
FPUAD2		
FPUAD3		
FPUAD4		
FPUTEL	University telephone number	021-359-3452
FPNKIN	Name of next of kin	Bloggs, J.
FPKAD1	Next of kin address lines	
FPKAD2		
FPKAD3		
FPKAD4		

| FPKHTEL | Next of kin home telephone number. | 01-892-2607 |
| FPKWTEL | Next of kin work telephone number. | 01-983-4982 |

| Entity : | PROJECT_EXTENSION |
| Description : | Details an application to extend a project deadline |

Attribute	Description	Example
FPEXACC	Accepted or rejected ?	ACCEPTED
FPEXDAT	Date extension was applied for	12/06/88
FPEXEND	New submission date	24/07/88
FPEXID	Student ID number	892324265
FPEXNUM	Number of extensions (incl. this ext)	2

| Entity : | PROJECT_REPORT / REPORT / THESIS |
| Description : | Written account of project work |

Attribute	Description	Example
FRASID	ID of project supervisor	861115703
FRDATE	Date that the report was produced	13/11/90
FREXMO	Name of the external examiner	Walter, H, Scott
FRID	Author's dept. ID number	795646556
FRRES	Level achieved (Pass or Fail)	P
FRTITL	Title of the report	A Comparison of ..

| Entity : | STUDENT |
| Description : | A department member taking a course |

Attribute	Description	Example
FSAL1G	'A' Level Grade (First 'A' level)	B
FSAL1T	'A' Level Title (First 'A' level)	Psychology
FSAL2G	'A' Level Grade (Second 'A' level)	C
FSAL2T	'A' Level Title (Second 'A' level)	English
FSAL3G	'A' Level Grade (Third 'A' level)	B
FSAL3T	'A' Level Title (Third 'A' level)	Latin
FSAL4G	'A' Level Grade (Fourth 'A' level)	A
FSAL4T	'A' Level Title (Fourth 'A' level)	French
FSAL5G	'A' Level Grade (Fifth 'A' level)	C
FSAL5T	'A' Level Title (Fifth 'A' level)	Mathematics
FSALEVP	Total 'A' level points score	21
FSAPNUM	Unique application number	000678
FSCOUR	Course code	G500
FSGCOL	O'level or GCSE	GCSE
FSID	Unique student ID number	861115703
FSLEDES	Last educational establishment	King's School Oxford
FSOLCOMP	O'level Computer Science Grade	C
FSOLENGL	O'level English Grade	D
FSOLMATH	O'level Maths Grade	E
FSOTQUAL	Any other qualifications ?	City & Guilds in....
FSSTAT	Student course status	BSc
FSTUT	Personal Tutor	P. C. Smith
FSUCCA	UCCA candidate or not	UCCA
FSYDEP	Estimated year of leaving	1990
FSYENT	Year of entry	1986

| Entity : | STUDENT_COURSEWORK |
| Description : | Links the STUDENT and COURSEWORK entities |

Attribute	Description	Example
FCSID	Unique student ID number	861115703
FCSTITL	Official title of coursework	MSL Compiler

Entity : STUDENT_EXAM_PAPER
Description : Links STUDENT and EXAM_PAPER entities
i.e. A student taking a paper

Attribute	Description	Example
FSEPID	Unique student ID number	86111570
FSEPNUM	Exam unique ID number	000634
FSEPOCC	Number of attempts	4

Entity : STUDENT_MODULE
Description : A student taking a module as part of a course

Attribute	Description	Example
FSMCODE	Module code	CS310
FSMID	Student unique ID number	861115703
FSMTERM	Term module taken	3
FSMKEY	Virtual key of FSMID/MODULE	

Entity : SUPERVISION_HISTORY
Description : Record of periods of project supervision

Attribute	Description	Example
FSHEDATE	Date supervision ended	12/01/89
FSHSDATE	Date supervision started	11/06/88
FSHSTID	Unique student ID number	861115703
FSHSUID	Unique supervisor ID number	795635643

Entity : SUPERVISOR
Description : Person that supervises a project or assesses coursework

Attribute	Description	Example
FSUID	Supervisor ID number	664563423
FSUPOD	Position in the dept.	Admissions Officer
FSUPORG	Position within research group	Convenor

Entity : UCCA_CANDIDATE
Description : Application via UCCA

Attribute	Description	Example
FUCOUR	Course applied for	G500
FUCAPNUM	UCCA application number	674764764
FUCAST	Aston position on UCCA form	3
FUCINTD	Interviewed ?	No
FUCINDAT	Interview date	12/11/87
FUCOFF	Offer made to applicant	Conditional
FUCRES	Candidates response	Reject

In developing the information system, the co-operation of colleagues was and still is required, and the prospective carrot of an information system to help administrative work, although neither guaranteed nor short-term, proved tempting to academic and non-academic staff alike. Colleagues agreed to help both the academic staff leading the project and the students requiring advice when investigating the application area. Such co-operation was agreed informally, through discussions, and formally, in a departmental staff meeting.

In general, those colleagues teaching information systems and other teachers of computer science, administrative staff, and technicians have proved willing to be interviewed, participate in the prototype development, use the prototypes, comment on the design and attend formal presentations.

Figures 15.5 to 15.9 show the set of structure charts for the processing of UCCA applications. These are applicants for undergraduate courses who apply through the standard channels. Figures 15.10 to 15.12 show the data flow diagrams that were constructed representing this processing.

General consensus between groups working on the project is required for much of the planning and development stages and the role of the database administrator is essential to ensure that the various applications do link and integrate with the overall database. Agreement on the establishment of the goals of the overall system and common standards, such as naming conventions and screen designs, is essential. However, groups worked reasonably independently when modelling 'their' part of the department, mapping this onto a database and developing the prototypes.

The prototype has been designed for different types of user:
- Database administrator
- Head of department
- Senior tutor
- Admissions officer
- Course tutor
- Timetabling officer
- Examinations officer
- Careers/job placements officer
- Project supervisor
- Lecturer
- Member of non-academic staff
- Research student
- Student.

A user data model is provided for each of these user views. This allows the same data to be seen by different users in different ways; simplifies the user's perception;

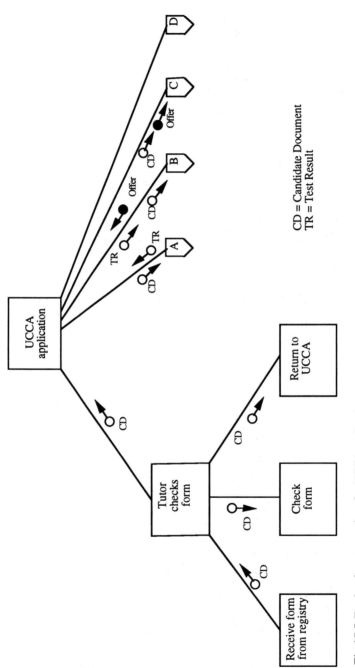

CD = Candidate Document
TR = Test Result

Fig.15.5. Top level structure chart for UCCA application

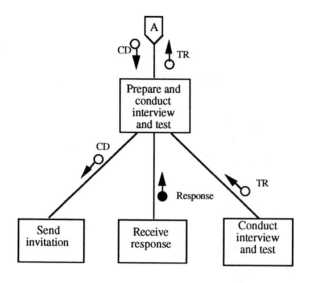

Fig. 15.6. Structure diagram for interviewing and testing applicants

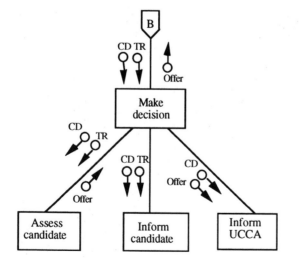

Fig. 15.7. Structure diagram for making a decision and informing applicants

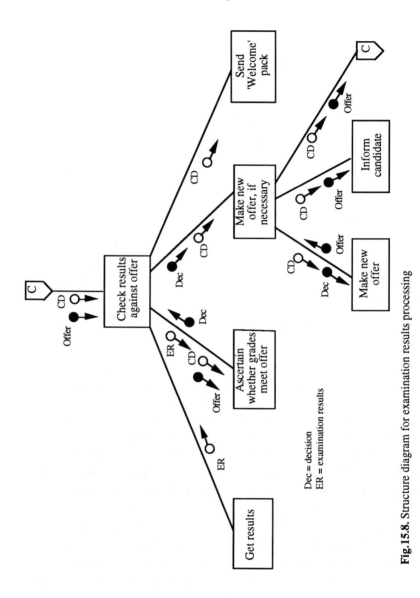

Fig.15.8. Structure diagram for examination results processing

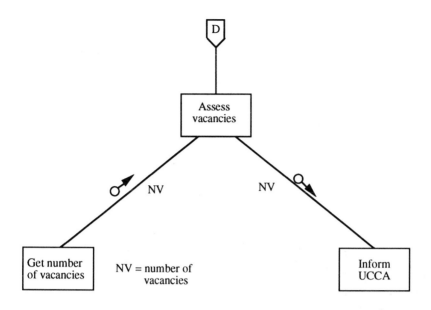

Fig. 15.9. Structure diagram for course vacancies

provides a certain amount of logical data independence when restructuring the database; and provides automatic security for personal data, as some data will not be available in a particular view. With the exception of the database administrator's view, which is the complete database, all these views are subsets of the data held in the DIS database.

An example user view is shown as Figure 15.13. It shows the data model for the admissions officers. There are three sub-views, those for the admissions officers for undergraduate courses, postgraduate courses and research students. The user model links to those parts of the database relating to the candidates, the courses (or research programmes), funding, and lecturer or supervisor. The admissions officer will be restricted to those aspects of the database, though if that person wears other 'hats' such as course tutor, then access to those parts of the database will also be permitted.

The applications are menu-driven, and the user chooses the preferred option through a series of menus, which can be by-passed by the experienced user. The basic menu structure is shown as Figure 15.14. Figure 15.15 shows the first-level menu for admissions officers and is therefore the first option in Figure 15.14. The first three selections will lead to a second level menu being set up for the appropriate admissions officer, which will involve a choice of screens or reports. Choosing option 1 in the first-level menu will lead to the display of the screen with the ID 18 (Figure 15.16). Assuming that the user wishes to print out reports concerning candidate details, option 2 will provide the various list of reports (Figure 15.17). Option 7, described as a

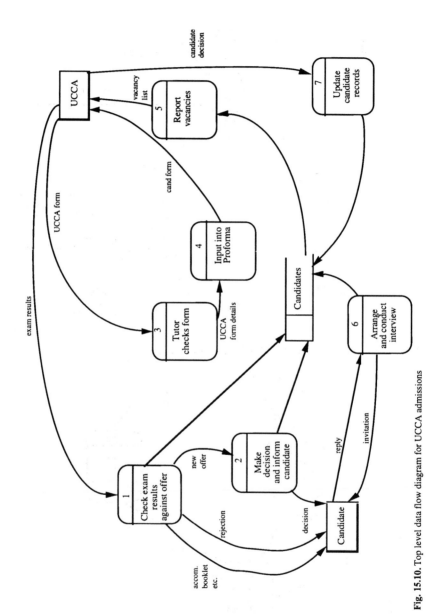

Fig. 15.10. Top level data flow diagram for UCCA admissions

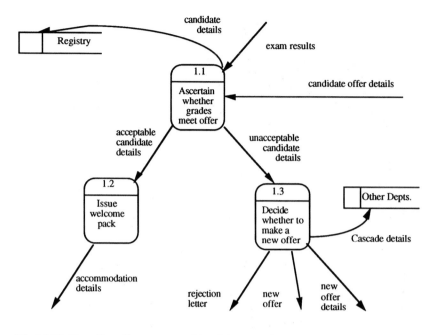

Fig.15.11. Data flow diagram second level (process 1)

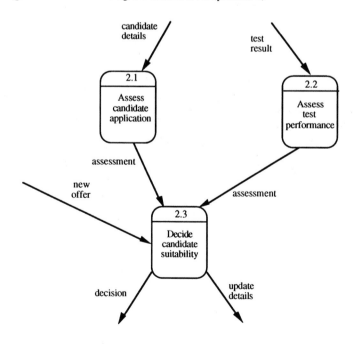

Fig.15.12. Data flow diagram second level (process 2)

ADMISSIONS OFFICER USER DATA MODEL		
UCCA ADMISSIONS	**MSc ADMISSIONS**	**RESEARCH ADMISSIONS**
CANDIDATE DETAILS	CANDIDATE DETAILS	CANDIDATE DETAILS
Candidate	Candidate	Candidate
UCCA-Candidate	Non-UCCA-Candidate	Research-Candidate
STUDENT DETAILS	STUDENT DETAILS	RESEARCH STUDENT
Student	Student	Research Student
Person	Person	Person
COURSE DETAILS	COURSE DETAILS	PROJECT DETAILS
Course	Course	Research Project Research Programme
FUNDING DETAILS	FUNDING DETAILS	FUNDING DETAILS
Funding Funding body	Funding Funding body	Funding Funding body
SUPERVISOR DETAILS Supervisor Person Area-of-interest Lecturer	SUPERVISOR DETAILS Supervisor Person Area-of-interest Lecturer	SUPERVISOR DETAILS Supervisor Person Area-of-interest Lecturer

Fig. 15.13. Admissions officers' user data model

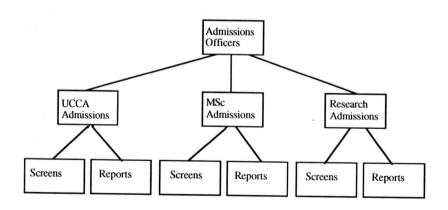

Fig. 15.14. Menu structure for admissions officers

```
┌─────────────────────────────────────────────────────────┐
│                                                           │
│  15 July 1989                         Screen ID 17        │
│                                                           │
│       DEPARTMENT OF COMPUTER SCIENCE AND                  │
│             APPLIED MATHEMATICS                           │
│                                                           │
│       DEPARTMENTAL INFORMATION SYSTEM                     │
│                                                           │
│  Admissions Officer Applications Menu                     │
│                                                           │
│  Select from the following:                               │
│                                                           │
│  1  UCCA Admissions Officer: Admission Details            │
│                                                           │
│  2  MSc Admissions Officer: Admission Details             │
│                                                           │
│  3  Research Admissions Officer: Admission Details        │
│                                                           │
│                                                           │
│  H  Help                                                  │
│                                                           │
│  R  Return to previous menu                               │
│                                                           │
│  Q  Quit                                                  │
│                                                           │
│  Enter your selection _                                   │
│                                                           │
└─────────────────────────────────────────────────────────┘
```

Fig. 15.15. The first-level menu for admissions officers

'statistics breakdown', gives information such as this year's figures compared to last year's, the proportion of female to male students, the proportion of home to overseas applicants, the average GCE 'A' level grade, the percentage of offers against the total number of applicants, and the percentage of offers which are accepted. Another option is Standard Table Two (option 9). This is presented as Figure 15.18. The option and report name is rather unhelpful, but it is the choice of the present admissions tutor and can, in any case, be changed easily.

The soft copy form for capturing and updating basic student information is shown as Figure 15.19. It shows the screen for adding, updating and deleting data relating to students (option 3 of the menu in Figure 15.16). The menu for the actions in this case is placed at the bottom of the screen. The user has to key-in the first letter of the options: thus A for Add, and so on. This screen is designed for experienced users. They will be used to completing these forms and do not need detailed prompting (though there is an option 'help' which shows the user what to do if required).

The data dictionary is used to describe every component of the database; locate the data areas; verify that requested modifications to the descriptions are permitted; co-

```
15 July 1989                                        Screen ID 18
             DEPARTMENT OF COMPUTER SCIENCE AND
                     APPLIED MATHEMATICS

             DEPARTMENTAL INFORMATION SYSTEM

        UCCA Admissions Officer Applications Menu

        Select from the following:

        1  Candidate Details - screens
        2  Candidate Details - reports

        3  Student Details - screens
        4  Student Details - reports

        5  Course Details - screens
        6  Course Details - reports

        7  Supervisor Details - screens
        8  Supervisor Details - reports

        H  Help

        R  Return to previous menu

        Q  Quit

        Enter your selection  _
```

Fig. 15.16. A second-level menu for admissions officers

```
15 July 1989                                        Screen ID21
             DEPARTMENT OF COMPUTER SCIENCE AND
                     APPLIED MATHEMATICS

             DEPARTMENTAL INFORMATION SYSTEM

        UCCA Admissions Officer: Candidate Reports

        Select from the following:


        1  Overseas candidates list
        2  EEC candidates list
        3  Disabled candidates list
        4  Acknowledgement letters
        5  Offer letters
        6  Address labels
        7  Statistics breakdown
        8  Standard table one
        9  Standard table two

        H  Help

        R  Return to previous menu

        Q  Quit


        Enter your selection  _
```

Fig. 15.17. A third-level menu for admissions officers

STANDARD TABLE TWO

WEEKLY BREAKDOWN OF UCCA ADMISSIONS PROCEDURE

Week	Ends	Rec	Unc	Con	Rej	Pen	PAc	FAc	Enr
1	07/01/90	1		1				1	
2	14/01/90	1		1				1	
3	21/01/90	3	1	1	1		1	1	1
4	28/01/90	3	1	1	1		1	1	1
5	04/02/90	3	1	1	1		1	1	1
6	11/02/90	3	1	1	1		1	1	1
7	18/02/90	3	1	1	1		1	1	1
8	25/02/90	4	2	1	1		1	2	1
9	04/03/90	4	2	1	1		1	2	1
10	11/03/90	4	2	1	1		1	2	1
11	18/03/90	4	2	1	1		1	2	1
12	25/03/90	7	2	2	1	2	1	2	1

Rec = Applications received   Unc = Number of Unconditional Offers
Con = Number of Conditional Offers   Rej = Number of Rejections
Pen = Number pending Offer   PAc = Number of Provisional Acceptances
Fac = Number of Firm Acceptances   Enr = Number of Candidates Enrolled

(These figures are cumulative.)

Fig. 15.18. Standard table two

ordinate restructuring tasks that must be performed on the database; control all access to the database; catalogue back-ups; and keep track of users and programs that access the database.

Security in the DIS is important, particularly as the database will contain personal information, and the system has a number of security features. Only registered users can create or use a file. Users are assigned an ID and password and will be registered with certain 'sign-on' privileges (for example, to read, create, change or delete a file) and a priority that defines the way in which they can use the system. At the user data model level, privileges that can be granted to an individual user include exclusive use of a file; the right to 'unhold' a record held by another user; rights to hold, delete, modify or add a record; and rights to modify the value of an individual data element. Privacy directly relates user access permission with the access constraints assigned to record types, view types and data elements. Privacy codes are assigned to record types and elements, and view types and elements. Tests compare these codes with user read and write codes, which are assigned by the database administrator to a particular user when

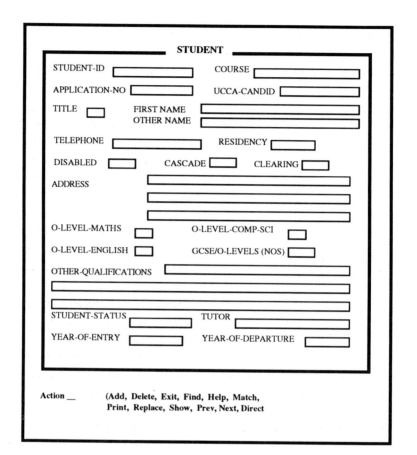

Fig. 15.19. VDU form for adding, updating or deleting data relating to students

he or she is authorised to use a model. When a database is shared by a number of users, it is also essential to maintain the integrity of the data. Again, it is not appropriate here to discuss this in detail, but the system provides a wide range of validity checks and integrity constraints.

The role of the database administrator and computer officer includes:

• Setting up that part of the database to be implemented next
• Ensuring that the subsystem to be implemented fulfils the requirements of the particular users
• Performing a training role
• Fine-tuning aspects of the system already implemented to ensure that it continues to meet changing usage and demand of the users
• Ensuring the human-computer interface is suitable for the various types of users

- Ensuring that security and privacy requirements are met
- Evaluating software packages and hardware as they become available
- Coordinating the departmental information system with the development of the university management information system.

Tutorial systems have been designed for each user type, improving help facilities, and making the menus and screens more appropriate - in general making the system more usable. Usability in this context means making the DIS as easy to use as possible and ensuring that each user interface is appropriate to each of the thirteen different user groups. Users can now enter the system by typing 'DIS' and thereby going straight to the top menu (assuming that the user has the required access rights), whereas early versions required the user to follow a complex set of commands. Wherever possible, the interface design needs to be flexible, even within a user group, as a naive user can quickly migrate to casual expert through to being an experienced professional. The extra facilities required to enable inexperienced users to find their way round a system will be time-wasting and irritating to professional users.

Although the prototype, which has been developed on a large computer using a large and complex software package, has shown that it is possible to set up a DIS using a database which will fulfil many of the information needs of staff and students and ease the administrative load on staff, there are many question marks in the prototype relating to ease of use, ease of learning, flexibility and speed of developing applications. We are constantly looking at other possible directions, such as the provision of an icon interface on a microcomputer which is linked to the mainframe. Here all accesses relating to data will be intercepted by the interface software:

- Receiving data requests from the user
- Processing those requests
- Transferring the requests to the mainframe system, executing the request and transferring the results back to the user
- Displaying the results in a suitable screen format.

The most likely direction is to implement the database on the mainframe and also link this with the microcomputer version of the database management system which will be implemented on the departmental network of microcomputers. This has a number of advantages:

- The use of the familiar icon interface, which the users prefer
- The availability of a number of tools which will speed up the development of some applications, in particular reports and screens
- Connections with the departmental network and the university local area network
- Easy transfer of information to other microcomputer packages for viewing in a number of ways, including graphically, and for data manipulation.

Figure 15.20 shows a screen used as part of a prototype system for student feedback. The use of buttons (for the various options) and icons (for help and return), gives a screen which seems a considerable improvement on the conventional menus of Figures 15.15 and 15.16. The input document shown as Figure 15.21 for recording students' general comments, also seems an improvement on the type of form illustrated as Figure 15.19. The up and down arrows for each window allow the user to extend the amount of text held beyond the actual window size. Thus the user could 'scroll' up (using the up arrow) to go to the top of the message or downwards using the down arrow.

One final comment. The experience with conventional database systems has shown that they are inappropriate to some aspects of this application, and their inappropriateness, by implication, extends to aspects of many applications. Conventional databases assume that all information can be classified and retrieved in tabular (relational) form. This limits the use of the database to a specific range of types of application and users. Some information may not suit this tabular representation, it may be better represented graphically or in image form. Information related to the DIS might be in the form of hand-written and annotated application forms or photographs. In the long term, we need to develop multi-media databases, with their user interface much more flexible. The relational database and associated query languages will be part of this, but there will be other aspects. The process of storing other types of information has already started as the students' photographs are scanned and are included for display in each student's computer record (Figure 15.22).

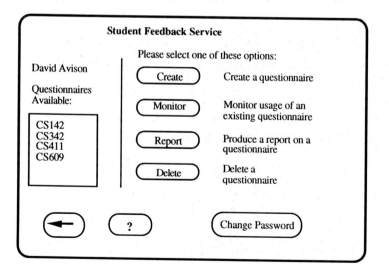

Fig. 15.20. The student feedback prototype - analysing student questionnaires

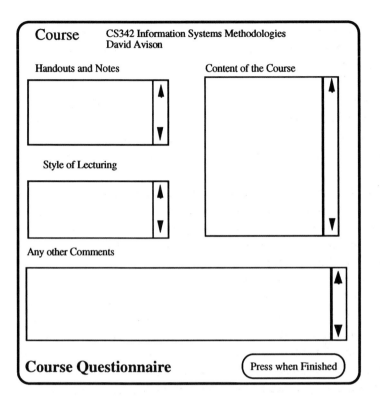

Fig. 15.21. Student feedback prototype - recording students' general comments

Fig. 15.22. Student record with photograph

Bibliography

Ackoff, R. L (1967) Management Misinformation Systems, *Management Science*, **14**.

Ambron, S & Hooper, K (Eds) (1990) *Interactive multimedia,* Microsoft, Redmond, WA.

Andrews, T & Harris, C (1987) Combining language and database advances in an object-oriented development environment, *OOPSLA*.

Andrews, T, Harris, C & Sinkel, K (1991) The Ontos Object Database, Ontologic, Burlington, Ma.

ANSI/X3/SPARC (1975) *Study Group on Data Base Management Systems, Interim Report,* ACM SIGMOD Bulletin, **7**, 2.

Avison, D. E & Catchpole, C. P (1987) Information Systems for the Community Health Services, *Medical Informatics*, **13**, 2.

Avison, D. E & Fitzgerald, G (1988) *Information Systems Development: Methodologies, Techniques and Tools*, Blackwell Scientific Publications, Oxford.

Avison, D. E & Fitzgerald, G (1991) Information Systems Practice, Education and Research, *Journal of Information Systems*, **1**, 1.

Avison, D. E & Golder, P. A (1991) *Tools supporting soft systems,* In: Jackson, M. A, Flood, R. L, Blackham, R. B, Mansell, C. J & Probert, S. V. E, Systems Thinking in Europe, Plenum, New York.

Avison, D. E & Wilson, D (1991) Controls for Effective Prototyping, *Journal of Management Systems*, SA-58.

Avison, D. E & Wood-Harper, A. T (1990) *Multiview: An Exploration in Information Systems Development*, Blackwell Scientific Publications, Oxford.

Avison, D. E (1981) Techniques of Data Analysis, *Computer Bulletin*, **II**, 29.

Avison, D. E (1989) Action Learning for Information Systems Teaching, *International Journal of Information Management*, **9**,1.

Avison, D. E (1990) A Departmental Information System, *International Journal of Information Management*, **10**, 2.

Avison, D. E (1990) *Mastering Business Microcomputing*, 2nd ed, Macmillan, Basingstoke.

Avison, D. E, Fitzgerald, G & Wood-Harper, A. T (1988) Information Systems Development: A Tool-kit is not Enough, *Computer Journal*, **31**, 4.

Bachman, C. W (1969) *Database management: the keystone of applied systems architecture*, In: Gruenberger, F (Ed) (1969) Critical factors in data management,

Prentice Hall, Englewood Cliffs.

Bachman, C. W (1973) The programmer as navigator, *Communications of the ACM*, **16**, 11.

Bachman, C. W & Daya, M (1977) *The role concept in database models*, Proceedings of Conference on Very Large Databases, ACM, 1977.

Baskerville, R (1988) *Designing Information Systems Security*, Wiley, New York.

Beer, S (1985) *Diagnosing the System for Organizations*, Wiley, Maidenhead.

Bemelmans, T. M. A (Ed.) (1984) *Beyond Productivity: Information Systems Development for Organizational Effectiveness*, North Holland, Amsterdam.

Benbasat, I, Goldstein, D & Mead, M (1987) The Case Research Strategy in Studies of Information Systems, *MIS Quarterly*, February, 1987.

Benyon, D (1990) *Information and Data Modelling*, Blackwell Scientific Publications, Oxford.

Benyon, D & Skidmore, S (1987) Towards a tool-kit for the systems analyst, *Computer Journal*, **30**, 1.

Bertalanffy, L von (1968) *General Systems Theory*, Braziller, New York.

Beynon-Davies, P (1992) *Relational Database Design*, Blackwell Scientific Publications, Oxford.

Blackman M (1975) *Design of Real-Time Applications*, Wiley, New York.

Blumenthal, S. C (1969) *Management Information Systems: A Framework for Planning and Development*, Prentice Hall, Englewood Cliffs.

Boar, B. H (1984) *Application Prototyping: A Requirements Definition Strategy for the 80's*, Wiley, New York.

Boehm, B, Gray, T. E & Seewaldt, T (1984) Prototyping versus Specifying: A Multiproject Experiment, *IEEE Transactions on Software Engineering*, SE-10, 3.

Booch, G (1991) *Object-oriented design with applications*, Benjamin Cummings, Redwood City, Ca.

Borovits, I, Ellis, S, & Yeheskel, O (1990) Group processes and the development of information systems, *Information and Management*, **19**, 2.

Bowers, D. S (1988) *From Data to Database*, Van Nostrand Reinhold, Wokingham.

Bradley, J (1987) *Introduction to data base management in business*, 2nd ed, Holt, Rinehart and Winston, New York.

British Computer Society (1976) *Data Dictionary Systems Working Party Report*, BCS, London.

Budde, R, Kuhlenkamp, K, Mathiassen, L, & Zullighoven, H (Eds) (1984) *Approaches to Prototyping*, Springer-Verlag, Berlin.

Bullen, C. V & Rockart, J. F (1984) *A Primer on Critical Success Factors*, CISR Working Paper 69, Sloan Management School, MIT.

Burns, R. N & Dennis, A. R (1985) Selecting the Appropriate Application Development Methodology, *Data Base*, **17**, 1.

Cardenas, A. F (1985) Database Management Systems, 2nd ed, Allyn and Bacon, Boston.

Ceri, S & Pelagatti, G (1984) *Distributed databases,* McGraw-Hill, New York

Checkland, P. B (1981) *Systems Thinking, Systems Practice,* John Wiley, Chichester.

Checkland, P.B & Griffin, R (1970) Management Information Systems: a Systems View, *Journal of Systems Engineering*, **1**, 2.

Chen, M, Nunamaker, J. F & Weber, E. S (1989) Computer-aided software engineering: present status and future directions, *Data Base*, Spring.

Chen, P. P. S (1976) The Entity-Relationship Model - Toward a Unified View of Data, *ACM Transactions on Database Systems*, **1**, 1.

Codasyl (1971a) Programming Languages Committee, *DBTG Report*, ACM, New York.

Codasyl (1971b) Systems Committee, *Feature Analysis of Generalised Database Management Systems*, ACM, New York.

Codasyl (1973) Data Description Language Committee, *DDL Journal of Development*, ACM, New York.

Codasyl (1975) Programming Languages Committee, *Cobol Journal of Development*, ACM, New York.

Codasyl (1978a) Data Description Language Committee, *DDL Journal of Development*, ACM, New York.

Codasyl (1978b) Programming Languages Committee, *Cobol Journal of Development*, ACM, New York.

Codasyl (1981) Data Description Language Committee, *DDL Journal of Development*, ACM, New York.

Codd, E. F (1970) A relational model of data for large shared data banks, *Communications of the ACM*, **13**, 6.

Codd, E. F (1972) *Relational Completeness of Database Sublanguages*, In: Database Systems, Courant Computer Science Symposia Series, 6, Prentice Hall, Englewood Cliffs.

Codd, E. F (1974) *Seven Steps to Rendezvous with the Casual User*, In: Klimbie & Kofferman (1974).

Codd, E. F (1979) Extending the relational model of data to capture more meaning, *ACM Transactions on Database Systems*, **4**, 4.

Codd, E. F (1987) Codd's 12 rules for relational DBMS, *Relational Journal*, **1**, 1.

Comer, D (1979) The Ubiquitous B-tree, *ACM Computing Surveys*, **11**.

Crowe, T & Avison D. E (1980) *Management Information from Data Bases,*

Macmillan, Basingstoke.

Curtice R. M & Dieckmann, E. M (1981) A Survey of Data Dictionaries, *Datamation*, March.

Cyert, R. M & March, J. G (1963) *A Behavioral Theory of the Firm*, Prentice Hall, Englewood Cliffs.

Daniels, A & Yeates, D. A (1971) *Basic Training in Systems Analysis*, 2nd ed., Pitman, London.

Date, C. J (1984) A critique of the SQL database language, *ACM Sigmod Record*, **14**, 3.

Date, C. J (1987a) What is a distributed database system? (part I), *Relational Journal*, **1**, 1.

Date, C. J (1987b) What is a distributed database system? (part II), *Relational Journal*, **1**, 2.

Date, C. J (1990) *An Introduction to Database Systems, Volume 1*, 5th ed, Addison-Wesley, London.

Date, C. J & White, C (1988) *A guide to DB2*, 2nd ed, Addison-Wesley, Reading, Mass.

Davenport, R. A (1978) Data Analysis for Data Base Design, *Australian Computer Journal*, 10.

Davis, G. B (1982) Strategies for Information Requirements Determination, *IBM Systems Journal*, **21**, 2.

Davis, G. B & Olsen, M. H (1985) *Management Information Systems: Conceptual Foundations, Structure and Development*, 2nd ed, McGraw-Hill, New York.

Deal, T. E & Kennedy, A. A (1982) *Corporate cultures - the rites and rituals of corporate life*, Addison-Wesley, Reading, Mass.

Dearnley, P. A & Mayhew, P. J (1983) In Favour of System Prototypes and their Integration into the Systems Development Cycle, *Computer Journal*, **26**, 1.

DeMarco, T (1979) *Structured Analysis and System Specification*, Prentice-Hall, Englewood Cliffs.

Dodd, G. C (1969) Elements of Data Management Systems, *Computing Surveys*, June.

Dowgiallo, E (1989) The art of distribution, *DBMS*, **2**, March.

Downs, E, Clare, P & Coe, I (1988) *Structured Systems Analysis and Design Method: Application and Context*, Prentice Hall, Hemel Hempstead.

Draffan, I. W & Poole, F (1980) *Distributed data bases - an advanced course*, CUP, Cambridge.

Earl, M, J (1989) *Management Strategies for Information Technology*, Prentice Hall, Hemel Hempstead.

Eason, K. D (1984) Towards the Experimental Study of Usability, *Behaviour and Information Technology*, **2**, 2.

Elmasri, R & Navathe, S. B (1989) *Fundamentals of Database Systems*, Benjamin/Cummings, Redwood City, Ca.

Fagin, R (1977) Multivaried Dependencies and a new normal form for relational databases, *ACM TODS*, **2**, 3.

Fröhlich, D & Krieger, H (1990) Technological change and worker participation in Europe, *New Technology, Work and Employment*, **5**, 2.

Galliers, R (1987) *Information Analysis: Selected Readings*, Addison Wesley, Sydney.

Galliers, R. D & Sutherland, A. R (1991) Information systems management and strategy formulation: the 'stages of growth' model revisited, *Journal of Information Systems*, **1**, 2.

Gane, C. P & Sarson, T (1979) *Structured Systems Analysis: Tools and Techniques*, Prentice Hall, Englewood Cliffs.

Gibson, E (1990) Objects - born and bred, *Byte,* October.

Gillenson, M. L (1982) The State of Practise of Data Administration, *Communications of the ACM*, **25**.

Gillenson, M. L (1990), *Database: step-by-step*, 2nd ed., Wiley, New York.

Gradwell, D. J. L (1983) *ICL's DDS, DD Update*, British Computer Society, London, April.

Gretton-Watson, P (1988) Distributed database development, *Computer Communications*, **11**, 5.

Hekmatpour, S & Ince, D (1986) *Rapid Software Prototyping*, Open University, Technical Report, 86, 4.

Hirschheim, R & Newman, M (1988) Information systems and user resistance: theory and practice, *Computer Journal*, **31**, 5.

Holloway, S (1988) *Data administration*, Gower Technical Press, Aldershot.

Holloway, S (Ed) (1990) *Fourth generation systems - their scope, applications and methods of evaluation*, Chapman and Hall, London.

Horowitz, E (1985) A Survey of Application Generators, *IEEE Software*, January.

Howe, D. R (1989) *Data Analysis for Data Base Design*, 2nd ed, Arnold, London.

Hsiao, D (Ed) (1983) *Advanced Database Machine Architecture*, Prentice Hall, Englewood Cliffs.

Hull, R & King, R (1987) Semantic database modelling: survey, applications, and research issues, *ACM Computer Surveys*, **19**, 3.

ISO (1987) *Database language SQL*, International Standards Organisation document ISO9075.

Jackson, M. A (1983) *Systems Development*, Prentice Hall, Englewood Cliffs.

Jeffery, D. R & Low, G (1989) Productivity Issues in the Use of Current Back-end CASE Tools, *Third International Workshop on Computer-Aided Software Engineering,* London, July.

Kassapis, A. K (1989) *Distributed databases,* unpublished MSc project report, Department of Computer Science, Aston University.

Kent, W (1983) A Simple Guide to Five Normal Forms in Relational Theory, *Communications of the ACM,* **26,** 2.

Kent, W. A (1978) *Data and Reality,* North Holland, Amsterdam.

Khoshafian, S (1990) Insight into object-oriented databases, *Information and Software Technology,* **32,** 4.

Kim, W & Lochovsky, F. E (Eds) (1989) *Object-oriented concepts, databases and application,* Addison-Wesley, Reading, Mass.

Knuth, D. E (1973a) *The Art of Computer Programming, Vol 1,* Fundamental Algorithms, 2nd ed, Addison-Wesley, Reading, Mass.

Knuth, D. E (1973b) *The Art of Computer Programming, Vol 3,* Sorting and Searching, Addison-Wesley, Reading, Mass.

Kroenke, D (1977) *Database Processing,* SRA, Chicago.

Lacroix, M & Pirotte, A (1977) *Domain-Oriented Relational Languages,* Proceedings of 3rd International Conf. on Very Large Databases, Tokyo, October.

Land, F. F (1982) *Adapting to Changing User Requirements,* In: Galliers (1987).

Land, F. F & Hirschheim, R (1983) Participative Systems Design: Rationale, Tools and Techniques, *Journal of Applied Systems Analysis,* **10.**

Langefors, B & Sundgren, B (1975) *Information Systems Architecture,* Petrocelli, New York.

Langham, M (1989) A distributed dilemma?, *Network,* January.

Lantz, K. E (1985) *The Prototyping Methodology,* Prentice-Hall, Englewood Cliffs.

Law, D.T (1985) *Prototyping,* NCC, Manchester.

Lawson, R. W (1988) Distributed databases, *HP World,* **1,** 2.

Lederer, A. L & Mendlelow, A. L (1989) Information systems planning: incentives for effective action, *Data Base,* Fall.

Liebenau, J & Backhouse, J (1990) *Understanding information: an introduction,* Macmillan, Basingstoke.

Lindop, N (1978) *Report of the Committee on Data Protection,* HMSO, London.

Lobell, R. F (1983) *Application Program Generators, A State of the Art Survey,* NCC, Manchester.

Longworth, G (1985) *Designing Systems for Change,* NCC, Manchester.

Loomis, M. E. S (1990a) OODBMS: the basics, *Journal of Objected Oriented Programming,* May/June.

Loomis, M. E. S (1990b) OODBMS vs relational, *Journal of Objected Oriented Programming*, July/August.

Lyon, J. K (1976) *The Database Administrator*, Wiley, New York.

Maciaszek, L. A (1990) *Database design & implementation*, Prentice Hall, Sydney.

Markus, L (1984) *Information Systems in Organisations: Bugs and Features*, Pitman, London.

Martin, C. F (1988) Second generation CASE tools: a challenge to vendors, *IEEE Software*, March.

Martin, J (1977) *Computer Data-Base Organization*, 2nd ed, Prentice Hall, Englewood Cliffs.

Martin, J (1982a) *Application Development without Programmers*, Prentice Hall, Englewood-Cliffs.

Martin, J (1982b) *Fourth Generation Languages, Vol 1*, Prentice Hall, Englewood Cliffs.

Martin, J (1983) *Fourth Generation Languages, Vol 2*, Prentice Hall, Englewood Cliffs.

Martin, J (1991) *Rapid Application Development*, Macmillan, New York.

Martin, J & Finkelstein, C (1981) *Information Engineering, Vols 1 and 2*, Prentice Hall, Englewood Cliffs.

Martin, J & McClure, C (1984) *Structured Techniques for Computing*, Savant Research Institute, Carnforth.

Mayhew, P. J & Dearnley, P. A (1987) An Alternative Prototyping Classification, *Computer Journal*, **30**, 6.

McCririck, I. B & Goldstein, R. C (1980) What do Data Administrators do?, *Datamation*, **26**, August.

McFadden, F. R & Hoffer, J. A (1991) *Database Management*, 3rd ed, Benjamin/Cummings, Redwood City, Ca.

Mehlman, M (1981) *When People Use Computers*, Prentice Hall, Englewood Cliffs.

Misra, S. K (1990) Analyzing CASE system characteristics: evaluative framework, *Information and Software Technology*, **32**, 6.

Mumford, E (1981) Participative Systems Design: Structure and Method, *Systems, Objectives and Solutions*, **1**, 1.

Mumford, E (1983) *Designing Human Systems*, Manchester Business School, Manchester.

Mumford, E (1983) *Designing Participatively*, Manchester Business School, Manchester.

Mumford, E (1985) Defining Systems Requirements to meet Business Needs: A Case Study Example, *Computer Journal*, **28**, 2.

Mumford, E & Henshall, D (1979) *A Participative Approach to Computer Systems Design,* Associated Business Press, London.

Mumford, E, Land, F. F & Hawgood, J (1978) A Participative Approach to Computer Systems, *Impact of Science on Society,* **28,** 3.

Naumann, J. D & Jenkins, A. M (1982) Prototyping: The New Paradigm for Systems Development, *MIS Quarterly,* **6,** 3.

Nelson, K (1985) Technical Requirements of a 4-GL, *Data Processing,* November.

Nolan, R (1979) Managing the crises in data processing, *Harvard Business Review,* **57,** 2.

Olle, T. W (1978) *The Codasyl approach to data base management,* Wiley, New York.

Olle, T. W (1991) *Information systems methodologies - a framework for understanding,* 2nd ed, Addison Wesley, Wokingham.

Olle, T. W, Sol, H. G & Verrijn-Stuart, A. A (1982) *Information Systems Design Methodologies: A Comparative Review,* North Holland, Amsterdam.

Olle, T.W, Sol, H.G & Tully, C. J (1983) *Information Systems Design Methodologies: A Feature Analysis,* North Holland, Amsterdam.

Open Systems Group (1981) *Systems Behaviour,* 3rd ed, Harper & Row, London.

Oxborrow, E (1989) *Databases and database systems,* 2nd ed, Chartwell-Bratt, Bromley.

Ozsu, T & Valduriez, P (1989) *Principles of distributed database systems,* Prentice Hall, Englewood Cliffs.

Pactel (1979) *Distributed database technology,* Wiley, Chichester.

Pergamon (1987) *Analyst Workbenches: State of the Art Report,* 15,1 Pergamon-Infotech, Maidenhead.

Porter, M. E (1985) *Competitive Strategy - Techniques for Analysing Industries and Competitors,* Free Press, New York.

Porter, M. E (1985) *Competitive Advantage - Creating and Sustaining Superior Performance,* Free Press, New York.

Pratt, C. J (1987) *Database Systems: Management and Design,* Boyd & Fraser, Boston.

Pressman, R. S (1982) *Software Engineering: a Practitioner's Approach,* McGraw Hill, New York.

Quang, P. T & Chartier-Kastler, C (1991) *Merise in Practice,* Macmillan, Basingstoke (translated by D. E & M. A. Avison from the French *Merise Appliquée,* Eyrolles, Paris, 1989).

Reinsch, R (1988) Distributed databases for SAA, *IBM Systems Journal,* **27,** 3.

Rickards, T (1974) *Problem solving through creative analysis,* Gower Press, Epping.

Robinson, H (1989) *Database Analysis and Design,* 2nd ed, Chartwell-Bratt, Bromley.

Rockart, J. F (1979) Chief Executives Define Their Own Data Needs, *Harvard Business Review*, March-April.

Rock-Evans, R (1981) *Data Analysis*, IPC Press, London.

Rock-Evans, R (1989) *CASE Analyst Workbenches: A Detailed Product Evaluation*, Ovum, London.

Senn. J (1984) *Analysis and Design of Information Systems*, McGraw Hill, New York.

Shave, M. J. R (1981) Entities, Functions and Binary Relations: Steps to a Conceptual Schema, *Computer Journal*, **24**, 1.

Sherif, M. A (1988) *Database Projects: a framework for effective management*, Ellis Horwood, Chichester.

Shipman, D. W (1981) The functional data model and the data language DAPLEX, *ACM Transactions on Database Systems*, **6**, 1.

Smith, J & Smith, D (1977) Database abstractions: aggregation and generalisation, *ACM Transactions on Database Systems*, **2**, 2.

Son, S. H & Choe, K. M (1988) Techniques for database recovery in distributed environments, *Information and Software Technology*, **30**, 5.

Stevens, W, Myers, G & Constantine, L (1974) Structured Design, *IBM Systems Journal*, May.

Sundgren, B (1985) *Databases and Data Models*, Studentlitteratur, Lund.

Symons, V & Walsham, G (1988) The Evaluation of Information Systems: A Critique, *Journal of Applied Systems Analysis*, **15**.

Tozer, E (Ed) (1984) *Applications Development Tools - A State of the Art Report*, Pergamon-Infotech.

Tsichritzis, D. C & Klug, A (Eds) (1978) The ANSI/X3/SPARC Framework: Report of the Study Group on Data Base Management Systems, *Information Systems*, **3**.

Ullman, J. D (1988) *Principles of Database and Knowledge-Base Systems, Vol 1*, Computer Science, Rockville.

Ullman, J. D (1989) *Principles of Database and Knowledge-Base Systems, Vol 2*, Computer Science, Rockville.

Van Duyn, J (1982) *Developing a Data Dictionary System*, Prentice-Hall, Englewood Cliffs.

Vasta, J. A (1985) *Understanding Database Management Systems*, Wadsworth, Belmont .

Veryard, R (1984) *Pragmatic Data Analysis*, Blackwell Scientific Publications, Oxford.

Waters, S. J (1979) Towards Comprehensive Specifications, *Computer Journal*, **22**, 3.

Waters, S. J (1979) *Systems Specifications*, NCC, Manchester.

Watt, J (1987) *Applied fourth generation languages,* Sigma Press, Wilmslow.

Weldon, J. L (1981) *Database Administration,* Plenum Press, New York.

Willcocks, L & Mason, D (1987) *Computerising Work,* Paridigm, London.

Wilson, B (1984) *Systems: Concepts, Methodologies and Applications,* Wiley, Chichester.

Wood-Harper, A. T & Fitzgerald, G (1982) A Taxonomy of Current Approaches to Systems Analysis, *Computer Journal,* **25,** 1.

Yalonis, C (1988) Data dispersal starts as a trickle, *Computerworld: Spotlight,* **22,** March.

Yourdon, E (1989) *Modern Structured Analysis,* Prentice-Hall, Englewood Cliffs.

Yourdon, E & Constantine, L. L (1978) *Structured Design,* 2nd ed, Yourdon, New York.

Zani, W. M (1970) Blueprint for MIS, *Harvard Business Review,* Nov-Dec.

Zloof, M. M (1977) Query by Example: A Database Language, *IBM Systems Journal,* **16,** 4.

Zloof, M. M (1978) *Design Aspects of the Query-by-Example Data Base Management Language,* In: Shneiderman, B (Ed) Improving Database Usability and Responsiveness, Academic Press, New York.

Index

Items in italic refer to names of cited authors (see also Bibliography), products or companies; page numbers in bold indicate principal references.

Abstract data type 144
Abstraction 146
ACF2 300
Ackoff, R. L 73, 74
AD Cycle 274
ADA 274
Adabas 204, **217-219**
Address 150, 157, 160, 218
American National Standards Institute
  (ANSI) 127, 223, 258
Analogy 61
Analysis (see Systems analysis)
Analyst (see Systems analyst)
ANSI/X3/SPARC **30-32**, 37, 40,
  138, 148, 164, 165
Apollo 234
Apple 234, 235, 236, 239
Application 31, 34, 37, 75, **164-196**,
  242, 326-27
Application backlog 14, 19, 180, 259
Application Factory 274
Application package (see Package)
Arthur Young 274
Assembler language 204, 215, 260
Assumption
Aston University 309, 328
Attribute 78, **80**, 91, 101, 117, 278,
  287, 314, 315, 323-324, 332-338
Auto-Mate Plus 274
Automated tools (see Tools)
Avison, D. E 40, 64, 65, 74, 96, 97,
  182, 184, 195, 196, 272, 279

B-trees 36, **154-156**
Bachman, C. W 143, 145, 296
Backhouse, J 74
Baskerville, R 306
Batch 18
Benyon, D 30, 74, 113, 146
Beynon-Davies, P 147
Binary chop (or search) 150-151
Binary trees 158
Blumenthal, S. C 68, 74
Booch, G 144, 147
Borovits, 178
Bottom-up analysis 99
Boundary 59, **62**

Bowers, D. S 114, 146
Boyce-Codd normal form (BCNF)
  111-112
British Computer Society (BCS) 284,
  286, 292, 294
Britton-Lee IDM 242
Business analysis 6, 31, 33, 34, 35,
  43-74, 279
Business model 6, 33
Business universe 49

C 18, 220, 277
C++ 142, 220
Cardenas, A. F 104, 114
Cardinality 101
Case study 34, 39
Case tool 19, 22, 142, 259, 272, 274,
  275-278
Case2000 276
CATWOE **65-67**, 189, 190
Ceri, S 245, 252, 258
Chain (see Circular list)
Chartier-Kastler, C 86, 140, 146, 280
Checkland, P. B 188
Chen, P. P. S 77, 78, 114, 142, 143,
  282
Choe, K. M 251
Circular list 158
Clerical system 3, 4, 7
Client (see Customer)
Cobol 18, 19, 25, 127, 135, 138, 139,
  200, 204, 208, 212, 215, 222,
  223, 260, 266, 277
Codasyl 77, 78, 135, 140, 147, 156,
  200, **209-214**, 217, 284, 292
Codd, E. F 77, 78, 99, 103, 108, 114,
  118, 123, 126, 142, 222, 248, 258
Communication 36, 89, 177, 290
Compaq 234
Competitive advantage 44, 52, 57
Computer Corporation of America 252
Computer-aided design 142
Computer-aided manufacture 142
Computer-aided software engineering
  (see Case tool)
Comshare 309, 311
Conceptual model 6, 30-33, 34, 36,

75-114, 201, 280, 286
(in Multiview) 189, 190
Conceptual schema (see Conceptual model)
Concurrency 249, 300
Connector records (see Link records)
Control 24-25, 26, 53, 54, 186, 194, 195, 202, 245, 255, 285, 298
Conventional systems analysis 3, **8-15**, 21, 75, **166-168**, 176
Cost-benefit analysis 59
Critical success factors 73

Daniels, A 39
Data 18, 44, 46, 75
collection 46
flow 170, 289
integrity 24-25
model 141, 201, 343, 346
(see also Entity model; Conceptual model))
shareability 24
Data administrator 254, 256, 304, 305
Data analysis 5, 6, 20, 33, 36, 37, 51, 69, **75-114**, 174, 284
Data Base Task Group (see also *Codasyl*) 135, 138, 147, 156, 209
Data collection 45, 69, 99
Data definition language (DDL) 116, 133, 138, 139, 223
Data dictionary 18, 28, 29, 34, 39, 89, 174, 202, 217, 248, 255, 264, 266, 275-280, **284-294**, 298, 300, 313, 347
Data duplication 181, 246
Data flow diagrams **169-171**, 191, 276, 278, 339, 344-345
Data independence 4, 13, 25, 31, 154, 164, 201, 202, 246
logical 31
physical 31, 154
program 164
Data manipulation language (DML) 116, 117, 133, 138, 139, 213, 223
Data processing 4, 5, 12
Data processing department 4, 8, 22, 285, 303
Data steward 304-305
Data storage description language 138
Data usage diagram **97-98**
Database 19, 20, 26, 69, 199, 297
(see also Database management system)
justification **23-26**
maintenance 186, 194, 195, 300-301
microcomputer **233-241**
multi-media 20
Database administrator (DBA) 28, 34,

39, 58, 69, 116, 117, 118, 127, 145, 148, 154, 162, 201, 202, 203, 204, 210, 214, 217, 245-246, 257, 278, 281, 284-285, 288-291, **295-306**, 350-351
Database machine 17, 34, 38, 145, **241-242**
Database management system (DBMS) 6, 18, 19, 24, 31, 34, 37, **115-147**, 166, **199-221**, 263-264, 280
hierarchical 36, **129-133**, 144-146, 319
network 36, **133-139**, 144-146, 320
relational 20, 36, **116-129**, 144-146, 253, 267
Datalogical 30
Date, C. J 108, 112, 113, 114, 146, 154, 155, 156, 163, 221, 222, 232, 246, 247, 252, 258
Daya, M 143
DB2 117, 127, 128, 129, 204, **214-217**, 222, 232, 254, **293-294**, 309
dBaseII 233
dBaseIV 117, 182, 222, 235, **236-238**
DBMS (see Database management system)
Deal, T. E 50
Dearnley, P. A 183, 196
Decision 45, 46, 53, 73
Decision support system 23, 29, 45, 52, 177
Decision table 173-174
Decision tree 21, 173
Degree (of a relation) 119
Degree (of a relationship) 101
DeMarco, T 169, 171, 175, 195
DesignAid 275
Desk-top 261
Determinacy 104
Device and media control language 138, 212
Direct access files 152-153, 204, 208-209
Distributed database 17, 34, 38, 220, **244-258**
DL/1 (see also *IMS*) 204, 208
Document-driven data analysis 95
Documentation 10-11, 14, 20, 36, 89, 167, 180, 263, 275, 278, 284, 288, 292, 300, 313, 314-317
Dodd, G. C 162
Domain 101
Dowgiallo, E 254, 258
Draffan, I. W 252
DSL Alpha 126, 127, 222

Earl, M, J 71, 73, 74
Efficiency 301
Eiffel 142
Elmasri, R 114, 140, 146, 163, 220, 221
Entity 20, 76, 78, **80**, 89, 90, 117, 191, 287, 316, 332-338
   occurrence **80**, 117
Entity Model 75, 191, 313, 331, 333-334
   (see also Entity-relationship diagram)
Entity-relationship diagram 20, 36, 89, 95, 96, 276-277, 280, 309, **310-317**, 333-334
Environment 49, 50, 53
Event 85, 86, 88, 93, 287
Event-driven data analysis 86
Excellerator 274-275
Exception condition 9, 14
   (see also Management by exception)
Executive information system 23, 29, 52, 69
External view 31-32, **164-166**, 230

Facilitator 22, 181
Fact finding (see Systems investigation)
Fagin, R 113
Feasibility study 8, 9, 10, 33
File 36
File access 33, 36, **148-163**, 202
File management system 233
File organisation 33, 36, **148-163**
Fitzgerald, G 40, 195, 272
Focus **267-270**, 271, 272
Form 166, 200, 277
   soft copy 19, 200
Form-driven systems 166
Fortran 18, 25, 215, 260, 277
Fourth generation language (or system) 19, 22, 23, **259-272**, 281
Foxbase 235
Fröhlich, D 179
Function 79, 313
Functional analysis 86, 311
Functional decomposition 21, 168, 169, 191, 278
Functional dependency 104, 106
Future analysis 193

Galliers, R 40
Gane, C. P 169, 170, 174, 175, 196
GemStone 146
Generalisation 146
Gibson, E 146, 147
Gillenson, M. L 294, 303, 305
Goals (of the firm) 44, **46-50**
GoldenGate 275
Golder, P. A 279

Goldstein, R. C 305
Gretton-Watson, P 252

Harris, C 219, 220
Hashing algorithm 153
Hawgood, J 196
Henshall, D 178
Hierarchical sequence 132, 207
Hirschheim, R 180
Hit rate 149
Hoffer, J. A 114, 147, 163, 221, 243, 304
Holism 43
Holloway, S 282, 305
Homonym (of data name) 88, 96
Horowitz, E 282
Host language 25, 28, 32, 164, 200, 212, 215, 217, 219, 222, 231, 327
Howe, D. R 85, 114, 146
Hull, R 142
Human activity 64, 184, 185, 187, 191
Human-computer interface 184, 185, 186, 187, **188-191**, 194, 256, 282

IBM 204, 208, 233, 234, 252, 274,
ICL data dictionary system **292-293**, 294
Icon 166, 234, 352
Identifier (see key)
IDMS 135, 139, **209-214**, 292, 318-319
Implementation 25, 35
IMS 133, **204-209**, 213, 214, 318
Index 150, 151, 152, 160, 226, 278
Indexed file 150-151
Indexed sequential file 151-152, 153, 154, 204, 208
Infological modelling 30
Information 44, 46
Information analysis 35, 184, 185, 187
Information Builders 267-272
Information centre 180
Information Engineering (IE) 272
Information Engineering Facility 274
Information Engineering Workbench 273-274
Information model **62-63**
Information modelling (see Information analysis)
Information retrieval 186, 194, 195
Information system 45, 48
Informix 232, 235
Ingres 116, 126, 222, 232, 234, 252, 309, 318, **319-327**
Integrity 24, 203, 256, 285, 295, 298, 300
Interface 62

Internal schema 31-32, **148-163**, 296
Interoperable Database System 252
Interview-driven data analysis 95
Inverted files 36, **160-162**, 204, 217-
219

Kassapis, A. K 255
Kennedy, A. A 50
Kent, W. A 108, 114
Key (of record) 79, 81, 101, 117, 145,
152-153, 217, 278
  candidate 101, 106
  composite 102, 106
  foreign 102, 122, 145
Khoshafian, S 142, 147
Kim, W 144
King, R 142
Klug, A 30, 40
Knowledgeware 273
Knuth, D. E 154, 155, 163
Krieger, H 179

Lacroix, M 128
Land, F. F 53, 193, 196
Langefors, B 30
Langham, M 245
Lawson, R. W 250
Lederer, A. L 59
Liebenau, J 74
Life-cycle (see System development
  life-cycle)
Link records (in network DBMS) 134,
137
Linked lists 130, 157-158
List processing **156-160**
Lochovsky, F. E 144
Logical model 6, 33, 34, 36, **115,
147**, 149, 164, 199, 280, 309,
318-319
Logical schema (see logical model)
Look-up 150,
Loomis, M. E. S 141, 147,
Lyon, J. K 305

Maciaszek, L. A 280
Machine code 260
Maintenance 4, 9-11, 15, 22, 25, 194-
195, 281, 294, 300-301
Man-machine interface (see Human-
  computer interface)
Management **51-55**, 71, 177, 285
  middle 12, 23, **51-55**
  operational 12, **51-55**
  strategic 12, 23, **51-55**
Management by exception 53, **54**
Management by summary 53, **55**
Management information 12, 23
Management involvement 28

Manual systems (see clerical systems)
Mapping 31, 115, **139-141**
Martin, C. F 282
Martin, J 259, 274, 276, 282, 283
Mayhew, P. J 183, 196
McCririck, I. B 305
McFadden, F. R 114, 146, 163, 221,
243, 304
Mendlelow, A. L 59
Menu 164-165, 234, 238, 261-262,
277, 346-348
Menu-driven system 343
Merise 86
Metaphor 61
Methodology 29-30, 272
Methodology workbench **272-274**
Microcomputer 17, 38, 233-241
Misra, S. K 276, 283
Mission statement 47
Model 4, 5, 6, 28, 29, **30**, 35-36, 76
Monitoring 194-195
Mouse 166, 234, 239
Multi-media 20, 144,**278-279**
Multivalued dependency 113
Multiview **184-195, 328-353**
Mumford, E 178, 179, 196

National Computing Centre (NCC) 3, 8
Natural language 164, 200, 260
Navathe, S. B 114, 140, 146, 163,
220, 221
Nelson, K 262
Network **130-139**, 158, 209
Newman, M 180
Nolan, R 23, 40
Normalisation (of relation) 5, 88, 97,
103-113, 174, 278, 282
Nunamaker, J. F 282

Object 143
Object Lisp 142
Object Pascal 142
Object-oriented 22, 36, **219-220**
Objectives (see also Socio-technical:
  objectives and Goals) 47
Office automation 142
Olle, T. W 56
Omnis 182, **239-241**
Ontos 146, **219-220**
Open systems architecture (OSA) 16,
257
Operations 85-86, 89, 94, 287
  synchronisation of 86
Operations documentation 10
Oracle 116, 127, 222, 232, 235, 252,
254, 275-276, **277-278**
Organisation 4

culture 49, **50-51**, 72
Organisation chart 68
Organisational learning 72
OrionII 146
Overflow block (for files) 152, 153
Oxborrow, E 147

Package 29
Packing density (of files) 153
Pactel 245, 255, 258
Paradox 235-236
Parallel running 11
Participation 22, 37, 73, 167, 168,
    175-181
Pascal 142, 222, 260, 277
Pelagatti, G 245, 252, 258
Performance 256
Physical model 6, 7, 30, 34, 36, 116,
    148-163, 164, 280, 309
Physical schema (see Physical model)
Pirotte, A 128
PL/1 200, 204, 212, 215, 222, 260,
    277
Planning 53, 68
Pointer 129, 134, 150, 152, 156, 158,
    160, 209
Poole, F 252
Porter, M. E 48
Pratt, C. J 221
Primary task 185, 189
Priority (of systems development) 59
Privacy 139, 203, 217, 219, 288, 292,
    298-299, 349-350
Problem situation 188, 189
Process (see also Function) 170
Program generator 22, 265-266
Programmer 27, 303
Programming language 18
Project leader 58
Project team 58
Proteus 252
Prototyping 22, 37, 167-168, 178,
    181-184, 278, 280-281, 339,
    351-352
Pseudo code 172, 273

QBE (Query by Example) 118, 128,
    144, 145, **215-216**, 235, 236,
    264
Quang, P. T 86, 140, 146, 280
Quel (see also Ingres) 126, 128, 145,
    222, 319-327
Query language 7, 18-19, 28, 31-32,
    38, 53, 164, 200-201, 264-265,
    288-289
Questor 318

RACF 300

Random access file 153
Randomising algorithm 153, 209
Rapport 116
Real-time 18
Recovery 194-195, 248, 256, 299-300
Referential integrity 122
Reinsch, R 249
Relation 21, 86, 103-113, 323-324
Relational algebra **118-125**, 222
Relational calculus 118, **125-129**
Relational model **75-114**
Relational theory 20
Relationally complete 118
Relationship 76, 78, **81**, 86, 92, 117,
    130, 191, 278, 287, 317
    cardinality **81-84**, 85, 140
Report generator (or writer) 22, 32,
    164, 182, 214, 265, 267, 326-327
Resistance to change 71
Review (of system) 9
Rich picture 21, 35, 64-65, 188-190,
    279, 328-330
Rickards, T 60
Robinson, H 85, 114, 146
Rockart, J. F 73
Root definition 35, **64-67**, 189, 190,
    279

Sarson, T 169, 170, 174, 175, 196,
    276
Schema (see also Model) 138, 209,
    211
Schema data definition language 138
Screen painter 22, 182, 265
SDD-1 252
Security 203, 217, 219-220, 257, 262,
    285. 288-290, 296, 298, 300-301,
    349
Semantic data model 142-143
Sequential file 149-150, 204
Serial file 148-149
Set *(Codasyl)* 135-137, 140, 211
Sherif, M. A 296, 305
Shipman, D. W 142
Sinkel, K 219
Smalltalk 22, 142, 146
Smith, D 144
Smith, J 144
Socio-technical approach 184, 185,
    187, 192, **193**
Soft boxes 76, 171
Software 27
Son, S. H 251
SQL 7, 34, 38, 127-128, 142, 145,
    200, 214-216, 220, **222-232**,
    238, 254, 258, 264, 277-278, 293,
    319, 322
SSADM 272

Standards (see also documentation) 11, 25-26, 203, 285, 291, 296
Stepwise refinement 168
STRADIS 272, 275
Strategy (for information systems development) 59, **67-71**, 73
Structure charts 171-172, 340-343
Structured English 21, 172, 266, 280
Structured systems analysis and design 167
Structured walkthroughs 175
Sub-schema 101
Sub-schema data definition language 139
Subsystem 60, 71
Sun 234
Sundgren, B 30
Sutherland, A. R 40
Sybase 252
Synchronisation 86
Synonym (in data names) 88, 96, 278
Synonym (in file keys) 153
System 8
  human activity (see Human activity)
System R* 252
System2000 204
Systems analysis 8, 9, 10, 21, 33, 76
Systems analyst 27, 37, 51, 58, 76, 167, 303
Systems approach 43
Systems design 8, 9, 10, 33, 37, 167
Systems development cycle **8-11**, 37, 166-168, 183
Systems development team **60**
Systems implementation 8, 9, 10, 33
Systems investigation 8, 9, 10, 33, 60
Systems life-cycle 3, 37
Systems planning team 56, **57-58**, 67, 71, 74
Systems thinking 43

TAB 275
Teradata DBC 242
Third normal form 88, 103, 104, **106-110**, 313
Tight English 172
Tool 34, 38-39, **259-283**
  evaluation 281-282

Top Secret 300
Top-down analysis 69, 95, 99, 168
Total system 70
Tozer, E 283
Traits 142
Transactions 54, 86
Transitive dependency 107
Transparency 248
Tsichritzis, D. C 30, 40
Tuple 101, 117

Unify 222, 232
Union compatibility 119
Universe of discourse 87
User 10, 13, 14, 27, 57, 59, 176, 201, 285, 339
  casual 56, 201
  dissatisfaction 13
  documentation 10
  involvement 22, **71-74**, **175-181**
  professional 56, 201
  regular 56, 201
User interface (see Human-computer interface)

Van Duhn, J 294
Vbase 219, 220
Veryard, R 114
Virus 299

Waterfall model (see System: life-cycle)
Watt, J 259, 283
Weber, E. S 282
Weldon, J. L 305
Weltanschauung 188
White, C 232
Wilson, D 182, 196
WIMP 234, 241, 261
Wood-Harper, A. T 64, 65, 74, 96, 184, 196
Workbench 259, **272-274**
Workstation 17

Yalonis, C 247
Yeates, D. A 39
Yourdon, E 276

Zloof, M. M 128